THE LETTERS OF NOSTRADAMUS

SECOND EDITION

THE LETTERS OF NOSTRADAMUS

REALIZING A PROPHECY OF JESUS CHRIST

SECOND EDITION

Translated, edited and introduced by
ROBERT TIPPETT

ISBN 978-0-9801166-0-1

Published by Kartina Pearls, LLC

CONTENTS

PART 4: THE CONCLUSION

DEDICATION

On August 1, 2005 I moved to Waveland, Mississippi to write and promote my first book. On August 29, 2005 Hurricane Katrina completely destroyed the house I was living in, as well as many more in Waveland, Bay Saint Louis and Pass Christian. The entire Mississippi coastline was devastated, and much of the southern half of inland Mississippi did not fare much better. As I have been writing this book, I have watched the people of Mississippi show tremendous resolve to not be defeated by a natural disaster. They have shown great patience in the face of the federal agencies that are faster with excuses than assistance. They have exposed the insurance companies that coddle foreign investors more than local refugees. I dedicate this book to the thousands of good-hearted souls who have come to Mississippi to help the recovery, by volunteering to build and clean and provide the most basic of services. I dedicate this book to the Mississippians who have smiled as they helped their neighbors, fighting back tears because of their own woes. I dedicate this book personally to Lyn Stabler, who has sheltered me in the wake of the storm so that I could write this book. I dedicate this book to Hurricane Katrina, as it was God's way of showing all of us what we must do in the times of emergency.

GUIDING SCRIPTURE

And we have the word of prophecy made more sure; whereunto ye do well that ye take heed, as unto a lamp shining in a dark place, until the day dawn, and the day-star arise in your hearts: knowing this first, that no prophecy of scripture is of private interpretation. For no prophecy ever came by the will of man: but men spake from God, being moved by the Holy Spirit.

2 Peter 1:19-21

PART 1

LETTER AND
INSTRUCTION

INTRODUCTION

I would like to spend a few pages setting up the contents of this book. Obviously, from the title on the cover, this book is about the Letters of Nostradamus. However, before I begin to present to the reader what that means, it is important to get a feel for Nostradamus. By that, I do not mean that I want to present a biography that will expose previously unknown information about Nostradamus, or a hidden letter that explains everything he wrote. I mean I want you to get a true feel for Nostradamus the man, before you learn what Nostradamus wrote.

People who know me know I like to talk when a topic interests me. When I talk about Nostradamus and the areas that surround his work I can generally leave many people lost in silence because I love to talk about this topic. Some might call it preaching. Still, they don't get lost because what I have to say is too technical and difficult to comprehend; they just get lost because I tend to ramble a bit, before reaching a point. These ramblings often take me down seemingly disassociated paths, which leave the listener scratching their heads, while smiling politely.

I generally am able to snap the listener out of his or her fog when I remind them why I made that short side trip. Those who like listening to me just usually patiently wait for me to explain how I wandered onto that topic; while those who are not aware of my wandering style will interrupt and pose a question, returning me to the topic. I am about to wander onto one of those paths now.

Since the written text does not allow for immediate feedback, I am giving you fair warning now that this introduction, which is intended to give you a feel for the true worth of Nostradamus, might seem to be off the subject a bit. If you bear with me, I will show you what I mean when I say that everything that you thought you knew about Nostradamus is wrong. Hopefully you know very little to begin with; but, if you think you are versed in what Nostradamus wrote, I will change your perspective considerably.

Most people don't know much more than the name "Nostradamus." Some people think they know more, particularly the people who have earned an income presenting themselves as knowing of this man. Still, there seem to be a lot of internet sites that make it appear that there is a clique of people who actually study Nostradamus; but, I am certain that every one of those who thought they knew something more than most are actually more wrong than those who know nothing. You should be surprised to find out that everything previously thought to be known about Nostradamus is mostly useless tidbits of sensationalized trivia.

My point is this: knowing Nostradamus is unimportant. What is important is to feel the essence of the man and feel the purpose of his work. This book is designed to take you to that level of feeling. Now, as promised, it is time for a brief sidetrack.

I remember when I was a kid; perhaps ten years of age, my best neighborhood friend and I read a book of *Peanuts* cartoons. They were all 4-frame, black and white cartoons, which had appeared in newspapers over a period of time, reproduced as a book to continue the popularity. My friend and I both got hours of pleasure from reading those humorous encounters that the *Peanuts* gang has perennially been known for. Charles Schulz was a very funny man, not only for his caricatures and witty dialogues; but, he also had a gift, knowing how to capture a humor that both kids and adults could equally enjoy.

My friend and I read that book from cover to cover, several times. We never failed to laugh out loud on occasion; and, we would make our parents and siblings read the ones that we thought to be the funniest. I remember we would break out laughing just at the facial expressions that Charlie Brown would make, or the sight of Snoopy dancing, regardless of what dialogue accompanied the drawing. Still, from all of that laughter that we shared, I would probably laugh all over again if I read that book again today. The reason is I have forgotten the vast majority of those cartoons; but, then I have a hard time remembering jokes that are funny too. I'm just easy to please that way.

From reading *Peanuts* in the Sunday funnies for years and from watching the Charlie Brown specials on television over and over, I know a lot of the basic settings, characters and general situations of Schulz's series. I know in that book there were cartoons of Snoopy as the Red Baron, Lucy as the five-cent counselor, as well as the girl who would always snatch the football from Charlie Brown at the last minute before he would try to kick it. Still, for all of that memory, there is only one complete 4-frame cartoon from that book that I still remember: setting, characters, dialogue and punch line.

In that one cartoon Charlie Brown and Linus were leaning against the stone wall that they would occasionally meet at. It seemed that the wall was a quiet place where they could meet to privately discuss the deeper issues of a kid's life.

13

In the first frame, where we saw them both, Linus had brought a book with him this time. He began to read it out loud to Charlie Brown. The first frame said, "A man was born." Charlie Brown elbows on the wall with his hands holding up his head, just listened.

In the second frame both Charlie Brown and Linus were in the same positions, as Linus next read, "He lived and died. The end." This led to the third frame, where Charlie Brown and Linus maintained the same positions, but nothing was said. In the fourth and final frame, Charlie Brown finally reflected, "Gee. It makes you feel like you knew the man."

I remember that I laughed hard when I read that cartoon, because it seemed so ludicrous that Charlie Brown could draw that conclusion from such lack of detail. My friend laughed too. However, now that I remember that cartoon, after more than 40 years of knowing it, I can finally see the true talent of Charles Schulz in that cartoon. He so simply captured the essence of feeling, versus rational thought; and, he did so with one simple word, "feel." That word requires no external change in Charlie Brown's position, leaning against that stone wall.

Looking back at all of the figures in history that I have learned about in my lifetime, it now seems that most do fit this synopsis. For all that is written or said of the lives of the rich, famous and powerful, none of the details of exploits can create a feeling of importance. Simply put, they were born, they lived and they died, just like all of us will eventually do. The end is the only true point in time that the sum of the effect can be determined. However, when that end has been reached, we find that there have really only been a special few whose lives evoke such deep feelings, the kind that Charlie Brown expressed. When we realize no matter how much detail about someone's life we absorb intellectually, we never really feel we knew them. What Linus read was devoid of all of that intellectual clutter; and, simply from knowing of one out of billions, Charlie Brown was moved emotionally.

One man whose name can have such an effect is Jesus Christ; and, believe it or not, another is Nostradamus. I imagine anyone who was ever close to someone who died – a sibling, a parent, grand-parent, aunt, etc. – would be overwhelmed by the same emotional feeling, with no detail even required to bring out that emotion. Just the memory of the name of someone close, who was born, lived and died, is all that is needed to spark one's heart to feelings. In this scenario, where we do actually know the person who died, it is the same depth of feeling that comes when we learn about someone very important, someone we actually didn't know; but, these people are rare. For me now, and hopefully for many others, Jesus Christ stirs such emotion.

While there is detail about the life of Jesus Christ, in what some have called the "Good Book," that detail is unnecessary to recall in order to feel the power of the name. When I am moved just by His name, I am protected from any and all external influences by those who do not feel the same about Christ as I do.

In these times, there are growing numbers of those that do not believe in Christ and do not call themselves Christians. There are several reasons for this growth; but, to these people, the same details I have learned about the life of Christ have no effect on them. In fact, it is the intellectual level that keeps them from an emotional connection and the details of Jesus Christ seem contradictory to them. They can point out what they believe are errors and contradictions, even in the words written by one apostle, compared to another; and they can dispute the details of His miracles as defying the laws of physics and improvable. When all is said and done, the argument based on the intellectual properties of the details cannot be the basis for belief and faith. If I had become dependent on those details for strengthening my belief in Christ, I could easily be influenced to think that I really knew nothing about the life Jesus Christ lived.

I can say that I know Jesus Christ was born, without any argument from non-believers; but, some will question where the manger was, whether it was truly a virgin birth, the actual date of Christ's birth not being December 25th, and/or I could even hear of the impossibility that a one-time star could lead the wise men to find the baby Jesus. I feel the importance of Jesus Christ because he was born, regardless of the details.

I can say that Jesus Christ lived, and include some of the detail that surrounded three years of his life; but, many question the miracles that were written of, as though there was a trick involved that the trained eye did not catch, causing those who wrote of them to be fooled. I would be unable to prove that Jesus raised the dead, gave sight back to the blind, fed the multitude with twelve loaves and fish, walked on water, turned water into wine and anything else that was written as miraculous. The non-believers can argue that these things have never happened since, or there is scientific explanation for similar instances being misunderstood. None of that matters when it is simply agreed that Jesus Christ lived and had followers who believed in those miracles. I can feel the power of

Christ without analyzing His accomplishments.

Finally, I could say Jesus died on the cross for the sins of mankind; and, as a Christian I could say that Christ rose from the dead and ascended into Heaven. However, many do question the resurrection and many do not believe that he is seated at the right hand of the Father. With all of these doubters to contend with, and to keep from arguing opinion that cannot be backed up with sufficient evidence to sway the unbelieving, the only detail that can be agreed upon by all is that this man named Jesus was born, he lived and died. To the non-believers this is the end of the story; but, to many like me, we feel like we personally know Jesus Christ, even though we have no personal memory of having ever met this man. I feel absolved of sin when I pray to Christ for forgiveness. This is the power of Charles Shultz's statement in the cartoon. It speaks volumes for feelings.

For all of the feeling I have developed for both Jesus Christ and Nostradamus, this has become more solidified in the last four years. That was when I began to have an awakening about Nostradamus, which led to a rebirth of Christ in my heart. As far as the intellect is concerned, I have known about Jesus Christ almost since I was old enough to know my name; and, I first learned about Nostradamus when I was in my early twenties.

By the time I was ten years old and reading that *Peanuts* book, I was already well aware of Jesus Christ, from Sunday school and going to church four times a week, beginning shortly after my birth. With that upbringing I was well aware that I was a Christian; but, my knowledge of religion did not assure that I felt Christian. Since I was raised a member of a Pentecostal Church (Assemblies of God) and none of my friends outside of that church shared the same religion (Baptists and Methodists mostly) I pretty much was a Christian only in that church environment. In my other environments I adapted to less religious ways of living. While I had feelings for religion, I was caught up in the mentality of peer groups, where religion was very secondary. I stopped going to church at the age of 14, basically because I thought I saw hypocrisy in others; but, it was really the hypocrisy in me. Over the course of the majority of my adult life I struggled to maintain my inner feelings for God and Christ, while having to blend with a world that seemed cold to religion. It seemed that I encountered more people who questioned Christianity than I encountered true believers of Jesus Christ.

This has sent me on a personal path to justify my belief, which I always maintained privately, but that path was basically through the use of rational thought. I felt that it was important to understand other views on religion, so I could explain my beliefs to others. After encountering all the arguments of question, I learned many ways to turn arguments around to my benefit. This was not from any course I took, but more of a natural way of incorporating the logic of seeing both sides of an issue and looking for weaknesses. From this practice I felt I was quite adept at making a case for my beliefs, even if I made no case to convert someone else. Therefore, I mostly kept my views private and only unsheathed them to cut down a non-believer when necessary, by exposing his or her lack of rationale for not believing.

Over the past four years I have come to realize a much deeper belief in Jesus Christ, which does not require any of my rational swords for protection. I have come to fully understand that faith is all that is required, as all doubts and questions need not affect me. Jesus Christ is real to me and I have such a strong faith now that I can only feel pity for those that still do not believe. Where so many people feel a need to go door-to-door preaching to people unwilling to listen, I choose to let those people make their own mental decisions; because, when they feel that they know Christ they will also realize all of the faults of their rationale. I cannot argue anything to bring about this change of attitude, because I cannot add any new detail that will make someone feel how important Jesus Christ is to them. It follows the principle that only the seekers are willing to listen; and, as a seeker myself, I feel that true seekers follow their hearts, even when it leads to seemingly foolish pursuits.

This is where my work with Nostradamus comes in and becomes important. I feel people will be led to read what I have to say. At first I thought that everyone would rush to read what I had to offer, but that was not the case. I know, from my inner voice, that my words will be read when I have perfected what it is I have been trying to say. I cannot write from the mind to do this. I must write from the heart. This is a burning desire for me now, because I feel a responsibility to somehow make people aware of how much they do need to feel this importance of Christ. My renewed faith in Christ has come from my work over the last four years, studying the writings of Nostradamus; and, it is through Nostradamus that I rekindled the spirit of Christ within me.

Nostradamus is another man, like Jesus Christ, where relatively little is known of his life; and, what is believed to be known is not free from argument and questioning. Unlike Christ, Nostradamus actually wrote documents that were to become his legacy; but, aside from these strangely worded poems and prose, there is very little known of his life that is agreed upon as true and not embellished lore. There is not much that I can add to the history of Nostradamus, as far as facts of his life that would appeal to one's intellectual curiosity; but, it is important for me to restate some known facts.

Nostradamus is known to have published a yearly set of poems, called his *Almanachs.* Several of these are still available as documented evidence, some as copies of the originals, but some have been lost. We know of these lost editions only from references in other literary works of that period that mentioned them specifically. These *Almanachs* were Nostradamus' yearly predictions; and, they were similar to what is still found today, in the *Farmer's Almanac.* Both use astrology to make predictions; and, while farmers have used the information in the *Farmer's Almanac* to schedule their planting of crops and the like, there were people in Nostradamus' day who swore his predictions were just as beneficial and accurate. Still, for all of the practical use that was found at that time, last year's almanac is like yesterday's newspaper. It has little value for the coming years. This means while Nostradamus became popular writing these predictions, they were not designed for long-term use.

Nostradamus' present legacy is based primarily on the largest work he produced, named *The Prophecies*, which some simply call "The Centuries." That legacy is because it is assumed this larger volume, so similar in style to the *Almanachs*, is making predictions of much greater importance, for a much more distant period of time. The irony of these two legacies is that Nostradamus was revered by his contemporaries for his writing of the *Almanachs*, but he was largely shunned for writing *The Prophecies.* He was shunned because, unlike his words in the *Almanachs*, which were understandable, thus predictable, *The Prophecies* was unintelligible. An unintelligible work of writing, just as back then, still makes last year's bestselling author this year's has-been.

In Nostradamus' case, this rejection led Nostradamus to become more reclusive over the last five years of his life. Rather than going around explaining what he wrote, to make *The Prophecies* intelligible and maintain his dignified reputation, Nostradamus did not help anyone find any clarity. So, for all of the celebrity Nostradamus once enjoyed, for some reason he threw it all away.

Today, Nostradamus' name is familiar to so many people, roughly 450 years after *The Prophecies* was first published because some people claim to have found that clarity. These people have been coming forward to speak up for Nostradamus, when he chose to remain silent on what he wrote. This means the popularity of Nostradamus today is not based on the intelligible writings he produced, but the unintelligible ones. The popularity is then the mystique that has come from others claiming to know what Nostradamus left unknown. This practice of doing the thinking for Nostradamus began shortly after his death; but, it has gained more momentum, and thus seeming importance, in the Twentieth Century.

It is this speaking out by others that has made the topic of Nostradamus a very popular one today. This becomes evident by the way the print, radio-television and the film industries continue to produce a steady stream of programming which, directly or indirectly, uses the name of Nostradamus to promote their media product. All of this promotion of the name of Nostradamus can only lead one to believe it must be a profitable name, or we all would have forgotten Nostradamus was ever born, lived and died. Still, it must be realized that all of this promotion is intellectual, with nothing designed to bring about deep feelings.

This recent popularity is because Nostradamus blends into one very hot topic these days, which is the End Times. This wave of shock media began in the late -1990s, when the dawning of a new millennium neared. Besides the fear that was generated in the computer world with Y2K, that was a good time to brush off all of the old prophecy stories that had been previously produced and draw new attention to them. I remember one hosted by David McCallum that mentioned Nostradamus' predictions, among several others.

Recently, at least for the past two years, it seems we have entered the period of "the Codes." I say this because the History Channel has a regular feature named *Decoding the Past*. This series covers everything in the pre-2000 productions; but, they do so with a more scientific and research minded air, including interviews with seeming authorities and experts. I assume this title came from the popularity of *The Da Vinci Code*, which now has a feature film in release, to follow up on the popularity the book generated.

Dan Brown's book is a work of fiction that pulls together about a dozen conspiracy theory ideas involving religious sects; but, instead of Nostradamus being the old name to rehash, they make Leonardo Da Vinci a mastermind of deception. Still, another program that has been run recently is named *The Bible*

Code. This theory says that just about any major event can be found predicted in a systematic way of sorting letters from the Bible's words, with amazing accuracy. This is then paralleled to the accuracy of Nostradamus; although, one of the "experts" of the Bible Code wrote Nostradamus off as pure idiocy.

The point is, if you watch enough of this type of programming, as I have, you find the name of Nostradamus pops up very regularly these days, at least as a segment of a full show, if not a full feature on what Nostradamus wrote. This brings Nostradamus to our intellectual forefronts; but, it does nothing to give an accurate feel for the man himself.

In this realm of information about Nostradamus, few seem to agree on the different aspects of Nostradamus' life, other than his having written predictions. One program was solely dedicated to disproving much of the lore that had been attached to his life: the curing of plague victims; being a degreed physician; and, why Nostradamus purposefully wrote enigmatic verses designed to come true, to some degree, if enough time were to pass. Still, so little history of Nostradamus is actually known as fact that most media simply focuses on the translations and interpretations of others. These are the people who are speaking for Nostradamus, who appear in interviews, with impressive titles listed, giving the impression this is expert opinion; but, they can only speak for Nostradamus by using the intellect, because Nostradamus chose not to speak for himself.

The result of every one of these programs is they sensationalize a select few of the quatrains (four-line verses) that are part of *The Prophecies*. It is widely accepted that Nostradamus wrote 942 of these quatrains (some, like me, believe this total is 948 or more), but even a program that is dedicated exclusively to painting Nostradamus as an accurate forecaster will present no more than ten of these quatrains as evidence. Add to this those programs which focus on none of Nostradamus' quatrains being accurate, due to being too vaguely written, and the result is that no one really believes Nostradamus did anything important. Amazingly, when this entire gamut of media is summed up, the only summation the majority of the people could possibly make, as known truth, is: Nostradamus was born, he lived and died. The end.

With this style of promotion there are no Charlie Browns who would reflect that they feel like they knew Nostradamus. For someone who lived and died over four hundred years ago, without any truth given to elicit that feeling of closeness, it seems remarkable we even still pay any attention to Nostradamus at all. The way the media seems to be so non-committal to making anyone completely believe anything, besides being a sign of reflecting a complete lack of trust in anything, it shows intellectual stimulation, rather than emotional attachment, is what the media panders to these days. It is that intellectual approach which makes everyone seem the same. Someone was born; someone lived and died. Tune in tomorrow for another meaningless intellectual pursuit on (fill in the blank).

I must admit I am now very emotionally attached to Nostradamus; and, it has been through this development that I have come to be a firm believer in Jesus Christ, without any doubt at all. In this development I have had very little influence from the media, other than to have their tidbits of information act to support my feelings. For as much as I have learned from these various outlets for intellectual pursuits, it has been a swell of feeling that has come from within that has had the most influence on me. It is this heartfelt sensation which has opened my mind to greater heights of understanding of God and Christ, to levels that cannot be learned otherwise.

I can quickly sum up the first 26 years I knew about Nostradamus as the time that I really knew nothing. I had one book I would occasionally pull out to look through, before closing it and putting it back on the shelf, having solved nothing. While I intellectually knew nothing about Nostradamus, I still felt something was there. I just didn't know what it was.

This all changed shortly after September 11, 2001. I pulled my one book down and began looking through the quatrains once again; but, this time was very different. I can only explain it by analogy, as it was like a doorway appeared which I walked through. Behind the door was a hallway and doors off of it, which I would open and peek inside. Each time I did this I was amazed to find a new revelation of exactly what Nostradamus meant. At that early point, with the outer doorway still within sight, I had two choices: I could leave the hallway and go tell everyone what I had found, hoping the doorway would still be open when I got back; or, I could continue going down the hallway, hoping that someone would eventually realize I was missing and come find me. I chose to keep exploring the doorways and now that I am out, I know everything Nostradamus meant in his writings about *The Prophecies*. More importantly, I feel the true spiritual essence that is there; and it is there beyond a shadow of a doubt.

Nothing that has been previously interpreted about Nostradamus' writings is accurately presented, even though some things have been attached to the right events and historical figures. Overall, none of my views are shared by anyone I know of; as I am the only one who sees Nostradamus the way that I do, so far. I have tried to explain what I have been allowed to know about Nostradamus, in a clear and forthright manner which avoids sensationalism; but, people tend to be more willing to listen to hype than listen to reason. The style that I first chose to use to explain the true meaning is most appropriate in an educational setting. There is a wealth of information to explain; but since there are no institutes of higher learning that teach how to understand Nostradamus, I have not reached many minds yet, to touch their hearts.

Let me just make it clear to you that everything Nostradamus wrote about *The Prophecies* is explainable, in clear and logical methods; but, that is merely an intellectual pursuit. Explaining the details cannot make you feel the purpose of Nostradamus. Therefore, I will try not to bore you with explanations in this book.

This book will jump you right into the lap of Nostradamus, where he will write to you two most important letters. It will be those letters which will let him explain everything needed to be known about his book. While part of the words will be mine, they are not mine by intellectual manipulation. Think of it as me channeling the thoughts of Nostradamus, so that my words become his. That will make everything appear to come from Nostradamus, to you; and, when you have finished reading what Nostradamus has to say to you, none of the details will be the primary importance for you to gain. The primary importance will be what you feel inside, when everything has been read.

Keep in mind that everything presented in the media is designed to hook your interest, to get you to read or watch a book or show. Once hooked, they will not try to convince you to believe. That would be bad business. They want you to be intrigued. They want you to be confused when everything is done, by leaving you with more questions than you began with, or in complete denial that anything of importance will come from the words of an old man, 450 years ago. They want to addict you to viewing or reading, so that you will continue to come back for the same information being redistributed, over and over again. This, if not brainwashing, is what psychologists call desensitization.

This process will get you to believe that there is a coming danger, by promoting a book or program that advertises that it will shed light on a known danger.

Once you get involved in this light, you will find out that the intellect can defeat this fear. Exposure over and over to this up and down ride that plays on the emotion of fear will leave you emotionless, thinking that the danger was all make believe.

The danger now so frequently promoted is the End Times. Call it Armageddon or the end of the world or what have you. The source is Biblical; but, you will find that these programs will also add several different claims of similar end, from non-Biblical sources. Nostradamus is believed by these promoters to be non-Biblical; and, when they discredit one claim, it has the effect of discrediting all claims.

They also understand that your interest is based on an inner belief. This is the danger to them, and why they desensitize you to your inner feelings about this danger. You have to feel to act against its coming; but, without feelings you will fall prey to your intellectual programming.

Nostradamus does fall into the Biblical category, and he is not as easily written off as has been believed. You will find in this book everything that you will need to know that will confirm this Biblical connection. It is clearly there, but it has been ignored or overseen for as long as interpreters have tried speaking for Nostradamus.

Nostradamus was, in fact, a true Prophet of God, having encountered the spirit of Jesus Christ, who then dictated a Prophecy for him to write. When you have read this book, regardless of what you think, it is important that you make contact with how you feel about what is written.

If I have done my work properly, when you have finished this book you will know that Nostradamus was born. You will know that he lived, too. It can then be assumed that he died, as the dates on the letters are so far in the past. His story is about the end of mankind; the end that each one of us knows is coming, one way or another. However, this end is not as concrete as many have believed, from the biblical texts. When you feel the connection between Nostradamus and Jesus Christ, you will feel the power that is within us all to avert this end, as it is written.

The most important thing that you must come away with is you must feel like you knew Nostradamus. If I can accomplish that goal, then you will also feel that you know Jesus Christ. This feeling will make you pause. It will make you reflect; and, this feeling will be in a way that you have never known before. This feeling will be important for your well being, and that of a great many others.

A PERSONAL LETTER TO YOU

Hello. My name is Robert Tippett and I have been trying to write a book that would be attractive enough for you to read for quite some time now. If you have read this far, please don't put this book down and walk away. You will not regret it if you keep reading, as you will see, well before you finish this book. In fact, after you have read it from cover to cover, you will need to give this book to someone close to you and then let them give it to someone else after that. This is because what you are about to read will affect you deeply, on a very personal level, whether you realize it or not at this time. So, please, continue reading.

I know this must sound odd, and believe me when I say that this is not some ploy to sell books, but I have written this book just for you. By that, I mean that this is the third book that I have written in the past four years, all on the same topic, with each book telling the same important message, but you have not read any of those. So, this book was written just to appeal to you, and here you are.

Please don't feel badly that you did not read either of my first two books. The first book was never published. It wasn't like I didn't try to publish it, but there were some issues to deal with, such that to make a long story short, it just wasn't time to put the story out. I needed to refine my thoughts a little more, which I did to produce my second book. That one was published, but it was way too long for most people, and it was much too expensive for the casual reader, like you. That book, *Pearls Before Swine, Volume 1: Predicting the Past*, was written like a textbook, designed to teach students how to properly analyze Nostradamus and what he wrote. Since you didn't enroll in that course, this book is designed to boil all of that information from books one and two down to one easy-to-read book, while still conveying the importance that has to be known.

This importance is actually not found in any of the quatrains, or 4-line verses, that Nostradamus wrote. This is not meant to mean that the quatrains are not important, as they are very important. Everything that Nostradamus wrote, which is associated with the book he wrote, *The Prophecies*, is very important; but, that importance pales when compared to the true purpose of his book. This is what makes my book special, and personal to you, as no one else has ever figured out what that purpose is. This, then, means that you do not know what that purpose is either.

This is the purpose of this book. I have written this book to make it very clear to you why Nostradamus wrote *The Prophecies*. The purpose of my second book was to make it clear how I came to the conclusions I came to, of what the quatrains mean and how others can come to the same conclusions. To do that, there are the lessons that have to be learned, to learn how to understand Nostradamus' words. These lessons involve a logical method – I call it the systems of Nostradamus – which makes that understanding possible. But here, in this book, I am not trying to teach you any lessons. I am here to convince you to believe in God and Jesus Christ. That is why Nostradamus wrote *The Prophecies*.

I know that you feel a little uneasy right now, for any number of reasons, but please don't panic. Keep reading and you will see exactly what I mean. I know you have never heard the name of Nostradamus associated with Jesus or God before, and that is why no one has ever been able to understand what Nostradamus wrote. I have seen this connection, and I will show you that Nostradamus himself even wrote that he only produced the physical manifestation of *The Prophecies*, while Jesus Christ was the true author who dictated every word that Nostradamus wrote. This means that Nostradamus is actually a true prophet of God and that *The Prophecies* is actually the equivalent of a biblical book of prophecy.

I assume there will be those who will see that claim of mine as some form of heresy, since most people have thought that Nostradamus was some kind of magician with a brass cauldron and wand. Some think he used some form of evil practice to be able to peer into the future. I will show you, in Nostradamus' own words that this was not the case at all. Nostradamus was a saint, even though he has not been given this title; and, he was a servant to the Lord Christ, to save your soul. That is the ultimate purpose of what Nostradamus wrote. However, that salvation is dependent on faith, and belief in what Christ told the world, through Nostradamus.

So, this is why I am writing this book to you personally. I want to help you find that faith; enough to cast away any shadow of doubt about what Nostradamus wrote, so that you will have everything that you need to save your own soul. After all, no one else can save your soul for you. You are the only one who can do that. Therefore, I am completely committed to help you as much as I can, by telling you what Nostradamus said, when he defined the general meaning of *The Prophecies* in two letters of explanation. However, it has taken me a while to figure out the best way to tell you what you must know.

Let me say that I have wanted to get you this message of importance for the last four years; but, I thought you would want to know all of the *why's* and *how's*. That led me down the path I have taken, writing two prior books; but, that path was not as much for your benefit as it was mine. I had to be able to answer all of these questions for myself, before I could confidently tell you the basics. I have seen just how marvelous the documents are that are associated with *The Prophecies*, and the quatrains are like rosebuds, which appear small, but unfurl into beautifully detailed blossoms. It is not the story that is beautiful, as it is one of great sorrows that mankind is facing; but, the beauty comes from realizing how only God's influence could have produced such depth of meaning, from so few words written. My work has solidified my belief in Jesus Christ; and, God and has convinced me that Nostradamus wrote, as his title indicates, the true prophecies of God. My conviction is so strong that it has to be this strength which leads you to believe in God and Christ, stronger than you ever have before.

In this book to you, I have foregone the depth of explanation I put in my other two books. I want you to know there are few questions I cannot answer about Nostradamus, but I will spare you most of this explanation. If you feel the urge to want to know more about how I come to my conclusions, feel free to pick up a copy of my second book. Just know now that my second book is subtitled "Volume 1," which means it does not tell everything about every quatrain. As far as my interpretations of the individual quatrains go, I only interpreted 111 of the 948 quatrains which have been attributed to *The Prophecies*, in volume one. The average length of interpretation for each 4-line verse is about four pages. As you can see, that is a lot of explanation. So much that the size of the book (740pp, 81/2x11, over 3 lbs) has been intimidating, and the suggested retail price for such a large book ($41.95) is prohibitive to most.

This means that this book, *The Letters of Nostradamus*, is designed to give you an in-depth overview, without all of the explanation that could be added, in a shorter, more manageable book, for a reasonable price. Please know that I do not believe that I have been allowed the enlightenment I am passing on to you, which comes from God and Christ, in order to become a wealthy man. That is not my motivation at all. If I could afford to print out a million copies of this book and then give them away, I would. I feel that strongly about completing this assignment for God, to make sure you know what He wants you to know. However, as I'm sure you know, I cannot afford to do that.

27

So, since you have paid good money for this book, I want you to get a return on your investment that exceeds what you paid for it. If I can help you find your faith, that return will be accomplished. However, on top of that, if you don't forget to pass this book on to someone else, someone important to you, when you have finished reading it, you will find out just what my true return is. Just a hint … it is not becoming rich.

In fact, over the past four years I have been faced with a series of financial hardships that would have made most people cringe to think of such things happening to them. In that time, I have lost almost everything that I once had, and let me emphasize the **thing** part of everything, as my health has been excellent and my family has not been affected. This is really what matters the most, so losing a job during an economic depression, selling most of my major household furnishings at auction (for about 9 cents on a dollar), having the most expensive possessions that I didn't sell get stolen from me, and having to move in with my elderly mother or face homelessness at the age of 49, didn't faze my determination to write two books, which brought no financial reward to me. When I was about on my feet again, with my second book available to the public, I then moved to coastal Mississippi, to promote its sales. I did this just in time to have everything that I didn't carry with me to the shelter get swept away by Hurricane Katrina.

I believe all of the things I have lost are meant to show me just how little things mean, especially towards a goal of happiness. I have been happier these last four years than ever before in my life. My happiness comes from knowing that God is real and that Jesus Christ has led me to my understanding of what Nostradamus wrote. Ever since I first became aware of what *The Prophecies* truly held, I have been moved closer and closer to total understanding, as more and more has become perfectly clear to me. None of this has been by a conscious attempt to understand Nostradamus, as there was no mental design on my part to write the books I have. It does not influence my plans for those books I will write in the future. I have been called to do this, as I have been called to tell you.

When you think about the connection between Nostradamus and the annihilation of the world and the misery which his book tells of, it can be somewhat difficult to see how this can bring me happiness. Be assured that this is not what makes me smile, as I have shed many tears while reading and writing about some of these horrific events to come. The happiness has come from me being chosen to make this important exposure to you and the world, and the happiness has come from feeling that closeness with God and Christ. When something new dawns on me, it comes from the whispers which come into my mind. I go from that insight and research something I knew very little about before. This method has led me to find my research has just placed another piece of the puzzle into the proper place for me. When this happens, well I can't help but smile. The whole of *The Prophecies* is such an amazing piece of work, with so few words, but so much meaning, and with such confusing style that unfolds into a consistently repeated pattern. It impresses me each time I discover some new facet that I missed before; and, it is so remarkable that it can only come from Heaven. I feel my heart warm when I have been led to understand Nostradamus, and I want to give you that feeling too.

Still, with all of that warmth of feeling, I have also felt a sense of urgency to get the message that Nostradamus wrote out to the public. I have been frantic at times. At first this was because I saw the possibility of that proverbial "line in the sand" being crossed or "the point of no return" passed, leaving no time to prevent a tragedy. I worried that current trends in international affairs would escalate, before I could get the word written and out for common consumption. However, just as I had to learn that losing my possessions was all part of Jesus' plan for me, I also had to learn that this message would get to you when you were ready to hear it. You would not see what I have to say until I was ready to write it the right way.

My haste to write book one meant that, by the time that I had finished writing it, I had learned more about the systems and nuances of the style than I did at first. These new adaptations meant I would have to rewrite it, to add the consistency of what I later learned to the former. The same thing happened as I wrote book two. As I was at the halfway point, I realized more that had not dawned on me, so the editing took twice as long as it took to write book two. Even now I am still realizing more of the refinements, as I was preparing this book for you.

All of this means there is so much meaning in *The Prophecies* and so much detail, that schools could offer degrees, in multiple disciplines of study, covering all aspects of what Nostradamus wrote. There is so much to tell about this work that I believe it will take years for me to realize what I have still missed. You do not need to know all of that detail. When this future begins, you will not want to be living it, so all you need to know is enough to bring out your faith.

It has taken me a while to realize that. God knows I am committed to see this project through; but, He also knows I need to fret over my impatience and practice getting the attention of people, so when the right time comes I will be ready to do what He really wants me to do. All of this practice has prepared me to make this vital point of belief that I am making to you now. And let me reiterate that I do not take credit for having figured that out all by myself.

Christ leads us by sending people into our lives to tell us how to approach our problems. Usually, at least in my case, these people tell me what I don't want to hear, so I only actually listen to what they say after I have beat my head against a wall a few times. Christ has sent people to tell me how to live, all of my life. I have marveled at the synchronistic comings and goings of people in my life, and how they affected me at the time of appearance; but, usually I have only realized this importance in hind sight. It has been these casual visitors, in and out quickly, leaving a fast impact I have been most aware of. It has been the people who have been closest to me who have acted in the same manner; but, I have tended to be looking for something more exotic to take notice. At least, take notice before I fall on my face and remember someone close told me not to fall. Three such friends (maybe more) have told me you want to read this book, which means Christ knows you want to read this book; and, you are not so interested in the scholastic textbook explanation. You are ready to believe, without all of the details.

Still, in these times of anguish over how I was going to do this book, I have been reminded of two fairy tales, or fables, which have seemed to symbolize all of my difficulties in getting this message out. I have only now finally understood how they precisely represent what I have been going through. It finally dawned on me what the true meaning, or concept is that is at the core of these stories, which has been there for us all to realize, from the beginning. I am going to tell you these two fables; but, before I fully explain them to you, I want you to think about them by yourself first. See if you can feel the full meaning on your own before you read what I have to write about them. The fables are *The Boy Who Cried Wolf* and *Chicken Little*.

In the story of *The Boy Who Cried Wolf*, it should be fairly understandable that this applies to me, as I have been crying out for people to listen to what I have to say for some time now; but, no one has been responding. Of course we all know the story, such that a shepherd boy is given the responsibility of watching over the town's flock of sheep. He is told if the sheep are not watched, a wolf can come in and eat the sheep. This is not a desired outcome, so the boy is instructed to call out "Wolf!" should the wolf come.

Well, the boy begins to test the town and this emergency response system, by crying "Wolf!" when there is no wolf around. The people of the town all come running, with clubs to beat the wolf away, but the boy just admits there was no wolf. He just wanted to see if the system worked. He then does this so many times that when the wolf actually does come, his cries for help have no effect on the people. Sadly, in the end the boy and the sheep are eaten by the wolf.

Now, while I have easily been able to see the parallel to the end of that story, where no one comes running, it hasn't seemed a perfect fit for my situation. I say this because I haven't been misleading anyone, since the time I first began crying "Wolf!" The moral is supposedly that no one will believe a liar, even when a liar is telling the truth, so always telling the truth is paramount. That seems appropriate; but, I have not been lying, so the fit did not set well with me. Still, I kept being reminded of that story.

It finally dawned on me that the moral is not about lying at all. The moral is not about the boy getting eaten, it is about the people of the town allowing the boy to get eaten. Boys will be boys, so a boy testing the system should be expected a few times. If the people of the town wanted someone completely trustworthy watching the sheep, they should have sent a man, or one of themselves. A man could have fought off the wolf without needing to call for help; or, if more than one wolf came, he could then call for help and be expected to really need help. This seems so obvious to me now that it really seems amazing that the "don't trust a liar" moral ever stuck.

I want you to look at this fable in a new light now, as I want you to look at the symbolism that is all through this made-up story. The boy is the shepherd over a flock of sheep. A boy, as a child, represents innocence and purity. The sheep represent the meek.

Now there is another parallel to this, which we all recognize as Christians, where Jesus Christ is the shepherd of our souls. The sheep, therefore, are the souls of all of us who need to be watched, so that they will not be stolen by the wolf. It is our souls that are meek and in need of care. The reason all the people of the town were to be called is because they are the bodies which own those souls. When their souls were to become endangered of being lost, they wanted to know, so they could save their souls from the wolf that would steal them and consume them.

Now, think about the people of the town being in the town, away from their souls. The town represents the conscious state, or reality, or the material world. That is what is more important to the people, although they also put importance on their souls, even though they do not physically watch over them. In other words, we have to live this linear life that we are born into, even though our souls are the source of that life and must be protected. This takes us down to the ending, which is the source of the true moral.

The people have been called to protect their souls, over and over, even though the people, who run to see the wolf, cannot see the wolf. Since the boy, or Jesus Christ, has told them there really was no wolf present, the call was a test. The truth has been told. The boy did not lie about there not being a wolf, because when the people got to the boy and the sheep, no wolf was there. The boy was testing the system, just as Jesus Christ will test our faith in Him. It is no different than a fire drill, which is an intentional false alarm to make us act with a sense of urgency. Such practice of that urgency is by design and will make a real fire become less of a danger to us. So, when the people finally give up responding, due to these test calls, their souls have been stolen by the wolf. Think about that for a moment.

As we go about our daily routines as human beings, in whatever it is that we do, we must always guard our souls, especially whenever we hear the cry. Since the sheep are our souls, and the boy is Jesus Christ, these are not figures in the dimension of reality. They exist in our minds or near where we work and play; but, they are close enough that we can always hear the call. The cry of "Wolf!" is our conscience, which tells us when we have sinned. We run to church, or pray for forgiveness, or believe that Jesus Christ is watching over our souls; and, when we feel that comforting sensation of relief that there really is no wolf, we go back to our world and carry on.

The moral of this story is to never stop worrying about our souls, and to never leave them unguarded. We must always trust that voice inside our heads, the one which tells us that what we are doing is drawing the wolf near. Obviously, the wolf represents Satan, who acts deceptively, like a wolf is known to act in fairy tales. Like a wolf to sheep, Satan is always watching for lost souls to grab.

Now, that moral makes more sense to me; and, if you are seeing where I am coming from with that, you will have no problem understanding what Christ's message is, coming through Nostradamus. For these past four years I have been thinking of that fable; but, it only now makes perfect sense why I have been thinking of it for so long. We are in the middle of the times when a cry of "Wolf!" will not be heard.

That's why no one has heard me so far, and that's why I have written this to you now. So many people will have forsaken Jesus Christ, God, and the concept of their souls, that they will not want to leave the town at all. They will have become so comfortable in the earthly plane, with all of its material things that preoccupy our minds. It will be those material distractions that they will not want to leave behind, even to save their souls.

These materially-minded people, who live for the physical pleasures, will have given their soul to the wolf; and, in return Jesus Christ will not be watching over them. That fable will be clearly understood by the time you finish reading this book. I have written this book for you, because you still have possession of your soul and you want to save it.

I hope you will give that fable some more thought later on, but now it is time to move on to the story of *Chicken Little*. This is another fable that has stuck in my mind for four years, all while I have been learning more and more about the meaning of *The Prophecies*. Now I will admit that I had less of an idea about why I was thinking about this fable, than I did with *The Boy Who Cried Wolf.*

The story is about a chick, Chicken Little, who gets hit on the head by an acorn and immediately screams "The sky is falling!" This incident is obviously important to Chicken Little, as she tells the same thing to everyone she meets along the path; and, while no one seems to be able to explain why the sky is falling, it still seems important enough to all of them to decide to go tell the king. After meeting seven other characters along the path, they all run into Foxie Loxie and tell him too.

Now Foxie Loxie does not see any importance in the sky falling; but, he does see a bunch of edible animals that seem pretty gullible. So, he tells them all that he knows the way to the king, which is a lie. He really wants to lead them to his fox den, so he can eat them all up.

This is where the ending gets muddled, as no one ending is said to be from the original version, because the original has been lost. But, the variations are: Foxie Loxie eats them all up in the den, but then the sky falls on him; or, the king's hounds come to save the day and run Foxie Loxie off, so that Chicken Little does get to tell the king that the sky is falling, only to be told that there is nothing to worry about. This leads to multiple morals, depending on which ending you use. One is to have courage and to not be a little chicken; and, the other is not to believe what you are told.

For me, the past four years have been full of telling people that "the sky is falling," with several people somewhat being behind me, by telling me that I need to go tell someone bigger than them. Still, I have not yet reached that point on the path, where I tell someone important like the king about what Nostradamus says is going to happen. Certainly, no one yet has told me that everything is okay.

I also have not met a Foxie Loxie yet, or someone who has tried to lead me to his lair to steal my book, or anything like that. I have had concerns that some power could try to misuse the information that I have; but, so far no warrants for my arrest have been issued. So, I have not really understood why this story has stuck in my head, as it really has seemed like a lame parallel to what I have been through. However, I understand that story now; and once again the symbolism is important to realize.

Here, we have to realize that an acorn is a seed, from the mighty oak tree. A seed is the potential for new growth; but, it has to find a fertile place to rest after it falls. This seed hit Chicken Little on the head. The head represents our thoughts and consciousness, so an acorn hitting Chicken Little's head become symbolic of a seed of thought. Chicken Little instantly knew what the seed meant, meaning that the seed's purpose was growing within her. The little chick represents our innocence and purity, as well as our meekness, such that it becomes important how well we trust our thoughts, as the voice of God's angles that will protect us. The path that Chicken Little commenced to walk is then symbolic of our life path, which we have to walk until our deaths.

The other characters that Chicken Little met along the path of life are those who believe our message, see its importance and want to help by going with us; but, the ones like Foxie Loxie are the ones who want to deceive us away from that path and destroy us. The king, just as the boy in the wolf fable, is Jesus Christ. Notice that a fox and a wolf are similarly foreboding animals which are symbolic of trickery. However, I have left out one very important symbolism, which makes everything come together for me now.

That symbolism is the statement that "the sky is falling." To make this point, let me say that I have translated every word of Nostradamus' Old French into English; and, before taking on that task, I knew nothing about the French language. I still don't consider myself as being able to understand French, without some tool to assist that endeavor; but, one word that I did translate several times, enough to remember it, was the word "ciel." This word translates as "sky." To say, "The sky is falling" in French, would be literally, "le ciel c'est tombant."

Now in French, that same word that translates as "sky" equally translates as "Heaven." Likewise, the present participle for the verb that means "falling" can also mean, "lighting upon." I don't know what language Chicken Little was originally written in, such that it would have been translated to say, "The sky is falling," but the same words in French can mean, "Heaven is upon us."

When you look at the story from that perspective, you and I are represented by the innocence of Chicken Little, such that the seed of thought that our souls receive is the joy of knowing that announcement. However, for it to be felt as a need to warn others, this has been precisely where I have been the last four years. The statement, "Heaven is upon us" is then found to mean, "Christ is returning"; and, this is the ultimate purpose behind *The Prophecies*.

The need to tell others is important to me, because I do not want my fellow souls to be lost when Christ comes. The believers are the ones of like mind, just as Chicken Little (a chicken) told two more chickens (one was a rooster), then told two ducks, two geese, and one turkey.[1] These represent people of like mind; and, they are the ones that the message will have importance to, just like you believing me, causing you to follow the message of Nostradamus due to its importance and tell others. It is the Foxie Loxies of the world that do not understand such a warning, because they are too caught up in the self-gratifications of this world, preying on the innocence of others, trying to steal their souls. The king is Jesus Christ, who is further symbolized in the tale as a lion. When these souls finally reach Jesus and tell Him that Heaven is upon them, He tells them that there is nothing to worry about. This is because Heaven has already arrived. It all makes perfect sense to me now.

---

1 The complete list of characters is: Henny Penny, Cocky Locky, Ducky Lucky, Drakey Lakey, Goosey Loosey, Gander Pander and Turkey Lurkey. All of these fowls are friendly. Foxie Loxie is non-fowl. This is like the different branches of Christianity. The fox is then the natural predator of Christians.

As for the morals the story of Chicken Little is said to convey, it is true that the courage and convictions of our faith and belief is what will place us at the throne of Jesus Christ, when Heaven has returned. Even in the negative outcomes, where the innocent followers have been devoured by the fox, Heaven does come to destroy Foxie Loxie. This is precisely what Christ told Nostradamus to write about. In that story Jesus is returning; but, those that do not have faith will be destroyed and not find Heaven. It will take the courage of Chicken Little to follow our faith in the face of this end.

In the version where the king's hounds come to chase Foxie Loxie away, they represent the angels of God that do protect us from the people who try to take advantage of us. The moral that we cannot always believe what we hear is not wrong, although it has to be tempered somewhat. We can believe in many things that are thought to be wrong by others. Most people would laugh at someone shouting, "The sky is falling!" About as many people would scoff at someone shouting, "Jesus is returning!" We can believe anything that we hear, if our hearts understand that believing is not wrong.

The danger for us lies in believing what the Foxie Loxies of the world tell us. They will say that they know the path to the king, when they really do not. They only want to mislead us, always to their advantage. It is that original "hit in the head" that prompts our belief in what is truly important, knowing it is something we must adhere to. Our hearts will give us the courage of our convictions, to not be swayed from them as we travel on the path of life.

Now these two fables have held significance for me personally, although I only just recently came to fully understand why. As you can see, and I do hope that you will reflect on these more later, the words of the stories do not change, although the message does. It is so often we are taught a story like these and told what they mean. Once told the meaning, we see no reason to think any more about them. Nostradamus is just like this. We are told he wrote a bunch of gibberish with no real meaning, so we don't put any effort into trying to solve it.

Usually, a moral is designed to assist us in being just that ... moral ... in the way we approach our lives. But, what I want you to do now is realize that the meanings are different, even though the same words have been spoken. What we once thought the meaning to be is now seen in a different light. This is how the words of Nostradamus have to be seen as well, to really understand the true meaning that is there. When you next realize that these are the words of God and Christ, you need to think about how this example of double meaning is precisely the way that God and Christ have historically spoken to prophets. Jesus Christ did not change this method when He appeared before Nostradamus.

In fact, as powerful as the Bible is, by conveying the messages that it does, which are the foundations for all Judeo-Christian morals, all of its books have been written in the same manner. All of the authors of the books of the Bible were led to write what they wrote by being in contact with God, whether directly or indirectly. Still, for all that we think we know about what the Bible says, just like we think we know what a fable means, if we allow ourselves to be directed to the true meaning, that meaning will dawn upon us in a personal way. Sometimes this dawning will be something very different than what we thought before.

Let me give an example of this, because it is important that you feel comfortable with this concept before I present you with what Nostradamus wrote, from Jesus Christ, for you to understand. A few months back, while listening to a talk-radio station, the conversation was centered on the war in Iraq. The callers were predominately presenting negative feedback, which was countered by the host, by quoting the scripture that says, "Judge not, lest ye be judged." Somehow, this was the argument that the host used to support the war. I understood this as I had previously learned that passage, which was the meaning expressed by the host. He meant it to mean that it is not for us to judge what God will judge. Such arguments will often stop a Christian cold, because they know the Bible as the source of our morals. The host implied that it was not our place to judge what our government had gotten our nation into. That, I believe, is how most of us have been taught to understand that statement. However, one woman called in to state that it was her parochial teaching that had led her to read that very same statement as meaning, "Don't judge and you will be judged for that lack of judgment."

For me, in the midst of trying to tell the world that we were approaching great danger by going into Iraq, that woman's point of view struck a chord within me. That different view of something that I thought I knew was precisely what I needed to know. That scripture is certainly telling us that it is God's responsibility to judge all souls, such that it is not our place to judge others for their sins; but it is also telling each and every one of us that we are responsible for judging ourselves.

If we see what others are doing and judge that as wrong, then we cannot let

37

their actions cause us to do wrong just because so many are doing wrong and it is not our place to judge. If we do wrong by failing to do right, God will judge us the same as He will judge them. We have full responsibility to judge ourselves, based on that wrong; and, if it is wrong there will be no justifying it if we do it too, or simply allow it to be done without acting to stop a wrong.

This means that every time our conscience tells us not to do something, but we go along with it, simply to not appear judgmental, we are making a mistake. This is a very important lesson to learn, and this lesson is learned by realizing that everything has double meaning, with us conditioned to only see one. Maintaining a connection to God will make these other meanings appear to us, when our souls are in danger. It is so important that you understand that.

As I have translated all of the words that Nostradamus wrote, concerning *The Prophecies*, I have had the greatest struggles when he would switch to Latin, from his standard French. I do not speak Latin either, so I would have to look up words in a Latin-to-English dictionary. Latin has some nuances that English and French don't have, even though French is mainly based in Latin, with English having a lot of French words in it, making it somewhat Latin-based. However, it is very clear that Nostradamus switched to Latin when he quoted from the Bible, or spoke in highly religious terms. This work has led me to realize yet another reason why we do not have a full grasp of the double meanings of the Bible.

One of the major elements of the Christian Reformation was spearheaded by Martin Luther. That movement occurred when he went against Rome, by translating and publicly presenting the Bible in German, or whatever language the local people spoke. The Catholic Church was adamantly against that; but, there were many other people who also believed what Martin Luther believed. The Bible was relatively soon translated into many other languages of the people, so that the people could understand what the Bible stated. This meant that the people were no longer completely dependent on a priest to tell them what it all meant.

The unfair restrictions and punishments that the Church of Rome doled out to those that broke its rules only acted to spur more resistance from the reformers; and, the result is what we have today – the fragmentation of one Church of Christ into many splinter organizations, under the general heading of Christianity. While I am not here to condone either the Reformation or the Inquisitions, I am here to tell you that there is some credence in keeping the

Latin intact; or even more importantly, keeping the original Hebrew and Greek intact, or whatever language the books of the Bible were written in, as that is where the total meaning lies.

I have found so many errors in the previous translations of Nostradamus' words, which people have made innocently, but made nonetheless, that what you may have read that was attributed to him as having written is, for the most part, not what he wrote at all. This is the basic problem that I have found with translation, such that there is not always one clear word that can be substituted for one written. I do not know if this was the reason that the Catholic Church opposed translating the Bible into multiple languages; but, when you look at the multiple meanings that so many words in Latin have, to select just one meaning then becomes a severe limitation on the whole meaning that is found in the Bible's Latin words. You will find that demonstrated in the letters at a few points.

Now the scholastic people who study religion and translations and the Bible specifically know that these errors exist; and, to some degree they let that be known. For example, on a couple of television shows that I have seen, which presented the Exodus of Moses, they announced that what the King James Version of the Bible's translation states, saying Moses parted the "Red Sea," actually translates from the Hebrew stating "the sea of reeds." In one other example that you will find here, presented in Nostradamus' Letter of Preface, the Latin word "virga" is used in the King James Bible to mean "rod." In reality, while this word can translate as "rod," it can equally translate as "a green twig." Depending on the usage selected the meaning of the statement changes significantly. So, I want you to realize that what I am going to tell you in this book is based on what was really written by Nostradamus, in a literal word-for-word translation. They are my translations for you, which you can trust or question.

You will find that the way I present Nostradamus will change any preconceptions you have ever had before. You will not find anyone else who presents Nostradamus the way I do, so there is no other source for you to go to for the truth. However, keep in mind that the same methods that I apply here can also be applied to the Bible, and anywhere else where someone has done the translations for us. It is my intent to have you to believe the Bible and I want you to believe me; but, I want you to be certain in your belief, above all. If you have any questions at all, you have to search for the true answers. This can be done by hours of looking up one word at a time in a dictionary, as I have done. Or, you

39

can look within yourself as you read what I have written, asking God and Christ for enlightenment. Either way, you must be willing to trust that the true answers will dawn upon you, as they have me.

I want you to know that it is okay to follow-up on what I say, since it is so new and different. I also want you to know that what I will present to you, as to what Nostradamus wrote in his words, is not totally dependent on faith alone to believe. What I state will be found to be valid, by the rules of true logic, as I have not and will not state anything that cannot be supported by those rules.

Let me just say now that there are many people who use the word "logic," and believe that they are very "logical," when they really do not know what all entails the process of critical thinking and the art and skill of logic. People most often jump to conclusions before they have completed the process of logic, coming to erroneous conclusions that seem quite logical to them. However, when their arguments, based on those faulty opinions, become exposed to some-one who knows how to properly use logic, their premises completely fall apart. Everything that I state about Nostradamus is based from logical opinions.

Now, I don't want to give the impression that I am some machine of logic that will only approach life from these rules. I did minor in philosophy in col-lege, but I never took a course in logic. I cannot say that I began to understand Nostradamus from a perspective of logic, as I did not. I completely stumbled onto what I found; and, it was my faith in Christ and God that brought the clarity to me, which then fortified my faith in them and the message that was being revealed to me. Logic had nothing to do with what I saw, at first, although everything that I was seeing made logical sense to me.

Faith is something that logic cannot prove. The history of the rules of logic states that they were constructed by the philosopher Aristotle, during an age of man when faiths and beliefs were frequently questioned. Some of the greatest philosophers in history tried to find logical proof of God, or at least some higher knowledge that was behind all that was known. This was based on their faith that this higher power must exist, because man was incapable of producing so much. None of the philosophers, so far, have come close to proving the existence of God, beyond a shadow of doubt. Beyond the shadow of doubt is purely where faith and belief lie. However, logic can be used to support that belief; and, in the case of Nostradamus, logic is what will defeat the arguments that have been used both for and against Nostradamus in the past.

It is not my purpose here to teach you the art of critical thinking and logic; but, it is important to understand just how important that is, when there are many people who will try to trick us, by presenting their illogical opinions as fact. I do suggest that you do a search of the Internet, by entering the key words "critical thinking" and "logic," and read up on this branch of philosophy. If you read the pages that are designed to give you an overview of all of the tests that something must pass to be deemed logical, you will find those tools will best help you approach my opinions. This will give you real reason to argue my points, from a perspective that is more than the simple illogical opinion of disbelief.

If you do as I have suggested you will be alarmed at just how illogical all of the views that have previously been presented about Nostradamus have been. The people who have made a living by attacking the views of people who appear to be in support of Nostradamus have not used logic to argue against that belief. They have just seen how illogical the opinions for Nostradamus are. Since they do not take the logical approach of a debate, or true argument, they have not taken any time to inspect what Nostradamus actually wrote. This means that Nostradamus has never really been the focus point of the debate. They have preferred to take the lazy approach, of simple disbelief, such that the issue of what Nostradamus truly wrote, and the meaning thereof, has never been addressed before. Everything you have heard or read previously has been one illogical opinion attacking another illogical opinion. This is nothing more than arguing for the sake of arguing, with nothing being accomplished.

This happens all the time, and you and I have both done this before, even if it was something trivial, like the great beer debate on television -- which is better? Tastes great or less filling? In a case like that there is no real reason to worry about an illogical argument. However, since the arguments, both for and against Nostradamus, have swayed many people to disbelieve Nostradamus, incorrectly, this issue does need to be justified.

We have a legal system that is very dependent on the use of logic, such that illogical arguments are usually stricken down, before they can begin to sway someone's opinion. If the argument over belief in Nostradamus was actually tried in a court of law, none of the evidence that has been presented so far, as reason for believing, would be admissible. They have a legal term for what the believers of Nostradamus would present, which is "hearsay."

If you are like I was, I was first interested in the notion of Nostradamus

because I thought the idea of some man being able to see the distant future accurately was interesting and worth investigating a little more. That was a long
time ago, when I bought my first book on Nostradamus (and only book I owned
for 25 years); but, way back then I could not read the French text and understand what it said. That made me totally dependent on the English translations
that the English-speaking author provided in the book. Admittedly, reading the
English translations made very little sense to me either, but at least I knew what
most of the words meant. Some of the translations, according to the author,
made little sense to her also; and she was the one interpreting them all. However,
many of the quatrains were accompanied by a paragraph or two, telling what
those strange poems meant.

Well, let me tell you that after I wrote my first book part of the reason it could
not become published was that I did not do my own translations. To use the
work of another author, who had taken some time to translate the Old French
to English, was then necessary for me to write about Nostradamus at all. But,
to do that I was faced with going through the painstaking process of getting the
permission of that author's publisher, which had since ceased to be a publisher.

With all of the corporate takeovers, mergers and rights acquisitions that had
resulted since that author first published, it was not an easy matter to simply
find out who owned the rights, so I could ask for permission. Add to that the
requirements of having to produce another copy of my 25-year old book, highlight each translation that I wanted to use in my book, and send that to the legal
department of a publisher, with a letter explaining why I wanted permissions,
I realized that it would be much faster for me to consider another solution. I
decided to do my own translations and completely rewrite the book, according
to my own abilities to translate French to English. Besides, by that point, as little
as I knew about the French language, I had already found some glaring errors in
the translations in the book that I had used as my only source.

It took me four months just to translate all 948 of the quatrains that are attributed to Nostradamus and *The Prophecies*.[2] As tedious as that task was, what
kept me vigorously going down that road of translating a foreign language was

---

2   There are 943 confirmed quatrains. Some authors also include 5 other quatrains that
are believed to be by Nostradamus' hand, but so many forgeries came out that it is unsure.
I am convinced that these 5 are actually Nostradamus' work.

the fact that in quatrain after quatrain I found that the translations that I was producing were significantly different from what was found already translated for me. This wasn't just in the one book that I owned, but in all the books I had since purchased on Nostradamus. By then I had purchased, or had given to me, about ten other books on this topic. All of those authors basically had published the same translations, with minor variations; but, very few of theirs matched mine exactly. There are several reasons for that.

First of all, I was doing a literal translation, word-for-word, maintaining the case and tense as the word was written; but, all of the other translators were taking a few of the words written and then paraphrasing the rest. Remember, in a court of law this type of altered evidence is hearsay. The reason they have done that is the literal words do not make complete sentences, in a nice, easy to understand way. To solve that problem, everyone has made up what they thought a sentence makes sense from those words. This means that everything you have read that Nostradamus wrote is wrong. You just read what someone thought Nostradamus wrote. Returning to what I said about the use of logic, that is an illogical opinion and not fact.

Second, every other author has admitted in their forewords that they do not have a clue where Nostradamus learned to punctuate, because all of *The Prophecies* is punctuated like done by an illiterate madman. To alleviate this problem, every author that has published a book of translations of Nostradamus has done so by putting in their own punctuation, changing or omitting the punctuation that Nostradamus wrote. This again is not presenting what Nostradamus wrote, with the accompanying explanation, it is making up something, attributing the influence to Nostradamus, and then explaining what they just made up. This is not fact, but highly illogical; and, is not admissible as evidence for or against Nostradamus.

Finally, there are many words Nostradamus wrote which are not words in either Old French or Latin. Many of them may be spelled similar to another word in French, or another language, such that the translators have made the automatic change to the word known. However, many more words of this nature do not even come close to matching a known word in language.

To solve this problem, the translators have all admitted that this and that word is unknown; but then proceed to present wild guesses about what those words mean. This leads some to believe that Nostradamus actually did mean that. After all, an expert suggested it. This is faulty reasoning, as the only way any unknown word can be guessed at is with a consistent logical method, making it an educated guess. Once again, none of this is fact, thus none can be entered as evidence for what Nostradamus wrote.

The people who have spent time arguing against all of the faulty opinions of the believers have historically put forth explanations against Nostradamus that served no purpose other than to defeat faulty opinions. Those who have acted to argue against Nostradamus have actually presented no logical approach to what Nostradamus actually wrote. They have only defeated the people who have guessed wrongly about what Nostradamus wrote, or what they think he meant by writing it. If all of those people who call for belief in Nostradamus were true, with valid arguments, the only way that disbelievers could reach logical agreement on a difference of opinion is to actually know what Nostradamus did write. A valid disagreement can only be solved by approaching the argument from that perspective. They do not do this, as this would require some effort researching something that they simply automatically reject.

Automatic rejection is another form of faulty reasoning, and although some automatic rejection can be correct, it proves nothing without supporting reason. To simply deny belief, because one's opinion has automatically rejected the possibility that seeing the future is within the realm of human achievement, would not hold up in a court of law.

There the laws require that the factual reason be presented as grounds for rejection, such as an example of a previous case that proved that specific impossibility. Since it is commonly accepted that weathermen see the future in their 5-day outlooks and stock brokers see the buying and selling trends of future stocks, one cannot simply reject belief in seeing the future. Acceptable forecasters utilize detailed statistical analysis or computer generated movements and trends to argue the accuracy of their abilities. To argue against Nostradamus' predictions, one must be prepared to specifically argue why that is impossible, should that be their opinion.

Now, if Nostradamus was alive and well today, all of the prior opinions would become moot. To really argue whether or not Nostradamus could see the future, it would all be a matter of asking him, "What does it all mean?" Since he is the author, he is the one person who can speak for himself, to answer what the meaning is. If that answer were obtained from Nostradamus everyone would be forced to come to an agreement of the meaning. From that point of agreement, different opinions could be made, based on that stated meaning. However, Nostradamus died in 1566 and there is no way he can personally tell us today what he meant; or, at least that seems to be the case.

Nostradamus actually did tell us what he meant in *The Prophecies*, before he died. When *The Prophecies* was first published in 1555, it came with a preface, which appeared to be a letter to his son, Caesar. As a preface, simple definition states that this is an author's foreword about the book it appears in, mapping out what the book is about. That is Nostradamus' own words about what the general concepts that will be found to follow. However, very few people have been able to make much sense of this letter, especially as far as connecting it to what is found in the quatrains. But, there is another letter that Nostradamus wrote, which he wrote for the express purpose of explaining everything that he wrote.

Three years after the first publication of *The Prophecies*, everyone was having a very hard time understanding what the verses meant. This included the King of France, Henry II. Henry paid Nostradamus to write and publish, so he was expecting more of an understandable work from Nostradamus. Everything Nostradamus had written before had been understandable and judged highly accurate. He was a very popular astrologer and many called him a prophet, due to his accuracy with astrology. But, with *The Prophecies* being so difficult to understand, Henry requested an explanation, and Nostradamus replied with a letter. This Letter to Henry II is clearly an explanation of the meaning of *The Prophecies*.

The problem with this letter has been that it is even more difficult to understand than the Letter of Preface. Many authors on Nostradamus do not even attempt to interpret this letter as it appears as if it was written by someone insane. Rather than attempting to understand this letter, past interpreters have simply disregarded it. This means the two letters of instruction which accompany *The Prophecies* have not been used to support the claims of what the quatrains mean. This is absolutely irresponsible, as figuring out how to understand the explanations is what will act for Nostradamus being alive today to tell us what his quatrains are all about.

This is what I have been able to do, and this is what you are about to read. When you have finished reading the rest of this book, you will know more about what *The Prophecies* mean than anyone who has ever professed to be an expert on Nostradamus. It will be these letters that will serve to draw out your faith, as they are remarkable documents. Together, they fully explain what is found in the quatrains, when they are properly interpreted.

The Letter of Preface states the theme of *The Prophecies*, including the prime theme that the work is truly from Jesus Christ. It places only a minimum of focus on the actual story, while giving important clues about how to read the document for meaning. The Letter to Henry II, as a letter of explanation, confirms the preface; but, it goes into great detail about seeing the future, as well as the distant past, while giving solid astrological timing clues. The majority of the letter then gives an overview of each different element of the story that the quatrains tell when they are placed in the proper order. When these letters are understood, everything about *The Prophecies* becomes clear.

This is the only logical way to solve Nostradamus. All interpretations of *The Prophecies* have to match what he said it meant. I have done this for you. Of course, you can take what you find in this book and come to your own conclusions. In my case, I have spent about four years making the quatrains fit these explanations, and vice versa. I have done this so you will have this logical approach to provide you with ample reason to believe in Nostradamus. However, you are more than welcome to double check my work; but I do not believe that you will want to spend that time doing that.

Let me assure you I have done all of the background work necessary for properly presenting these letters. I believe I have finally been led to present this here in a manner that best makes it possible for you to understand them. The original presentations of the Letter of Preface and the Letter to Henry II were written such that they were designed to confuse the readers; but, this confusing style is also built into the quatrains themselves. It is this style that has mystified so many people for so long; and, although some of the content has easily been captured by others, the style keeps them from getting to the depths, where the true meaning lies. I remove the necessity of having to learn to read through this style, while I still make it possible for you to learn it.

In order to present them in this manner, so that the true meaning becomes clear, I have had to modify the letters to varying degrees. In that respect, they do not appear in this book exactly as they originally appeared. I will explain more about that when I introduce each letter; but, one modification is the separation of text into more readable portions. The Letter to Henry II requires a more extensive modification, which calls for its readable portions to be reordered.

Still, it will be found that even with my modifications I remain true to what Nostradamus actually wrote. While I have sorted large blocks of text into smaller ones, none of the words have been changed, replaced or altered. While there are places that sections have to be moved and fit in with other sections, I have maintained the order of the original words. In this sense, everything has been kept intact; and, this will all make more sense once you begin to read what I present.

I am not making the mistakes that others have made before, because my modifications come from understanding the quatrains. It is the quatrains that the letters explain; so if one understands the quatrains, the letters can make sense. While the reverse is usually the case for solving a riddle – the instructions tell you how to solve it – in the case of Nostradamus the instructions are as much of a riddle as are the quatrains. Since I solved the systems of the quatrains first, it became possible for me to solve the letters. Still, there are aspects in the proper ordering of the quatrains which require having the Letter to Henry II solved first.

The way I present these letters is totally based on my four years of enlightenment; and, from all of my efforts I have been allowed to correctly interpret a significant number of the quatrains, although I have not had the time to concentrate on all of them. Some I have not yet interpreted, although I have translated them and have a general feel for their placement. Some I have sorted into a grabbag of "not sure yet" quatrains (less than 5%, or under 50); but I understand the correct method for gaining that understanding. The majority I have been able to place well enough to establish a firm order of story, even though most I have not yet written an interpretation on. I am able to sort them based on just a few key words that each quatrain contains.

All of my ability to sort and match and categorize into story sections is based on being able to see what Nostradamus actually wrote, while converting that into an understandable language for myself. Before I began my own translations, I was able to see some of the most basic elements of a system that was incorporated into the writing style; but, the time spent translating brought out more elements, and the time spent writing interpretations brought out the rest. I have realized enough of this system to be able to know what Nostradamus meant; and, this system I have discovered is the foundation for the logic that will defend my findings. I wrote about these systems in *Pearls Before Swine, Volume 1*, so I will not explain them here. But, Nostradamus explains most of them in his letters, which will then be more specifically defined for you.

It is important for you to realize that my work with the quatrains preceded my work with the letters. It has been from my understanding of those that I have been able to make sense of the letters. What has become so pleasingly simple to me is what has been so difficult for others to understand, for quite a long time. These are the doorways I kept peeking in, each time learning something new. I was certain the systems worked in the quatrains; and, I trusted the systems would equally apply to the letters, making them more understandable, which they did. What you are about to read of those letters is a result of all of that knowledge having been applied to them.

In *Pearls Before Swine, Volume 1* I applied this same knowledge to the Letter of Preface; but, I presented that letter differently than I will present it here. In my first explanation, I made separate explanations of each block of Nostradamus' words. This means I showed you what Nostradamus wrote, then I explained what that meant, one portion at a time. This method, while maintaining the integrity of Nostradamus' words, is too much of an educational approach for easy understanding. It becomes easy to get lost and makes it prohibitive to the casual reader. For this reason, as this book's purpose is to give you the full impact of what Nostradamus meant in his words, it becomes necessary for me to add my own words to Nostradamus' words, as part of his text. This is done so the words that Nostradamus wrote flow in the true communicative style that they were intended to represent.

All of my word additions are solely influenced by the meanings and definitions of Nostradamus' words; and, you must always remember that Nostradamus' words were carefully selected by Jesus Christ. My words are clearly identifiable and will be found to be attached to the individual words or phrases that Nostradamus wrote. This addition acts as the necessary explanatory words for the meaning intended, based on definition and knowledge of the quatrains. As Nostradamus wrote these letters in the first person, I maintain that perspective. In essence, I am using Nostradamus' words along with my words to speak for him, to you.

I also want to assure you that I am not smart enough to figure this entire thing out by myself. If intelligence was the key to understanding Nostradamus, it would have been solved a long time ago, by much brighter men than I. I do not take any credit for having figured anything out alone; although it was my brain that functioned to figure it out, and my body that typed it all out. I clearly contend that there was a higher mind at work, leading me through this entire experience. I want you to know that I have been led to this point of presentation by Jesus Christ and God and the angels who serve them.

I have not been chosen for this task because I need to be a star or a celebrity, or because I seek great wealth and riches. I have been chosen simply because I had certain basic qualifications: believing in God and Christ and prayer; being receptive to my inner voice; and, having a strong interest in poetry, mythology and metaphysics, which includes Nostradamus. My status as an astrologer also helps, such that I am able to understand the mechanics and symbolisms of the astrology Nostradamus used. Still, with all of those qualifications, I was primarily chosen to understand so that I would be able to give you a warning from Jesus Christ. That is the whole purpose for my being here right now – I must make you aware of this message.

Finally, I want you to remember for just one moment, before you begin reading the Letters of Nostradamus, the two fables that I told you about before. I want you to envision me as the boy that is crying "Wolf!" Also, see me as an oak tree beside you, dropping an acorn on your head. You should hear the call of importance and feel an awakening to something that you had never thought of before. It is now time for to you to react accordingly. You have to ask yourself, "Am I ready to respond to this danger?" You have to ask yourself, "Do I have the courage and desire to respond?"

You now are armed with enough information on this matter to not be fooled by others ever again. The letters that you are about to read will be all that you will need to know for your soul's salvation. You will not have to take a course on how to understand Nostradamus. Just read the explanations that Nostradamus wrote, telling us what *The Prophecies* means. It says enough, even if it does not say it all. Then, listen to your inner voice as you read and then again when you are through with the whole book. Let it lead your thoughts, and trust them. Your prayers and dreams are the assistance that you need to get in touch with your faith; and, hold on to that faith. Release your guard and open yourself up to receive the word of Christ, as written by Nostradamus and enhanced by me.

ABOUT THE LETTERS

Of the two letters, the Letter of Preface is the shortest. It is almost exactly half as long as is the Letter to Henry II. By modern typeset standards, the Letter of Preface amounts to roughly four pages of single-spaced, 10 point type. The Letter to Henry II is about eight pages, typed in the same manner. This makes it appear that the letters are brief, especially when compared to the quatrains. However, looks are deceiving, especially where Nostradamus is concerned.

In these two letters that Nostradamus wrote, they are so compact because every word is packed in tightly together. Think of it as Nostradamus speaking in rudimentary words, where only the most important words to understand were written. In my method, where I separate each segment of text so that it becomes a separate line, determined by Nostradamus' use of any form of internal punctuation or symbol, this expands the length. When I then double space at each period that Nostradamus wrote, this spreads each document out even more. Without anything added to explain the words, it doubles the page count of the Preface to eight and turns the eight-page Henry letter into a 20-page document.

When my explanation is added, you find that what appear to be two relatively short documents actually unfold into two very detailed dissertations. In addition to my words, I turn the letters into manageable sections, with headings. This adds some extra blank spaces, but it makes everything more easily digested. As proper letters of instruction and explanation, these documents must be able to tell everything that is needed to know, towards understanding what is contained in the quatrains of *The Prophecies* and how that understanding is gained.

In that growth, the four pages of the Letter of Preface will be found to turn into a 100-page foreword, in multiple sections. It becomes the explanation of how *The Prophecies* were conceived and how to properly read them. The Letter to Henry II will expand from eight pages to take one hundred seventy-nine pages to properly present, again in multiple sections. This document is actually a full explanation of the story that the quatrains tell; but, it holds some extra information and a twist, which are not specifically in the quatrains.

Each of the quatrains is a microcosm of this kind of hidden length, such that all are produced by writing in the most basic concepts of language. This is opposed to writing in the form of common speech that we naturally expect to find, when reading. In my book *Pearls Before Swine*, I averaged writing about four pages of text for each four lines of verse. This length was mostly due to the explanations that I followed each quatrain with, showing how I came to the conclusions that I reached. Here, instead of doing that style of explanation, I will simply add the explanations as if Nostradamus himself had fully written the letters, without need for explanation.

Since the Letter of Preface was published first, placed before the first sets of quatrains released in 1555, I will present it here first. The Letter to Henry II was an "after the fact" document, written in 1558, so I will present it second. However, what I am not including in this book are the quatrains, which followed the preface and then prompted the letter to Henry. This is important to know, because both letters directly reference the quatrains. The quatrains contain all of the amazing detail that is generalized in nearly 300 pages of explanation here, requiring an estimated 3,500 pages of interpretation, when all is said and done.

A letter was written to the King of France because nothing of *The Prophecies* made sense to the people that expected to gain from such a large work. Those people were the "investors" of Nostradamus, which were the King and the Church. While Nostradamus had written yearly almanacs, which were somewhat like puzzles by not clearly stating the details, they were not hard for these men of wealth, position and intellect to figure out. These predictions were found amazingly accurate; and, in the way that they teased the reader to figure them out, it made them more appealing. But, this new work was different, as it was immediately way too hard to figure out. Explanations were demanded because the verses had some fairly obvious calamitous words in them. This made Henry suggest that Nostradamus come to him and explain more about what this work was about.

Of course, since Nostradamus wrote a letter to Henry, he did not go to the King to explain anything. Had he done that, it would have been possible that Nostradamus could have been detained, until he talked clearly. That might have resulted in some pain, so Nostradamus wasn't about to do that. He instead fulfilled his obligation to the King in a letter. That letter actually does fully explain *The Prophecies*; but, it was as easy to understand as were the quatrains, which means that everything returned to square one. Nobody had a clue what anything meant; and, until now, basically everything has stayed just as confusing as it was then.

I will tell you now that, as far as the contents of the two letters are concerned;

the Letter of Preface is a very straightforward document. If you understand the basic principles of the systems that make the quatrains make sense, then a simple application of the same principles makes the preface fairly easy to make sense of too. The Letter of Preface actually confirms those principles, instructing the reader how the following text should be read. The difficulty comes when you get to the Letter to Henry II, as this letter is much more complex in its presentation.

I will explain more about that complexity before I present my version of the letter to Henry; but, let me state here that the finished result that you will read will have removed all of the complexities, of both letters. I also want you to know that when I began working on this book I had done nothing towards fully understanding the Letter to Henry II. I had translated the Old French into English and in doing that I was able to see how it related to the quatrains. However, I had no clue that the finished result would be as powerful as it is.

A lot of the confusion seems to come from the writing style that Nostradamus used in both letters. I have recently been told that the paragraph is a relatively modern invention, such that it was not a formal writing tool in the 16th Century. This makes sense, as there are basically no indents to speak of, which would indicate paragraph breaks. For the most part, when Nostradamus began a letter, he wrote until it was time to sign his name. I am not certain if this style was typical for most 16th Century works of literature, or not. You will see both letters presented, so that they are broken into blocks of text that will act much the same as paragraphs, although not perfectly. Some blocks are actually quite long, too long for a proper paragraph.

This inability by others to break these documents down into separated, bite-size bits of information does explain some of the difficulty that so many have encountered when trying to interpret them. Still, besides this continuous flow of text, which appears to not be separating groups of thought into individual sections, Nostradamus wrote in what my English teacher would call "extremely complex sentences." My English teacher explained this to me because I can fall into a "put everything into one sentence" streak, which is from not editing a free-flow of thoughts. Nostradamus takes this style of long-windedness to new heights, making it appear to be impossible to follow his frequent leaps in thought.

Nostradamus wrote as if he was limited to the number of periods he could use. This made for some very long-winded statements, where the capitalized first word would be followed by an inordinate number of words, separated by many other forms of punctuation. These statements would then weave through what appears to be several shifts in thoughts, to finally end with a period. It reads like he took a deep breath and then spit out as much language as he could, before having to place a period and take another deep breath.

For instance, the Letter of Preface has only 36 periods in it, for a 4-page document. The Letter to Henry II only has 68, at roughly eight pages. Obviously, book publishers in 1555 must not have been as concerned about editing as they are today. This is also seen in the volumes of other punctuation that is used, many seemingly incorrectly, which completely magnifies the low numbers of periods that were used. I gave up trying to count, but there are roughly three times as many commas, at least twice as many colons, and more ampersands than you can shake a stick at, compared to the number of periods.

I jest a little writing this assessment of Nostradamus' writing style, partly because sometimes I wake up and realize that I need to change what I have written. What I originally write as one complete thought often gets edited into two sentences. I also know the hoops that a writer must jump through to get published. I doubt that Nostradamus would get the attention of the biggest name agents and book publishers today, with that style that he used then. However, the amazing thing that I want to point out is that every mark of punctuation and every limited period is precisely the correct form of punctuation. Every mark was written with intent and is necessary to make everything understandable.

Nostradamus' use of punctuation was very much by design. It served two purposes, the first of which was to confuse the reader. This worked very well in 1555; and, this confusion has persisted throughout the centuries. In the year 2000, for the millennium edition of Henry C. Robert's book on Nostradamus, he footnoted his presentation of the Letter to Henry II, at the bottom of the first page the letter appeared on. In that footnote Roberts stated that if it was up to him the book would not include the Letter to Henry II. He stated that the letter was impossible to make sense of; and, to put it in the book was a waste of paper. If not for the demands of his publisher, he would have omitted it from the book.

While I think some other authors should have also tried to keep it out of their books, the reality has been that no one has ever brought forth an intelligible interpretation of this Epistle. This brings out the second reality of Nostradamus' seeming misuse of punctuation, which causes so much confusion. This is actually the most important key to unlocking the meaning of what was written, as the punctuation is not marking a properly written sentence (there are none of those to punctuate), as much as it marks the direction to the next series of words.

You will not be able to notice this "impossible" punctuation in what I will present to you here, as I have eliminated all of Nostradamus' punctuation, except for the periods. All of the other punctuation that appears is mine. The punctuation of Nostradamus becomes invisible; but, if you have a copy of the letter that shows the punctuation marks, then you may be able to detect the direction statements in the text that I add. Once you understand how to read Nostradamus, the mysterious punctuation can disappear.

In the quatrains, the greatest number of them (I imagine over 95%) end with a period. Within the four lines of each quatrain that does end in a period, various other punctuations are used internally. They appear in the middle and at the end of the lines. One of the common mistakes that have been made, when people have interpreted Nostradamus' verses, is that they see one period and assume that those four lines equal one sentence. As this is not the case at all, the same attempts to make Nostradamus' rambling "sentences" in the letters as connected in one long thought become equally error-prone.

This simplest way for me to explain this to you here is that the use of a period in the letters, and likewise in the quatrains, is designed to be the point of reference that acts to separate thoughts, like a paragraph. Therefore, the period marks a complete block of my text for the letters. However, there is a little more to it than that, as a colon also marks the end of a separate section, as does the "comma ampersand" combination. The colon shows where a following block will clarify a previous block; and, the comma before an ampersand shows where a separate block will emphasize an important point made in the previous block. The use of a semi-colon is not as often used; but, it too will separate a block, to show a different view of a related topic. These all become the paragraph separations.

All of the singular commas act more like a period, showing where the end of the "sentence" structures is found. The majority of these "sentences" are generated simplistically, many from only one word. This is especially true when commas will be found to separate three consecutive words. The one word in the middle becomes a "sentence" by itself, which highlights how all of the words have this capability. Any series of words between punctuation marks can yield as many "sentences" as there are words. This expansion of only one or a small few words into several sentences is, in essence, the "paragraph" of Nostradamus.

I know this may be difficult for some to grasp. If it is, please do not feel alone, as no one has been able to grasp it in 450 years. It is a completely different way of communicating than the way we have all been taught in school. We are taught to recognize syntax when reading; and, we learn it so well that we begin to automatically make what is written transform to fit that mold. This is what has kept people changing what Nostradamus wrote, as they felt the urge to make it fit their concept of language; and, this is what has kept it a secret message for so long. However, it might help to think of Nostradamus' text as that uttered by a caveman.

Presuming that cavemen spoke in rudimentary concepts, without the refinements of language like punctuation and flowery adjectives, a caveman statement would be grunted in spurts. At the very beginning of time for language, the dictionary was much shorter. Rather than stating, "I am hungry. I think I would like chicken tonight." a caveman would grunt "hungry," then look around and point at a chicken (if they had them then) and then grunt "chicken." This means that one or two words would be uttered at a time. The caveman might include hand gestures and facial expressions, to make sure the word grunted was understood. This would come before going on to grunt the next one or two word expression.

Now, if a stenographer was at this make believe scene, to record the caveman's "sentences", all of the pauses and unspoken gestures would occasionally be noted with marks, or punctuation. In the end, one would find a series of words, with seemingly unintelligible punctuation, resulting in an equally difficult to understand transcription of what was actually communicated. This is how Nostradamus wrote everything associated with *The Prophecies*. Everything has purpose, based on the most basic of meanings.

Whatever punctuation shows in Nostradamus' text, other than a period, is then not necessary to become the actual translation of what was stated. For example, the placement of a comma in the text does not mean that the intended translation is required to have a comma, which follows the grammatically correct use of a comma. The same applies to the placement of colons and semi-colons. Ampersands have a specific purpose, like in the game of Charades, when someone makes the symbol for "new word." All of this acts to show where shifts of thought come in, with everything before the period relating to the overall concept of the paragraph's theme.

Everything other than a period is actually not punctuation at all, but a mark of reference. Since the period denotes a reference for a group break, something like a paragraph, all other marks denote breaks in the statements that make up that paragraph. The words presented between two internal marks, or from the first capitalized word to the first mark, are not indicating that a complete "sentence" must be constructed from all of these words. Each individual word can generate its own sentence, simply by defining that word in sentence form. The marks of punctuation act to indicate the perspective which must be used to view the text that follows.

That view is determined by what defines the use of those marks, meaning that as much as grammar does not apply, the application of definition does. For example, the use of a colon directs attention to what follows, such that an example of what was just stated or a clarification can be expected. Likewise, a comma acts to separate one thought from another. A semicolon acts to show that two related statements that are somewhat dissimilar are combined, expanding one thought. In all of these cases, once the purpose of the symbol is understood, the actual use of that punctuation in a sentence structure is unnecessary.

The use of an ampersand is particularly important in the work of Nostradamus. An ampersand is a symbol used to replace the words, "and per se." This means that it shows an intrinsic value that is applied to that which follows. More than simply stating the meaning of the simple conjunctive word, "and," it symbolizes that what follows stands on its own measure. This shows the significance and importance that must be realized in any word of text that follows the ampersand.

All of this means that punctuation is the key to understanding, as it acts as the commands by which all of the text is read. Once that command is properly understood, it becomes meaningless as actual punctuation, except for the period. Therefore, in the texts I have prepared for you, only the words of Nostradamus are presented. I add the proper punctuation, along with the necessary words which will convey the meaning of what Nostradamus wrote, in a grammatically understandable form.

As far as the words of Nostradamus are concerned, the nouns usually create their own separate sentence, while verbs and adverbs create separate statements of action, based on the sentences created by the nouns. Prepositions and adjectives act to guide the sentences along; but, they are not necessarily connected directly to one of Nostradamus' words. Only the articles act in conjunction with either the nouns or the verbs; but, in the quatrains the article "the" has significance, especially when capitalized. Nostradamus' use of conjunctions is most frequently found at the beginning of a new block, as a form of connecting two blocks together. In this manner of writing, each word written has a much higher impact of purpose and meaning.

You will notice that I present Nostradamus' words in bold print, while all that I have added are in regular type. This will allow you to follow the basic concepts of Nostradamus, from a glance, before you become immersed in reading what my words are telling you that he wrote. Since the punctuation marks of Nostradamus' "sentence" fragments are missing, you will not be able to see how the fragments clearly separate. However, I can tell you that I do not combine the words of two fragments in one sentence of mine. If Nostradamus' words are separated by his punctuation, the words that follow punctuation will be in separate sentences.

To denote Nostradamus' use of a period, I have double-spaced at the end, as if a new "paragraph" has begun. These double-spaces will then be followed by the first word in bold type, capitalized, like Nostradamus wrote it. Whenever a block is separate and not begun with a bold, capitalized letter, then this is a separation created by a colon, semi-colon or comma-ampersand combo.

You will notice that most of these blocks are not proper paragraphs, as you have been taught to construct and recognize a paragraph. Some of the "sentences" or groupings of words between periods can contain well over ten other marks of punctuation. In these cases they then yield large blocks of statements. Since each fragment, between separating marks of punctuation is where Nostradamus wrote most lucidly, on one narrow topic, it is possible that everything could be worded to indicate separate paragraphs, making it all comply fully with literary standards. However, this would make recognition of the original documents too confusing; and, it would defeat the purpose of presenting the true work of Nostradamus' letters. Remembering that paragraphs were not used widely in the 16th Century, I have decided that it is best to present each block of sentences in the way that I have explained, to maintain the integrity of the original work.

One other clarification I want to make is about the use of capitalization. A word Nostradamus wrote that is capitalized shows the significance of that word. Since it is customary to capitalize the first word of a sentence, some first words have been overlooked or seen as less important, even though they have been capitalized. It must be known that all capitalized words have significance, no matter if it is a conjunction, adjective, preposition or article. For this reason, I have tried to avoid capitalizing a word that Nostradamus wrote in lower case, just to begin a sentence.

Further, at some times Nostradamus wrote words in all-caps or words where every letter is capitalized. These words show an obvious greater importance than a regularly capitalized word of name or title. These all-cap words must be noticed and understood, particularly in respect to all aspects of that word's definition. In those cases, all contexts the word can be used in must be considered with the surrounding text. In most cases this will cause one word to generate multiple sentences, based on multiple definitions and contexts.

Keep in mind these letters, just as the quatrains themselves, were written as they were directed to Nostradamus by Jesus Christ. Every word Nostradamus wrote is then a perfect word, in the perfect case and tense, and cannot be altered by mankind's desire to make them fit a grammatical mold. The language of French has no bearing on the understandability of these documents, as the mold of syntax has kept the French from making sense of what was written for 450 years. Christ has carefully chosen all of the words, specifically for each word's full scope of meaning; and, when a literal translation is applied, the language of origin becomes insignificant.

There are also no misspelled words found anywhere in the texts of *The Prophecies,* including these letters. In particular, there are manufactured words which were written; and, usually these manufactured words were created both to confuse and to add depth of meaning. All of these constructed words come as combined forms of existing words; and, the root language will either be French or Latin, but not a mix. No other languages are applied to the texts of Nostradamus, with the exception of the Greek-based names of places and mythological figures.

To better show the reason for manufactured words, consider how any new word gets added to our vocabulary. For example, prior to the invention of the telephone, the word "telephone" did not exist in the English vocabulary. It became a word by combining forms of the Latin words that held the root meaning for what a telephone does. The use of Latin was due to the fact that English is primarily a Latin-based language. Alexander Graham Bell did not search Turkish, Arabic or Sanskrit for potential sources of root words to name his invention; so the same principles of reason can be used to defend the Latin-French sources in Christ-Nostradamus' creation of vocabulary.

Finally, it must be noted that neither of these letters were given a title by Nostradamus. I have given the impression of title by my reference to them as "The Letter of Preface" and "The Letter to Henry II." You will find that some authors will refer to the preface as "The Letter to Caesar Nostradamus," and the one to Henry as "The Epistle to Henry II." I have purposefully avoided such references as these, although I understand how they get these titles. I believe that those titles draw attention to the misleading elements, which have kept both letters in obscurity.

Nostradamus is dedicating *The Prophecies* to his son, Caesar; but, the purpose of the letter is to preface the work for all readers. It is therefore a letter of preface, disguised as a personal letter to his son. While Nostradamus leads the letter to Henry with the all-caps word "Epistle," this word is surrounded by the symbols of brackets. As nothing is misspelled, neither is anything inconsequential. All has meaning; and, by definition the appearance of brackets means to separate or classify. While the word "epistle" is French for "letter," the all-caps and brackets yields that something more important is the source of what is to follow.

This separated "EPISTLE" is actually referring to the separated document that is an Epistle of Jesus Christ. This is then identifying *The Prophecies* as the document that has become the motivation for the letter that follows it. The letter is not the Epistle, but the explanation of it. Still, I refer to each document as a letter because each is signed and dated by Nostradamus at the end, which is customarily how one would finish a letter.

Each letter also has a heading that precedes the text which follows it. The headings are clearly separate from the text; and, they have been written in separate lines, unlike the continuous flow of words which appear in the bodies of the letters. These heading lines include the use of punctuation and capitalization, which makes them very similar in appearance to the quatrains. In both, the separated lines of text are punctuated, which gives the lines and words increased meaning and purpose. This means the headings are also open for interpretation, based on the same rules which apply to the text of the letters and the verses of *The Prophecies*.

One last thing I will mention is in reference to the French of Nostradamus. Other than a few footnotes and some of the proper names or manufactured words, I do not list anything in the language that Nostradamus wrote in. It becomes unnecessary in an English text, especially when I am trying to keep you from being confused as much as possible. Just know that in some places my translations do not match what others have written in translation.

To this difference, all I can say is that I have triple-checked my translations, using an Old French source. I am confident my uses are accurate. Further, you may notice I will sometimes use alternative translations in following sentences, restating something already stated. These will be restating a word that has a dual translation or meaning; but, only the first use will be in bold type. Feel free to buy a book with the Old French text and follow along with my translations.

I hope these instructions are helpful for you. It is not necessary you research what I have written to confirm how I came to the determinations that I have. It is not the main focus of this book to teach you how to read Nostradamus. However, these instructions are designed to assist you, should you feel that need. Moreover, I want you to know that I am certain of what I am writing about here.

There is a very logical explanation for everything I have written; and, I can explain everything in such detail that your head will ache. So, just read what I have written just for you, as I have tried to make it simple and easy. Then, you will have to prove to yourself what more proof and reasoning will be necessary for you to have faith and believe.

PART 2

THE LETTER OF PREFACE TO *THE PROPHECIES*

THE HEADING

This document, or letter, will serve as a **PREFACE**, which means that it precedes this book of quatrains as introductory remarks about the contents held within. However, as I have written this word in all-capital letters, the word "Preface" also carries a deeper meaning. It should also be recognized for its Christian meaning, as used in the Eucharistic liturgies. The all-caps represent that this preface is for a document that will act completely as one's true rite of communion with Jesus Christ, with the words His body and the message His blood. Found within the document to follow will be the words **of** Christ, as spoken to me, **M.** (Mr.) **Michel** de Nostre Dame. My father came from the city named for Our Lady, the Virgin Mary, Mother of Christ. I have commonly been referred to by the Latin derivative of my name, **Nostradamus**. This preface is in reference **to the** title of this work, *The Prophecies*. This title is by no means a misnomer, as it does not contain any calculated predictions, such as I have previously been known to publish. I have capitalized the word Prophecies to show that this work is truly from the inspired declaration of divine will and purpose, as they were indeed told to me by Jesus Christ. I dedicate this work **to Caesar Nostradamus, the son of mine** that was born while I was receiving these divine words. In this work I will occasionally address Caesar, to personalize this dedication; but, this preface holds the instructions that will be necessary for future understanding. That understanding will show the divine purpose of Christ's message to humanity, which is the preservation of **Life** on earth. I capitalize this word because it does not refer to any one individual life, but to the sustained Life of all mankind. The continuation of Life will become threatened in a distant future. It is also the purpose of this work to explain the true value of Life, and what measures will be necessary to ensure that each individual's soul will survive eternally in **bliss**, as one with God and Christ in Heaven. Life on earth is separate from true bliss, as only in Heaven can the soul find life and bliss in unison.

THE SOURCE

Your birth has come **late** in my life and just as Christ was **arriving** to show me the future of mankind. **Caesar Nostradamus** you are **my** first-born **son** to your dear mother; and, as such you will become the keeper of this document when I will have left this world. **I've done** this work for Christ **to put my** name on it, and it was not something that was done quickly. Christ made visits to me over a **long** period of **time, by** appearing before me on a **continuous** basis. He had me **keeping watch** for Him, during the **night time** hours, **to refer** me to the visions that I have been allowed. It has been these visions that I was instructed by Christ to put **in writing**. Since your birth last year (1554), I have not been able to tend to **you** as much as a father would like. I have had **to neglect** some of my husbandly and fatherly duties. While I have not been able to assist your mother in her care for you, you have been in my **memory**, such that my thoughts are of you now. As you are not yet walking, you are still too young to know of my past, where I have produced public predictions on a regular basis. I have regularly produced these the last several years. As you grow older you will find that you are recognized as my son, from the popularity of those writings; but, my name will not be as popular for these that I have now written for Jesus Christ. You are to neglect the outside opinions of others, who will have memory of the marvels of my older work. Likewise, disregard all that bring up memory of this work, believing it to be produced by a crazy man. This later memory will be due to my pledge to Christ that I would not give clear explanation of what *The Prophecies* mean; and, to honor that pledge this will include you as well. This document is intended to remain an enigma until well into the future. This period of nebulosity will not only last until **after the bodily extinction of** me, but beyond your passing, and beyond that of **your** siblings and their **offspring**. I want you **to** always know that regardless of how little is known, and what wild guesses will become, the true contents of this book are for **the common benefit of** all **human** beings that will come later. As all humanity is in common, I must keep this message **from those that** hold uncommon power today. These are the royal rulers that are already dedicated to the influence of Christ. The time of benefit will be for those common people that are yet unborn into this world, who will be in need of this influence. The words of this book are all completely from **the Divine**, and thus this work is a true Prophecy. It is as holy as any of the books in the Bible, written by God's Prophets. I have been instructed to give this work the **essence** that it was obtained **by** the calculations of the **Astronomic** planets and their **revolutions** through the zodiac. I have done such calculations by **myself**, based on the positions that I have witnessed, **having** found everything true, as determined by those mathematical laws of motion. However, none of that would have ever been possible, had I not been **gifted** this power of **cognizance** by Jesus Christ and his assistant angels.

And since my experiences with Christ, I have come to understand the source of all knowledge and awareness. All of this is from God. All that mankind knows is a gift from God, such that even **when** we learn from teachings or observations and think we have found the answer to **it** which we question, it is not our minds alone that have created knowledge. Knowledge is given to mankind **in** small quantities, like the sprinkles of **rain**, which moistens the earth and then soaks in. This keeps the earth fertile and growing and is equally important to humanity. All of our insights come **from the** same source as the rain, which is **God**. His **immortal** being knows all that will be known and has been known, and He imparts small parts of that knowledge to mankind, when we are in need of the moisture of knowledge to keep our minds fertile. To think **that** a thought is only held by **you**, as one individual, and **not** also known by many others, at a similar time, in separate places, is purely egotistical. To think that you alone have unique knowledge is giving too much credit to **yourselves**. All that mankind is capable of **coming to**, as far as our own instinctive **natural wisdom** is concerned, is so very little that we are no more intelligent than are the animals of the wild. Our capability of higher thought comes when God enters **inside** our minds and speaks to us in the whispers of insight. Still, for all of the knowledge that all of mankind knows, **it's** only a pool, compared to the ocean of knowledge that God knows. In our **earth born** existence, our knowledge has no greater depth than the laps and waves of water that sweep onto the **beach**. **But**, as little as man truly knows, the natural inclination of man is to the **Martial** actions, where thinking is on its most primitive level. These actions are territorial, and put their thoughts only to the development of physical strength, for the purpose of manipulating and controlling others for material gain. This is what so many people see as true power. It is the continuing presence of these warrior mentality people, who are the **incapable** ones **of** mankind, which will eventually condemn mankind. They are unable **to receive** such knowledge that Christ has to offer.

These are the ones who these words are to be hidden from, as they would either be found destroying them out of fear, or manipulating them for their own gains. At **your** young age, Caesar, you have a **weak understanding** of **those** types of people; but, it is because of people like **that** that **I am constrained** from making this message clearly stated. This does not mean that it will never be understood. This is because **after my days** on earth have come and gone, there will come a time when someone will be able **to define** the true meaning of all of the words that Christ has instructed me to write here.

There will come someone who will view what has been written and realize that there is a way to make sense of everything. This way to understanding will be realized as possible by the way that the quatrains are written. While that way will be the reason it's not being possible to understand them now, at that time it will be realized you cannot trust to leave something of this nature in clear style of writing. This is because there will be those that are not in need of understanding, and knowing the true meaning would cause them fear. Still, there will be those who will need to understand, when this future comes. That time of need is not now, and by worrying those this future will not affect, the abuse or injury of their pain could do harm to them and to this document. Only when the times of this future have arrived, and the past times have been obliterated, can the true message come forward. Until that time, the vast majority of the message contained here will be undecipherable.

The most important element which will be realized, **for** the clarity of these words to appear, will be the understanding of the unusual manner of **speech** my verses are presented in. The written word will be read wrongly as the oral word normally used. Language is normally a **hereditary** process of understanding, where communication is passed from one generation to the next. These are the accepted ways of communication, and they form the standard rules of language. Even though the manner **of** speech we accept as normal now is easily understood, in time our way will be seen as **the occult** way. It will not then be as easily understood, due to the generational changes in speech. In the future, people will see these words I have written as indicative of those changes, thinking my unusual manner was indicative of a typical use of language. Because our style of speech will be occult to them, they will feel free to change what was written, to meet this future's normal manner of speech. They will also look at each quatrain as a separate **prediction** of the future; but, each quatrain is a separate prophecy, which can only be fully understood in the context of the whole of the quatrains. The only way to gain the proper meaning **will be** to see each quatrain as being one part of many, **inside** the whole, where each links like an ordered chain of verses. The quatrains link to tell the story of this future; with groups of quatrains linking to tell separate stories, all within this whole of the overall story. The time will come when people will realize the choices of **my** words are purposeful, and they cannot be altered in any fashion. Each and every one of them has been spoken to me, by Christ, with each word designed to touch the emotional center of one's **stomach**. This will not be felt in the future, until one realizes each word is so carefully selected that it must be read as if **enclosed** by parentheses. This makes each word stand out and require being separately read. Each word must be fully understood before attaching the meaning of that word to the next word. My words will be symbolic of a pregnant woman, who carries a child in her stomach. At first, the woman will not show her pregnancy, even though she feels the life that is enclosed within. As the child's growth accelerates, the stomach begins to grow; until the time has come for a new life to be born into the world.

Once the true meaning of my words have been born into the world, it will become clear the stories of *The Prophecies* are **confiding** the secrets of the Martial peoples. By that time, these people of base intellect will have built a vast history of secrets, and a brotherhood of manipulation. The quatrains which tell these stories will be of this future generation's past, so they will be recognizable to them. As that part within the whole will lead to that present, there will **also** be quatrains that will be telling of **the adventures** these Martial people will currently be involved in. These will be recognizable as exposing those who will be endangering peace on earth. The people **of the** future will show the nature of **human** beings, which is to doubt; but, when my words will be correctly understood, by **defining** their full meanings, they will expose a time corrupt of leadership. With this corruption **being** deeply ingrained in all of the societies of the world, mankind will be in great danger and in need for immediate change. This demand for change will draw out the **uncertainties** of the common people; as by that time many people will have begun to question the value of religion. This work's greatest purpose is to reach those seeking proof of God and Jesus Christ; so they will be able to have a renewed faith **that the whole** of this work **is royal**, as the Prophecies of Christ the King. These words come from the most sovereign of all rulers, as it is **guided by the power of God**, through Christ. The lessons contained here teach of the sins of mankind, who will have been led away from God. In the Old Testament the prophets warned of a similar sin, where mankind worshiped idols. In this future, mankind will be led to worship man and his philosophies. That which will be found exposed in these verses will be the most **invaluable** asset possible for those truly seeking salvation. *The Prophecies* will provide the truth that will be necessary for one to again believe, to restore their faith in God and save themselves from the loss of their souls. While it will be hard for many people to accept that **we**, as human beings, are not as intelligent as we like to believe, this message from Christ will be **inspiring** to many who truly seek signs of God's reality. Salvation will **not** come **by** refusing to act on faith, when faced by those who will be exposed and the threats they will make to maintain their control over the people. Those who will be exposed will become like a **furious woman** who has become enraged over a lost lover. They will act angrily at the potential for losses of worldly controls and fortune; and, they will make threats to keep the weak under their power. The actions of these Martial people will **not** be overcome **by** people who agree with the prophecies, but show **lethargic movement** to act on their beliefs. Most believers will lack the fortitude of Shadrach, Meshach and Abednego; **but**, there will be some who will make sacrifices solely based on faith. The accuracy to be found contained in some of the quatrains, **by** the specific references to the **Astronomics** of fixed planetary movements, will convince several to find faith and act on that. Other quatrains will make clear **assertions** that will be seen to have come to pass as predicted, with others showing a clear future which will not be one to chance happening.

THEY ARE NOT LIKE THE ALMANACS

It is important to understand that this work is different from my previous works of prediction. Those predictions have been made solely from astronomical calculations. The **whole** of this work is from the **deity** that is Jesus Christ. However, this is not to lessen the accuracy of prediction, as my past predictions have been found highly accurate. To that success, I must give the praise to the one deity, God, as it is He that **daily** sends **breaths** of guiding insights to me. These breaths come to me in the form of whispers, as my inner voice or conscience. He does the same for all of us, in various ways, at various times. We all have heard **them**, often at the moments that we are in need of warning. These whispers of God are how we feel **presentiment**, such that one feels that something is necessary, as a premonition. These moments of foresight are also highly accurate; and, they act like predictions to amaze both us and those who we tell of them. Still, this is not something that can be duplicated or replicated by the designs of thought. They just come when needed. In this sense, these whispers cannot be proven to others, although we all experience them. It is the strength of our feelings that accompany those experiences that becomes the source of our inner faith. I have learned to listen to these whispers when I calculate the astrological charts that I have cast, to produce my almanacs. Through knowledge I see angles and aspects; but, from prayer I hear guidance that has led me to those accurate predictions. While I have enjoyed some success with this method in my past predictions, this work, *The Prophecies*, is not a work of this nature. This work is entirely from true **inspiration**, by divine influence; and, it is different from prediction by being truly **prophetic**. The difference is stated aptly in the title. *The Prophecies* means that my work here is of the divine will and purpose of God. It has been produced to inspirationally declare a warning, as **a foreboding** future will be at hand. The will and purpose of a prophecy, as is found **in** this work, is to save human life, or moreover the soul. This makes it wholly **proprius**, or the proper use of prophecy, where the future will be found infallibly predicted. Nothing of my past works has been infallible, as accurate as they have been deemed.[3]

---

3   Everything in this block was written in Latin. Nostradamus used Latin often to directly state Biblical quotes, particularly in reference to quotes of Christ. I could not find a particular Bible quote to match this, but my Latin is worse than my French. Feel free to check for this on your own.

I had not known just **how much that** ability to accurately predict was assisted by God, because my almanacs only predicted one year ahead of time. To go beyond this period and expect **the** same level of accuracy of predictions over **long** periods, where **times** can radically change, is impossible by mankind alone. Knowledge of this distance can only come directly from God; and, this is entirely at His discretion. I have been chosen now, **by** Jesus Christ, because I have had **several** yearly almanacs which I have successfully produced. The accuracy of my predictions of the **times** to come has enabled me to develop a reputation for being able to see the future. This reputation **that** I have gained is because **I've predicted** events that have been helpful to the people of France. I have been assisted in this accuracy as **long** as I have not sought personal gain. As God knows all **times**, He has known **of the** need for me to establish a credible record, in **advance of** my being encountered to write *The Prophecies*. The whole of my accuracy has been due to **this** need of attracting readers of my words, due to my reputation as a gifted astrologer and predictor of the future. I am certain that had I not been given **that** level of accuracy in the past, the magnitude of what I present now would not be as widely interesting, enough to survive well into the future. However, **since** I have become a popular figure, *The Prophecies* **has become** just as popular, in anticipation.

Christ has presented me a vividly clear future, **in** the detailed **particulars** that make it up; but, I was not witness to every detail of everything that is to come. This book has a narrow perspective, as it deals only with the **regions** that will be the most in need of warning, when that time comes. These regions are those that will be **attributing** to the development of **the whole** story of this future. This is where **being** able to see the changes, which will be **made** in the future **by the** people and leaders of these regions, will prove the **virtue** of this work, proving it can only be possible from Christ and God. Only from the **inspiration** of the **divine** can this story unfold as accurately as it will unfold. This accuracy will make all of my **other** works of writing pale in comparison. The depth that each quatrain will be found to have will be so amazing that, when each is linked together, the great **abundances** of detail that will come will make it realized that this work can only be judged as a miracle of epic proportions. Many of the quatrains link to tell the sub-stories of the most **sinister** peoples that will rise to power and cause **adventures** that will lead to the worst hazards imaginable. The stories **of** the advent of these sinister peoples will begin slowly; but, once they will have taken hold, the dangers to mankind will be increasingly **accelerated**. At one point in time, their hold will be so great over the masses that they will act with great **quickness**, leading to more and more **pronounced** changes. It will be **that** suddenness that the people will not be able to adjust to, **since** many of the people will have become enslaved to the sinister peoples. So many will think they **are** those who will be the **chanced** ones, where their fortunes will have come to pass by the virtue of luck. However, these sinister people will control that luck **by** their power of manipulation. This control will extend to all **the climates** that these regions will cover, which will cover a large portion **of the world**.

These people who will have risked their souls, for the fleeting promise of wealth and power that is possible in the material realm, will be forced to trick many other people to give up their souls. The influence that will have caused this loss is the same that has existed since the original sin, **having** always delighted in turning mankind away from God. This influence is just as present today; but, in this future there will become an increasing acceptance of the influences of evil. For this reason, Christ has **required** me **to conceal** the message of this book from those who would see its purpose and destroy it. It is imperative to know that the purpose of this concealment is not **to abandon** mankind, and leave mankind to blindly face this future. Nor is it **for** the purpose to **cause** actions **of** anger against those who now have God-given power, as royal rulers. These rulers of nations and the leaders of the Church will eventually be **the** ones who will be attacked, weakened and destroyed, without the benefit of my words to predict this. The future holds the rising of the common man to power, elevated by the influence of evil; and, that rise will **injure** the balance of power that has survived now for many centuries.

THE OVERVIEW OF THE THEME OF CHANGE

It is important to know that the nebulosity of this book is a necessary restriction, to protect the innocent. This protection is **not so much** to **only** protect those **of the times present**, because such influential changes are still some time away; **but**, the mystery of my words is **also** designed to protect those **of the** institutions that must continue to operate as the influences for good, until the times of change begin. There will come to be elements of mankind that will assume **greater** power than kings, such that mankind will **part** from these institutions of good influence. This lack of good influence will be the causes **of the future**, such that the greater part of *The Prophecies* will tell the stories of the result of this coming evil influence. As this future unfolds, **some** of the key events and personalities which will have brought about these changes will need to be commonly recognized, as figures of past history. This will act **to put** the reader in the middle of the story's timeline when understanding comes. At that point in time, part of what I have put **in writing** will be verifiable and the rest predictable. When the future will have come to the point that needing to understand is imperative, the ability to look back at the past and begin to understand their future will be vital for establishing belief. Understanding the writings of those quatrains which denote known past events will be key to understanding those quatrains which tell of events still to come. At this future time, the past will be recognizable by the changes that will come in three areas. The first area of change that will be important **for** belief to follow will be **those** changes to come to the monarchal structure of Europe. It will be undeniable **that** all of **the** holders of **reigns**, or the royal leadership of the kings and queens of nations, will have fallen, with little semblance to the power of reign they hold today. The second area of change that will be clear to see will be found in the power of those who comprise the **sects** of support, who now cater to those royal figures of power. By this term, "sects," I do not intend for it to be used in a narrow context, denoting religious zealots. The sects are the groups of people with the power of influence, which adhere to the specific principles or doctrines of any one leader or philosophy. For example, I am a member of one sect, as an astrologer, and a member of another sect, as a doctor. Some other sects now include: artists, architects, philosophers, craftsmen, the military and specialized orders of religious zeal. There are many others; but, the identifying characteristic of a sect is it is a group of common people with a particular specialized talent. All are dependent on commissions, grants and stipends from the two wealthiest elements of the population, the Kings and the Church. Their power of influence comes from their skill, such that each is given a level of freedom to express that talent, for the ultimate purpose of supporting the principles and doctrines of the Kings and the Church. This subservient area of life will become changed, such that they will gain greater power, once the royal figures will have been displaced. Finally, of the three areas that will face change, the third will take place in the **religions** of the world. By this I am most concerned with the monotheistic religions that adhere to the one God; and, I am specifically referencing the changes that will be coming to the religions of Christianity. All of these religions **will make changes**, which will be so great that no one now would find them recognizable in the future. The changes that will occur in the world's religions will be **so** great that anyone now who could see them then would think of them as having become complete **opposites** of what they now stand for. If these could all be **seen in the** light of now and then, the **respect of** religion that exists in **the present** day will be clearly different at this future time. Religions will clearly appear **diametrically** opposite to the fundamental purpose that religion serves today, to both God and mankind. It will be **that** element of radical change in these most important institutions of present day life that will be **so** dangerous to these future generations of mankind. The power of the Church has worked in unison with the power of the Kings, but the loss of royal power will cause the Church to become an island, with less influence over the people. It will be that decrease of religious influence that will jeopardize mankind. These three drastic changes in mankind's hierarchy of influence which **I have** stated here will be made the first stories of the quatrains, to **come in** this order I have listed here. The order of these changes will be to the reigns first, followed by the sects second and the religions last. When religion is no longer able to function to save souls, mankind will begin to be in need of higher assistance. Additionally, the stories in my quatrains are of specific cases, designed **to refer** the reader to the most profound and recognizable examples of these diametrically opposite changes. The verses which are **those** of reference to **that** element of change will be more indirectly presented. The details of the upheaval that will come **to them** who will change is not the point of this book, as this is **to happen** by the result of their failures to God, as the protectors of mankind. The stories the quatrains detail **will be** found to be those which will come after this point of change, after the initial changes will have already set in. This will especially be found in **those** many quatrains that tell the stories **of** the common man's rise to power and its lust for **reign**. This change will promote the people of the **sects** of philosophy to the height of power, allowing them to take over the reigns of nations. While these changes will initially be hailed as good for the common man, seeing change as having righted the wrongs of kings, they will not have the blessing of God, as they will not welcome the Church by their side. This will lead to the beginning of the Church's change, for the worse. The quatrains that tell the stories of this change that will come over the sects will be those that will put focus on the events that mirror these negative developments. Finally, and most importantly, the changes that will come to the world's **religions** will then be seen spelled out in the words of many quatrains. When it is agreed the purpose of religion is to assist God, and to guide mankind to higher morals for the purpose of the salvation of one's soul, this purpose will no longer be maintained. For a religion to change diametrically, this means that an institution which was once designed to serve God, for good purposes, will have been changed to serve Satan. It is with great sadness that I have written so deeply of those changes, especially those affecting the Catholic Church. The time will come when the people serving that **faith** will be **found** unfaithful, with the name of all Christianity **smeared** by the opponents of Christ. There will be **so** much **evil** connected with the Church, which will be found **agreeable** to its highest ranking members, that many of the faithful will lose faith in the Church and God. This will be attributable **to** those corrupted leaders, who will care more about **their** dreams of **fantasy**, than to the **auricular** of confession. The confessions of the people will be pointless, when those hearing the confessions will have not themselves confessed to God their sins. These men will let their ears block out the whispers in their hearts. With the world's largest sect of Christianity facing **that** change in the Church, the people will have lost their influence for good, putting their souls at risk. Without a guiding light, **they** will be easily seduced by Satan's tongue. The Church **will be** still seen as holy in the eyes of many, but the **coming** of this future will find Jesus Christ's return **to damn this** church. This damnation will be the one **that** was foretold **by the** last appearance of Jesus Christ, **centuries** ago, to John the Evangelist. For that **to happen** to the church that bears the name of Jesus Christ, it will have committed the greatest sin and greatest shame that a church can commit. The damnation will come because the sins of the Church will have endangered the souls of all humanity. The Church will have hidden its sins from the public for some time, although some will have believed this corruption to exist. The rumors will circulate about all of these failures; but, when **one** begins to understand the language of *The Prophecies*, then all **will be cognizant** and aware. With these sins **being** exposed and clearly **seen**, the Church will be warned to confess and return to the glory of Christ. It is very important to know that the quatrains which tell of this atrocity will not be questionable, as all will be **apparent**; but, at that time the Church will be firmly in the grasp of Satan, and breaking free will become a tremendous challenge.

THE CHALLENGE OF PEARLS BEFORE SWINE

To most simply state why the message of this book cannot be made clear, **considering** the advent of these sinister peoples, with their Martial attitudes and **also** the changes that will come to the institutions that are on earth for the betterment of mankind, one needs to understand **the maxim of** who can be given such wisdom. This decision is made for the protection of the message from such people, who would keep **the true** message from ever being known by those who would believe. The maxim is one which was stated by the one true **Savior** of humanity, Jesus Christ.

Christ is quoted by Matthew, where he told of Christ's warning to us, to **be unwilling** to allow that which is **holy to** be given to the unholy. Christ symbolically stated that we should not **give** that which is holy unto **dogs**. The use of dogs is symbolic, as it is not representative of the pets known as "man's best friend," but instead the animal minded people of the world, who gather in packs of like mind, as beasts trained for the protection of their masters. They are the Martial peoples, who do not act from a higher sense of inspiration. They only respond to the base desires of self-gratification. Since this book is holy, coming from the mouth of Jesus Christ, I am unwilling to give this work unto the protection of warlords who would destroy it for the sport or, shred it, looking for material contents of sustenance. People of this nature thrive only on an inferior level of existence, and are incapable of recognizing the importance of a holy work. Christ then warned one **not to send** out to the world **all** of one's **pearls** of wisdom, **before** the people that are depicted as **swine**.[4] Here, the symbolism of swine represents the contemptible people who are of a sinister nature. Unlike the dogs, the swine have the intellectual ability to understand such pearls of wisdom; but, they would purposefully use that knowledge for their own benefit, keeping others from accessing such knowledge. They would manipulate the words, to alter the understanding so that it could be a tool by which to falsely lead the people. Christ then warned that **lest** one uses this care with holy words, they will be **trampled**

---

4   This is the source of the title for my series on Nostradamus: *Pearls Before Swine*.

under foot by these unsavory characters. Under foot means as far away from the mind and heart as possible, where the words become smeared, making them appear unholy. The dogs and swine would stand on the word of Jesus Christ, to stamp out any threat to their exclusive power over people of lesser means. Finally, Christ foretold what the result would be if one was to disregard this wisdom of His. He said this ignorance will cause those unprepared for such holiness, the dogs and swine, **to turn around**. This redirection will come when their attention has been gained. This turn around will then lead away from the direction that the unholy will have been going; but, it will not represent a change of heart. Instead, they will turn around from their preset goals, to put new focus on the elimination of that distraction. It will stop them, making them take notice of a new wisdom that has not been controlled to their advantage. This, in turn, will cause the unholy to use its power **to break** up anything that keeps them **apart** from their goals and aspirations. This does not only include the object that is holy, but **you** who would present such holy wisdom. This is precisely what happened when Jesus Christ walked the earth as a human being, as the presentation of the holy will attract such violent opposition. This is why I must leave *The Prophecies* alone now, knowing that Christ and God will protect them until the time that its wisdom must come out. At that point in time, the dogs and swine will be presented with the pearls of holy wisdom, where they will react with the same natural instinct; but, they will not be able to protect themselves from the results of their actions.

My reputation, **which has been** fairly successful these last few years, is based on both the accuracy and the clarity of my past predictions. The obscure way that this book is written, where the powerful and intelligent will not be able to make sense of the words, will be **the cause** that will raise several people **of** power somewhat against me. In the past I have worked **to make** my predictions fairly clear; and, these people of power will want me to make this work equally explainable. Still, **to refer** this work to those expectations which my past works have created, where **my** past **language** has been designed **to** meet **the** demands of being **popular**, I cannot do this now.

It must be understood that I have no control over this work, as **the quill** was guided **to the paper** by Jesus Christ; although I held the quill. This was **then** an automatic writing experience, where it was not **myself** who authored

78

this work. I was fully aware of what was being written and what everything meant; but, the thoughts and visions were not my own. In this regard, it also applies to this preface, such that I have **been required** not to give a clear overview of the meaning of the quatrains. I have been instructed **to dilute**, or weaken this introduction which is **announcing** the purpose and contents of *The Prophecies*. Again, this is **for the common** good of mankind, as this way will ensure that the document survives the test of time, until it is needed to be understood. While there is confusion now, **becoming** the source of the wildest leaps of imaginative thought and completely illogical interpretation, the removal **of** everything confusing will one day come. At that time the **blockage** that will have made everything uncertain will turn and act to make everything crystal clear.[5] The whole of this work is designed to be a collection of **puzzles**, where each of the quatrains is its own **puzzle**; but, a quatrain is also representative of one piece of the overall puzzle, which is how to recognize the order of the whole story. This organization is the overall puzzle of the quatrains. This preface is only another puzzle among so many puzzles, where all need to be solved both individually and collectively. For example, each line of each quatrain will then be separate piece of a 4-line puzzle. This will confuse many, as the words of each line will be seen as **sentences**, instead of realizing that they do not follow the rules of grammar. Each word must be defined separately before attempting to gain meaning from them together. This misunderstanding will come from people not recognizing that the text is dependent on the most basic concepts of language, with grammar being a more complex element that is not actually written, but implied. The ingrained processes of automatic reading by the rules of grammar will be **the causes** for people to read each verse individually, as a series of words in one extended sentence. This will cause them to see one thousand different **futures** in the quatrains, rather than many thousands of elements in a much more limited scope. By failing to realize the connection between the quatrains and the importance of the wording, most of the quatrains will make little sense and this will cause many quatrains to be read totally wrong. Still, while the

---

5   In this section of Old French, Nostradamus wrote, "pour le commun advenement," which you see in bold as, "for the common becoming." Another way of reading this is as "the advent of the common (man)." Both are accurate to interpret, but you will notice I have already made that statement of the coming of the common man prior to this point here.

same errors will repeatedly be made over the years that will follow, there will be some quatrains that will be seen as **the** ones that are **more** clearly written; and these will be the ones which appear to tell of an **urgency** that will come. In those quatrains the wording will most easily be identified, allowing them to convey this urgency more clearly.

These quatrains are important to realize, as there are **those** quatrains that are **that** easy to get a feel for a clear sense of urgency. This comes by the instant recognition of the verbiage. While **I've made** those quatrains very **apparent**, many are clearly predicting events that have never happened before and will not happen until that time comes. This makes **some** of the quatrains appear as if I have shown my **human** frailty, by the areas and regions mentioned being too stable to ever **change** or mutate to meet **that** quatrain's prophecy. Unless mankind makes the necessary changes in itself, the events that are so clearly stated, but seem so impossible to ever manifest, **will happen** as stated. Many more of the quatrains have been stated in ways that they will not be recognized easily. This will especially be so with those that tell of the corruption that will befall the Church. This is done so that the Church will **not** suffer from a prophecy which will still be a long time coming. If these were stated clearly, they would act **to scandalize** a Church which will have still been dedicated to Jesus Christ and the salvation of souls. The people must not be swayed away from **the auricular**, as the confessionals of the Catholic Church are important outlets for the people to ask for forgiveness of sins. The rite of the confessional should not be lost from the people; but, the Church will, by its own accords, become scandalous. At that time the priests will be without ears for hearing sins; and the lusts for fancy trinkets that will be worn on the little finger will show the **fragility** of the papal crown.

As easy and as difficult as the quatrains will be found to interpret, it is vital for you to know that **the whole** of *The Prophecies* is **written under** the direction of Jesus Christ. Everything composed within is by design and purpose. While there will be those who will imagine the shape of the quatrains, and claim to have found insights, they will have all figured wrong. Nothing of these works is so clearly written that the full scope of the contents will be known, before the time for knowing has come. I have written everything in a **figure** of speech that is purposefully misleading. One even has to doubt the use of a numerical figure, as nothing is wholly as it seems. What one thinks one sees will become nothing more than a mirage, as the **nebulous** nature of the words will make knowing this document as tricky as holding a cloud. There is **more** than first meets the eye; and, **that** nebulosity is what must be mastered, before the hidden understanding will come out. Faith in the unseen is the design **of the whole**; and, the design of the unseen will apply to everything written about the work. Faith will make it all appear. Just as God and Jesus Christ must be believed as real, *The Prophecies* must be believed to be truly **prophetic**. This will be **how** so **many** people will fail to read the words properly, as they will miss **that** most important point: *The Prophecies* is a title of divine inspiration that is truly prophetic. It makes the words of Jesus Christ, to the apostle Matthew ring so true, when he praised the ways of God, saying: **Thou hast hidden this**, these things **a wisdom**, with regard to the wise. True wisdom is found in those that can see obscurely, as anyone can claim to be wise by knowing only that which is clear.

Most importantly, those who are truly wise will be separate from the cause of hiding wisdom. Wisdom appears to those who look deeply, beyond the surface features. They will know that wisdom comes from patience, and not from quick judgment. Christ also stated to Matthew that God also hid wisdom from the **prudent**, as these are the wise people who are silently pondering, using sound judgment. It will be this nature of prudence which will make everything clear, as these words of wisdom are themselves prudent. The use of language here is restrained, just as was the philosophy of William of Ockham. In Ockham's Razor he proposed that less is more. This understanding of prudence will make *The Prophecies* come vividly alive, with tremendous depth of field.

The passage in Matthew concludes that God made His revelations of wisdom to children, or babes. The purpose of hiding wisdom from the wise and prudent is because the wise and prudent seek the power of knowledge. They are the ones who will have sought to know the meaning of **this** prophecy. To have this knowledge **is** to wield the **might** of future knowledge. However, a baby knows nothing of power and might. True wisdom is true power and the true children of God are **to be ruled** by the wisdom of God. This wisdom has generally been departed to the prophets of kings, so the royal levels of influence can prevent a prophecy from becoming fulfilled. This prevention is gained by the necessary changes being ordered and then carried out faithfully. The leaders of the churches would also be told of prophecies, as they hold the power to elicit change too. However, in this future which comes, many of the children of God and Christ will be left alone, without true leaders; and, they will be in need of this wisdom for themselves alone to carry out the preventive changes.

It is very important to understand that a leader is not always one who holds the power of true wisdom. Simply possessing earthly powers of influence does not make one wise. To make the words of wisdom so **plainly** clear, to the Martial and sinister peoples, **this** would empower them **to** then **drive out** those who might see their power as corrupted. God is more concerned with protecting the **feeble** people of the world, from the mighty, than He is with giving one a gross advantage over another.

This principle of God empowering those who are trusting and faithful, loving and gentle, applies not only to this book, but **to** all of **the** biblical examples of **Prophecies** which have been given to mankind. Prophecy has always been conveyed to humanity in this manner, **by** the selection of those who have shown these childlike qualities. These are the people God chooses to serve Him, as **the medium** between mankind and Heaven. These people do not seek to act as a medium, or seek the power prophecy holds. Instead, these people are selected to become the Prophets **of God**, without any prior conception of what that entails. It is God's **immortal** being that has known of this end, from the beginning. As such, He can be found having told a variation of the same message to all of history's Prophets, regardless of the historical time and the circumstances surrounding those times. God has repeatedly warned mankind to live according to His Law, or face the consequences of living in sin. However, in the periods between these episodes of prophetic wisdom being imparted to mankind, mankind is still influenced to act in reverence to God, by another medium, which is also immortal.

THE WHISPERS OF ANGELS

This immortal assistance comes to mankind by **the good Angels** who serve God and mankind. These are the daily mediums which whisper guidance to us, when we are in need of direction and when we ask God for assistance. In my life I **had** found that the more I gave to others the more I **received** in return. This return was not measured in the material realm; but, it was measured on a heightened spiritual level, one which brings personal satisfaction. I felt a strong sense of reward, for trying to live my life as close to **the spirit of** life that the New Testament models, by the lessons of Jesus Christ. It has been this practice of living in peace with my neighbors and helping others with my knowledge of medicine that I was led to put more efforts into astrology. I have always known of the values of astrology; but, I always kept it personal and private. I also always knew that astrology was a way for all to benefit, on an individual level. When I first began **making** predictions for the people I was **foretelling** events to come by the methods I had learned before, of planets and angles and aspects. These first predictions had an uncanny way of coming true, beyond any of my expectations; but, this accuracy was not from my restating the formulas that I had been taught, as standard occurrences from a particular aspect between planets. I looked at the aspects and **by** letting my mind go quiet, listening to my innermost thoughts, I wrote predictions that no other astrologer would have risked making. I realized the accuracy was not based on what I had learned, but instead on that **which** transcends the intellect. These connections are those which we make with our guardian angels; and, **they** whisper to us in our thoughts, to help us achieve success in our daily lives. A trained astrologer is able to **see** the daily motion of the planets; and, they can calculate the times of coming events that are normal in people's lives. This ability to see **the things** which are natural in our lives allows us to forecast events at some **distances** of time, but well within the expected life span of the one whose chart is being read.

This is not mystical or magic, as human beings are relatively the same, in that they generally evolve over the same developmental stages, between birth and death. At my age, **having seen** these patterns repeated over and over again, this knowledge of normal human development had become ingrained **in** my ability **to** make sound predictions. It would be easy to predict that a baby will crawl and then walk on two legs; just as later it could be predicted to marry and have children, before dying of broken health. Astrology is not necessary for a prediction of this nature; but, astrology allows an astrologer to see when to **expect** these typical growth periods to occur. In this way, predicting **the future's happenings** is far from being impossible. The accuracy of such predictions is not perfect, however, as this is where other guidance is needed.

I have learned as a doctor that making a diagnosis of illness, based on the physical signs and symptoms, calls for standard prescribed medicines and treatments. This alone does not guarantee that a recovery can be predicted. Likewise, as an astrologer I know that certain planetary arrangements show the signs for a particular life circumstance; but, there can be no guarantee that what will follow will be that. There are so many variables in life that **nothing** can be known to occur, precisely as predicted to occur. This is because it is beyond **oneself** to know what is yet to come. Mankind's **power to** see the future is based on knowing the past; but, that hindsight cannot **perfect** foresight. Man's ability to predict so accurately that others see it as perfect cannot be achieved **without** external assistance given to **him**. God is the source of all knowledge, **which** is passed on to His Angels, **so** that they can whisper it to human beings. This is how the faithful know how **great** God **is**, as the sick can become well, despite the predictions of doctors. This is because of the faith which people have in **the** empirical **power** that God wields.

For all the power God has, God delights in using it with **the** greatest degree of **kindness**. This is most shown **to the** ones of humanity who **subjects** themselves to this power, by respecting that power is His and having faith that that power will be used for good. It is **that** subjection to the power of God which is important to all of mankind, as our souls are **pending** their time on earth, in our physical bodies. They wait till they can return and share in that kindness with God, in Heaven. Life on earth is **that** time of pending, when mankind loses its sense of Heaven, causing our need for angelic assistance. It is **they**, these Angels of God, which stay with our souls, **remaining by them** until it is time for our souls to leave our bodies and return to God. All the time, these Angles are whispering guidance to our minds, to keep us remembering our subjection to the power of God, **albeit** that God has given man the power of free will. The gift of free will is mankind's test of subjection, as our minds are also open **to the** whispers of **others**, who are seeking to influence us to different **effects**. These alternative impressions are dependent on the level one **subjects** oneself to God, and they are designed more **for** confusing our minds over these matters of subjection. The two influences both share **the similarity** of whispering advice to us, at times when we have reached points of moral decision in our lives. It is up **to** each of us to properly make **the** correct decisions, by recognizing the thoughts which **cause** us to consider sin as an option. These thoughts **of** acting against the rules of God must be defeated, turning us back in the direction of **the good** whispers we hear. As difficult as these decisions may be, as the pains and suffering of a worldly existence can seem unbearable at times, the measure of one with true **genius** is as one who bears pain for a greater reward. The genius of cunning, which tells us we can ease the pain with no one knowing, is the same genius that convinced Eve to eat of the forbidden fruit. It is when we have overcome **these** tests of our inner fortitude that **warmth** comes over us, by the loving arms of Jesus Christ holding us. This warmth is how I have felt, when I have helped others in need; and, it lets me know I have done good and that I am protected. This is the motivation that we need to succeed; and, as such it is a transfer of **power**, from God to us, so we can continue on this path. That power has enhanced my abilities to predict, and it makes me more than simply a **skilled** astrologer. By learning to listen to the inner voice and ignore the urges to seek self-gratification, my skills allow me to elevate my words to that of a **prophesier**, more than a predictor. This power is a gift, or a talent, which is earned from a true desire to help others; and, **he** who also understands this principle can elevate any natural talent to amazing heights, by following the model of Jesus. God wants to help us all; but, it is up to each of us **to approach** him with prayer, asking for that assistance. God's Angels have already come **to us**; and, they will give us the advice we need, to find God's way for having our prayers answered.

This warmth I mentioned, when Christ has made contact with me, is **like** that of a warm summer day. I feel **he** is with me daily, so strongly that I feel **we** are one. When I have written my almanacs of yearly predictions I have prayed that my words will tell the truth, to help guide our nation's leaders. At times when I have struggled to find the words, they **became** apparent when I ceased my worry. It was like **the rays of** light which come from **the Sun** had illuminated my mind's eye, allowing me to see clearly what had been in the dark. Christ is like the Sun, **which** constantly sends light and warmth to the people of earth. His spirit has **come** to me many times, **casting** light on all the astrological elements and **their** symbolic natures. These enlightening periods have been the **influence** which has guided me to write such accurate predictions in the past. This influence is **in** the many aspects, natures and qualities which are symbolized by **the bodies** of the celestial orbs, where so much exists to remember. Most astrologers see the **elemental** functions of the aspects, which would lead most to predict the most basic of predictions. However, with this inner light guiding me, my predictions have **not** been **elemental** at all, having come from the trust I have in ethereal insights.

As for this ability to have ethereal insights, it is something that is not unique for me only. It is available **to** all of **us**, at any time, as long as we adhere to the laws of God and the lessons of Jesus Christ. Without myself showing such adherence, I would know nothing more than anyone else, **which** is a statement of mankind's overwhelming lack of true knowledge. This basically **sums** up the true intellectual capacity of **humans**, as without this spiritual assistance within us we are **not empowered** to know **anything** beyond our immediate environment. The extent **of our** mental powers is no different than those of animals, which share our innate ability for having an awareness of the **natural** surroundings and realizing physical needs. This low level of **cognizance** is how man happily lived, prior to eating of the fruit from the tree of knowledge of good and evil; but, it is still the way man would be, had Adam and Eve not accepted the power of mind into themselves. Since then, the natural **inclination** or tendency of mankind's thought processes has been **to engine**, or to invent. As one of the weakest physical specimen on earth, mankind now needs mental powers to develop tools which will help equalize the imbalances that exist between the many species of animals on earth. This makes man's brain more capable of higher thought processes, and causes him to seek an understanding of his environment. This inquisitive nature of man causes him to want **to know the secrets** of why and when things happen. The answers to these questions extend beyond the observable, to the **abstracts** of knowledge. Still, without God sending help to mankind, to allow people to expand their brains and survive, none of us would have any concept of anything abstract. Prophecy is one these abstract areas of knowledge which mankind seeks to understand; and, prophecy is one **of** the ways that **God** has given assistance to human beings in need of knowledge. God has explained many of the abstracts of the world to mankind; by making it clear we understand that God is **the Creator** of all things, for all purposes. Beyond what God allows mankind to know, mankind is not prepared to know. Remember the scripture, in the Book of Acts, where Christ stated why man must not dwell on what the future will bring. He explained that **because** mankind cannot see the future mankind should not worry about what will come. He said, "It **not is ours** (for you) **to know** the **times**." **And** to their questions about the return of Israel to its former glory, which could not be foreseen, Christ did **not** answer definitively. Instead, **he advises** that "you shall receive power, after that the Holy Ghost is upon you." The power of prophecy can only come after one has received the Holy Ghost, which will come upon us, and not vice versa. This advice is in effect **t**erra-cotta, or until countermanded. This is then how prophecy does occur, by the order of God, and not because mankind desires to know the secrets of prophecy.

This limitation does not mean God does not want mankind to know the future, which is evidenced by **how many** times God has given **that** gift of prophecy to mankind, through the Prophets of God. Still, with the assistance of our guardian angels, we **also** have a limited ability to imagine a foreseeable future, **from** a perspective which revolves around the **present**. It is from these insights about this near future that we **are able to** set our expectations and plan appropriately. In these instances, we have **become** aware of what will happen, before it does happen. However, it must be understood that these enlightenments are related to us alone, **being** lone **individuals**, separate from those who we know nothing about. With **that** sense of individuality allowed to us by **God**, He has allowed us to be **the creator** of our own futures. This allowance **has** been based on our diligence to meet the **required** conditions laid out for us by God; and, God is aware that this foresight is required for us to know these things we need to know, in order to meet those conditions. This makes us best prepared to properly address the future when it arrives. In our limited ability to see the future God does not appear to us to tell us personally what the future will entail. Instead, it is God's way is **to reveal** these glimpses of the future **by** using our **imaginative** senses. These are the **impressions** we get in our minds, whereby we are able to have forethought of something yet to happen. In **some** cases, **secrets** are exposed to us by premonitions and the impressions **of** dreams. Once we have had these unsolicited thoughts it is **then** up to our ability to listen to the inner voices, **to become** aware of the meaning. These fantasies represent the **agreements** we share with God, as the consistent abstracts of observable life situations. They are like our visual capacity for recalling memories of past experiences; but, these inner visions are not a review of our memory of real past experiences. Instead, they are symbolic analogies which reveal the secrets we need to know. Just as we can reach agreement on the meaning of dreams and visions, which are purely imaginative, we can also reach agreement on the physical signs that God provides to mankind, which reveals glimpses of an unknown future. God has promised to give signs by which to lead mankind, and the greatest physical guide is found **in Astrology**. God has placed the planets and luminaries in the heavens surrounding earth, for mankind to be led **judicially**.[6] Just as with dreams and visions, Astrology is not clearly showing us a fixed and real future; but, through it we are shown the symbols for how a future can become. This means that with both tools one has to learn to carefully consider the meanings of the signs. This careful judgment means the future will be **like** those times which have already been; so we learn to read the signs of the future **from** learning how to understand **the past**. When one has mastered **that** element of history, where we have seen one set of variables bring a high degree of predictability, Astrology has the same quality as mathematics, as a **certain** science. However, this **power** of certainty is different, just as people are more than numbers. Mankind has been given the gift of free will by God, and this makes that which has been predicted not fixed, but **voluntary**. The certainty is based on mankind's individual degree of **faculty**, where the power of the human mind can refuse to understand the symbols presented to it. One has to develop the voluntary faculty of receiving the whispers of guidance, where there is a willingness to leave the mind open. The greatest Prophets of the Bible tell how God **came to them**, to reveal the future's happenings or to show them the future in a dream. This is the openness of mind which believes in the unseen, without demanding proof the unseen exists. When the mind is centered in the heart, where true faith lies, one voluntarily acts, as if

---

6   Genesis 1:14 states this indirectly, where it says, "And God said, Let there be lights in the firmament of the heaven to divide the day and night; and let them be for signs, and for seasons, and for days, and years." These are the stars that make up the signs of the zodiac, through which the earth and planets move. This movement, especially with 1:15 telling of the Sun and Moon, tells us when the seasons will change. Horoscopes are based on these movements, for daily prediction, as well as yearly forecasts.

being watched and judged. When good people reach important points of decision, and are in need of assistance, the future's signs come to them **like** a **blaze** of blinding light. They will grab hold **of** the **fire** of inspiration which has **appeared** all of a sudden before them, casting light onto the darkness. It is **that** appearance which is recognized as the answer that was summoned from God, which is now returning to **him** who asked for help. This is how God bestows knowledge upon man; and, it is recognition which acts to warm our souls, **inspiring** us to know faith is duly rewarded. When **one** knows that God is there to protect mankind, from **having** had many such revelations **come** to one's imagination, faith is renewed. With God's guidance we are able **to judge** properly the paths we must take in the future. It is the wise man that allows himself to be assisted in those judgments by **the divine** whispers. This is the way God helps all **humans** glimpse the future, through divine **inspirations**, which are truly prophetic, but not true prophecy.

THE REALIZATION OF A PROPHECY

While God allows mankind to glimpse the future in small bits, **for** one to be a true Prophet of the Lord one has to be chosen for a reason that will serve many. This choice is not for the benefit of inspiring one human being to believe, but for all of humanity. When God gives someone a clear vision of **the** future it is to present someone with **tasks** which must be preformed for God, as this vision has **divine** purposes. That task becomes to announce the prophecy to others, and **that** divine task is the only reason God allows mankind to witness events which are yet to unfold. The visions shown are to be taken **totally** as what will happen, should not a warning be received and that warning heeded. The prophecy is then the warning mankind needs to avert this future shown. If heeded, this future will not occur as shown. However, if the necessary changes are not made by mankind, the future events which will have been shown to the Prophet **are** to become **absolute** prophecies. They will occur exactly as prophesized. In all of history's accounts of the Prophets of **God** it was God who saw in **them** a purity of heart and a conviction to God and their religion. From God seeing this elevated character, He **came** to them for the sole reason of warning mankind. The warning is **to perfect** a flaw in humanity, or else face this future that has been presented to the Prophet.

This is an important process to realize, for as much as the faithful will petition the Lord for assistance, he does not appear before anyone by summon. God chooses those He appears before, as does Jesus Christ. Those who claim to be able to favorably call upon the powers of the universe are using **the medium** of magic, which does not honor God. Magic, in all its forms, is **not** the medium God responds to, as **that** medium **is** the one **of** Satan, the prince of **the underworld.** Just as God does not directly answer calls by the faithful, Satan will also never directly respond to similar prayers; as he has sworn to never serve man. Still, God does not abandon mankind, as the will of God is carried by **the Angels** of Heaven, who are sworn to serve both God and mankind.

For those that practice magic it is the angels of **the third** kind that come to them. There are Archangels and Guardian Angels, who serve God and man; but, these others are the third of the angels that followed Lucifer, in the battle of heaven.

They are the demons who attempt to confuse mankind, by whispering cunning thoughts to us to make us turn our backs on God. These angels do not serve anyone but Satan. When they come to answer the incantations of magic, they are only concerned with **the bad** they can cause for mankind. They seek to destroy the souls of the foolish, by becoming an influence for evil.

But, there will be those who will believe I conjured up Satan, for the purpose of writing this book. They will have fantasies of me peering over a cauldron of boiling water, offering incantations to see visions of the future in the mist. Those are the fantasies presented by the bad angels; as I have done nothing of this sort. I have not used any such sorcery, or any means whatsoever to call upon the Lord to serve me. **My son**, you should have no fears wondering if I summoned God for personal gain. In my time spent with Christ **I** know you **yourself** will be **spoken** to, by the good Angles of God, after my passing. At that time, you will gain the understanding you will need, as you will know Christ came to me. I am comfortable with the fact I cannot express that clearly **here**, in this preface, where very **few** of my words will be properly understood before your life passes too. I cannot say **too much** that is clear at this point, not even to clear my name for you, as I must communicate **abstractly**.

I have stated that I have been instructed to write this book in enigmatic sentences, with nebulosity, by design; **but**, you must realize, as it is the Word of the Lord, it will be understood. The style of writing has allowed me to put **in as much** of the key terms **as** will be necessary for **the secrets** which have been hidden to be exposed. These key ingredients will make it clear I have been **prophesying** and not simply making senseless predictions. It will be known **that** my work is a true prophecy, when **one** is able to make sense of the systems that accompany my words, and use them to expand those basic concepts into standard language. The words which **came** to me from Jesus Christ are the necessary cornerstones in *The Prophecies*, from which a truly amazing work has been built. When this future time comes, and mankind is in need of knowing the full message this work contains, one will be ready **to receive** the necessary insights that it will take for total understanding to be gained. Those insights will come **by the** whispers of God's good Angels, who will lead the right person towards this understanding. They will do this through **subtle** hints and clues. This person will have the **spirit of** God within; and, the more which will be uncovered, the more a **fire** of passion will grow to continue on this path to make the message known. There is so much contained in so few words that all of the puzzles will not be quickly solved. It will be this depth **which** will appear to mean one thing at one time, but then **sometimes** change to mean something else, which will take considerable study to master. This person will see urgency in the message, **by** having gained **the understanding** of the overall theme; but, the first attempts to make the message clear will not be blessed by Christ, as the message must be correctly deciphered, before it will be allowed to be presented to the world. While this person will become **agitated** by premature failures, he will not be able to turn away from this project, due to the fire that burns within him. He will learn the value of **contemplating** the meaning of my words and listening to his inner voice. The more he trusts this voice **the more** clarity will come to him; and, this will make him feel so **high** that he will feel a heavenly connection. He will know the heavenly nature of Astrology, and he will know the meanings of **the stars** and planets. His views on the application of astrology will be much **like** mine, **being** that he will know how easy it is to fall into the practice of treating it as an intellectual science. This will keep him **vigilant** of the need for listening to the inner voice, before attempting to read someone's future. He will use a **similar** vigilance as **that** used with astrology, when he will attempt to take the words of my documents and fill **in the** necessary words which will complete the text. When this work has been perfected it will complete the correct **pronunciations** of the Words of Christ; and, the speech pattern used here will gain a distinct manner of verbal expression. This completion of *The Prophecies* in that manner, **being** the first time my words will have ever been truly presented in an understandable fashion, will have the people of the world **amazed**. Those **writings**, which will be **pronouncing** the exposures of so many of the Martial and sinister people of the world, while making the message of the end of mankind clearly known, will be put in a way that will be **without** the focus of **fear** motivating the necessary change. He will take a **less** formidable perspective, explaining that the true purpose of *The Prophecies* is to ensure the individual soul's salvation is **attained**. This will differ greatly **from** the people who will be **unashamed** by suggesting an inverse approach to these revelations. Some will be promoting the use of force to bring about the wrong form of change; while some will call for more time to believe, waiting for more proof to surface before committing to belief. Approaches of this nature will not have the effect of saving anyone's soul, as they will be designed to keep humanity unchanged. The new version of my book will have it addressed to each reader, one at a time, politely asking each reader to look within themselves and find reason for immediate faith and belief. Those who will be in touch with Jesus Christ will know of the holiness of Christ' Word; and, they will act to save their souls, by adopting the passivity of being that Christ taught. These people will be comforted in knowing their souls will be spared. The new version of Christ's message will spread, through the **talkativeness** of the people at that time, so the true message will be known by all; but, the message conveyed will make it clear that actions of faith will speak much louder than words. [7]

There will be plenty of people who will not believe, as so many will have wrongly proclaimed to know what my words say; **but**, this one believer will state the truth of **what all** will come to the world. He will have known nothing of what *The Prophecies* represented in the beginning; but, he will have **proceeded** to solve the most difficult puzzles with ease. This ability to solve the puzzle will be the confirmation that the solutions did not come **from** his own intellectual prowess, but instead from **the** ethereal **power** which assisted him. He will give full credit to the **divine**; and, he will affirm that the power **of** God far surpasses that of any of **the** world's **great** nations. Only **God** has the power of **eternal** wisdom, and His wisdom will make it shown how weak the great powers of earthly nations are. The message will call for all nations **to** seek peace. Those **who** believe in the power of God will comply, and **all** of the **kindness** of God will be **passed forth** to them.

Still, as certain as my words will be known, this future will not be yours to know now, nor will the people of your time know. As you are **my son**, you will be seen as an extension of me. As **that** first offspring of my name, you will inherit the legacy **I've** created with *The Prophecies*. My words will become **integrated** into the fabric of your being, as you share **the name of** Nostradamus. This name will become synonymous with the title of **Prophet**, based on the lore which will surround the works I have done. While **I** have certainly produced a true Prophecy with this book, it was **not myself** alone who came to such a high piece of work.

---

7   This sentence fragment written by Nostradamus ends, in French, "*d'inverecunde loquacité',*" which I originally translated as "of inverse one of talkativeness." Others have translated this as "minimum of verbiage." This fits as a description of the manner that Nostradamus wrote *The Prophecies*, however, the word "*inverecunde*" is questionable. Originally I looked at "*invers*" as the root, meaning "inverse." Now, I see that the root word is better attributed to "*vereconde,*" meaning "ashamed, demure, bashful," with the prefix "*in-*" making it the reverse, or "unashamed."

The **wishes** of some will be **to award** my name this **title**, which is a title **of** great respect. It is a title **so high** that it should not become **sublimated**, or seen as a socially acceptable replacement title, to become synonymous with the lower forms of prediction. This is especially true **for the times present**, being now called Prophet, more from the title of my work, *The Prophecies*, than from having claimed to be a Prophet of God. When my lifetime will have come to an end, nothing of my works will have been proven to be divinely inspired, justifying that title.

As an example **for that** misplaced title, I use a Latin axiom that states: **A Prophet**, or one who speaks for God, is **one** name used **to** determine those who can **say** what will happen **today**. However, only those **of the future** can properly assign this title to **one** so lowly, as any one human being is. The one who is truly the Prophet is the one who spoke to me, and has the **name** Jesus Christ. He is the true Prophet, passing His divine wisdom onto me, so I was **seeing** all of this future perfectly. Only when the future has seen the perfection of *The Prophecies* will I deserve the title of Prophet of Christ.

As you can see, it is semantics which loses the true impact **for** the word **Prophet**, Caesar; but, it is a holy title, so use it **properly my son**. For anyone who thinks a Prophet is something within the powers of mankind to become, through skill, ask them to **try this** exercise. Ask them to describe **that** which is **seen** by the eyes, by detailing all of the **things** found around a **distant** area. When all the descriptive details **of** that area are recorded, get close enough to see what is truly within **the** powers of cognizance. You will find that many obvious details, when viewed on closer inspection, were missed in the more distant view. This is the **natural** limit **of** mankind's ability to see anything at a distance, real or unreal. This includes the imaginations of a probable future, as well as **all** which is considered the world of reality. No **creature** can see all which is contained in the present material realm; but, man cannot see the ethereal realm any clearer, no matter what tools are used to enhance that vision.

And, with that inability to perceive a perfect future, there was no possible way **for** me to predict the high degree of accuracy which my astrological almanacs have achieved. I had no plan of **becoming** so popular **that** my predictions would cause several ranked officials to begin bestowing **the** title of **Prophet** on me. However, I fully understand now that there were higher forces **working** on my behalf to ensure my predictions would reach **the** level of acclaim they have **accomplished**. The guiding **light** of wisdom which my divine assistants shone into my mind allowed me to establish a record of believability, which has become the foundation **of** initial belief in **the** true **Prophecy** I was to be presented for publication. Without that background of approval, the state of presentation my work here is in would have never reached the light of day in the publishing world. This proves how God knows all, as he knew that Jesus Christ would bring **himself to appear** before me, with a message which would have to be received by one credible enough to make the message **publicly** known and accepted. This explains **the causes** of my accuracy, which had already brought me the title of Prophet. It has all been by **divine** means, for divine purposes. This foresight is precisely **like** its own Prophecy, where the title came to me, not from the success of my predictions but from the minds of the ruling powers receiving **gentle** whispers, telling them I would become a true Prophet. Of course, they would not know to admit **that** they were influenced by **these** gentle whispers, **not** thinking they **themselves** could be so ethereally influenced. These men are **powered** intellectually and believe they are able **to make** such designations from observation, rather than from heavenly hints. However, now that it is time for these powers to **view** the contents of my one and only true Prophecy, they will soon believe **that** they acted in haste with their titles and awards. They will want to know **the effects** my strange words will have **on the future** of them and on the future of France. Without the simple ability to make sense of the quatrains and this letter of instruction, they will cast aside the title of Prophet which they so generously gave before. Each quatrain will be seen as a **prediction** which will stand by **itself**, without the clarity a prophecy would be expected to bring. In order to make sense of what I have written they will begin a tradition of **reaching** to bring meaning to the words. These reaches will go **far** beyond what has been written; ensuring the secrecy of *The Prophecies* will be maintained.

THE SECRETS OF GOD

For the rejection which will come, as far as my work not being understood by the important people of France, I expect that. I know that God will comfort me through it all, so I am prepared. Still, I know that the work will maintain an aura of importance to many people, over the coming years. Just like the sword in the stone that awaited Arthur, there will be a steady stream of challengers who will try to unlock **the secrets** *The Prophecies* holds. I am completely confident no man will be able to find the keys to this holy work, without the blessings **of God**. Without that help, it will be impossible to gain the full impact of the many secrets which will be revealed, as a cloud has been cast over them, making them completely **incomprehensible** to man otherwise.

It is important to realize the secrets of God are kept from mankind to ensure **the virtue**, or the morality which would otherwise be lost. Just as in the mythological tale of Pandora's Box mankind is filled with curiosities of what is unknown; but, when Pandora peeked in to see what secrets were inside this released all the ills onto the world. **She that caused** so much grief to befall upon the world is representative of some people who would try to steal the secrets of *The Prophecies*. The virtue of mankind is **contingent** on its not being tempted to misuse the information my book contains, before the time it is necessary to be known by all. This has been the nature **of** mankind for as **long** as mankind's history has **extended, from** the first episode of Adam and Eve biting of **the** fruit of **cognizance**. Mankind has lusted for hidden knowledge since that time; and, rather than enjoying its **natural** state of ignorant bliss, **absorbing** the whispers of knowledge as needed, mankind struggles to consciously find its own answers. God does allows some of these answers to become evident to mankind, as these exposures will assist **them** in finding a **more** virtuous life on earth. This is because these enlightening experiences make mankind feel **near** to the **source**, from where the answers came, with that source being God. For this reason God wants **to** shed light to mankind, keeping it from **the** darkness; and, God is **liberal** with the knowledge He shares with mankind. Still, it is God's greater wisdom which allows Him to appropriately **judge** when mankind is properly prepared to receive

His gifts of knowledge.[8] God has **made** it possible for mankind to have flashes of brilliance; but, to some these inspirations seem **to appear** self-generated, as if originating within one's own mind, free of external influence. It is this type of ego which exists within some human beings, which becomes **the causes** of the sins of the world. These are the people **who** will take an idea designed for good and believe they are the owners of such intellectual property. This causes them to hide their secrets **from** others, such that it gives them an impression of power of mind over others. This is the similarity to Pandora and the opening of the sealed box, where just as **she** was only an innocent young girl, with no intention of bringing pain and suffering to the world, her ego was **the same** as that of mankind. Mankind has a tendency to think it can do as it pleases, as long as nobody finds out. Mankind is **not able to** control the urges that come over it, such that powerful inspirations become a danger to mankind. When one seeks **to acquire** the power of knowledge, one has to realize the important responsibility which comes with that acquisition. I have used **this** example of Pandora to be a **summary** of how our first instinct is to not do something, although our following urges tell it is okay to do it. When we give in to the urges this is when we find ourselves in trouble with other human beings, as well as in trouble with God. Those who will look **for** the answers that lie in *The Prophecies* , **being** solely driven for the purpose of gaining the recognition of being the one **known** to hold the truth, those are the **ones** who this message will be hidden from. The purpose of *The Prophecies* is **not** to give anyone an advantage over others **by** falling into **the** known traps that are natural for **human** beings. Many of these people are believers in the methods of **soothsayers**, where they seek to know the power of being a predictor or a conjecturer, believing I was capable of such magic. These are the people who will try to uncover these secrets; but, they will **not** create anything more than the necessary attention *The Prophecies* will need to survive. The message will be allowed to those who are driven **by other** motivations, where the **cognizance** they gain from these words will only act to strengthen their belief in God and Christ. Others will read the words of the message, but they will not be able to see **where** the believers find such strength

---

8 Nostradamus wrote, *"origine du libéral arbiter,"* which literally translates to, "source (origin) of the liberal judge." However, the words *liberal arbiter* together can mean "free-hearted will." This further explains why God must judge what knowledge is bestowed upon mankind, because free-will allows mankind to do what it chooses with it. That is the danger that God must control.

97

to believe. The believers will know the values of **virtue** and realize what must be done; but, the disbelievers will have lost touch with virtue and belief in prophecy will be **occult** to them. They would use their influences for personal gain, at the expense of the masses. The believers will know *The Prophecies* is **comprised** of words which do not operate **under the** same rules of grammar normal speech does. They will hear the whispers telling them to leave the linear plane of normal reading and **concave**. This curving inward will allow them to hear their heart telling them the true meaning **of the** words. This inward journey will let them know the words are not speaking to them; but rather, they will feel that the assistants of **Heaven itself** are letting them know Heaven is near. They will understand how mankind will have come **from** this beautiful place, so long before, and **the** acts of mankind, since leaving the Garden of Eden, will have **made** their **present** the time of danger. The ones who will believe in the message and make the necessary adjustments **to** prepare for **the** end of mankind will do so with a **total** commitment to Jesus Christ and the lessons he taught, for all mankind. These are the people who will spare their souls and find **eternity** with Christ and God in Heaven. It will be **that** desire for eternal bliss which the souls will know, as they each **came** into our bodies expecting this return. This is the voice that is **in oneself** and speaks to us all of our lives. This is the life source within us that tells us **to embrace** life as a miracle, and treat **all** human beings with love and peace. It is the element which knows **the times** that our bodies have on earth is miniscule to the totality of eternity. Those who will find the secrets within *The Prophecies* exposed to them will still have possession of their souls, as evidenced by how they will believe.

But, for those who will believe in my book's message, they will also know this future has been prophesized before **in** the Scriptures. There it promises that Christ will **return** and He will return **for** those souls which have prepared for **that** return. They will have prepared by having maintained faith in God and Christ and by obeying the rules of life handed down for them to follow. This maintenance is from understanding **that** following God's Laws and living with morals, according to Christ's teachings, is **indivisible**. There are Ten Commandments which cannot be divided up by humanity's interpretations, allowing for exceptions to those rules. When God spoke those commandments to Moses, saying "Thou shalt not kill," there were no implied exceptions which God would accept. Life on earth is a gift from God, and God has also given mankind the freedom to choose one's way of life; but, the time of the flesh is brief, when compared to the **eternity** of the soul. For that soul to enjoy both life on earth and life in Heaven there are basic restrictions that must be met. One must commit to desiring a return to God and the eternity of Heaven. However, **by** such a **committal** to God's ways, one must expect to face **agitation**, or turmoil, requiring **Herculean** powers of will to resist being shaken from that commitment. To resist **the causes** which could shake mankind from maintaining its commitment to God, man-kind must ask God to come to its aid. This help is requested **by the** confessions of prayer, asking God to grant His **heavenly** blessings and forgive the **movement** away from His graces. At times, man will forget realizing all of his actions are known by God; but, when man admits his acts of sin to God in prayer, it **is** then **known** by man that God returns the strength to surmount any obstacle.

THE STEPS AWAY FROM GOD

At this point **I** have **not** yet **said** the **step** we are at now, towards this future that comes. You are one step closer, as **my son**; and thus, you are my offspring who will outlive me. In the other steps which will lead **to** this **end that** comes, there will be many more steps; and, in these steps mankind will slowly begin to walk away from God and Christ. This path which will be walked will lead to the final punishment, where mankind will destroy itself. At that time, mankind will have traveled too far away to hear the calls for peace and brotherhood. Mankind will have caused an ending that will be **well** suited for it, as it will have devised **the means** of its own destruction. Those means **that** will be so destructive will those derived by **the cognizance** mankind will develop. The level **of this** awareness will be so deep that it will learn the secrets of **matter** and its most basic element. My present knowledge and your future knowledge are **not** enough to fully explain the intricacies of what this future mankind will discover; but, what mankind will create, from its own power of mind, will cause it to destroy **itself**. I am **able** to understand only the basic principles, such that mankind will **again** take a secret of the universe and turn matter into something which is dangerous. The terminology I must go **to print** with, to explain in my quatrains the result of this metamorphosis, can only be called a monster. This word is figurative; but, it is appropriate as the result will be well **inside** the parameters of the definition of that word. I have made an example of myself to you, as a physician and scientist; but, I want you to place more emphasis on the development of **your** heart. You must realize that mankind is **weak** compared to the other animals on earth. The success of mankind is said to be because man has a bigger **brain**; but Caesar, know that the weakest organ in the human body is the brain, as without God to guide it, it is no better than an animal's. I say this because this future mankind will believe **that** it has developed the powers of knowledge only God is capable of possessing. This belief that the brain will solve all of mankind's woes will actually become **the causes** of these **future** events. Their brains will see the **good** they will have created from knowledge, but, they will also realize the inherent bad their creations have brought as well. Instead of removing the monsters, their brains will believe that the danger is **remote**, and they will try **not** to permit their creations from **being** misused. This is the danger that is inherent **in the** brains of mankind, as the ego will believe it can be **cognizance of** the future; but, this is man trying to play god. Man is **the creature** God created in his image; but, God created man to be gentle and carefree in an idyllic existence. It was the serpent who seduced Eve, who then convinced Adam to eat of the forbidden fruit. From that point on, mankind has suffered and struggled over using the brain for being **reasonable**.

That power to reason is **so** strong in human beings that it sets man apart from the lower animals. But, this mental capacity is a detriment when misused by mankind. Some use it to their advantage, to confuse others and enslave people of weaker mind to their powers of reason. They believe their intellectual acumen makes them superior to others, thus developing a demigod status in their own minds. That status is what separates mankind from God; but when man thinks, he risks believing he has enough powers of reason to function without God's assistance. This is why most people **are not** able to find themselves **obtaining** the message of this work, as God knows some will over-think the words. Those who will under-think them will let others tell them the meaning. In reality, the words of this book are stated as **simply** as can be, while still communicating within the principles of language. They speak to **the creature** that man is, and not to his power to reason. It is this creature **of** God who is dependent on **the soul** for understanding. Man sees his power of mind as self-generated, with no need to consider the soul's insights. It will be men of this type who will be forcing my words to fit their **intellectual** preconception of **the things** which will come; but, they will base that perspective from how things are in the **present**. This will send them **far away** from the message contained in this book; and, the soul of man will not be getting through to **him**. The men of the future **are** not so different **from the** men of today, as on the **whole** most people are **not** able to comprehend **too much** beyond their daily lives and routines. The majority of the people in the world are not capable of understanding the **occult**, or the strange and unknown things. The masses will **not** put any thought into my words; but, a few will put **too much** thought into solving something that is simple. The simplicity is the words, which are **references** to the conceptual answers.

These references will be overlooked by the conscious mind; **but**, it must be understood that all of **the** words contained in this work are **perfected** by Jesus Christ. Many of **the causes** of this future, which the quatrains entail, have been written as 4-line **summaries** of events which can only be accurately seen from a past perspective. Without this perspective of the past, meaning that one is then in the middle of the main story line, one will **not** be able to properly identify any individual quatrains as reference to a coming future event that is plausible. The whole of *The Prophecies* is **itself** being one continuous story, told in chronological order. The stories within the main story show evidence of connecting together a series of quatrains, by key words being repeated or the use of synonymous words. This connectivity is what secures each quatrain to one specific event, such that this eliminates any other past events which could have appeared similar. The similarities of history's events make the conscious mind forget that history is said to repeat. Any one quatrain which is taken out of context, without seeing the other supporting quatrains that confirm the other quatrain's statement as true, makes it become impossible to understand any quatrain properly. The **ability** to put the quatrains in the proper order is the most difficult step, as for one **to acquire** this understanding requires subconscious thought. It will be impossible for those who only think objectively to solve the myriad of riddles that protect this document, as they will be **without** the most important tool for problem solving. That tool is to listen to **those** inner whispers, as they will provide the **divine inspirations** that are necessary for putting it all together.

Only when one will **want that** inspiration, by one's own dedication to God and Christ, will the door to understanding be slightly opened. Once one believes one is no more than an ordinary soul, seeking the redemption Jesus Christ offers, then, **all** of *The Prophecies* and its explanations will become understandable. It will not come from a selfish desire to understand, but from **inspirational** whispers. Trusting those gentle influences will lead one to find all of the words being truly **prophetic**. With these impulses **received** and acknowledged, then can one be found **absorbing** the true message of *The Prophecies*, and **its main** theme. This is the **principle** which will cause the words to be **changing from** cloudy to clear; and, nothing of this principle will depend on an intellectual approach to solving its riddles. Clarity will come from willingly accepting insights from **God**; and, once the clarity comes the whole will be recognized as holy. It can only be seen that no man could devise a work of this nature. Only God **the creator** could have created this prophecy. This message will unfold into a clear and present danger, as the times of understanding will occur when the times of danger will **then** be surrounding the reader. This understanding will mark the time of the beginning **of the** final **hour** of mankind. This use of "hour" is figurative, as it marks the time approaching a deadline. This hour is referring to the time allowed for mankind to accept this warning, admit its sins and make the required changes. This is the time which man has to save life on earth. Most importantly, accompanying this time of the beginning of the final hour, when worldly circumstances will have already created a sense of urgency, several significant acts **of nature** will have occurred, with more to occur in the near future. These events will not be manmade; but, they will signify the fragility of the earth, as well as mankind's inability to control the powers of the earth. This will be God's way of confirming the timing of the beginning of this final hour, which has been prophesized in my words.

By these natural effects the earth will be having, it will be God's way of showing mankind **what** true power really is and how insignificant man is, compared to that power. With such great events like these **being** prophesized as preceding the end of man, mankind will look for **the causes** of natural disaster and find mankind to blame. However, this will bring about the arguments of mind, where proof of man-caused changes of nature will be as difficult to produce as is proof of God. This will cause **indifferences** in humanity, where many will not believe in anything at all. Elements of mankind will thus prevent people from taking heed of the signs, just as they will try to prevent them from taking heed of *The Prophecies*, once they are understood. They will say that nature is **indiscriminately** a hazard to mankind, having always **produced** troubles for some.

Most importantly, they will claim that if God was all-powerful and all-loving, then these tragic events would **not** have **produced** the devastations which will have occurred. With God being all-knowing, **the** events would have had to have been **foreseen**; and, with God being all-loving, then the people affected would have been warned in advance. With warning they would have **departed** from those areas, before the natural disasters **happened**. These indifferent people will want to know **where** God was, if these events were known **to** have **been predicted** in biblical prophecy. They will ask why anyone was not warned beforehand, to save the lives of those who died and lost much of what they owned.

Doubts of this kind are always to be expected **for the** majority of the people struggle with **understanding** what the purpose of God's will is. A full understanding of why things naturally occur, many of which bring sadness to some of mankind, is not something that anyone can answer accurately, especially when separated from God. Man was **created** by God, to have some power of mind;

but, that power is designed to be **intellectually** dependent on God. Without faith in God, believing He brings to us what we need for soul growth, man rationalizes that God is **not** really there. Man is not **able to see** God; and, if God does not come to mankind's aid, in such situations as natural disasters, then God must not be real. However, God listens **closely** to the calls of mankind; and, when we ask for help, He responds accordingly. This is not by preventing a natural disaster; but, **by** sending the Angles who become **the voice** for God, steering people to safety. These actions are **done** to ease our worries and to console our losses, when one is **in the** state of **limbo** following such disasters. We hear these voices of encouragement which are **the means for** us to muster the strength that is needed to face our own personal circumstances by ourselves. When a natural disaster takes away **the** things we have worked hard to accumulate, we can **redeliver** things into our lives, if we ignite that **flame**, or spark of determination. That is where God comes **in**, as He provides us with that same spark **which** brought us things in the first place. For those human beings who have **departed** this life due to a natural disaster, they cannot be replaced. God knows the **futures** of everyone in this world; and, if it is one's time to pass on, then the prevention of an earthquake or flood will not spare their lives. However, the ones who will mostly find **themselves** blaming God for their material losses are those whose prayers were not asking for help at all. Those people will try **selling** their position **to** God, trying to convince themselves they are worthy of saving. They will believe they will not have to lose anything because they pray to God. However, the help these people pray for is to have God protect them alone; or **to bear good will** upon them, while the safety of others has no bearing to them at all. Those are the people who will say there is no God, because they lost a lifetime of material object in a natural disaster.

THE MOST DANGEROUS POWER

And knowing God does help those of us who believe, at all times, **also** know He knows how well we listen to our inner voice and use what He tells us. As you are **my son**, you are born a Christian and you will be raised to have a strong faith in God and Christ. As your father, **I** will guide **thee** in your overall upbringing, to lead you to become a man who serves God. In this upbringing, I will **implore** in my prayers for you **that** you will **never** blame God for your failures, nor fail to give God the credit He deserves. I pray that **you** will **not view** the directions God will send to you as your own cunning or intellectual acumen. You must take **them**, these whispers of enlightenment, **to use** for **your** own **understanding** of how to approach life, the way God knows is best for you. God will lead you **in such** matters, as long as you ask for advice through prayer. God will hear your prayers; and, He will know what you will need to know, in order for you **to succeed** in life. Remember that success is not measured by the amount of property you possess; but rather, as how well you served God and mankind. Always remember it is our own **vanities** that hurt us, such **that** when they surface in our outward appearance it causes us emptiness inside. It is this emptiness, from lacking the water of emotions, having **dried** the spirit within. This is a common ailment so many of **the bodies** which house the souls of mankind. You must always remember it is this emptiness that is **putting** one **in** jeopardy, as the dryness will **ruin the soul**. Without the uplifted spirit God brings to our souls, we are **giving** ourselves **trouble**. This will lead us **to** mental confusion and make **the** body **weak**. Without this extra **sense** God sends to us, we are unable to make just decisions in our lives.

This inability to think clearly is the **same** root cause for **the** uprising of **vanity**, which so many of mankind holds so dearly too. It is a vain man that thinks his powers of mind alone will lead him in the right direction. It is this vanity which makes some **of** mankind places themselves above God; but, **the more** this happens the more those people find Satan ruling their lives. It has always been **that** desire for having more, in the material realm, which has been the seduction of Satan. Satan has **cursed** more souls in the past with this seduction of material gains, than he has by the lure of black **magic**. Black magic has been **condemned** as evil by the Church, due to it being a craft which leads mankind away from

Christ and God, to worship Satan. However, there have been many more souls lost **in** the course of the **times** that have **past, by** those claiming to stand by **the** Church. They believe they have been **made holy** Christians, by quoting the **scriptures**, when they have become trapped by Satan by committing the sins of vanity.

One must always realize it is the sacred scriptures that the Church stands **by**, for without them there would be no Church. The Scriptures are recognized as the Word of God, spoken through the Prophets and **the** Apostles. Those **divine** words were inspired by God and Christ and have led to the Holy **canons** which rule the Church. The rules from the divine canons apply equally to all Christians, and the rules are given **to the leader** of the Catholic Church for him to protect. However, there have been some popes **who** believe the position of pope **is excepted** from those rules, as a separate holy entity, closer to God. Some of the past popes have made many of **the** people of the world suffer because of their **judgment**. They believe they are separate **of** the Laws of God. Some popes have also made it their judgment that Astrology is like magic and have banned it from the people. It has been this vanity which has attracted the present pope to seek **the** knowledge of **Astrology** from me. He sought to learn the power of Astrology, as a means for being **judicial**.

By this I mean I have been commissioned to teach the mechanics and methodology of astrology to the pope. He is aware of the accuracy of my almanacs, **which** have been attributed to my abilities with Astrology. Remember I have stated that my talents as an astrologer have only been successful because I have listened to the inner voice. The pope will find he will not have the same success with this God-given gift to mankind, as his motivation is for personal gain and reputation.

The rewards I have reaped, as far as possessing the reputation as a Prophet due to the accuracy of my astrological predictions, have been because I do not have those same motivations for personal gain. I have found success **in** the **return** of offerings because I molded my predictions **for** the purpose of **inspiration**. Equally important to remember is that when I receive a **revelation**, which has become a prediction, it has been assisted by **divine** accompaniment. Additionally, I have asked for help in such important matters **by** my **continual** prayers, for being able to make sound astrological **calculations**. It was from this assisted success that I have had previously which the Church **had** found reason to assist me financially.

Church officials have approached me, to have me teach selected members of its organization the art of astrological prophecy. From that training **our prophecies** would then be **drawn up in writing**, with the Church sharing the popularity.

And, it was this union between the Church and myself which demonstrated **how much** the Church wanted **that** popularity. It was comfortable seeking to learn the art of Astrology, if it could help them with their goals. They wanted to challenge **those** who had sought to subvert the Church, through **secret** organizations which study the **Philosophy not** singularly focused on the principles of religion. The members of the Church are not allowed to join such philosophical organizations, **being** because the focus of God and Christ becomes secondary to obtaining the powers within the grasp of man. Because of this, they have researched these matters **themselves**, and deemed it necessary they be officially **condemned** by the Catholic Church. They had made censures to include the practice of Astrology; but, they have become interested in exploring the possibility of this art being incorporated within the Church doctrines, to benefit the Church and the Catholic people. They found this evident because of the goodness they could see in my almanacs. However, due to the previous bans, the Church did **not** have any priests or ranking officials **having** the level of skill, as an astrologer, that I have. I have **never** claimed my success came solely from Astrology; but, the Church had **proposed** that I must **represent** the values of Astrology, by offering into their view how Astrology is not a secret Philosophy, inspired by evil. I am supposed to offer evidence which will overturn **their** judgments, which have previously lumped everything of this nature into one classification of evil. This associates astrology with the **unbridled** rites and rituals which are performed by people of pagan **persuasions** or beliefs, causing many to see Astrology as nothing more than witchcraft. I know **how much** persuasions such as **that** can cause the people to fear it, including the aristocracy; but, since I have produced **several** of my almanacs for public approval, the people have found that astrology allows for prophecy. The success of those **volumes** have given credence to the good use of Astrology, as a tool to guide mankind, **which** means I must now teach the Church how this is done. Because of the previous persecution against astrologers, many of the techniques **had** since **been** lost to many who sought to secretly learn it. The books I have learned Astrology from I have kept **hidden**, to also avoid persecution. Those books have been written **by** some of the greatest scholars of metaphysics, a **long** time ago. Those books have been passed down to me as family heirlooms, just as they have been passed on for **centuries**. I **myself** have known of the workings of astrology since I was a child, when my grandfather **had** me practice the lessons he had **been** taught. It is not something mastered quickly; but, having had been **shown** the true purpose and reasons for astrology's origin, I was well prepared to work with the Church and show them how the good of astrology can help mankind.

But, while I was prepared to teach the Church this benefit of astrology, I was encountered by Jesus Christ and instructed to write *The Prophecies*. With the Church already **doubting** that astrology was a gift from God for mankind, they expected **this** work for Christ to be a clarification of how well astrology can predict the future. They want to know the secrets the future holds, **which** my book does not make clear to them, or to anyone. I have written what **will happen** in the future; but, I did not write of a future which was predicted by astrology. The Church will be looking at the quatrains **in** this book, which they will **have** helped finance, expecting to be **made** aware of how the verses can be understood and how astrology led me to those predictions. I will not be able to do either for the Church, or anyone else, **after** this work is made public. When **the** Church has finished **reading** the confusing text of *The Prophecies* they will find nothing which relates to their **present** needs, and this will cause the Church to eventually present their final disapproval of the use of astrology. They will not see this document as being from Jesus Christ; but, they will point **to** references which I make in the verses and see paganism. One example will be a symbolic reference that is made to the Roman god **Vulcan**.[9] They will deduce **that** since Vulcan was one of the pagan gods, **this** reference will be evidence of a form of worship which has been banned. With this determination **pending** the pope's decision, and him knowing **that** I have been a devout Catholic, a compromise will be

9 Vulcan was the Roman god of fire, also known as Hephaestus in Greek mythology. He was mainly known as a blacksmith, working with metals. From metals he made the armor and weapons of the gods and heroes. In Greek mythology, Hephaestus had more roles in the myths, as he made just about everything for the gods. This was not completely restricted to metals, as he made tools from many materials, including the first human woman (Biblical Eve) from clay. As he ruled fire, his blacksmith forge was in a volcano. Nostradamus wrote of Vulcan in one quatrain which was in the original publication of 7 Centuries, along with one other using the term, *"vulcanal."* He added a 3rd reference in the final 3 Centuries. The 7th Century only has 43 quatrains, with 5 others being found being attributed to these censured quatrains.

made. The pope will say **he** has been advised on my work and there are several quatrains in **it** which will have **come** under considerable scrutiny. The pope will find there is no just reason **to devour** the entirety of my book with flames; but, the Vatican censors will remove many quatrains from the last Century. They will see this as preventing the conclusion from being known; but, the pope will be influenced by Jesus Christ, as to what quatrains should be removed. These last quatrains will be a part of the overall story, but their removal will not play an important role in determining the full message. This will allow *The Prophecies* to be published, keeping **the flame** alive, with the symbolism of Vulcan being very much appropriate. The fire of inspiration will keep people **licking** at the true meaning, thriving on **the air** of importance that surrounds this mysterious work. Meanwhile, the true message of *The Prophecies* will wear an invisible armor of protection, just like the one created by Vulcan for Achilles. The true power of *The Prophecies* will only be exposed when this protective covering has been **rendered** useless by Jesus Christ. At that time, **one** will be able to see, with great **clarity**, the message which is contained in the verses. This clarity will make the element of Vulcan further understood, as the story will show that mankind will come into an **unusual** machine, which will have the qualities of something produced by Vulcan. This machine will have **more** power than anything previously known to mankind, making it **clear** that a comparison to the god of fire and the manufacturer of mighty weapons is a well chosen metaphor. The source of this weapon will be fire, but it will be a greater fire **than** possible to be produced by a **natural flame**. Instead, this fire will be more **like** the fire of the Sun, as it will produce blinding **light**. As it is **of** the nature of **fire** to produce light, the light of this weapon will be more comparable to the light that comes **from** the **glister** of **lightening**. The power of this weapon will be so great that one would think only a god could be **causing** such a creation of light, so **brightening** that people will have to cover their eyes to keep from going blind. The beams of this light will be so **illuminating** they will quickly penetrate the darkest recesses. This will cause mankind to seek protection from such light in bunkers and basements, **under** the cover of earth. I say this because **the house** above the ground will be swept away by the rush of these rays of light. It will come **like** a flash, **so** fast that **it** will **burst forth** and immediately cover all. Those that will have **been** witness to this release of power and light, **in** the future's record of history, will know the **sudden** effects of this weapon. This weapon will bring a new type of **cataclysm** by fire, much greater than any volcanic eruption cause by Vulcan before.[10]

By that cataclysm, I mean **what** will be a part mankind's future powers, which will act **to end** his time on earth. Mankind will develop **that** ability for self-destruction by playing with the unseen fire that is **in** all matter. The gift of fire was Prometheus' gift to early mankind, to help **them to happen** protected and enlightened by the mystical powers of fire. This gift was **not** given to mankind so that it could develop **firesaws**, or weapons of fire which could be used to cut down an enemy. The creation of Greek fire was found so dangerous that its formula was kept tightly secret, so it would not be **abused**. The nature of mankind to be inquisitive will keep him **searching** to find out all of **the** secrets of nature, which have been **perfected** by God. When mankind finds out the secret to make this fire, it will mark a time of great **transformation**, when man will believe himself a god. It will change **all** of mankind, as this weapon will cause fear in everyone, as a threat to end **their own line** of humanity, due to **that** power of transformation this weapon will bring. This power will be so great it will become the most **solitary** weapon of fire ever produced, and it will be the one main cause for mankind's end.

Just as Vulcan kept his forges **under** the volcanoes of the earth, the material for this weapon will come from deep within the **ground**; and, it will have the qualities of **metal**. Once removed from the ground, these elements will be given a new classification, as the **incorruptible** elements, not subject to normal decay.

As difficult as this is to understand, this danger comes **in the waves** these elements cause, which are **occult** waves, meaning that they are secretly and unknowingly emitted. When future mankind will have perfected this form of transformation into fire, **they** will **have** turned all of the power **in** one small particle of matter into the power of the Sun. The burning waves which will be created will instantly turn all surrounding matter into **cinders**. The hidden coals of Vulcan

---

10 This block of the preface is one that appears to read very clearly, not as I have interpreted it above. This could be the actual source of the pope's focus on the use of the god Vulcan in the quatrains. In my book *Pearls Before Swine, Volume 1*, I interpreted this as Nostradamus' encounter with the Akashic Record and the illumination that he received from that experience. However, my inner voice now tells me that way is a secondary way to read this block, as there is more here to understand. Both interpretations are accurate. It shows how what appears to be the most obvious is actually just part of the surface clutter, which forms the invisible armor that surrounds *The Prophecies*.

will be **converted** into purely lethal waves, which will travel over great distances.

But at that time, **when** mankind has developed the capacity to release the power contained **in** such a small bit of matter, **that** conversion will have uncontrollable consequences. This manmade tool will become the harbinger of death, **which** mankind will eventually unleash upon **itself.** This power **came** to mankind, not from God's will, but from the evil seductions which approach man's mind. This development will precede the final acts of man, where initially its development will be seen as God-given, **to perfect** the developer into godlike status, as all-powerful. God will allow mankind this privilege to act like a god; but, **in return for** such acts which disgrace God, mankind must be willing to accept **the judgment** that will come from the **celestial,** or Heaven. God will know **that you,** future mankind, will have **wanted** the power of gods, **i.e. to show** what your minds can produce; but you will fail miserably as demigods.

For example, **by** having knowledge of **what** destructible force you will have created, and not to destroy it immediately, you will have proven your failure as a god. Being a true god means **to have cognizance** and awareness of all **the causes** which will result in **future** events. Future mankind will have been **reluctant** to void such a destructive power, and this reluctance will have persisted for a **long** time. There will be those who will present a number of **the fantastic** possibilities this power will offer; but, those possibilities will be nothing more than the **imaginations** of weak minds. By refusing to admit that degree of fantasy, **which** will not be a shared vision by most of humanity, mankind **will become** divided over the threat of this power. I have been restricted from telling everything clearly about this weapon, as Christ had me **limiting the** words and using symbolic names. The use of Vulcan is then designed to show a **particularity** that is relevant to this event. Likewise, I have listed some **of the** ancient names of **places,** where the history of those ancient times is important, as parallel events. These names act in this manner, more than to state a specific place on earth. All of this has come to me **by divine inspiration,** with my contact with Christ and the Angels, who have carried the will of God with them. This wisdom is **supernatural,** and is the true measure of a god. God can see far beyond the observable physical universe. Man cannot claim this feature. Everything I have written in this book is **according to** the Word of Jesus Christ; and, through Christ this does at times include the use of astrology. Christ has shown me **the** positions of several of the **celestial** planets, and reminded me of several of the mythological **figures**, all of which is for the purpose of symbolizing the story that is told. Christ has not hidden all from the text, as He has allowed me to clearly state some of **the places** which will be involved in the setting of this future. When it is time for understanding to come to mankind, **one part of** the story will become evident as having had already occurred, and perfectly predicted in the quatrains. This part will be well into the future from now, but then it will appear to tell of **the times** which will have already passed; and, **from** those parts which will have already occurred, the infallibility of those predictions will make the unfulfilled future quatrains believable. The **property** or characteristic that sets the language of the quatrains apart from normal speech will then be realized, as the only way the quatrains can be properly understood. When these properties are consistently incorporated, all previous interpretations will become pointless. While the words will still be as **occult** or as mysterious and obscure as they are now, they will be understood **by** the **virtue** of each word's definition.

It is still most important to realize that this understanding will not originate from the **faculty** of man; although once realized it will meet and surpass all of the tests of logic and critical thinking. The initial realizations will come from **divine** influence. Once this divine influence is **in** the **presence of** those reading the words, everything will begin to make perfect sense. This enlightenment will make the times recognizable, **which** will then be divisible by **the three** most basic measurements of the **times**. These **are** the times **understood**, when measured **by** the **eternity** of all time, to be the past, present and future. It will then be easy to realize in the storyline the element of **revolution**, or rebellion against authority, which will have been **tendered** by the common man as a viable method for dethroning royal rulers. That beginning, when the common man will have accepted the responsibility once held by the bloodline of Christ, as the protectors of mankind, will be the initial revolutionary events which will have led **to the cause** of their past, present and future states. But, this part of the story will not be foreseen, in advance of this period of revolution. It will only be recognizable when this period will be **past**. Once past, it will be understood as the root cause of the events happening in the **present**; and the quatrains which will deal with those present events will be partially predictive and partially proven prophecy. The parts of the quatrains that will refer to that present, and will not have been completely fulfilled, will be predictable as future outcomes; and, that predicted future will be seen as highly probable. But, while those events can be predicted, and thus tested for complete accuracy, this is where the danger will lie. This is because those quatrains, which will refer to still unfulfilled elements of a prediction, will forecast more significant events to come deeper in the **future**. While this future will be predictable, it will also be dependent on the present playing out as predicted. If the present then becomes changed, the future can likewise be altered. Still, all the quatrains will be clearly understood, before all will have come true. Once this understanding is known, mankind accepts full responsibility for whether or not the future will come to fruition.

With complete understanding of *The Prophecies* found at that time, the answer to how to approach this future can be found in the Bible, in the Book of Hebrews. In chapter 4, verse 13, it is said, "**Because all things are naked**," where "naked" is the way we all come into this world, when born. We are unclothed and bare; and, it is at these times that mankind is the most equal and the most vulnerable, epitomizing our frailties as human beings. It is this exposure which causes us to need clothing for warmth. However, this state is no different than the one found in the Book of Genesis, when Adam and Eve first discovered their nakedness. This exposure caused them to try and hide from God. Naked means the exposure and guilt of sin, which we feel when we know there is no way we can cover ourselves from God's eyes. God is the one who knows "all things," and the association to *The Prophecies* is that this future will be exposed. At that point the verse continues this exposure theme, by stating "**uncovered**." While this appears to be restating the same principle as naked or bare, uncovered means the act of exposing. This is the element of uncovering that which has been purposefully hidden. In other words, when we are naked we are seen in our natural state, as equals; but, when we are uncovered, we are exposed for what we have secretly done previously. This is what understanding *The Prophecies* will do; but, the purpose of this exposure is found in verse 16, where the passage concludes, "Let us therefore come boldly unto the throne of grace, that we may obtain mercy, and find grace to help in time of need." This acts as the solution to this problem, as it calls for a devotion to the true concepts of Christianity as the answer.

113

THE PATH TO HEAVEN

By that passage in Hebrews, you have to realize **what** going to the throne of grace and asking for mercy means. It means, **my son**, that God respects those who submit to His power, knowing He knows all that mankind has done, regardless of how hard they have **concealed** their sins from others. God whispers to us all, as our conscience, such that guilt brings out our **fears** of being detected. These feelings of guilt are **easily** recognized by all as present within them; but, these feelings **notwithstanding**, one who does not believe in God will continue to hide that which is personally known to be wrong, without asking for forgiveness. At **your tender** age you do not consciously know God and Jesus Christ. This is because your **brain** has not had time to develop and learn the principles of religion and the doctrines of Christianity. This means that as you grow you will not fully know the source of guilt, which will cause you to instinctively hide your mistakes. But, as you learn **to understand** the lessons of Christianity, such **that** your brain will then know the power of God, you will learn to admit your mistakes to God when you feel guilt and ask God to forgive you. God knows all of **the causes** of all sins. Some are common minor mistakes, **which** are easily forgivable; but, others are major mistakes, which cannot avoid punishment, although they may be forgiven. These major mistakes **are** the ones which break God's Law; and while God may grant forgiveness to those who commit such sins, punishment will still be **due**. The question then becomes when is this punishment **to happen**, as there are two choices. If one understands that God knows of these sins, and punishment can be either on the earthly plane or the eternal plane, the conscientious people will present **themselves** for punishment in this earthly plane. This is because **none** would dare wait to hear the **report** of punishment to be administered in the afterlife. For mankind to take these bold steps, to admit its sins and accept punishment on the earthly plane, mankind has required proof of God and the afterlife. This proof can only come when God speaks through Prophets, who then **prophesize** the future to the people and the prophecy proves to be accurately foretold. Some Prophets have been led to prophesize **by** God showing them signs in **the** dreams they have, during **nocturnal** rest. Others have felt the **celestial** presence around them and seen the **lights** of Heaven at the end of the tunnel of death; only to be sent back with a message to report from God. The means of God are many; and, He knows **which** of humanity will respond to

115

His revelations. The Prophets have spoken the truth on every occasion, warning the faithful of what is to come. Those who have disbelieved have had plenty of notice of God's reality, which many have woefully pondered in hindsight. It is only the **fool** who is forewarned of a danger, yet continues to proceed down a dangerous path. God speaks to us all through our thoughts, which appear to us **naturally**; and, it is this fool who believes those voices are his own, and refuses to heed his own advice.

This is so important to understand, **by** all mankind. The way to salvation is from faith that God exists; and, Jesus Christ is the Son who was sent to prove this existence. Just as the **spirit** of God daily speaks to us, Christ has spoken to us through the Apostles and the Prophet John. Those voices guide the holy of us to lead pious lives and to beg for forgiveness when we have strayed. However, for those who will deny this constant presence of God, or will deny that Christ is the way to salvation, when the proof **of** God's existence has been given to all through **prophecy,** in the infallible ways prophecy has proven to be true, denial will have dire consequences.

In this future which comes, there will be many people who will **not** have **that** connection with God, or any belief in true Prophecy. As much as **I** have been called a prophet by my contemporaries, including those who strongly believe in God, those were predictions I generated **myself**, without God speaking them to me as a prophecy. The **view** people have today will not be the same in the future; as **it** will not be a perspective of natural belief that prevails then, but rather one of pessimism. Many people in this future will not believe God exists; and, many more will confuse prediction with prophecy. While my name will survive until that time, for the people of today **to award** me the title of prophet, the future will see that **nomination** as proof of our ignorance. They will make that decision based on a comparison of our lack of knowledge, compared to their superior brains. Those who will have carried the torch of *The Prophecies* until then will have had **no effect** towards soliciting widespread belief in my work, particularly in reference to it being truly **prophetic**. They will instead believe I was a mystical charlatan; **but,** when my words will have finally been properly understood, **by** the grace of God, the true message will be **revealed** and mankind will realize a true Prophecy to heed. From understanding will arise the necessary **inspiration** which many will have sought, confirming their faith in Christ. This inspiration will be **like** I am there talking to them personally, pointing out the frailties **man**

116

is known to have. It will make those people aware that mankind is **mortal**, and all mortal creatures die. Mankind has always been living on borrowed time; **and**, this extends to all things of matter, including the earth and its heavenly spheres. Longevity of life is dependent on how one treats others and how one is **treated** in return. This principle applies clearly to how man treats man; but, it applies **no less** to how man treats the earth and God. Mankind must learn the value **of** this unity, and **sense** that mankind is but one cell **in** the whole of the body that is life. The soul of life is **the** ethereal life force of God and all which makes up **Heaven**. Without this force there is no life. A body would be no different **than** a corpse, which is only lifeless matter. God comes **to** breathe the breath of life into man; and as such, man stands at **the feet** of God, miniscule in comparison to the power of God. Man is just one form of life which God has placed **on earth**; but, man is the only life form which has been given the free will to deny God's existence. It is this power of mind which can make some believe that immortality lies in the material world.

Only God is immortal and eternal; but, God has allowed all of the souls He released from Heaven to take a material form and walk the face of the earth. This is the gift of physical being God has created for those eternal souls which are extensions of God. Mankind must remain centered on that soul influence, to stay focused on the objective of life. It is the responsibility of each one of mankind to safely harbor his or her soul, for its eventual return to Heaven. Without this focus mankind is lost. Jesus Christ was sent to earth as the Son of Man, to be the guiding light back to this focus. In the *Imitation of Christ*, by Thomas Kempis, he wrote how mankind should show its needs for Christ and ask for His grace as disciples. The message was Christ is the **one** who **can** comfort us, by helping us **not to wander** on earth in suffering. Without Christ in our hearts we so very easily become **deceived**, by others and by ourselves; and, this deception is allowed by one's failure to see the light of Christ. So often it is the pleasures of life which have **ensnared** us, leading us to turn our backs on Christ. When one has turned away from Heaven for the delights of sin, one has then **followed** the one who delights in luring one to become a **sinner**. The **more** one follows this influence to sin, the more one believes how **great** man is; and, when this belief is held, the pleasures of a worldly existence seem to be the goal of life. This is the trap of not following the guiding light of Christ, and instead following **that** influence to sin. That influence comes from the greatest sinner of all times, the fallen angel

Lucifer. The trap has long been set to steal our souls from God. Lucifer will not cease this enticement until **none of** mankind's souls remain faithful any longer. Lucifer's goal is to have all of mankind desiring to remain in **this world**. It is this source which seeks to make man's mind **subject to** his influence. And, as enticing as Satan's lures are, they are actually nothing more than traps. It is this evil influence that has forever causes **all** of **human** kind's afflictions. Satan only offers one a momentary comfort from the afflictions he has brought to us; but, the price required in return for this fleeting relief is way too high. It is an eternity for that lost soul in Hell.

But, even with those known afflictions and the prospect of Hell, there are many people who will be continuing to try **standing** upright alone, refusing to seek Christ for guidance. Without the willingness to listen to their inner voice's guidance from God, they find their steps are cumbersome; and, they are constantly **tripped by** unseen obstacles. In the **course** of these failures, God still stands by man, remaining **there** by his side, whispering encouraging thoughts. If it was not for God continuing to help mankind, regardless of the egos that refuse to honor God at all, mankind could not last **a week** alone. If mankind was left solely to the influence of Satan, the effect would be **maddening** to men's minds.

Such strains on our intellect can only be eased **by** God, as God knows it would take man **long** hours of **calculation** just to solve the simplest mystery of the universe. God watches those who understand these blessings of insight he gives; and, He sees the ones who act on their lessons of hardship, by **giving back** their knowledge to others. What God has afforded them they pass along to others, giving God the credit due Him. In my case, before I encountered Jesus Christ, I set aside time for **the studyings**, which are important to me. These are my readings of the Latin Bible, as well as my pouring other writings of knowledge, from medicinal herbs and medical texts, to astrological books, classical poetry, philosophy, history, geography and the ancient tales of mythology, to list a few. This is the course of my knowledge, as directed from within, and this has enabled me to help others from my knowledge. I have done this kind of study regularly, **by nights**; and as I do so I read **to** the **sweet smell** of burning incense, to make that time pleasurable and to open my senses to higher inspiration. This higher inspiration is why **I've written** yearly almanacs, as my knowledge from studies has made that seem to be a good way to give back what I have learned. In these yearly **books** I have told **of** how I see the coming planetary arrangements manifesting into coming events in our present society. The people who have read these books have called my poetic forecasts **prophecies**; but, these almanacs are really simply **containing** calculated predictions, based on my knowledge. I have done this for **each** year for a while now, such that I have written about a total of **one hundred quatrains** of this nature, so far. These have been prepared based on my knowledge of **astronomics**, and combined **with** the astrological meanings. Still, there is a sound historical perspective from which I have been able to base them on. It is not my talent which I claim caused those predictions to be found accurate. I simply listened to the voices within my heart, from God's good Angels, which activated the memory of what I have learned, which is stored in my brain. It was this recall of knowledge I had learned that was then applied to the forecasts. I know now they are truly **prophecies**, because I was divinely guided to such accuracy. However, those prophecies are seen as accurate because the events predicted came to pass and people understood the words I wrote, **which** were fairly clearly stated. By the use of poetic style, **I've** make them **a little** vague, as is **required** when one knows the future can take many shapes; but, I did not have **to plane** them **down** beyond understanding. By utilizing common metaphors I could state **obscurely** what was understood by most people, while maintaining a degree of safety, from anyone that might have taken offense.

These predictions I have written and published to so much acclaim **are** based on the **perpetual** events of mankind, such that life cycles continually repeat. If given the right conditions, then a correct result can be predicted, based on past results for the same conditions. The astronomics of the planetary movements mirror these life cycles, thus their placements and aspects likewise repeat, allowing an astrologer to forecast a typical event, for a typical astronomical alignment. As such, I was **foretelling** the coming of a modern version of past events. These predictions were **for** the public to enjoy, **from** my desiring to do something to give back to the people **here** in France. When I began to produce these almanacs, each book roughly contained one prediction per month, for thirteen months. This number was chosen **to** ensure that **the** full **year** was covered, before the next publication would be made available. With such a timely subject matter, I had to follow a consistent pattern for having work completed and sent to the publisher. This followed the requirements placed on me for publication, which included writing the material, getting the acceptance of my work by the publisher and printing the book for distribution. This meant I had to follow a **3 – 7 – 9** pattern for each year's writings. These numbers coincide with the number of the month, such that I began preparing them in March (month 1), to be finished and sent in to the publisher by May (month 3). The publisher would then set the press to begin publishing in the fall, or September (month 7), to be ready by November (month 9). With their availability not assured before December (month 10), this meant January would be the first month presented in the almanacs. I have followed this pattern now for **7** years.[11]

That process and schedule being in place for so long has made it **possible** for me to gain a more global notoriety, becoming known to many more people than ever before. This widespread recognition of my name, due to the understandability and accuracy of my works, **will make** it easier for *The Prophecies* to be published; and it will be in demand. However, without that prior record of achievement and popularity from the almanacs, there would be several people of importance who would act **to remove** this book from publication. The reason is this work is not like the others. It is longer and it is completely unintelligible to the people who will read it. Thus, the only reason *The Prophecies* will remain alive will be due to the **forepart** of my writing history, or my early period. From that record my book will be kept alive, enough so it will remain **in** the minds of **some** for a long time, particularly the **ones** who will see a challenge in solving my writings. This lasting life will be protected by the graces of Jesus Christ and God. Interest in its contents will be maintained for a long time to come, even though no one

---

11   In this sentence fragment, Nostradamus wrote, "*pour d'icy a' l'année 3797.*" This literally translates as, "for of here (hence) to the year 3797." This is where the Nostradamus popularists have gleaned their bold assumption that Nostradamus predicted the future until the year 3797. The use of a numerical figure is rare for Nostradamus, as he spelled out the words for specific years, both in the quatrains and in the letters. When one realizes that this use of numbers is something seemingly obvious that by itself says something else is the meaning. This is the only reference of this nature, so it is meant to be a puzzle. When one realizes that the text is about his almanacs (lower case "prophecies"), and not *The Prophecies*, the year 3797 becomes a meaningless date, as Nostradamus would not be expected to live that long to put out his 3797 predictions. This whole block follows the previous block, which ended with a colon, making everything in this block become a clarification about the almanacs Nostradamus wrote. However, I will admit that the perpetuality of planets recycling could mean a total of 3,797 years, which could be a reference to the previous extermination of humanity, during the Great Flood.

will clearly understand it. It will stay **in** the consciousness of these people due to it having the essence of a **clairvoyant** work, where people will sense it to be unusually perceptive. With this **so**, these people will study **long** on my words, trying to make them fit a standard model of communication. As no such fit will be found, the majority will resort to **stretching** the words to fit understandable sentence structure, making them seem to describe many events and times which will have become known. This effort to prove my clairvoyance will continue the interest well into the future.

Still, these efforts **by** so many who will feel the need to speak for me, wanting to prove my words were not written precariously, they will fall short of producing the real meaning. The real meaning is **under** the control of God, as to when they will be correctly understood. In this control, **all** who try to resolve the mysteries will fail; but, each effort will serve the purpose of stoking the fire of interest. In time, several will be able to stretch my words to fit many individual events which will come, due to **the concavity** of the quatrains. By this, I mean where the beginning and end of each quatrain appears to bend inward, keeping each separate. They will not be able to see how this inward bend is more like the curve in a link of a chain, looping first around one quatrain, then another, before returning to complete it singular purpose. This concavity will also present hollowness to the quatrains, as many will be seemingly without meaning. Other verses will be found only forming a shell of something that resembles an event; and, some quatrains will appear to tell **of** past events, before the present now. This element of past events will especially be found in reference to those quatrains where I have written about **the Moon** and the people who worship it. They will see those as references to the Muslims of the East; but, the accuracy of the words **will have** seemed to describe events which will have already taken **place**, long ago. This will be the problem people will find, trying to solve my quatrains, as this dependency on **intelligence** alone will cause them to fail to see the potential of a future which will repeat, similar to the past. Mankind will not find the answers to this work until God has found one willing to listen to His whispers; and, this will only happen when the proper time has arrived.

The importance of intelligence cannot be understated, as when **this** time of the future has come, mankind will have developed great pride about its overall intellectual abilities. The elements of mankind who will believe themselves to be the most intelligent, as shown by them having used their brains to grasp power over

121

the masses, they will be **extending** this intellect as godlike knowledge. They will demand respect **universally**, as the highest leaders of power, **by** professing to own the power of thought and the ability to conquer **all** obstacles. They will be the ones who will use their mental powers to bring **the earth** to its position of danger. Their minds will have come up with all the concepts and ideas that will become **the causes** of this future collapse of mankind. All of this, **my son**, is spelled out in *The Prophecies*.

That egotism for intelligence will drive men to try to unlock the secrets of the universe, several of which, once opened, mankind will not be able to control. This quest for the power of mind will cause **so** much grief to so many of mankind's wanderers. My son, **you** and I are of **the age** of man when mankind has a **natural** inclination to life, rather than a blind pursuit of knowledge. We can sense dangers without needing to understand them, because we have a strong faith in God. Above all, we accept our **human** position as being well below the powers of Heaven, trusting God will properly lead us, because we are weak minded. But, I can safely state that if **you** were to learn the things this future will have learned, when it **will see** so many things which are secrets to us now, it would **slant your** opinion of the values of intelligence. Life in our world is so different from the way it will be in this future world. The **climate** we now live in, in France, will become completely changed. I mean this both figuratively and **literally**, as the mood of the people of France will be much more hectic and the difficulties we now experience with the weather, in seasonal conditions, will be forgotten. To see some of the miracles these powers of mind will have created, you would think that future place to be **Heaven**. And, I mean if you were to appear in Salon, the city **of your nativity**, you would find it a whirl of advancements which your life, here and now, will never know. Still, for all of the wonders that will have been unlocked by **the** intelligence of these **future** peoples, those people of future France will see the evil those minds will have created as well. This evil will kill more people than the **undertakers** will be able to bury. Those minds will have been able **to** clearly **foresee** the dangers they will have created; but, once they will have created it, they will not be able to solve how to make the dangers disappear.

How many people will be killed because of **that** power of mind is impossible for me to say. Still, the damage this intelligence will cause to the body will be nothing compared to the damage it will cause to **the soul**. Upon death, the soul needs to return to **God** and find its **eternal** peace. But, at this time of death, when souls would ordinarily be **reaped**, the conditions for entry into Heaven will not have been met by the vast majority of people. Those conditions are **the same** conditions that have existed for the redemption of a **soul** since Jesus Christ, the Redeemer, died on the cross and promised to return again. The return of Christ, **which** has been **known** to all Christians for as long as Christianity has been alive, will be for rewarding **the** faithful and repentant with the promised **eternity** in Heaven. Jesus preached the true way **to** reach this end; and, the books of the apostles have represented those lessons, which stand as **the light** which shines to lead mankind to that end. Those souls which will be **passing forth** to the eternal bliss of Heaven and Christ will only be those who will have remained faithful **to him**. Those who will have lost the faith and placed more trust and value in the **selves** of mankind will have been lost.

I do not want this last statement to go without stressing just how important it is, as there will be many souls lost. In *The Prophecies* I have **said** all of the ways that mankind will place more importance in self, while neglecting to give God and Christ the respect they deserve. When my words are understood **clearly**, the degree of **that** importance will be so great that man will be worshiped as godlike, based on its higher level of intelligence. However, **to** put so much faith in man, while turning their backs to God, this is the greatest insult **which** will cause many to be punished by spending eternity in Hell. There will be so many people who will have lost their faith in God, unable to simply ask sincerely for the forgiveness of their sins and beg Christ to save their souls, that **the magnitude** of the consequences for their actions will be completely unexpected. The losses which mankind will suffer will be **immense**, from the worst imaginable abominations. People will be ravaged by the pains of war, disease, famine and flood, on a level **that** none will have been prepared for. There has never **been** anything, ever, close to this horror in comparison. The scope of this destruction and misery will be **without** any history by which mankind can attempt to **measure** the full impact of all the torture that will set upon the people of earth. It must be clearly understood that once this terror begins, no one will be able to beg for the mercy of Christ and be saved; so, to refuse to accept Jesus Christ as the Savior of souls, before all of this begins, and not act to prepare for the coming of the Lord is completely **incomprehensible**. I have stated **in** this book of quatrains all the knowledge which is **required** to be known for mankind to be forewarned and seek out God and Christ. My story is not a new story, as it has also been written before, **by** other prophets, **long** before I encountered the **inspiration** of Jesus Christ to write this Prophecy. Just as the biblical books have foretold this end, especially the topic of Judgment Day in *The Revelation of John*, this has been largely set aside by the churches, as it leads to **melancholy** in many. It is difficult for most to face thinking about such dreadful events; but, it is much better **to reveal** this future to them beforehand, so the only suffering possible would be the depression and anxiety caused by reading of a horrid future. It is no different than practicing a drill to escape from a fire, when there is no fire. It keeps the awareness of that potential on the forefront of the brain, so that if and when that emergency happens, one is prepared beforehand and knows how to act to save lives. It becomes a necessary study of the divine inspiration of Prophecy, which tells of that which will come to be. The drill is to stay committed to Jesus Christ and God. The revelations **that** have been exposed in the Bible are one's **working** guide to know there will be an end to life **here** on earth. It is written that Jesus Christ will be angry at those who will have refused to believe and pay respect. In my Prophecy **it** too reveals mankind will not reverse the core **cause** that results in this lack of respect. That cause will be the leaders who block the eyes of the masses from seeing God, establishing laws which forbid the practice of religion. These worldly leaders represent the **occult** factions, or the hidden elements of mankind, which will have **manifested** themselves as rulers of the world by then. This rule will be strengthened by them having amassing great wealth, at the expense of the people. Some of those rulers will even be seen as the most **divinely** led men and women on earth, so much so that they will be accepted and recognized as true leaders of mankind. But, those leaders will try to convince the people that sin is acceptable; and, they will call for the people to put their trust in them, rather than God. Those leaders will love power and the material realm so much that they will not willingly step aside, forfeiting their positions, to let the world choose a peaceful path. This refusal to let mankind guarantee its souls' salvation will **most especially** be seen in the corruption **of** the **two** greatest nations, which will share influence over most of the world. The powers amassed by these two nations will be so great that their unwillingness to relinquish control will lead to the **causes** of earth's demise. To keep the people from realizing the true dangers, both nations will hide the true extent of their powers. Both will have mastered the art of secrecy; and, in this process they will have become the **principal** initiators of the world's loss of religious values. Their power over

124

the people will be through their control of the material realms, **which** they will use to their advantage by enslaving the people to material addictions. They will amass great riches by taking advantage of the poor; but, they will appeal to the common people for their support, as if they **were** equally of common heritage. The masses will not know of the secret **inclusions** many people will have made with the ones in power. Those traitors against humanity will be seeking some of this power for themselves. In return for their support, the powerful will separate those supporters into a narrow class of elite, allowing them to work in unison, guaranteeing the slavery of the common class. Once exposed, they will speak **of the understanding** which will come from these words I have written here, showing them to be **of this** privileged rank. They will address my accusations because a growing number of common people will be **inspired** by the messages of *The Prophecies*; but, those leaders will begin to lose their control and become fearful. The messages of my book, **which** will be the same as those echoed by some of the Christian sects as **prophesized** in the Bible, will act to unite the religious sects together. The parallel to biblical prophecy is **the one** main reason they will support what **is** claimed here. They will not follow me, as they will know **that** the one responsible for *The Prophecies* is Jesus Christ. They will promote the message it was He who **came** to me with a warning; and, many will have been waiting for this sign to come, to confirm their belief in the return of Christ. The message **in** this book will not act to bring fear to the faithful; but instead, it will act **to infuse** them with the spirit of Christ. This message will be **brightening** the messages of the biblical prophets, by shining **the** new **light** which is required for them too to make perfect sense of biblical verse. To see these prophetic words and then to compare them to the language of the Bible will bring a new level of understanding to Christians. They will see the manner each book of prophecy was written is similar to mine, with all **supernaturally** inspired. This understanding will add **to the personality** of religion, such that Christ and God will be found as basic characteristics in each individual, which must be nurtured. Many will have seen astrology as an evil practice, by **which** the future could not be **predicted**. This belief will have been long influenced **by the doctrine** of the church. But, people will then become aware the symbolism **of the** zodiac's constellations of stars no different than the individually named brightest nighttime **Stars**, such as the Dog Star and the North Star. Both astrology and Stars represent important guides to set mankind's direction. Those Stars at night are the lights which shine in the midst of darkness, and can lead man to safety when needed.

The importance of signs and symbols has to be understood, as this is one of God's ways of communicating with mankind. The Bible's great Prophets wrote symbolically, of statues with feet of clay and seven-headed dragons with ten horns. This use of symbolism is similar to having **prophesized** an alignment of planets, such as saying Saturn and Mars will join. To most people, those kinds of symbolic statements which use signs as language have unknown meaning, making astrology occult to most. The ability to make sense of such literal words comes **by** allowing oneself to become **inspired** by inner wisdom, which one receives from God. This is how true **revelation** is achieved; but, awareness of astrology and the recognition of symbolism are important in understanding those inspirations. This is an important step to achieve before one is prepared to be given a revelation. One must also be aware of the presence of a Prophecy, **which is** given to only **one** of a group of people. This one is the chosen receiver for the many; and, this person is then known as a Prophet. This person will always be **certain** of the message the Lord brings and will know to carry the prophetic message to the people, for their **participation** in understanding. That message will never be so clearly stated that non-believers will understand; instead, it will come as symbolic riddles, where only those in alignment **with** God and Christ will see **the** meaning, by **divine** assistance. By understanding the divine message, those people can spread the news to others, thus saving the believer's souls for an **eternity** in Heaven. Faith and belief in the symbolism of Prophecy shows faith and belief in God; and, **in return for** this dedication an everlasting life of bliss is the reward. In that regard, one has to believe Jesus Christ is **the Prophet** of *The Prophecies*; and, one has to have true faith Jesus is the Son of God and the Savior of their soul. There must be complete trust that Christ first **came** to earth **to** save mankind from sin, by teaching and demonstrating the correct way to live in peace on earth. It also must be known that Christ will return to earth, at which time He will come **to judge** mankind. This judgment will be on the living's past abilities to abide by the Laws of God. One cannot have strayed **from** God's Law and find redemption; but, Christ will not only come to punish the wicked, as He will **also** come to reward the worthy. The judgment **that** Christ will serve upon mankind will be the redemption of the souls of the faithful. Those who will have followed **his** model and lived inspired lives, by welcoming the **divine** to blend with their **spirit**, those will be the ones whom **he** will come to save. Those are the souls which are **to** be **delivered up** to Heaven, assisted **by the** Angels of the Lord. The Angles will act as the **medium of** delivery, carrying those souls to **God**. Those who will have doubted God was indeed **the creator** of man and all things of matter will find out how powerless they are to create their own salvation.

This deliverance is importance to understand, as it will come only to those who are deemed worthy **by** the actions they have shown to others of mankind. It will not be because someone said Christian words, or quoted the verses of the Bible, if those words do not reflect a true understanding of them. Deliverance will be based on the way one lived by those words, and not contrary to them. Only the **one** who has found the way to integrate the meaning of the Scriptures into a **natural** way of acting in peace and love for the common good of others will be selected as worthy. There can be no verbal **instigation** that will change a man's heart, as forced actions breed resentment and thoughts of punishment being rendered. The ones who Christ will reward will be naturally caring and naturally faithful.

The Bible has spoken of **this**, by stating the number of souls which will be rewarded by Christ. The number **is** found **in** the Bible, in *The Revelation*, chapter seven. In verse 4, John wrote the number of 144,000, which will be the number of people who will be marked with the seal of God. It is imperative for the people of the future **to know** this number, as **that** is the total number of all people who will be spared. This will not be from one localized group, but from all the earth's populations. Future Christians must know **this** and adjust their lives accordingly, if they want to be a part of **that** number. This which has been **predicted** in the Bible **is** going to be found coming perfectly **true**, without exception.

It is also important to know that those who will be **in** this number who will be **taken** will have utilized their gift of free-will to make this happen to them. God has given this ability to mankind, to choose to follow **his** Laws or not. This situation has existed since the **origin** of sin, when Adam and Eve were first left alone to fend for themselves. God maintains contact with humanity **ethereally**, to not overtly put pressure on mankind to live without sin. Every decision we make is ours alone; and, we bear the responsibility of our decisions. Those who will not be taken will have caused this failure to happen by their own decisions; and, their decisions will become perfectly known to them, at the time of being left behind

Still, God does not want **such** a loss to occur. This is why Jesus Christ was sent to me, to shed more **light** on the necessity of mankind changing its ways. This is why *The Prophecies* have been written; and, it is why the **flame** of interest will burn until the time for understanding will have come. The purpose of the quatrains is to **redeliver** the message that **is** already present in *The Revelation* and other biblical prophecies, so this version will clarify the symbolisms found in those as well. All **of** those Prophecies have come from the same source, Jesus Christ; and, all are sent to **all** of the people of the world, not just to the people of one religion. Belief in these warnings will yield all the **strength** necessary for changing the one part of the world within their control. That part is themselves.

If one has complete faith in God and Christ, one will be capable **of** making the required changes within oneself; and, *The Prophecies* will clearly point out where change is necessary. Making changes will not go unnoticed by Christ, as He will be beside those showing a sincere desire to change. The spirit of Christ will allow one **such** inner strength that it will be easier to resist the urges which will continue to call one back to an insane world. Diligence will pay off, as each dedicated person will attain such a swell within them that each will feel at a **height none** could have ever imagined. Christ will accept no **less** of a commitment than **that** which is required, to seek love and peace as **the natural** way to live. Finding inner strength will bring a **brightness** to even the darkest days one may encounter. The love of Jesus Christ will shine through those who choose this way of living, and a **natural light** or aura will tell others they have **returned** to follow the way of the Lord. Through living the words of **the** one true **Philosopher**, Jesus Christ, all will be reinforced for their commitment. Those words of light were given to us **so** all could be **assured** of what awaits the **ones** who follow Christ. Know **that** this assurance is **in return for** those who adhere to **the principles** the Son of God preached. He taught us, as a servant **of** God the Creator, to believe in Him for our salvation. Those who will have denied God, or believed **the first cause** was from something other than God, will know this disbelief **was attained** from one who lurks **in a more** irresponsible place. An eternity in that one's **deep abysm** of Hell will give the unfaithful plenty of time to realize Heaven is indeed real. Doubt of this nature is intended to draw mankind away **from** the **more** responsible elements of humanity, which are reinforced by the **high doctrines** of Christianity.

THE END WHICH CAN BE AVOIDED

But, as important as the highest doctrines of Christianity are, the people of the Christian faith will not be held **to those** doctrines by church leaders, as the churches will not be able to maintain them themselves. This will be because the largest church of Jesus Christ will have failed the Son of God, helping this **end** come to mankind. The Catholic Church, **my son**, the church which is our church, will be forewarned of **that** coming end and it will not make the required efforts to stop evil from gaining momentum. The work **I** have prepared here, with the Church's financial assistance, will **not** be the source for it to gain knowledge to avert this change of heart; as, they will not be able to break the code of *The Prophecies* before the Church fails Christ. However, to fill the **void** that will set in, until my words are solved, there will be other clear prophecies to come, which will be sent to guide the Christian people. Other good people will **also** be encountered by the agents of Jesus Christ, to **secretly** pass warnings of the end of days on to the Church. Of particular importance to the Catholic Church is the Holy Virgin Mother of Christ. It will be her grace which will plead **for** the Church to take actions to prevent this end. With several important encounters between the Virgin Mary and the people taking place, her words will be told to highest ranking Church officials. Those officials will have **the capacity** to influence the leaders of all Christian nations, and ask for their assistance in these matters of concern. The Church will receive those warning, well in advance of this **future** coming; but, those secret matters **of** urgency will remain secret, under papal decree. Instead of taking the necessary steps to protect their flocks, the **tune** of the Church will be unchanged. They will cast doubt on the **judgment** of those who will faithfully bring those warning to them, but the Church will be unwilling to believe prophecy is still possible.[12]

With this lack of proper attention given a God-sent warning, the Church will then **also** play a role in **that** collapse of its own holy doctrines, by making other secret judgments. Those judgments will stray far from the Church's holy canons. In the times that **I** have made predictions, which have placed focus on the heads of state and important elements of the Church, those have had the **most-sight** possible by Church officials. There have been several holy minds contemplating them each time, to accurately judge their contents. To have the Church squelch something **that** will be identified as the Word of the Blessed Virgin, it will be breaking its own rules by sealing **the letters** sent to the Church from those that will be **making** those claims. The Vatican will be found keeping the information secret. The Church holds the responsibility of carefully considering the claims of prophetic wisdom; but for such claims to be taken **so** lightly, it will pave the way for those individuals who will become the **great** influences of evil over mankind. When I use this superlative, "great," I do not use it lightly as a value judgment of general goodness. It shows a magnitude of influence, and the Church will become **incomparable** to those leaders and nations which will be coming in this future as "the greats", as far as influence over the Christian people is concerned. The Church will have experienced such a **loss** of influence that it will allow elements of the common sects to rise so high that the Church will not dare to confront that power. The combination of **that** loss and the elevation of common men to the height of power, having almost complete control over mankind's souls, this book **I** have written will provide the **most-sight** of where

---

12 As these were secret visions, many will not be known commonly by all. However, the one most important of these has been named "The Secret Third Fatima," which Internet conspiracy theory buffs will be familiar with. The Virgin Mary appeared to three young Portuguese girls, at Fatima, Portugal, in the first part of 1917. That was before the Russian Revolution; but, over a series of increasingly publicized visions of the Virgin Mary, the girls were told that Communism would lead to the end of the Vatican, and at that end time much death would cover the world. One of the girls, now a well-known nun, was instructed to tell the Vatican; but, at that early time Communism was still new and weak. The pope was eventually told the Virgin Mary's message in two letters written during the Second World War, but he was unable to act. The letters were resealed and stored for later consideration. The third letter supposedly details all of this end's horrid events; but, no pope has acted on it, and it was not made pubic until after the fall of the Soviet Union. At that time, Pope John Paul II said the omen was no longer valid, and there was nothing to worry about.

the world will be headed, without leaders dedicated to God and Christ. My book will provide humanity with confirmations to the prophetic visions of what will come, as told by others Prophets and Prophetesses; and this confirmation will be known well **before** this future unfolds. It will place the responsibility of making **the universal** changes, which will be necessary to avoid this future's **conflagration**, in the hands of the common people, at the latest opportune time. At that time, the leaders of the world, including those of the world's greatest religions, will believe it will be best to leave the future **to chance**. This response will place **all of** the world's people in danger; and, the foreshadowing of this danger soon to come will be found symbolized by the coming of significant natural disasters, most particularly from **floods**. It must be realized these will not be typical floods, brought on by heavy rains which swell the banks of rivers and streams; but, they will be floods which will be **so** devastating, by the **high** rises of water, that the **inundations** will leave the people completely overwhelmed. While there are some natural areas where flood is a greater possibility, those areas will then find **that it** will have never before experienced this level of inundation. Since those floods will **not** have been witnessed before, the people **will be** dependent on history's records of flood, to be **guided** in their efforts to build in safe zones. Many people will populate the **land** which is accessible to the water, including land **which** has always **been** at the water's edge. They will have been prepared for the event of flood, knowing to keep their homes **closed** and articles covered, as they will know this is the price to pay for living **with** the beauty of the **water**. Many of those people **will be** the ones who will live off the water, **by** sailing and fishing the seas. They will have been in those coastal areas **so long** they will know the histories of the **times** when flood threatened them and their families and neighbors. Still, most will remember the times **when** they enjoyed their closeness to the water, **without** any fear having ever been **put** on them to leave. The lack of fear will make the water an attraction to visitors also, who will come to enjoy the **enographies** of the beaches. Many will come to enjoy and administer the areas promoted for swimming and exploring the corals, shells and marine life in the shallows of water. With this human interest in the element of water, the surrounding **topographies** will also become major attractions. This will be especially strong on the islands which will rise in the midst of the seas, where the barrier reefs and islands will help protect the mainland beaches. It will be **that** earthly elevation in the surrounding topography which will make **the whole** environment seem safe from the waters grasp; but, the people of this

131

future will find this safety is **not** as it seems. They will know danger is present, once the serenity of coastal existence will have **been** washed away, along with many of the people, landmarks and islands. All will have become **lost** from the floods.

Besides this loss and the misery the floods will bring, the misery will **also** continue well after the waters will have subsided. The damage will change the shape of the land and the lives of the people, to such a degree they will long for the way things were **before**; but, such a return will be beyond their ability to reconstruct. The people will try to circumvent nature, by building great walls and levees, at great expense; but, **after** so much effort, nature will create **such** greater waves that the **inundations** will destroy what was built and water will cover more land. The floods will spread around the world, **in many** areas, in many **countries**, such that it will be impossible for mankind to prevent the power of nature. Beyond this difficulty with the waves of the seas, **the rains** will also be showing a sign of change, with their regularity no longer being as it was before. All of this will be signs of the end nearing, **so** that mankind can become **redelivered** souls, realizing it is time to give God the respect that is due Him.

Without that redelivery of souls, mankind will witness much greater forms of rains which **will fall** upon the earth. Just like rain, it will come **from the** sky; but, this rain will not come from normal clouds. This will be a rain of fire which will spread over the earth, from a comet which will fall from **Heaven**. The heat from this fiery rain will be **so mighty** that no one will be able to find shelter from the heat. It will come in such **abundance**, as it streaks through the atmosphere, that all **of** the earth below it will instantly be torched with **fire**. This fire **that** will come **with** the comet will be from the friction created by air against **stone**; and, it will turn the stone into an **incandescence** ball of bright white heat. The brightness of **that** incandescence will be so great that **none** will be able to look directly at it, as it will **have** a blinding effect. All of people of earth who **will remain** at that time will be lost. No surface **matter** will continue to exist unchanged, as **that** thing which **it** was before. In just an instant, there will **not** be anything left which will not have **been consumed** by the heat of this comet. This will mark the final minute of mankind on earth.

It is very important to realize **this** last statement I have just made; so, let me expound on this for a moment. The consumption by heat, which is **to happen** when this comet strikes the earth, will be felt instantly. Once the comet has entered **in** the earth's surrounding zone of air, the time it will take to make impact with the earth's surface will be **brief**. That impact will create another powerful ball of fire and light, which will act to quickly heat all of the air surrounding earth, setting everything on fire.

It cannot be understated that this end is not as important as will be the time **before** the comet strikes. This time before will be **the last** opportunity for mankind to praise God, and beg for His forgiveness. God has the power to change this comet's path; but, He will not stand in its way, if mankind still does not change. The comet will come to earth, due to mankind's own selfish power of mind; such that man will even bear the full responsibility for this final **cataclysm**, which will cause its demise.

Because this cataclysmic end will be from mankind's inability to love properly and to live in peace with its fellow human beings, it will be a manmade end. It is astounding that so many of mankind will sacrifice their souls **for all that** agony and pain. The ones **who** will have had so much power over the others of mankind will have been the ones who will have sought war and might as its standards to live by. Of the millions of people left on **the planet** Earth on that fateful day, they will have paid more homage to the god **of** war, **Mars**, than to Jesus Christ. Ironically, mankind will have used its brain to reach out and actually touch this red planet, as mankind's mind will have **achieved** and accomplished so many fantastic feats by then. However, as powerful as man's mind can and will become, **his** ability to know what the future hold will never be within his reach, unless he calls on God for guidance. Mankind will have made tremendous advancements over the last **century** of its existence on earth. Unfortunately, many of those advancements will be offshoots of man's lust for developing new weapons. Mankind will become very adept at this skill; too much for its own good.

After one hundred years of terrible wars and terrible destruction, mankind will have not lost that taste for blood. The lust for war will be carried over into the new millennium of the Twenty-first Century. It is so important to know that **in the end**, when those **of** mankind who will still be left clinging to life, struggling mightily to maintain it, the ultimate decision to cause such struggle will have been **its** own. Mankind will have **denied** Christ's lessons, God's Laws, and the final warning of this prophecy, if that end comes. Awareness of this coming end will have allowed for a **period** of understanding, where significant changes could have been willed by mankind. As difficult as those changes would have been to accomplish, life would have been **so** much more than this end will prove to be. God will give **the** people what free-will will have allowed them to choose for themselves. Mankind **will receive** this suffering, if **it** will prefer suffering over eternal bliss with God.

It will not have been this way for all of this final century, before the new millennium will begin; **but,** the momentum will have been growing significantly over the last half of the Twentieth Century. This will be when mankind's mind will have unlocked enough of the universe's secrets to become most dangerous. As the intellect of man **assembles** more and more of the pieces of knowledge together, a broader view of the universe will become clear; although the whole scope of this knowledge will be far too vast to completely fathom. This wealth of knowledge will attract **the ones** who revel **in** such tantalizing elements of the unknown; and they will begin breaking them down to see how the pieces go together. Those people will display the characteristics of the astrological sign **Aquarius,** whose key phrase is known by astrologers as "to know." Those people of the Age of Aquarius will become the thinkers of a new age of intellectual pursuit. Under their intellectual pursuits the old methods of "trial and error" will have fallen to a new belief of "tried and true." This will be knowledge which will have been documented **by** a plethora of past experiments, with **many** yielding amazing results and new discoveries. Those developments will have mounted over many **years,** such that the changes which knowledge can offer to mankind will have grown exponentially. The world will begin going too fast for all of its people to keep up with the growth. This growth will begin to get out of control, causing the need for strict controls; but, the controls will not be sought to stem the advancements of knowledge. The controls sought will be to manipulate knowledge as a power over others. When one nation's academic specialists will have made a great breakthrough, they will be forced to adhere to the rules of secrecy that will be demanded. These rules will be designed to keep knowledge to oneself, and away from **the other** nations searching for the same academic results. This Aquarian quest for knowledge does not appreciate such boundaries and limitations, as all seeking the same thing are associates and colleagues in the same field, regardless of nationality. This demand for protecting the secrets of knowledge is a trait found **in** the sign of **Cancer**. That sign is protective of the home; and, as nations are homes to many, national worries of security have traditionally been a Cancerian motivation **for** secrecy. Often this is to defend against an enemy, to keep the enemy from gaining a military advantage against the homeland. This nurturing of national secrets has existed for many **more** years than this rapid advancement of knowledge will last; but, history has shown, over **long** periods of time, that spies are an excellent tool for finding out secrets. This has been the way the whole world keeps up with the latest inventions, developed one place and used everywhere; and, this is especially true about new weapons and their development. The purpose of knowledge is to work for the good of the people; but, when mankind tries to hide something from another, to gain an unfair advantage, God will make sure tongues slip and papers go into the wrong hands. Mankind has a **continuous** history of repeating these same mistakes, over and over again.

And, with this continuous repeating of mistakes seen **nowadays**, it will be no different in the future. The need for security now is ruled by **that** same Cancer urge, where the attempts to hide secrets **amounts** to the same failure to suppress them. One nation's desire for security, by keeping its advantages secret, is another nation's desire for security, by knowing what secrets its enemies hold. It is an inherent need for safety, **driven by** the emotional center, to find a place where calm can exist. However, as this emotional center is ruled by **the Moon**, which goes through continuous changing phases, this comfort zone is never maintained for long. The Moon also rules our intuitions, so secrets will always be sensed and eventually discovered. The emotional center is where our stomachs connect to the heart; and, this is where we come in contact with God and His Angels. Their voices lead us to these discoveries; but, this is not a reward of faithfulness, as much as it is **in return for** one finding out what another has in advance. God leads us to find out intuitively what is needed to know, to reduce **the total** impact of any knowledge advantage. This is what creates a balance of **power** in all **of** mankind and all of its nations. This is how **God** shows His love for mankind; and, it demonstrates that all knowledge should be shared with one another and not hidden for personal gain. If mankind can understand this one lesson, then the earth and humanity can find an **eternal** opportunity for life on the material plane. Unfortunately, it is **that** belief mankind longs to place in the material realm which keeps it losing what it so much loves. This loss is necessary to experience **before** one is capable of fully understanding the basic lessons of coexistence, in peace, love and brotherhood. Until **that** sharing concept has been learned, mankind will keep hiding secrets, **which** will continuously be stolen and used against him. Man **has** seen himself as an island and convinced himself only he knows his thoughts. This is man's basic flaw in reason, **by** failing to recognize God knows all; and, for those who try to serve God, He will bring about all of our failures, to show us how to better ourselves. This is how human beings become **perfected** in God's eyes. We learn with our brains not repeat the same mistakes; and, when we realize a mistake is ours, we must accept this was God's way of showing us that **his** vision of our future knows what is best. The **complete** good that will come in the long run is much better achieved by patience and honest reflection, rather than trying to repeat a failure on a path to a dead-end. The fewer dead-ends man walks down in life, the better he is able to complete the **circuit** or tour of his material manifestation and to return to God, from whence he came. The challenge of being able to understand that our thoughts are not our own, and adjust from our failures, comes from overcoming our own egos. This is a considerable challenge, which is represented astrologically by the Sun. The Sun is the only star in our sky which lights our paths. The glyph for the Sun is a circle with a dot in the center, which represents this circuit as all of the universal things which surround us; while we stand alone in the middle of this universe. On the lowest level, one will see oneself as the god of one's own world, in total control of everything; but, on the highest level, one knows that God, the true controller of the universe, is at the center of each of us. When this dawning **will come** to one, one is able to know that no secrets can be successfully kept, as all must be shared.

For Christians, only one man has been born into this world that had complete control of this ego. He knew the greatest protection and security comes from God. That man was Jesus Christ, and Jesus did not have to wander through life learning from his mistakes. The rest of humanity has had to learn the lessons that life's mistakes teach us, by trusting God will not send us down the wrong path. When we pray to God, we say, "Our Father," as God is the father who created all of humanity; but, He is also **more** than just that kind of father. God is the teacher within us; and Jesus Christ, as the Son of God, was our teacher, or rabbi, in human form. The role of teacher is traditionally held by the father as the teacher of his children. The father teaches the children how to correctly approach life. This comes from a deep love and affection, where the father wants to give the child his wealth of knowledge and wisdom. Therefore, the teacher is the father principle, which operates from a position of age and maturity; and, it represents one who has knowledge to pass on, which must be learned for successfully achieving life's goals. Whereas the Moon rules the mother principle and needs to nurture and protect, the concept of **Saturn** is to free the expression of the Sun, and let individuality shine. To learn individuality, each person must be free to learn how to apply the lessons taught to them as a child; and, the father knows these lessons are not quickly learned. There is an element of patience required. But, the lesson of discipline also must be instilled in the child, which comes in the forms of punishment and reward. Punishment relates to the mistakes we make in life; and, when we have reached a level of maturity we can look back in time and realize how many of our past mistakes actually ended up being great benefits to our development. In astrology, this father principle is shown in the planet Saturn, which symbolizes all of these elements of the teacher. So many have seen Saturn in the perspective of being harsh and cold, giving it the nickname of the Greater Malefic. Many see Saturn as the harbinger of hard times. But, this perspective is how many see God, when they have not developed the traits of true wisdom. This makes the nickname for Saturn, as the Grim Reaper, be the way they would view God, when their souls are not returned to Heaven; but, this is because of their own actions, which did not follow the lessons. When one has lived a life in honor of God, one reaps the reward of Heaven. This is not a grim time; but rather, it is a glorious recognition for having the stamina to achieve a goal sought after.

Considering that, how Saturn will represent both the return of souls to God, or the punishment of eternal Hell, this is precisely the view seen in *The Revelation*. In that book, **according to** John, in 13:13, **the** passage reads, "It will perform great **signs**, even making fire come down from the **heavens** to earth, in front of people." Many people believe that this tells of **the reign** of the antichrist, which is the second beast, marked by the number 666. While this is symbolic of the punishment which will be brought upon mankind, the man who becomes the antichrist is nothing more than symbolic **of** the nature of **Saturn**. The beast is thus acting as an agent of God, to show where mankind has made mistakes. The actions the antichrist **will be** leading on earth will be as a result of mankind's inability to learn the valuable lessons that come **from** God and Jesus Christ, as

137

stated in the Bible. Not having the patience to learn and work hard to instill those values will call for the **return** of Jesus Christ, with "his eyes ... as a flame of fire"[13] and "out of his mouth ... a sharp two-edged sword."[14] That return of Christ, to appear before John, was to warn mankind of **that** price which must be paid, in order to be returned with the Lord. For the same reason Christ appeared before me, to warn of this price. To prepare for Christ's return **it** will be necessary for mankind to understand His prophetic warnings, both here in my work and in *The Revelation*. This understanding will give **all** mankind notice of accountability for its actions, as a lesson from the Father which must be learned. All of this has been **calculated** by God, as seen in the many biblical prophecies which mirror many of the same warnings. This calculation is within the power of God; but, those who will be punished for refusing to heed the warnings will have shown the poor abilities of man to calculate, as many will have miscalculated that the end was not near. These warnings are not to be kept secret from anyone, as they are not just for Christians, but for all **the** people of the entire **world**. Mankind will be rapidly approaching the time when they will begin to destroy **themselves**, in ego-driven, emotional outbursts, with secrets exposed which will be revealing the knowledge that developed weapons of great punishment. Christ and God will reveal those Prophecies as those times are about to **draw near**, such that time will be of the utmost importance. The only response which will save mankind will be **to** cease the wars caused by the world's leaders, where the punishment will instead become **anarchic agony**.[15] This will be a rejection of all rulers and laws, on all levels, such that each man and woman will have to rule themselves, with only God's Law to lead them. This will be a call for a new **revolution** of the common man, where they will have to rebel against everything which would anger another and generate global destruction. The agony will be from the struggles to have everyone pull together, to help his and her neighbor, as this lesson will demand plenty of hard effort and discipline.

I cannot stress enough how important it is, understanding **that** need for revolution, as this represents the sweeping changes which will be necessary to save

---

13   Revelation 1:14
14   Revelation 1:16
15   The word written by Nostradamus was, "anaragonique," which is not a word in any language. This makes it a manufactured word, by combining two French roots, "*anarche*" and "*agonie*," with the suffix, "*-que*." This means that no Kingdoms will exist and agony will prevail.

138

the earth and mankind. However, this revolution has to come from the lessons learned from Jesus Christ, which means that it cannot be motivated by anger, with the use of weapons, and involving hatred. It can only succeed if it comes from the center of love, peace, sharing and caring, knowing Christ and God will support these changes. Still, the roots of this need for change are found in the trends **of** the **present**, where mankind is already moving towards **that** consciousness. There is now brewing a global desire to rebel against authority. The near future will call for **this** and use **that** ability to organize for revolution; and, this is the core change which mankind will make. The future will be find change coming, to become diametrically opposite the way things are now; and, **my writings** in the quatrains place focus on the elements of this change. Those revolutions which will take place will take mankind to the verge of ruin, when the revolution Christ will call for will need to return mankind to the way it was **before**. Still, the revolutions of mankind have been many, such that there have been others before now which mirror the revolution that followed the crucifixion of Jesus Christ. That revolution found the founding of a new religion. Additional revolutions within that religion have also occurred since then; and, they have been documented by writings. Two examples of this writing, which I will refer to, now, are by St. Irenaeus and John Wycliffe. These two men have shown two different ends of Christianity's evolution, stretching over 1200 years of church history. First, in the year **one hundred seventy-seven**, the Catholic Church was young and struggling with the agony of being under Roman empirical rule. At that time, France was a pagan frontier, called Gaul. St. Irenaeus defended the Book of Revelations, which before then was not accepted as a holy scripture. He saw it as a viable book of the Bible; and, he stated his justification for it to be preached. He believed such a horrid depiction of the end of mankind, as a Prophecy of Jesus Christ, was necessary to motivate the people to practice faithful religion. This view preceded the martyrdom which many Christians in Gaul suffered, in what is now known as Lyon, France. These early French Christians were attacked by local pagan peoples, who had not accepted Christianity as their religion. This savage element of mankind symbolized the need for a religion which would spread the message of love and peace, to control such savagery, as predicted to cause the end of mankind. From that savagery came the acceptance of *The Revelation* as the word of Christ. This was the beginning of a cycle, to preach that warning in the churches of Christianity, as motivation to follow Christ's principles. The other writing was one hundred seventy-seven **years** ago,

139

in the year 1378 AD. It was in that year when John Wycliffe criticized the Catholic Church as having had fallen into an impoverished spiritual state. He stated there was too much power given to the pope and to the councils; and, he stated papal power was secondary to that of royal Kings. This was at a time when the political affiliations of the Church had led it to a condition of opulence, with the papacy being held in Avignon, France. It remained in Avignon for 73 years; and, during that time the Church was served by only French popes. This lasted until the year 1378, when the pope to whom Wycliffe had addressed his criticism to died. With that death the papacy was then returned to Rome. However, **three months** before the end of 1378, and **eleven days** before the end of September that year, this arrangement was found not to be acceptable by the French bishops. This rejection was because an Italian pope had been elected in Rome. This caused the French to separate from the Church of Rome and elect its own pope. This pope became known as the first antipope, of what would be called the Great Schism of Western Christianity. Before this division was finished, in 1417, the Church had been divided for 39 years. During the time the papacy was held in Avignon, Europe was stricken **by** the black **plague**. The worst years occurred between 1347 and 1350. The result of those waves of death was nearly three-quarters of the population of Europe were lost. Before this plague, Europe had been stricken by a **long** period of **famine**, called the Great Famine. This lasted between 1315 and 1322. When these hardships existed, the Church had shown its opulent appetite. Wycliffe had pointed out the politics of the Church, showing how this was circumventing the King's law and failing to abide by God's Law. The Church was doing nothing to protect the people. With so much death and misery, many people believed that the End Times of *The Revelation* were near. This shows that a full revolution had been made, from the times when the Church began teaching this prophecy to the time it ceased teaching at all. The result both times was belief that the end was near; and, both times it was because of the savage nature of man, especially when given no true religious guidance.

There is no greater example of the savagery which mankind can show than that found in the **wars** it continually wages. Following this period, when the Church left Rome and ceased to provide proper care for the people, a growing dissent arose from seeing the imbalance of wealth and power. While the English and French had continual battles over a hundred year's period, the peasants of Europe carried out a series of rebellions because of this inequity. From Flanders, to here in France, Western European peasants rebelled against their rulers. It later occurred in England on several occasions, as well as in Bohemia, Slovenia, Hungary and the Germanic Holy Roman Empire. Most recently, it occurred in Sweden, in 1542. These wars of rebellion have been caused by the failures of both the royalty and the Church to care for the common people, so commonly called peasants. These are the roots of revolution, which have been set in the past's growing separation between the common people and those that feel elevated above others. In the future, this dissent will become manipulated by groups and individuals who will not have any intent to better the plight of the common man.

This resentment will grow greater after many **more** wars will be fought, at the expense of the lives of the common class. The commoners will try to achieve a level of respect, **by** giving their lives through military service; but, this respect will be found truly absent. This will be especially so when **the inundations** of flood waters will cover **the world**, destroying everything the poor will have worked to obtain. The separation **between** the rich and the poor will be completely uncovered when **this** devastation by flood comes. It is also very important to know that **this** exposure will present the awareness that this division must **end**; and, this period of awareness will be **prefixed** to the understanding of *The Prophecies*. The time to act on this peaceful revolution will be **before** this end will be unavoidable, as once the period of opportunity has passed it will be too late. The period which will come **after** this understanding will be marked **by** the beginning of the final war that mankind will wage. While this war will have **several** major battles, with **times** when a false peace will be reached, it will last until the comet strikes. By that point in time mankind **will be** starving, diseased, wounded and **so** weary the end will almost be welcomed. This **lessened** state of humanity is why it would be better to choose to struggle, with all people reduced to the same common class and seeking the same objectives of survival, than to continue to be enslaved by a class structure which has the wealthy stand on the shoulders of the poor.

By this time of decision, there will be **so** many more common people in the world than those that rule over them; but, most people will have so **little** they will feel they have to fight for their masters. At the same time, the advancements of the powers of mind will have made **the world** a smaller place, as there **will** be nowhere out of reach, thus nowhere to hide. It will be **that** smallness of the world that will endanger all of **the** people on earth, from the weapons which will have the capacity to strike from great distances. This will include the **one** nation which will have the greatest wealth and resources of all nations; but, this nation will have **not** shared with those in need, such that all could be equal. This nation's people **will find** this arrogance, **which** will have made the world **view** it as only filled with wealthy people, will make it a target of **these** weapons. When the attacks begin and panic strikes, instead of all coming together to help each other out of despair, the poor will try **to take** the possessions left behind by the dead. This nation will have a bounty of agriculture; but, when these attacks begin, they will find that **the fields** of plenty have gone barren. Without their crops, **which** will have been sold to feed the world's hungry, the people of this nation will begin to face their own starvation, like it will have never faced before. The leaders of this nation will be known for their art of **misleading** their own people, as well as others; but, over time they will have sold many of the world's peoples on the benefit of their philosophy of mind, which makes them believe that they are **free** peoples. This concept of freedom will act as the spell that will have all of the poor unknowingly enslaved, making them beasts of burden for the rich. They will have **also** tried to sell this concept as a just reason to invade other nations, those which will not have allowed their people to believe in freedom. This imperialism will produce examples of nations which will have been successful under this philosophy; but, while it will be wholeheartedly successful **for** some, this great nation will try for **a long time** to duplicate those successes, without success. The nations **that** will have been successful adopting this plan of freedom will have been those which had previously been thoroughly defeated in war. This great nation of people will believe **they** are the model of success, as they **were** once fledgling peoples at the hands of a master too; but, they will say that by **being** peoples of strong dedication to liberty and freedom they will have become the world's greatest power. This story of success will not carry much weight in several of the nations this great nation will put **in servitude**. This enslavement will have not been for the promised goal of liberation; but, instead it will be for the leaders of this great nation to increase their own power and wealth.

It is important to know that **this** forced servitude will be seen **in regard of** how this nation will use its mind to get **in the** governments of these other lands. This great nation will seek the support of its dominions, and it will use lies to gain international support for repeating these actions. These lies will be **apparent** to several other nations of the world, such that they will not side with the **judgment** of this one nation. The great nation's own people will be divided over the judgment of its leaders as well. To make a clear example of how this will come to be, it is best that I present the symbolism found in astrology. The **celestial** planet which rules judgment is Jupiter; and as such, judgment is expansive and difficult to hold back. Judgment is not the same as justice, and in **that** celestial regard the planet Saturn represents the patience to see how well judgment is administered. Saturn becomes representative of the symbolic aftermath of judgment, as the test of time following a judgment rendered. This is then measured by the **returns** of the judgment, where reward shows good judgment and punishment shows poor judgment. In essence, the Jupiter-Saturn polarity will explain **that** measurement simply as, "**we** reap what we sow". If we put effort into preparing the ground and plant good seed, with the correct amount of water added, then we will have a good bountiful harvest. However, if we simply toss seeds to the wind, onto hardened ground, the punishment will be a harvest of weeds. The judgment of this one nation will be found poor, as its own people will become the **reaped ones**. I have stated before of this element of reaping, which is symbolic of the planet Saturn. Each of the orbs **in the** heavens has a numerical order and value. In this, the lower numbers, one-two-three-four, are more personal, and the higher numbers, five-six-seven, are more impersonal. Saturn is the **seventh** in this system of **number**, and it is thus the most distant from our personal being.[16] Due to this distance, like the father away from the child while the mother stays near and cares for it, Saturn's involvement is **of** a limited nature. While the Moon, like the mother, will act **a thousand** times in the child's life, Saturn will only act a few times, making those time it acts become quite profound. Jupiter, **which** represents good fortune and good luck, is also closely related with higher learning, including the rules of religion and international understanding. When these principles of growth have been **fully achieved**, one learns that good fortune and luck are blessings from God, for good behavior, based on the higher values one has learned to apply. Saturn represents the discipline to take this understanding and convert it to true knowledge, where one does not count on luck, but on

---

16 1-Sun, 2-Moon, 3-Mercury, 4-Venus, 5-Mars and 6-Jupiter are numbered in order of magnitude/size as seen from earth (1, 2) and then distance from the Sun. Saturn was the seventh and last number in traditional astrology, which only deals with planets visible to the naked eye.

God. These outer planets judge and administer justice for our actions, which is ruled by the planet Mars. Mars acts in response to the inner personal self, such that **the whole** of the solar system symbolizes the life forces of any entity, human or otherwise. Our natal chart represents the whole of **us**, individually, and shows us all where our strengths and weakness lie. From that understanding we can know what tools God has planned for us to use, and which He knows will serve us for no good. Astrology has remained a solid tool for learning the self, since God presented it to mankind. However, we are **approaching** a time when mankind will be expanded, **from** this outer limit of Saturn, to the addition of **the eighth** planet of number, which is yet unseen. When this planet is found, it will lie further away from the earth than Saturn, and thus more distant from our personal being. This discovery will mark the time and place **where** mankind will break from the restrictive elements of Saturn and find a quest for freedom. This planet is not visible by the naked eye, but **it** is suspended in **the firmament** now, waiting for the time it will come into mankind's awareness. At that time **of** awareness, **the** discovery of an **eighth sphere** will mark the advent of the common man to power over kings, through revolution, seeking freedoms and individualities. These will be the events **which** will symbolize the qualities of this planet, astrologically. This planet **is** beyond Saturn's orbit, and is only slightly smaller **in size** than Saturn, so that size will allow it to break the chains of Saturn. In times to come it will be found that this planet has a very unique feature, which is that its polar axis is **latitudinal**, rather than longitudinal.[17] This is an important feature, as this symbolizes how breaking the restraints will affect something of this great size. Mankind will be breaking its Saturn restraints as well when this planet is discovered; but, this quest for freedom and individuality will still be held accountable by the wisdom of Saturn. In these times to come, when this one nation will be using the concepts of freedom and independence to cheat its way into another land, mankind will have not used good judgment. The result will be that this same feature to be found on this new eighth sphere will also come to happen on the earth. This sudden change, **where** the poles will shift horizontally, will be when **the great** floods will cover the earth. The

---

17   This is a perfect description of the planet Uranus, which was not discovered in 1781, between the American and French Revolutions. It was not until Voyager 2 sent back pictures of Uranus, in 1986, that we realized that the polar axis of Uranus is east-west, rather than north-south. As far as the astrological number of Uranus is concerned, it is the "eighth" of ten orbs (including the Sun and Moon).

comet will strike the earth, causing great heat, which will melt the polar icecaps, and the earth will shift its poles. You should know the impressions which lead souls to spot a lie come from **God**; but, it is up to those who know when one is lying to stop the acts founded on lies from happening. If mankind is to have a chance for keeping the earth **eternal** and a place for human life, then this forced servitude must be stopped. If it **will come** without any resistance to stop it, then mankind will be at the final step. Once that step is taken, it will not be long before the comet hits the earth, bringing all life to a fiery end. Either way mankind chooses, this will act **to make an absolute end of** the wrongs which will have come from poor judgment, based on **the** lusts mankind will have found in the element of **revolution**.

This element of revolution needs to have some closer inspection, as it will be the downfall of mankind. The revolutions which will coincide with the discovery of this revolutionary planet will be violent and designed to destroy the elements Christ put on earth. Christ came to save mankind; and, the spread Christianity was a revolution designed to keep mankind from coming to such a disastrous end. However, this period of revolution will differ from the one coinciding with the discovery of the eighth sphere, as the revolution of Christianity will have safety elements to keep this revolution continuing towards this direction of salvation. These safety elements are: the royal rulers of Europe, who represent the holy blood of Jesus Christ; and, His Churches, which represent the holy body of Christ. These institutions are just as symbolic for Christ, as are the sacraments which keep Christians saved. Since their conception, the kings and the Church have held full responsibility for the souls of man, as the role they play for Jesus Christ. Together, they act as the impersonal ruling bodies which are symbolized by Jupiter and Saturn. The revolutions that will come and overturn these institutions, causing their ruin, will leave all of mankind fully responsible for its own acts and each individual's own soul salvation. This responsibility will not only be to rule over one's own individual life; but, more importantly, the responsibility will be for each person to rule over the safety of his or her own soul. This cycle of revolution will lead to this final point of decision, when mankind must again find its love for sudden change and change itself, beginning from this individual perspective. If not, then the revolution becoming the sudden and final event of mankind will be one also changing the revolution of the planet earth. But, know that this revolution will not be caused by God, as the comet which will come to earth will have been brought by man's own mind. This will be from mental exercises, **where** man will have devised a way to send one of his weapons into the orbits of the planets. This will have been done for the purpose of capturing **the images** of a **celestial** comet, just as it will be hit by this weapon in flight. When those images will be **returning to** the people who will have awaited them on earth, those people will be proud of **themselves** and their mental accomplishments. They will feel as powerful as gods, for having been able **to move** such a distant object. However, it will be most important to realize that **the movement** of this comet will be changed by this impact. The comet will change to a much more **superior** orbit than before, and this movement will have not been expected. The effect of this weapon's use will cause the comet to have more of a trajectory change than the designers of this project will have planned. It has been said that to err is human, **which** is why **we** should not be surprised when the impact of this comet on earth will have been man-caused. Another revolution will have then been caused by mankind, one sending a comet which would have otherwise revolved safely around the Sun, making it to be **returned** to **the earth**, bringing mankind its death. This folly will have adjusted the comet's **stable** course, sending it heading towards earth; and, when it comes to earth it will be moving **fast**, posing the eternal question: what happens when the irresistible force meets the immovable object? This question is best answered by remembering what David wrote in Psalms 103:5. There, David wrote that God is the one "Who hast founded the earth upon its own bases: **it shall not be moved for ever and ever.**" This means the stability of earth, on its polar axis, was set by God and it should not be altered. If it is not changed, the earth will be stable for all eternity with God. As long as mankind continues to recognize God as the founder of earth and all its life, and makes a personal revolution to commit to God's Law, this polar axis will remain stable.

To clarify this quote by David, this condition of stability would last forever **except** for the fact God has **put** mankind in control of its own destiny. Destiny is then controlled by the gift of free-will. That is what will have allowed for mankind's revolutions for freedom; but, mankind's acts of freedom can limit the "for ever and ever" part of **that** quote. David has stated what God's wish is; but, mankind must also make **his** desire its own, by honoring God's power to provide eternal safety. Mankind has **to desire** God's presence in his life, so man is free to act as God leads. With God in our hearts, the earth **will be** eternally stable. As long as mankind has **accomplished** the conditions of peace, love and adherence to God's laws, this stability will always remain set; **but**, the exception is that **no point** short of these conditions can ensure this outcome. Mankind is free to act **differently** than has been God's wish; and thus, the eternity of earth is not assured.

To clarify exactly **how much** mankind will act differently, with **that** gift **by** God to act with free-will, the quantity is **ambiguous**, as there is uncertainty. The objectivity of such an answer can only come when all of mankind will have acted individually, to answer this question for themselves. This leaves it up to the **opinions** of each of us, where our personal beliefs and judgments cannot be founded solely on material proof. Proof can only be felt by the faith which permeates us. If the majority of the opinions are found **exceeding** the obvious, transcending and going beyond the observable world, then the overall opinion of **the whole** will be to limit one's capacity to act as one pleases. Still, the human brain needs **reasons** to be assured of these opinions; and, these intellectual justifications come from the rational and logical deductions gained from one's **natural** environments. This is man's freedom to seek proof for the improvable, by observing the miracles of nature which show that things are greater than the sum of all parts. Just as we all are affected **by dreams**, where the imaginary seems so real, the actions of those dreams are not bound by the laws of physics. It is our freedom to interpret our dreams and to develop our opinions, backed up by our reasoning of nature's way. In this way one can establish a philosophy which becomes mutually accepted by many others. This is how religions come to be, by **Mahomet-like** philosophers who explain the mysteries of the universe. Men can put God in terms that are understandable to many, while different from the observations of others. There are **also** other "prophets" who have led many people by their philosophical thoughts, instructing the world on how humanity must control its freedoms, for its own good; but, it must be realized that at **no times** has **God**, as **the creator** of mankind and the universe, wished to frighten mankind into submission, to force His desires on man. This has often been the case presented, **by** several of **the ministers of the** various Christian sects. Those preachers have felt and will continue to feel the importance of *The Revelation*; and, by preaching that prophecy they will have acted as Christ's **messengers**. Still, by failing to emphasize righting the seven churches of which Christ spoke, those messengers are not for focusing on the true message of prevention, through peace and love. They will preach the fear **of fire** and brimstone, making fear become the reason to honor God and Christ. To see Christ **in** a setting of **flame** is contrary to His true spirit, which is **missive** by the Epistles which **came** from the Apostles. Christ returned to tell John *The Revelation* as another sign of his love. The purpose of *The Revelation* is to show what the state of the world will be, when Christ will come back again. The world will then be **in** a terrible state of need; and, Christ will return to call on the faithful to save the world. For people **to propose** that Christ will come to punish the unfaithful, this makes more of a comparison between Christ and Satan. This is not the case, as it is Satan who delights in creating misery for mankind, while Christ as all-loving. Christ will be angry at a world which will have forsaken Him and God; but, His wrath will be directed at Satan, for having tricked mankind. Promoting Jesus Christ as vengeful does nothing to lead one **to the understanding** of love for our enemies, as Christ taught. The **outward** appearances make it seem Christ approves of punishment against those who sin against God. This makes it **especially** difficult to turn the other cheek when this sin is **in our** presence and meets the **eye**. It must be realized **the causes of** this **future** suffering of mankind, as has been the **prediction** of several true Prophets before, are not found to be the predictions themselves. They predict the causes. They do not cause what is predicted. A prediction of prophecy is quite separate from the actual causes; such that, the predictions are the **significators** which make the causes known. The causes lie in mankind; and, the seven churches are responsible for guiding mankind to peace and love. Because Christ saw the scenario of churches doing wrong, this is **to be the case** in this future. This wrong is clearly presented in *The Prophecies*, as well as by the biblical prophets. This story of the **future** is told from the perspective of mankind continuing to act, without heeding the warning of prophecy. The necessary changes which will be needed to correct this predicted course are not factored into the predictions. This prophecy has to be told in this perspective, as a worst-case scenario, **which** can have no other outcome if **oneself** feels too insignificant, as one in a world of many, to bring about change. Everyone **has to** understand the outcome will affect each person directly, if they do nothing to save themselves. It is this lack of positive change **which** has been **foreseen** as the reason the predicted results are **to manifest**. But, the individuals who make changes in themselves, to honor God and Christ, they will not suffer through this tragedy.

Seeing that this end has been foreseen and presented to mankind in an incoherent manner, **the** power of this **presage** is clearly not based on the creation of fear. That power to create fear will have already been generated, long before this document will be understood and the end time will come. Instead, the power here comes from assuring those of mankind who desire salvation, by letting them know that it can be attained; but, the responsibility of salvation is in the hands of each individual, when the churches fail to represent God and Christ. From this awareness, everyone has the control to avoid this end. The message is then personal, as to **what oneself** has gained from it and the changes which will have to be **made**, to adapt to it. To those finding value from the message, coming from out **of** the obscurity it once held, **the clearness** of how the message will then be obtained, as it is intended will be found, will make perfect sense to them. The **outward** action of true believers **comes** from this understanding; and, it is positive action that becomes a testimonial to each person's belief in the **infallibly** of a true prophecy. Knowing this future has been infallibly predicted; and, knowing infallibility can only be achieved by Jesus Christ, as the true Son of God, is a step towards belief and faith. From there one is able to go **in** a direction that honors God, and **to** accurately **judge** his or her own past and future. The prophecy will have **parted** the people, or divided them into groups, **with those** who believe on one side, and those who do not believe on the other.

It is so important to understand that the believers must begin **working** towards making all people come to this understanding and belief. This is one of the actions which must be taken. One must not try to hide this understanding from others, or feel special because one knows something others do not. The prophecy is an important message all must know, such that spreading **the light** of understanding **outward**, to others, must be done.

Let me clarify this spreading of light, as people do not always respond favorably to forced preaching. The light is in the message, so it will speak for itself; but, it will matter **how many** read the message and **truly** believe. The message will need to be passed on to others, by the ones who believe. This should first spread to friends and family, the ones who they care for. My **part** to play will be in the initial attraction of readers, as it is my name that many will find recognizable; but, the initial readers will not be expecting what they will find or know what my understood words will hold. There will have been no true understanding of the contents of *The Prophecies* before, although a core of interest will exist. Some will

149

feel that my name is associated with accurate predictions, but know nothing specific. When Christ will release the proper way to gain understanding from this book, the true meaning, **which** will have for so long been misrepresented, will **seem to have** suddenly appeared. There will be a radically different meaning at that time, attracting back those who will have known of my work, but dismissed it for lack of clear meaning. Those previously interested people will have known of *The Prophecies* **by** those who have used **the eye** to come to meaning, rather than from listening to their hearts. Those who will truly understand this different approach will want to share the message **of** *The Prophecies* by passing it on to **the** most knowledgeable interpreters of my words, to see if they will agree with this new **understanding**. By doing **this** they will remove **that** previous understanding, admitting they were **not** correct. They will find that every word, every mark, every letter **is by** the design of Christ; such that all is perfect and cannot be changed. They will realize I have been instructed to minimize the words so only the conceptual meaning remains. When this is realized, **the damage** caused by previous misinterpretations will be removed. The ones who will initially find the true understanding will be those **of** a prior belief in Jesus Christ, as Christians desiring **the** truth of God to come into them. Those people will **sense** the emotion of the words, through the intuition; and, the visions of this future will easily appear to the **imaginative** sense. They will see the true meanings come alive and understand *The Prophecies* is truly a living document, just as is the Bible. The ones who will test *The Prophecies* for tricks and shams will find the words do not rely on imagination to understand; but instead **the art of reason** or the rational approach of true logic will confirm the meaning for them. They will see this logical approach will expose all the errors which will have been previously made, yielding a much greater work than was ever imagined. They will uncover so much that **it** will be known to have great depth of meaning, with **too much** accuracy for it to have been chance. All of the meaning found will then be based on the **obvious**, rather than conjecture. They will confirm all of these methods of logic and reason apply to **the whole** work, and not just to selected passages. With the depth **being** seen as a complexity of simplicity it will be realized as way too ingenious for any one man to have devised. None will be able to duplicate this work. This includes any machines which will have been devised by man to assist in such duplication endeavors. They will admit the work can only be a true prophecy, where the past will have already been **predicted** infallibly. They will let it be known this could have only come **by** the means of divine **afflatus**. It will be agreed it is from the inspiration **of** the **divinity** who is Jesus Christ.

The importance of this recognition, from a thorough testing by those of intellectual prowess in such matters as logic and language, is this will expand the presence of the message, helping mankind choose to avoid the end which is foretold. For all who find the proof of Prophecy as reason to believe in God and Christ, their commitment to change will be assisted **by the means** of mankind's guardians. Those assistants are **of the spirit** which surrounds our souls, connecting us to God and Christ; and, this spirit is truly **angelic**. The angles know when one is truly **inspired** to change and in need of help to do so. They will come **to** your aid, giving strength to **the man** and woman who is seeking to remain focused on God and Christ. By the **prophesying** of Prophets mankind has proof of God's existence. This is enough reason for **committing** one's life to honoring this presence, and acting to change in accordance of that prophesized. Those who find commitment will be the **anointed** ones of Christ, as they will become the new priests **of** His new Church. This will have them spreading these **prophesying** words to others, so that the world will know of **the coming** of Jesus Christ. The words **in** the Bible were meant **to illuminate** the hearts and minds of Christians; but, when Christ appeared to Saint John, **he** was unable to comprehend the visions that were **moving** before his eyes. It was difficult for John to write of **them** distinctly. Christ appeared to me at a time still well **ahead** of this future; but, this time we are in now is close enough to this future time to make better sense **of the** machines mankind will then use. In Christ's version of *The Revelation* to me, much of the symbolic **fantasy** has been removed. This means **by** comparing the symbolisms of *The Prophecies* with those of *The Revelation*, as **diverse** as they may seem, the two will be found telling the same story. This comparison will show my work with Christ, which I have stated came during the **nocturnal** hours, was a series of **apparitions** of the Holy Ghost, and not conjured images coming from a boiling witch's cauldron. Some will have believed **that** I talked to the dead spirits of the future **by** some form of satanic incantations. The comparison with *The Revelation* will prove the **divine** presence in *The Prophecies*; and, the infallibility of the part which will have become the past will make this a **certainty**, as no man can see the future that perfectly. Christ is then the one who would **prophesize** to me, **by** giving me instructions, the same as he did with John. As I was allowed to see visions of this future, I was taking notes during this **administration** of Christ's Holy Word. The timing of events has been explained to me in

Astronomic terms, which I easily understood; and, this will be something skilled astrologers will be able to confirm, once the system of understanding is revealed. When many disciplines are **conjoined**, such as astrology, history, and mythology, **with** the arts of language and logic, **the** effect will be a holy **sanctification** of *The Prophecies*. Christ has come to me to show me the **future** because of my past accuracy of **prediction**; and, He has come to me for the purpose of helping mankind save itself. However, Christ has **not** limited mankind to just these two tales of the end of the world. Mankind must be open to **considering** other possibilities and other claims which will have surfaced **elsewhere**, telling different versions of **that** future and the changes that will befall the earth. Mankind will **have** all of the warning it will need to save itself; but, the question will hinge on the **courage** of each individual. Each person will be **free** to judge the validity of this message and be responsible for making a sound decision.

THE MISTAKE OF NOT FINDING FAITH

Freedom **comes to** mankind only when its souls have been released from the material realm. Anything less than this ultimate freedom is simply an illusion. When mankind will have reached **this hour** of decision which will come in this future I have been allowed to see, it will be most necessary **to understand** just how limited one is. The only true freedom one has is to choose one's own course towards that ultimate freedom. You will find, **my son** that you will have to choose a course in life. That course will not make you free; but, it will make your time on earth spiritually rewarding. You will find **that** same understanding of life **I** have **found**, where our physical lives are more pleasantly lived when we are giving back to others. Ultimate freedom comes by creating peace and happiness in our surroundings; and, it is not rewarding when one strains to achieve something as impossible as physical freedom. You will be able to discern true freedom is happiness, caused by the warmth of the soul; and, this comes **by** sensing that God and Christ smile down on you. In **my** life I have experienced many **revolutions** of self, from all the highs and lows of my life experiences; and, it has been those emotions generated by a soul trapped in a physical body **which** have shown me what my strengths and weaknesses truly **are**. Each of us, as individuals, has our own particular set of assets and liabilities, which are our **accordant** traits; and, these traits are well fitted to our life path needs. Each of us **has** a purpose for being given life on earth; but, that purpose is only **revealed** to us by the power of internal **inspiration**. It is those revealed inspirations **that** whisper to us in our thoughts, which urge us to make the correct life choices; and, those whispers ultimately lead us to trust in God that we will find the knowledge we need to fulfill that purpose. Having an eternal soul which is born into **the mortal** limitations of a human body means we are loaned our spirit for the enjoyment of the physical plane, but that loan must be repaid. It is our choices in life that will be judged; and, judgment is relative to how well we have protected our souls for its return. All our life choices are then like a **sword**, which cuts two ways: one offensively and one defensively. If **one approached** all life choices the same way, we would not be able to distinguish any right **from** wrong. If **we** are forced to make a decision **presently**, at this very minute, our basic nature would be to show caution first, and become defensive. This automatic fear of the unknown causes us to initially reject change. This would be even though we

153

feel an urge to move towards change. When we have learned to trust our instinctive traits we know we must move beyond our natural guard to hesitate and stay defensive. By trusting that our inner voice will let us know when it is time for us to go on the offensive and act, we will be filled with confidence once we begin those acts, even when we have had no prior experience in that direction. Take a day to consider what this document says, when it gives reason for change. The world will face suffering **by** a **plague**, which will sweep across vast areas, killing large numbers of people. If you are faced with a plague, would you act as I have in the past and act to treat the sick? Or would you run to save yourself? If you would prefer to run away from a real and present danger, would it not be better to walk away from that which will cause the plague to come? The world will be facing **war** also, where war is synonymous with death. All war originates from a disconnect between the leaders and God, when nations believe the outward cut of the sword will easily cut down a defensive enemy; but, the decision for war must always be well advised, because war turns the defensive offensive. This future outbreak of war will not see the dangers of unnecessary killing, as the leaders of the most powerful will see war as nothing more than a nuisance in their quests for taking what they want. This attitude will lead to an unexpected war which will be **more horrible** than any war ever waged by mankind before; and, it will be fought with weapons **that** will cause the horrible conditions of plague. Those horrible weapons will make it difficult **to live**, even in places far removed from where the soldiers will do battle. There will be **three** types of weapons which will be withdrawn from their sheaths; and, these will kill **men**, women, children and livestock, by the use of poisons, diseases, and explosions much greater than a cannon ball. Those weapons will represent the culmination of weapons training, from the past experience of three world wars. Those wars will all have been fought within one hundred years time, with larger and larger numbers of dead left in their wakes. However, the number of dead will have **not** stopped men from seeking new ways to destroy life. Will you want **to** see this war come, when the world will have had the chance to decide not to have it ever have **been**?

As far as chance goes, some will be able to avoid the plague and the wars; but, the vast number of people who will die after this final hour has run out will be from the slow and miserable death which will be brought by **famine**. The war will unleash powerful weapons which will destroy the earth's capacity to produce food. One weapon in particular will be used so numerously that the smoke from its discharge will create a cloud which will stretch three hundred miles and repeatedly circle the Northern Hemisphere. This cloud will contain the poisons of that weapon, **which** will continue to make it lethal. This cloud will produce a poisonous red rain which **will fall** from the sky. Everywhere this cloud goes the vegetation that will have been **on** the **earth** will soon die; and, as time continues on with this rain, there will no longer be enough vegetation left to support life. Will you make a choice that will kill millions, just so you can die with millions more, from hunger?

The leaders of the nations which will have stockpiled these weapons for use, and who will be sending millions of soldiers to die in the war, will make decisions that will depend **on** the choices made by the people they rule. Without the consent of the people they will not be willing to fight alone. If the people are afraid to oppose their leaders, those tyrants will begin a course of events which **will turn** the world into an uninhabitable place. Each person must ask themselves how **often** they have personally experienced the death of another human being. Have they ever held a loved one in their arms as they passed away? How will they be able to handle dozens of new deaths, close enough to touch, each day? Will they be able to bury all the dead? As **for** help in these matters, those future people will not be able to count on **the Stars** of humanity, or those whose egos will have shone the brightest. As the leaders will be leading the lambs of the world to slaughter, those people of privileged rank will have secured a place just for **themselves**, where shelter, food and medicine will be prepared for their arrival. Those of common stock will be restricted from entering those secure zones, as entrance will be **according to** wealth and position of power, with only a minimum of common slaves necessary. Those leaders will have been the descendants of **the revolution** which supposedly gave the people the right of freedom; but, those descendants will be the ones who will use freedom as a yoke, to quell the right of the people to choose another revolution. Will those people choose not to change, due to fear of those Stars? Will they put their faith in their leaders to save the world, forgetting the power of faith in God?

As this future will have to contemplate its own personal revolution, and which way its sword will cut, they must **also** remember the warnings repeated several places in the Bible. Those warnings are meant to make it clear what will happen **to** man when God sees an imbalance of power and the misuse of wealth to punish others. It is written in Psalms 89:33, "I will visit their iniquities with a rod

155

(of iron [Psalms 2:8]): and their sins with stripes." This translation of the Latin is accepted to be the meaning of this passage; and, it makes sense for an Old Testament view of God as one who will punish the wicked. However, it is not totally correct, as God actually **said** this:

I shall see power only on the condition that it is equal, with no more of an imbalance than **a firm green twig.** This is all the power a father needs to whip his son to obedience; but, anything beyond a green twig **is** an unfair advantage. For those who will seek to have unfair advantages of power, I will see **their unfairness** as abusive if it is meant to be used against one weaker. Knowing I will not accept unfairness, if so much as one stroke is used **upon** one unfairly, **I shall see** it as just punishment to give the means to strike back to the other, **to whip** the one who is **to strike** first as **hard** as that one struck **those.** This is a warning for all of those who will try to abuse others with their might, on any level of power. All of those who abuse power can count on being equally abused in return, just as powerfully. This is, again, symbolic of the revolution of Saturn, as the repayment of debt owed, which can be harsh; but, this repayment is specific to the work done prior, which caused one to deserve it.

Considering that scripture, see how it shows how **the mercy** and compassion which is known to be the nature **of God** will **not** be given to those who will wage this war and kill God's children. This goes for all times; but, this lack of protection will especially be found if this final hour ends without a decision for change. Without change, those inhuman tyrants will begin the end; and, at that time it **will be** too late for mankind to save itself. This **by no means** says God will not have pity for those that will suffer; but, only those who will have maintained strong faith in God, as demonstrated by their actions, will have **since proceeded** to Heaven. Those left behind will have turned their backs on God, the **one time** it will have most mattered not to do so. You will hear the cries of those future lost souls, **my son,** as they beg for forgiveness; but, it will be too late then. Their true faith will be shown when their pain and agony becomes so great their cries turn to epitaphs. They will cry out that God is dead; and, they will shout out curses against God and Christ for having been left in such misery. And, by **that** time of procession to Heaven, when only the lost souls will remain on earth, **the most part of** the quatrains of **my Prophecies** will still be yet unfulfilled. Some of those lost souls will find themselves **being** believers in Jesus Christ and God, as more and more of the most horrific quatrains become **fulfilled** ones. Their belief will be such that they will know what will be **coming** next, as prophesized; and, they will expect **to be** finding more misery coming into their lives. They will envy those who will have stood **by** Christ and drew faith and conviction from realizing the prophetic words of *The Prophecies*, before it will have become too late. Those believers will have drawn strength from the **accomplishment** just a few past event quatrains will have proved to them. Those believers will be the last **revolved** souls which will be returned to God.

At that time, when those of faith will have returned to be with God, **by** the failures of so **many** to have the courage to believe the **times** of man will turn on him. The evils of those inhuman tyrants will have been left **continuing**, unchanged, while the world reads the unsealed words of my book. The power and lusts of **the sinister** peoples will cause them to attack these words of Jesus Christ. They will attack them from a position of fear: fear of the masses turning on them and stripping them of their wealth and glory. They will cause **storms** of anger to rain upon the people; but, the truly faithful will have no fear, regardless of the anger shown to them. They will only need to look at the words of the Prophet Ezekiel, where it is written in 25:7, "**I will destroy thee** and thou shalt know that I am the Lord." Those sinister peoples and their Martial henchmen will have no power to remove this faith; but, in this passage the Latin words, "Conteram ego," actually mean, "I shall see (you) destroy (your) self." This will be the actual case, as God will have no need to destroy mankind. Then, in Ezekiel 5:11, it states, "**will say the Lord** God, Surely, because thou hast defiled my sanctuary with all thy detestable things, and with all thine abominations." This says the end is a certainty, because man will have raised idols of worship to the material realm, while corrupting the Church of Christ. All of this will have been done for the right to destroy the earth, in denial of God.

This verse then continues, with a repeating of the destruction which mankind will bring upon itself, using a slightly different descriptive word for destroyed. Here, the Lord will also see mankind, "**broken to pieces**". There will be no safety in numbers when every man or woman must fend for themselves. They must fend for themselves under the threat of disease, when no doctors or medicine are available. They must fend for themselves under the threat of war, when neither soldiers nor civilians will have protection against the weapons being used. They must fend for themselves under the threat of famine, when the only food available can only be afforded by the rich. Wherever it was believed unity existed and the laws of man ruled, there will be found the worst forms of anarchy rising. Every man will become an island, with survival of the fittest being the only law of the lands.

It is most important to know the final line of this series, in verse 11, as Ezekiel concludes with, "and my eye shall not spare, and I will **not have any pity**." This then leads to verse 12, which states, "A third part of you shall die with the pestilence, and with famine shall they be consumed in the midst of you, and a third part shall fall by the sword round about you, and a third part I will scatter to all the winds, and will draw out a sword after them." Chapter 5 ends with verse 17, stating, "So will I send upon you famine and evil beasts, and they shall bereave thee; and pestilence and blood shall pass through thee; and I will bring the sword upon thee. I the LORD have spoken *it*." As you can tell, this story has been told before; well before the time Christ told it to me. This example of Ezekiel shows how others have seen this same future.

It is so important to know that the Bible holds no less than **one thousand** such verses, told by **other** Prophets, detailing the same **adventures** mankind will take. The message of these passages repeats that **which will be coming** at the end of time. I have told you of the floods; and, the Bible also tells of a cleansing **by water**. It tells of the destruction of the earth at the time of Noah, when **continual rains** fell for forty days and forty nights, covering the earth. I have not written of anything that has not been already stated by other Prophets, one way or another; but, while my prophecies are **like** those others, Christ has given me **more** of this end's detail **to** present. When these words are clearly understood, by the systems which are implanted into the writing style, it will make those previously foretold warnings become clear. It will be **plain** to see, from understanding how to read what **I've written** in the quatrains, how to reach the intricate detail which is also in the books of the Bible. It will be **by** understanding this **writing** style **of mine**, which is the same style that has been used in the **other** true **Prophecies**, which will make everything become clear. All of the prophecies are supporting one another, telling of the same end, **which** proves they **are composed** by the same author. Only an eternal spirit could have encountered **all** of the prophets, **in the long** spaces of time between each, to have them all share in the same vision. It will be realized that my words **in** the quatrains are keywords, which require words of **explanation** to be added between them. This is the only way **prose**, or common speech, can bring the full meaning to the words written. I have **not** written the quatrains in prose, so they cannot be made into prose in any other way.[18] In many instances I have written what appears to be the name of a city or area; but, those names were intended to be **limiting** the vision of the people trying to interpret the quatrains. One has to look at the meaning of the name first, as the root word which gives the name meaning. This is often the way to approach **the places** I have named. I have also played with my use of dates, as the **times** are not ever clearly stated in the quatrains. Many will not realize this, causing some to state I was wrong with a time. However, when one looks carefully at what was written, just as one has to look at the names of places, the precise times will then appear, having been clearly written. It is so important to know all was done with purpose, and **the** period of misunderstanding has a **term** of time **prefixed** to it. This means **that** it is now known some true **human** beings will make sense of everything, **after** this term has concluded. Christ will send His angels to those people of humanity to have them **coming** to *The Prophecies*, such that this work will be **seen** clearly in a new light. Those people will not be guessing about what they are seeing, as they will be **knowing** Christ has chosen them to explain **the adventures** which will have befallen mankind. This prefixed term will come to an end after some of the quatrains will have already **happened**. It will be those quatrains which will tell of past events, which will be recognized as **infallibly** predicted. This infallible history, which could only have been predicted so accurately by Christ, will act as the true test of faith in the believers. At that time, there will already be many who will have interpreted *The Prophecies* over the years. Some of the correct interpretations will make some look **like** the previous interpretations, as **has** been **noted**, or written down in books **by the other** interpreters. However, the previous interpreters will have missed much of the depth of meaning that goes along with proper understanding. Those who will have captured the true depth will have been led by the whispers of Christ. This Spirit will be **speaking** the truth of the words written, making them **more clearly** understood.

To clarify how clearly *The Prophecies* will be made, some will claim the new

---

18   Only for this fragment of this block did Nostradamus write in Latin, "*in soluta oratione.*" Nostradamus used Latin to quote Jesus or the Bible, or generally to make a religious statement. To me, this is how Jesus explained his style to Nostradamus. The ending, "*-ne,*" of "*oratio-ne,*" makes this state the negative, which others seem to have missed. It translates to, "in explanation not prose." This is what confirms the style that I have used throughout this book, filling in between the words written in bold.

interpretations are **notwithstanding**, without close inspection. They will point out **that** others will have equally claimed to know what *The Prophecies* meant, only to crumble **under** closer scrutiny. They will notice the **cloud** of mystery which has surrounded the quatrains for so long; but, after they apply the principles of logic to the verses it **will be** clear the new interpretations show merit. A complete testing of how the methods of language lead to those **understandings** will prove this work is well beyond the powers of reasonable man. The pieces of the puzzle will fall into place, proving this work surpasses **the** most advanced of mankind's **intelligences**, who will have failed for centuries to properly put it together.

Many people will have seen this work as an intellectual pursuit, and used that to discount its value; **but**, this argument will no longer hold value, **at the time when** world events will be quite in line with the message of *The Prophecies*. The understanding will come when it is time for mankind **to move up** to the front of world affairs, **from under** the cloak of deception which will have been thrown over it. The people will realize they will have been misled, and to continue on this path **will be ignorance**. The world will know **the case** the quatrains make; and, with the secrecy removed it **will be** possible to demand **more clear** representation **in this matter** which urgently threatens the end of mankind.

THE CONCLUSION TO THE PREFACE

Making sense of this preface will make it easier for many believers to face this end, with faith that Christ will save their souls. And, when this end has come, my son, prophecy will no longer be necessary. So, as I end this preface, I want all believers to take heed and, therefore not worry about those who will choose to live for today, letting tomorrow be forgotten. Take this book of quatrains as a gift from Jesus Christ, to demonstrate the true power of God and the importance of living your life by the Laws of God, the true father of all mankind. Christ is the Son of Man and the Savior of those souls which do not lose touch with Him. Christ has blessed one Michel Nostradamus, by allowing me to become a servant to this salvation. God, Christ and the spirit of myself will all be hoping everyone who reads these words will realize their importance, and move them towards a strengthening of faith. This letter will make it possible for you to compare the interpreted quatrains to these instructions. With proper understanding you will be able to declare at least one of the quatrains supports each of the blocks of statements found in this letter. This will help direct you to realize The Prophecies is indeed a work of true Prophecy. While all of the quatrains are not stated in the blocks which are contained here, when the same process of understanding this letter is put to them, all will become clear.

Praying will be necessary to bring you the assistance needed, as the intellect alone will not be enough to bring forth the correct understanding. If you truly desire to uncover the secrets **to the** quatrains and the message **God** has sent to mankind, you will find you will be touched with guidance when you sincerely request it. You will receive all the encouragement you will need to save your **immortal** soul. You must remember **that** this element of immortality is dependent on your care, just as you must care for the mortal state of your body. The salvation of your soul is more important than the physical state, as **it** holds that immortality for **you**. You must be **wanting** Christ **to lend** you a helping hand, to pull you up to a **life** after death. Eternity is a very **long** time. It will either let one forget the pains of a short mortal life, or cause one to remorse the decisions one has made, for the moment a long time before. Life **in** Heaven is where only **good** exists, away from the trappings of the material realm. There, you will find the true meaning of the word **prosperous**, as Heaven represents the golden realm of peace, which will bring the prosperity of **happiness** and love.

From my heart I write to you in **Salon**, our home, on **this** 1st day **of March,** in the year of our Lord, **1555**. This letter is now completed while the Sun is in Pisces, the sign of selflessness and faith. May those qualities find their way to these words.

SUMMARY OF THE LETTER OF PREFACE

Hopefully, after reading my version of the Preface, you were able to block out what I have written, allowing your eyes to only focus on the bold words. This practice will allow you to see how well you can guess the true meaning, before going back and reading what I have added. Try reading it again if you did not try this exercise and see if you get a feel for the flow of the words. Some people will get a different feel for what some of the words say, perhaps missing how I came to what I have written.

This method of writing allows room for great depth of meaning; and, I have not covered every possibility by any means. I will assure you that there are multiple ways to read many, if not most of the sections, with all making valid points supporting the main theme of this letter. However, I have tried to maintain a consistent flow on the deepest level, often choosing the hardest meanings to see, at first glance; but, I am confident this version speaks well for what the preface was intended to present.

I have given you the most thorough reading of the strength this letter holds. I was not able to do this alone, from a purely mental approach. I had help writing what I have written; and, as you ponder the words of Nostradamus, you will need help too. Just be patient and trust that Christ will assist you in finding the meaning, as that meaning will ignite faith.

As a preface or foreword to The Prophecies, this letter makes its strongest points in stating very clearly that Jesus Christ is the author. From that point being made clear, Nostradamus wrote quite a bit about the title being very appropriately chosen. The work is indeed from the divine inspiration of Christ, rather than mere prediction. While Nostradamus admitted he was known for his predictions and even called a prophet for that, this work is much more than a calculated future.

The overview of what mankind can expect to find coming, which is spelled out in great detail in the quatrains, is really secondary to the reasons why that end will come. A significant portion of the preface was designed to show that this future is avoidable; but, only faith in its claims will spur the necessary actions which will make it be avoided. The conclusion is this document is not to frighten people into believing; but rather, it is designed to uplift the believers of

Christ and God. We all must feel assured that we will not suffer because others have failed. Understanding this letter makes reading the specifics of the quatrains, beyond those which tell of the past, completely optional. The quatrains which tell of the past, proving the element of infallibility, are more for those who need a little more proof to find that faith.

For proof to be unveiled, the preface also serves as a tool for realizing many of the hints for completing the puzzle which the quatrains are the pieces of. Once the preface is read so it makes sense, it tells us generally what can be expected to come. The preface presents a logical and ordered overview of the downfalls the Christian world will face, leading to the advent of the common man and the eventual corruptions which will take the world to the verge of ruin. This is important to realize, because the random presentation of the quatrains shows a need to place them in the proper order, simply to match the order of the preface. Aside from that order, the preface includes valuable instructions for making sense of the words in the quatrains, so that they can be understood, and so ordering is possible.

In my past work with the quatrains, I have found there is an order of story which they must all fit into. Some of the quatrains combine to tell of the past, which has led up to the present times. These conjoining stories are of some of the known important events of our history; but, they do not tell of all important events that have occurred. The preface tells of the fall of Kings and Church, with the rise of Sects; and, there are quatrains that tell of significant events which are representative of these falls from grace. The events which are the earmarks of those falls make up a significant part of the section that is now past and verifiable.

This then gives rise to the "sinister peoples" and their "Martial" partners, which will create inhuman tyrants. This part of the past is where others have seen accuracy in Nostradamus' work. The quatrains clearly tell of Hitler, Stalin, Mussolini, Franco, and even the Shah of Iran, Muammar Khadaffi and Saddam Hussein; and, several writers on Nostradamus have recognized key quatrains of these series of stories. However, they miss most of the supporting quatrains, which adds the details which solidify the ones they have spotted as indeed related to that one specific event in time.

When Nostradamus wrote in the preface about the Kings, Church and Sects becoming "diametrically opposite," the tyrants show the movement in that direction. However, the completion of this change is done within these three institutions themselves, rather than from tyrannical force. In the quatrains there are three stories which give the clearest evidence of this change; but, only conspiracy buffs will readily recognize the stories. These events are not concretely known by everyone. All are recorded deaths of important figures, one for each category, with Nostradamus telling us they were all murders which were covered up. This part of past history tells the corruption of these institutions, as the prefaces mentions.

While this past is shown infallibly predicted, all the events he wrote of occurred well after his death. Still, for those who will want a still future event to be clearly predicted, before it comes true, those come from the quatrains which tell of the current events we are going through now. In the preface, Nostradamus told us to look to the signs, especially the floods which will occur before the final hour comes. The quatrains tell of September 11, 2001, the invasion of Afghanistan and the occupation of Iraq, along with the capture of Saddam Hussein; but, they end with the beginning of this point of no return. In that sense, enough has been proven to demand some future prediction come to fruition before belief can be justified. Only a fool would wait for a predicted war to become real war, simply to think that was ample proof.

In my book, Pearls Before Swine, Volume 1, the subtitle, Predicting the Past, deals with those quatrains which tell the story up until the year 2000. This 445-year period of time, since the original publication date, is told in only 111 of the 948 quatrains; and, this includes several quatrains which act as an Introduction, retelling much of what Nostradamus wrote in the Letter of Preface. Volume 2, when it is completed, will begin with the quatrains telling of the events of September 11, 2001 and take us up to the verge of another world war. That war will not be hundreds of years away from now. This much briefer period of historical time, less than a decade from now, is covered in approximately the same number of quatrains as it took for Nostradamus to cover the first 445 years.

This increased density in the story line tells us we are into this future, and the final hour is about to begin. Once that war starts there will be no turning back, and the time left for mankind on earth will not be long. However long that period is, there are still over 725 quatrains remaining unfulfilled at the point of no return, which tell of the misery which will have begun once that war commences. If mankind is to avoid entering the end time, it has to realize the perfection of these letters and the stories the quatrains tell of the past. Only faith in God can help mankind turn back time; and, to do that mankind must change.

Near the end of the letter, when Nostradamus appeared to be speaking to his son, Caesar, he actually asked each one of us to find the individual quatrains which support each of the blocks of information he presented in the letter. This is a way of stating the confirmation for everything he wrote in the preface will be found in the quatrains. It becomes important to know, from my own personal experience interpreting the quatrains, that when those quatrains are found, which match the terminology written in the preface, they will all have several other quatrains linked to them. This combination then gives a very deep and detailed explanation of what Nostradamus wrote here.

In the length of this letter it becomes amazing how this style of writing makes the whole become tremendously expanded. In Pearls Before Swine I included an appendix which listed the bullet points of what was stated in this letter. In a single-spaced, 10 point font, the bullet points went six pages long. Remember the original form of the Letter of Preface was similarly reproduced into a 4-page document. Those six pages of summary notes show all of the important points Nostradamus made here. Obviously, there is a lot of information passed on in this letter; but, it is so much I will not go over anymore of it again here.

The main point that I want to leave you with, before proceeding to the Letter to Henry II, is to let it all sink in for a while. Do not dwell on any of it. When it has sunk in, you will begin to have flashing thoughts of what the important points are to you. If you have questions about a particular point, then find where that point is stated and reread what I have written. It is not a bad idea to keep a note pad nearby, to jot down thoughts while you read. You even have my permission to write in the book and dog-ear the pages, to remind you to follow-up on what makes you feel uncertain. Remember that prayer will assist you in understanding what I have written for Nostradamus.

PART 3

THE LETTER TO HENRY II

SPECIAL INSTRUCTIONS FOR THE LETTER TO HENRY II

At this point, you have read the instructions I have written for my approach to the letters of Nostradamus. You have been able to see how this applies, from having read the Letter of Preface. I have approached both of the letters of instruction Nostradamus wrote in the same basic vein, where each word written expands to include some necessary explanatory words. This is how the proper understanding is obtained. In both letters, some of these explanatory words come from a dictionary, where a word written is defined in the text; but, many of the explanatory words come from understanding the story the quatrains tell. That understanding then has been transferred to the letters which explain the quatrains. However, the Letter to Henry II differs from the Letter of Preface in some regards.

The Letter to Henry II is a much more complex document, although it follows the same principles that will be found in the whole of the book which preceded it. The complexity of *The Prophecies* created the need for a letter of explanation to be written. The complexity of this letter thus matches the complexity of the quatrains themselves, in the sense both can make clear sense; but, this clarity is only possible if one knows how to find order in chaos.

While the Letter of Preface clearly stated the purpose for *The Prophecies*, with general details about the quatrains, the Letter to Henry II goes beyond stating purpose and generality. It reinforces the theme that everything is from Jesus Christ; but, it also puts more focus on giving the reader greater details, including many of the specifics that are found in the storylines of the quatrains. However, it is the way these specifics are given which adds to the complexity of the letter.

The Letter of Preface put forth an orderly presentation of what was then and what would come, in general terms. The broader strokes at the beginning were followed by slightly more detailed strokes at the end. Simply put, that style was indirectly stating that a chronological order existed in *The Prophecies*. The obvious incongruence of the individual quatrains, by them not matching that chronological order of the preface, tells us some reorganization is required for the two to match. Without a reconstruction of order, it becomes very difficult to know all the complete details which fit the generalities of the preface.

The Letter to Henry II is not as straightforward as the Letter of Preface. By this, I mean it does not follow the approach of starting out with broad strokes and then coming back with smaller strokes to finish the picture. The Letter to Henry II will follow a path like this to a point, where it then lurches off to some other point of direction and follows that path for a while. After several of these wild branches off topic, it then comes back to one of the previous topics and begins to again give more details to that. This style has thus been seen as impossible to understand, with many researchers calling it pure gibberish; and, some authors have refused to even try to make sense of it. However, as difficult as that wild ride is, this style is used with purpose and intent; and, the manner of presentation the Henry letter makes is actually a clue to the puzzle *The Prophecies* holds.

Just as the quatrains were rearranged from their original order, making it confusing, Nostradamus rearranged the statements he wrote in the letter to Henry. This is where the confusion about the meaning of this letter comes from; and, it is this irregularity which acts as a parallel to *The Prophecies*. If you understand that to make sense of the letter it requires the procedure of reconstructing it into understandable groups, then you just made the first step toward understanding how to make sense of the quatrains. Simply by rearranging the elements of the Letter to Henry II, into an understandable order, you will find that it does make perfect sense. As a letter of explanation, this overall form of presentation explains that the quatrains are incomprehensible because they are not placed in the proper order.

Just as I have done in the book *Pearls Before Swine*, where I have reordered the quatrains to tell a story which is chronological, I have reordered the statements of Nostradamus here, to make the Letter to Henry II make perfect sense. The bold type words presented in my rendition of the Letter of Preface are exactly in the order Nostradamus wrote them. Each block of text represents the words of Nostradamus in the order they were written, separated only by one of the punctuation marks that represent a break. This separation by punctuation has given it the appearance of something like a paragraph. However, the clean way that the Letter of Preface becomes divided is different in the Letter to Henry II. The same punctuation marks indicate the same break points; but, once the letter is divided like this, it becomes a puzzle which must be rebuilt into the proper order.

In most of the blocks of text the Letter to Henry II produces, from capitalized first word to the ending mark (period, colon, ampersand, semi-colon), some of them will tell a perfectly chronological story, without a need to move them. Some of the pieces are then preset into the proper order, in positions which to build the others from. These blocks are on one select topic; but, once the letter has begun this block may or may not fit the chronology of the surrounding blocks, before or after. The task is then to slide the pieces around, until they interlock correct with the proper matching context.

Some of the longer blocks cover a very wide range of time, with information of many events, some of which will not match the others. After much painstaking prayer and trial and error, I have found that this letter must be fragmented and rearranged into a completely new presentation, for it to tell the story of the quatrains. This is precisely how the stories of the quatrains come to life in this letter.

I will tell you that there is system to this madness; but, this book is not designed to instruct you on this matter. This will be presented in a more educational book still to come. Here, I will not train you for something you will not understand, because to make you understand I would have to take timeout in the story telling to discuss what just happened. I also will not make any references to let you know where I have made movements of the text, to piece the parts together. I actually saw no need for this in *Pearls Before Swine*; but, the quatrains have their own serial numbers (Century & Number) which allows for that reference, unlike this letter. I state this now for anyone who might expect to follow along with another work which has translated this letter, as another author's letter will be difficult to find in my letter.

Just know that the Letter to Henry II takes the Letter of Preface to new heights of explanation. It adds more detail and more elements, many which the Letter of Preface did not put bright focus on or even mention. Nothing in the Letter to Henry II contradicts what was contained in the preface's statements. However, it takes that straight-forward foreword, about what can be found contained within the pages of *The Prophecies*, and repeats that information, expounds on that information, and adds new information. The result, as you will find, is a greatly detailed outline of the stories within the main theme of *The Prophecies*. This letter explains the future parts of what the work holds, as seen from our present perspective.

Please be forewarned, since the length of this letter is almost double that of the preface, there is much more detail and specifics than you have read so far. While the Letter of Preface told a general overview of a horrid story of cataclysmic war and destruction, with floods, famine and disease, the Letter to Henry II gives more gruesome details. Logic tells us that this letter, as the explanation of the meaning of *The Prophecies*, is telling us what the quatrains tell. My own personal experience, working with the quatrains, confirms beyond any shadow of doubt for me that the quatrains themselves takes these gruesome details and personifies them, so that one can feel the pain the words carry. The emotion of this letter is amplified even more in the work it explains.

Without further explanation, please read for the first time the correctly paraphrased Letter to Henry II. This version is what Nostradamus intended us to read from it. That intention was designed to be well after the days he constructed it; and now is the time it must finally be understood.

THE HEADING

[Important to understand first: This letter is in reference to the document known as *The Prophecies*. That document is the recorded words of Jesus Christ, just as were the **EPISTLE**S of the apostles, found in the Bible. Therefore, *The Prophecies* is also an EPISTLE of the words of Christ.][19]

The words of this letter are mine, but **FROM** Jesus Christ, as told to me. Jesus Christ is the **MOST INVINCIBLE** man that ever walked the earth, as he is the only man to have died and been resurrected with immortal life. He did this before taking His throne, alongside God, the Father of all mankind. God, our Father is the One God, **ALL POWERFUL**, all seeing and all loving. Christ, the Son of God, has come to me with His power of prophecy, just as He has brought His power to other Prophets before. Jesus Christ had me pen *The Prophecies* as He dictated them to me, for the purpose of saving the souls of mankind.

AND, Christ sends His blessing to those that carry the torch on earth, in His name. Closest to Christ's heart are **all** of the people who are **Christian**. This number has steadily grown to great size in numbers; but, it would not have reached this height had it not been for the people called to serve Christ, in the churches of Christianity. Christ blesses those who are completely dedicated to living model lives, from the teachings of the New Testament. Jesus Christ also sends His blessings, equally, to the royal bloodlines of the Christian nations, as are you **Henry**. You sire are of Jesus Christ's bloodline, which has elevated you to the position of **King of France**, from birth. You are from the bloodline of the Holy Grail; and as King, you are responsible for those of the common ranks of France. Jesus Christ sees that your kingdom allows the Church an equal power of influence, to also assume this responsibility. Both you and the Church acknowledge your earthly positions of power are **Second** to Christ, the One King. Christ is also close in the hearts of those who are from neither of these two royal ranks;

---

19   The first word of this letter is surrounded by brackets. The defined use of brackets is to separate a comment that is apart from the document that the bracketed information shows in. As the word bracketed is the all-caps EPISTLE, this is reference to *The Prophecies* as the Epistle of Nostradamus. The all-caps shows the full definition of the word Epistle must be understood, which gives it a clear religious meaning.

but, His appreciation goes to those of the sects, who influence the common class to serve your needs. He blesses this class that I, **Michel Nostradamus**, am one example of.[20]   Together, this class brings special talents which serve the Lord, through your direction. Christ sends **his** love for the dedication and loyalty that religion and country have shown in bringing His words of teaching to the common people. The model of Christ shows the common people the merit of being **very humble**, realizing the earthly plane of existence is lowly. The veneration for maintaining a spiritual direction during a hard life is eternity in Heaven. The model of Christ also shows the common people the need to be **very obedient** to the laws of God, as well as to the teachings of Christ and his actions while incarnated. Christ is always close to those who follow these humane models, by acting as a **servant** to the Lord. In one's life of service, through humility and obedience, one serves mankind while serving Christ. With Christ in one's heart, one will **subject** to the will of God and Christ and listen to one's inner voice. This reflection from humility allows the message of love, peace and brotherhood to be spread. For those who can make these sacrifices for the Lord, they will be the ones who find ultimate **victory**. They will win over the temptations of the earthly plane and find the ultimate reward in eternal **bliss**, as a soul returned to be one with God and Christ in Heaven. Christ speaks to those that have proven their servitude and subjection.

---

20   These three classes were told of in the Letter of Preface, as Church, Kings and Sects.

EXPLAINING THE ELEMENT OF CHRIST

For the purpose of responding to your highness in reference to your request for an explanation of *The Prophecies*, **here** in this letter I have presented a heading which symbolizes the statements of my Letter of Preface to that document. You may read **this** as being an overstatement of my **supreme** admiration for your highness; but, my superlatives are reserved for the one who is even more supreme than you. My **observation** is based on the strictest definition of **that** word "supreme," as **I've had** the pleasure of personally observing Jesus Christ. The surprise of this visit was **oh** so wonderfully unexpected. I can only say that I have been blessed by having the wish that only the **most Christian** of people could ever imagine come true for me. I have witnessed Jesus Christ before my passing beyond this realm. Christ has truly been **most victorious** over my heart; and, as much as you are Henry, King of France, to whom I owe allegiance, Christ the **King** has won my loyalty, completely and absolutely. That title has been given to Christ, as ruler over the Kingdom of Heaven; but, **since** being in Christ's presence I have realized just how true **that** title of King is for Him. His presence filled my whole **being** with joy and admiration, and a smile beamed across **my face**. I cannot tell you how much I have wanted to tell the world of this meeting; but, Christ has willed that this cannot be so. For that reason, I have held my tongue for a **long time**, keeping this meeting **overshadowed** and secret. Still, for **oneself** to be **presented** with such a gift of presence, I have since been overwhelmed with lingering emotion. Christ coming **to** such a simple man as myself has left me in debt, as **the** one receiving a gift, **owing** Him a gift in return. It is difficult for me to fully explain how it feels to possess such a gift of sensations. It is difficult to put into words how it feels to be in the presence **of the** single most important **deity of** one's religion; the one whose blood is in **your** royal highness' veins, and the one you call **Majesty**. The feelings which burst forth within me are completely **immeasurable**. The elevation I first felt has **since** gone higher, and I have remained **in this** continuing escalation of feelings. This height **I've** experienced has **been** so unending thus far that I trust it will last **perpetually**. I will forever be **dazzled** by this encounter I have had. I was put into such an instant state of illumination when Christ first appeared that I was not frightened at all. I did **not** want to hide from Christ, **withdrawing from** such an encounter. In the presence of Christ I felt it my responsibility **to honor**

Christ and welcome His presence, even though I was overwhelmed with the honor which that presence gave me. I have always tried to live my life **worthily**, and **to venerate** all who perpetrate the religion of Christianity. I have tried to serve others the best I could, knowing **the one day** would come when my mortal existence would end. I fully expected **that** the day of my death would allow me **for the first time** to see Heaven and Jesus Christ. Many times **I** would drift into thought of how I would **present myself** to Him, knowing I would be **before the one** whose life has changed so many lives. There are several religions **like** Christianity, where many people feel changed by the prophets who began them; and, Christ wants all of mankind **to** serve God by the principles of religion. Jesus Christ is the **one** Prophet of Man who preaches the **singular** message of peace on earth and goodwill towards men. While he is accepted as the **Majesty** of the Christian world, Christ cares for **all** the peoples in the world, of all races and all religions. Christ has come to me because of this **humane** concern He has for all of the world's peoples. He has come with a message for all mankind and that message is contained in the quatrains of *The Prophecies*.

Now, that work I have produced for Christ is not well understood and you are **searching** for an explanation for the meaning of my words. You are aware that I have done **some** work for you on **occasion**, and I have willingly explained peculiar references to you before. I have been permitted, **by** Jesus Christ, to send you this letter of explanation, **which** will fully explain everything contained in *The Prophecies* and more. However, **I** can only explain it in the same manner as it was written, so I am well aware that this letter will make little sense to you now. Christ has complete control over when both *The Prophecies* and this letter will be correctly understood; and, there is **little himself** can do to cause this meaning **to manifest** without the assistance of Christ. When that time comes, I am assured that **the** one who Christ enlightens will be one with a **good heart**. I say that because the message contained in our document will expose those of bad hearts, in very **frank** means. Having a good heart, with strong faith in Jesus Christ, will give this person the **courage** that will be required to make the public aware of the message. Christ will enhance **that** level of courage for the one **working** so hard to understand my words. Before **he** will be able to present **my** name to the world as a Prophet of Jesus Christ, he will have to be given the **power** to see that a true Prophecy is in *The Prophecies*. The power to understand those words will come after this person will have **had himself** been **made** prepared for this understanding. This will have taken the course of a lifetime; such that, he will have shown **ample** knowledge and interest in the basic elements that compose *The Prophecies*, including such things as astrology, poetry and mythology. This one will then act as an **extension of** me, at a distant time in the future. Having this **knowledge** already instilled in him will allow him to be more easily moved **towards** the necessary and correct understanding. That time of understanding will not be **ours** to be concerned with, Henry, as France has now entered into a **most serene** period, under the rule of your **majesty**. This is why I do not take the time to travel and visit you personally, sire; for I cannot make the message any clearer now, than the way this letter will appear to you.

Now is not the time to make *The Prophecies* clear, as it tells of another time. Therefore, **seeing** the future now can upset **that** serenity of your majesty's reign. It would upset it **by** exposing you to the horrible **issues** and effects of a future world, which will be so bad simply knowing about **it** could cause you **to declare** my book must **not** be made public at all. I realize the only reason this work has been made public is the reputation which precedes **me**, having **been** successful predicting the future by the stars. That success will make it **possible** for *The Prophecies* to remain as an enigmatic source of interest until this future comes; but, this condition can only be met as long as the book is left unexplained. My book is so **joined with** the future that **my** own understanding of it would have been impossible, had it not been for the accompaniment of Christ. Still, this work from Christ will become the most **singular** source of hope that future generation will need; because, at that time they will be able to clearly understand my words. Your **desire** to know the meaning **of** this which Christ has placed in **my** protection will gain you the respect of my loyalty to your highness. In that regard, I will fully explain the contents, as you desire, as best as I am allowed by Christ. However, as I know this letter will not make sense to you or your court, I also know a lack of clear explanation will become the catalyst, which will send **so many** on a quest to solve the riddle of *The Prophecies*. This quest will last for a **long** time to come; but, instead of making things clearer, the wild guesses which will come will cause an **obtenebration**.[21] Still, for all the **obscurity** this lack of light will bring, it is as certain as is a mountain top, even though that top is obscured by clouds. There is a very distinct message **being** hidden in this fog,

---

21   Obtenebration is the act of darkening, meaning that less light will be shed upon the meaning.

which will **suddenly** appear when the fog has lifted. In that new light, the book will be found having sharp edges and multidimensional detail. Once the **bright** light of Jesus Christ comes to burn off the fog, it will be all made clear; but, before that time comes there will be an **interval** or period where the shadows in the clouds will play tricks on people's eyes, making them see shapes of things that are not there. These are the imaginations of the mind, **transported** from its storage in the memory, of such shapes and figures, **to the** nebulous vapors which surround my words. The brain cannot make sense of that which is cloudy in this kind of intellectual way, as the solution to this puzzle will come from the psychic center in the **forehead**. This is where the "third-eye" is located, making it a part **of the** physical features of the **face**, instead of the brain. This sensor **of** the highest vibratory elements of sight is the physical gland which connects the brain to **the sovereign** being that is God. The power to use this **eye** has been lost by most people today; but, those who can naturally exercise this muscle will know this connection to God can make one all-seeing.

Let me make it very clear that this exercise includes the commitment **of** one's soul to God and all the good that God holds. This is **the first** step which must be taken, towards achieving this ability to see all. One has to have sworn allegiance and proven loyalty to the one greatest **Monarch**, who rules not over one kingdom, but the whole **of the Universe** which He created. There is **so much** to behold in **that** universal expanse, which includes all knowledge and all times. **I've been** able to see the times of Man; but, it was so much to see that it has left me **in doubt** of my abilities to comprehend what all I have seen. Christ has witnessed my dedication to Him and God; and, this is the reason **for** my being chosen to view the history of mankind. Mankind has survived on earth for **a long time**, but **at** one point in the future it will be faced with extinction. Jesus Christ is the one **who** has been sent by God to save mankind; and, **I** am the benefactor of His great desire to help mankind. Christ **came to** me to assign me the task of carrying a message to mankind, in this pursuit of salvation. My book, *The Prophecies*, has the **sanction** of the Father, the Son and the Holy Ghost, such that **these** quatrains amount to verses of a Holy Scripture. I have recently supplied the last **three** divisions of this Book of Nostradamus to the publisher, again under the sorting as **Centuries**. Some call my book "The Centuries," but this is not the title. Those chapter separations merely mean a grouping of 100 verses is in each chapter; and, the word "Centuries" is not in any way a reference to time.[22] These last three Centuries released were all written at the same time as the others; but, they were not released with **the last** edition, in 1555. This separation of three years will give a **trace of** suggestion that the additional three years have been needed; so that I could complete **my** calculations of the future times, to make more predictions. This suggestion will be purposefully designed to mislead, as the title of my work states the truth of its source; for the quatrains are all divine **Prophecies**. The previous seven segments have enough information contained in them to tell this story of the future, from beginning to end; but, these remaining verses will be **perfecting the** totality of the detail. This detail is quite deep, with **thousands of** lines and segments in the quatrains, yielding an amazing depth of meaning.

Christ instructed me to wait until **after** the first release of *The Prophecies*, so that the three additional Centuries would make the quatrains appear **to have** been written in the order they have been published in. Everything has actually been written **for a long time** and simply not published all at once. They were also written in a chronological order, then separated and reordered to have them presented in a random order. At this time, the proper order is **known** only by Christ and myself; but, when this future time comes, the proper order will be known by all. If all **of** the quatrains had been published at **one** time, it would have given the impression the verses were prepared with **reckless** abandon, causing some to become more **daring** with their powers of censorship. It is known that you, sire, allow the Church an equal power, to rule over the souls of the land you serve; and, I have **had** the opportunity to have **taken my skill** and trade, as an astrologer, to both you and the Church, with good success. I have leaned **towards** the fairness of **your majesty** and the kindness of your Queen, as this has allowed me to be more open and frank with my observations. While the Church has been supportive, they do **not** appreciate any language **being** written that does not first meet the approval of their censors. *The Prophecies* has thus been placed under your authority **for** the purpose of preventing the Church from exercising **that** primary role, as censor. I understand you have been **surprised** by the seemingly unintelligible contents; but, you have the ultimate power of decision, as King, and you have seen how my misunderstood words have a way of later making

---

22   The initial publication of *The Prophecies* (1555) only contained the Preface and seven "chapters" called "Centurie I," "Centurie II," etc. The final three Centuries were published in 1558, the same year as this letter of explanation.

perfect sense. With this reign of yours having a binary system of equal powers, it is **like** in the days of ancient Sparta. I know this because the story was **told** long ago, by **the gravest** or most serious **author** of Greek antiquity, **Plutarch**. I am reminded of the passages **in the** story Plutarch recounted, of the **life of Lycurgus**.[23] In **that** story, he wrote of Lycurgus' return to Sparta, after a period abroad, when two kings were fighting for control of the same land. No one was **seeing** a solution for this conflict, so they came to Lycurgus making him **the offers** for gaining the power to lead a unification of Sparta. Those offers led him to see a need to change the commonwealth. So, Lycurgus **presents** a plan **that** would make Sparta **one** nation, with two leaders. To ensure that the graces of the gods would protect Sparta's unification, he **made** this secured **by** making holy **sacrifices, at** one of **the temples** of Apollo. That was the temple which housed the Oracle of Delphi, who was known to only tell the truth to those who questioned her. The oracle confirmed that Sparta would indeed be best with **the two** kings, along with a Senate of 28 landowners, and with all sharing equal power. This arrangement was favored by **the immortals** then, just as Christ smiles at your willingness to share rule with the Church now; but, it is also important to know how Lycurgus' intent, based on the knowledge bestowed upon him by the deities **of his times**, was not understood by everyone.

Even **with that** support of the gods during times when rule of **one** needed to come to an **end**, there was fear for either of the chosen co-rulers to act as ruler. Lycurgus gained the support of the leaders and requested the majority of the people bear arms, to ensure that the unity would be agreed upon. The fear of **that** action led one of the Kings to believe that the people were arming to bring his claim to reign to an end. He believed Lycurgus was **the one** who was leading a conspiracy against him. That King knew he **himself** did **not** have the power to defeat such a conspiracy; and, fearing for his life he sought refuge in the temple of Minerva. With the other King in hiding, Lycurgus returned to the temple of Apollo to get more answers; and, on that visit he was told to build two temples, one to Jupiter and another to Minerva. This would settle all disputes. When this was done, Lycurgus engineered the division of the lands of Sparta into equal

23 Plutarch was a Greek biographer and essayist that was the priest of the temple of Apollo at Delphi. As the Delphic Oracle he accepted offering from those seeking to know the truth about what the future held. Lycurgus was a character that Plutarch wrote of, and who was known as the Father of Sparta. Under Lycurgus' leadership, Sparta was known for its unique philosophical doctrines, which promoted true equality.

amounts for each group of leaders. To some this was **surprising; by** the way this division was being **too** generous to some. Those losing land became angered at Lycurgus and he was then chased. One youth, **often** known to display reckless and rash actions, caught Lycurgus and struck him with a stick. The stick damaged one of Lycurgus' eyes. Still, Lycurgus did not fight back. Instead, he **retracts** to his home, to make his wound heal with **cool** treatment. The point of this story is that the changes designed for Sparta were **set** by the gods, and **not** by Lycurgus. He acted as the gods had commanded, such that he **himself** was not to profit from the changes. In the end, he lost the use of his eye, simply from **daring to present** the plan he envisioned, **to** build **the temples** and unify the people.[24]

And, I too am daring to present something which will unify the people, as commanded by God and Jesus Christ, in a way that some do not understand. Since the story of Lycurgus shows natural reactions of people, based on fears, those same fears today could jeopardize the safety of *The Prophecies*; but, your highness is the one king who can influence the Church to follow your lead. In reference to the temples of Lycurgus' days, it was the temple of Apollo that Lycurgus consulted. Plutarch was a priest of the same temple. Further, it was the temple of Minerva which the second king sought refuge in, when he was in hiding. These temples were built for the gods, but available to **the whole** of the people. Apollo was the god of truth and **Minerva** was the goddess of wisdom; and, while these may seem to be two similar qualities of knowledge, the truth is not always understood by all and wisdom is not always the truth.[25] Each is **independent** of the other, although they are both of knowledge. I mention this because, figuratively, the two temples of France today are your royal highness and the Church.

As independent as the two of you are, you are **not unwilling** to work together for the same goals. You both have supported the almanacs I have produced; and, it is known that I have done these by **calculating** the movements and aspects of the celestial orbs. Unfortunately, this support is not **nearly as much** now as it was before, with the publication of a most mysterious book. The format **of the** presentation, in 4-line verse style, makes it appear to be the **same** as my other

24 See The Internet Classics Archive: Lycurgus, by Plutarch, translated by John Dryden at http://classics.mit.edu/Plutarch/lycurgus.html

25 Minerva is also known as Athena, who is known as the goddess of wisdom and the patroness of the arts and sciences.

works, which have predicted the **adventures** I saw the kingdom would face. The wisdom of the Church knows those predictions were **chances** taken, where probability was a factor. I have taught them that the return **of the** same aspect can produce the same effect, over and over again. If something has happened several **times** before, this makes it more probable it is **to happen** again. This is the mental approach of wisdom, where one believes that what has happened before will happen again, making the future **like** the past. The Church believes man is able to predict a stable future today, by knowing **of the ages past.** However, it is this form of **understanding** which is a danger to the safety of Christ's message. This has kept me **from** approaching the Church for their approval of my document, such that I have written this explanation to **present** to you, your highness. As king, you have the true power to save this work.

But, as I come forward now to present an explanation of what *The Prophecies* means, I offer **such** in the manner of Apollo.[26] The truth about its contents which your majesty has requested will be presented; but, no one will be able to understand them in the present times. The first clue is stated in the title, where I have capitalized the word "**Prophecies.**" This word, by definition, tells the reader that the book is multiple verses which have **proceeded from** a divine source. This is then generally spoken from **the mouth of** a Prophet, who has been in contact with **the holy Spirit.** In no way does this title mean the contents came from independent thought, as would be a calculated prediction. That **which** I have produced, *The Prophecies*, **has been** entirely composed as dictated to me by **the sovereign** Christ Jesus, our Lord. He has the **power** to see beyond the present, knowing all the future and the past, as his vision is **eternal.** Christ has the ability to see all times. I was an **assistant** to Christ, but there were other assistants who were still more capable than me, for seeing the future. Christ has other spirits working **with** Him, and those assistants are those who operate by His commands. Those helpers are also members of **the celestial** realm. Those celestial assistants are commonly known to be angels, and people have been **in** touch with numbers **of** them in the past. Many people have reported having had prophetic experiences as a result of meeting their angel. Over the ages of history, **some of** those people who have reported **this** type of prophecy have been placed

---

26 The Greek god Apollo was the Sun god. When one reads the introductory quatrains that set up the story, there is made the symbolic comparison to Jesus Christ, and thus Christianity, as the religion of the Sun. This is because Christianity offers the truth that goes beyond wisdom, which lights the path for our souls.

in with a **number** of prophets who have not encountered Christ; but instead, they met with another equally all-knowing spirit. The Bible tells of angels who have appeared in this manner; and, another famous figure of post-biblical prophecy is the Virgin Mother, Mary. The people who they have encountered have **had** the gift of prophecy given to them, and those people have made that which was **predicted** publicly known. When the prophecy came true, they were given a reputation as one of the **great** prophets of mankind. Those are true Prophets; and, the stories they have told have been seen as **miraculous** events, in that those could have only happened through spiritual assistance. Those Prophets have helped prevent mankind from taking some terrible **adventures** into areas where mankind should not tread. Likewise, *The Prophecies* ventures to repeat the same purpose of prevention.

While **my** book will have that same purpose, let me clarify that point somewhat. I have played a part **in** the physical writing of *The Prophecies*, but **that is** simply because Christ saw me as worthy of performing that task for Him. My name does appear on the **face** of the book for that reason. However, **I** am **not** the originator of the text, as an author would normally be. For what I **myself attributed** to the making of this book, or any input which came from me, aside from quill, ink and parchment, I have no basis for claiming credit. Certainly, **by no means** did I seek to fabricate a document, said to be from divine inspiration, to gain **such** a title as Prophet.[27]

---

27   This is Nostradamus repeating the same disclaimer that was made in the Letter of Preface.

EXPLAINING THE SYSTEMS OF UNDERSTANDING

This title bestowed upon me **notwithstanding**, the title *The Prophecies* does not convey, to the people who already call me prophet, any connection to God. I am but a common man, neither seeking nor deserving of great praise; and, I would not be so bold as to assume my predictive abilities were prophetic. I am satisfied with my rank, and I have no need to be idolized. I am moved by **seeing your splendor**, your highness, at those times when I have been summoned to serve you. I am in awe of the aura which emanates from your **Royal** being, as you are justly elevated to a position of honor. You cast a glow that says you are indeed from the blood of Jesus Christ. Because you have allowed the Church its degree of power, you are not fearful as a solitary ruler; but, you allow this benevolence because you feel **accompanied** by Christ in all of your actions of state. Christ sides **with** you, and with **one** so **incomparable** leading you, you are loved by the people of France. You are a true king of mankind, showing kindness, patience and **humanity** for all to model. Additionally, you are united with a queen who is like no other. She is one who seeks to have the best guides surround you, to influence you properly. This influence of good which you demonstrate **has** willfully **taken** me and my services to you. The Queen's admiration of **my skill** as a prognosticator has caused her to summon my skills to be used for your benefit, on several occasions. The relationship we have shared, between astrologer and king, is **not like** the relationships that are found **with the** most renowned astrologers who exist elsewhere today. Those astrologers serve the **Kings** in and around the land **of Persia**. In **that** arrangement **it** has **not been** the luxury of the court astrologers to have such a pleasant relationship. The astrologers in Persia are **by no means** given **permit**, or license, **to go** freely **with** their findings and present **them** to their kings. They do not have the freedoms we enjoy here; **nor**, by **less** means, can the astrologers **themselves** request an audience **in** the king's presence, or dare **to approach** with advice, without an invitation. This is a testimony to the trust you have shown me, and you have been well advised in the past by me, on serious matters which have required your attention.

But, as an exception to this past relationship which I have had with your highness, I have since provided my services **to one very prudent**, or one wisely discrete entity. By this I mean I have dedicated my greatest loyalty **to one very wise Prince**, or Jesus Christ, the Prince of Peace. During this time I have spent with Christ, **I've devoted my nights** to listening to His words. Those words have been **prophetic**, telling me what the future holds and the warnings which must be given to mankind. These have led me to my daily **calculations** of confirmation. Those calculations have taken place after I have had aspects **composed** for me, by Christ, so that I could check the possibilities of cycle for the information Christ has given me. My calculations are not the origin of the text; but **rather**, I take the information which comes **from** Jesus Christ and then use my own abilities to project what future timeframes could be produced, based on the present methods and knowledge of calculation. I have been chosen as the **one** to receive this gift because of my **natural** talents with astrology and my trust to follow my **instinct**. By this instinct, I mean that I have been able to look at the planets and their future movements and then listen to the inner voice, the psychic sense, to predict from that. I did not realize that the accuracy of my predictions were due to my being **accompanied** by God's assistant Angles; but their assistance in my thoughts is what made those compositions seem prophetic. However, I have written *The Prophecies* **with** the total assistance of Jesus Christ, who is the **one** who all credit must go to. He is the source of the **poetic** style that has been attached to the quatrains; and while I have also used this style in my almanacs, the sheer number of poetic verses created, at such speed, with so much depth of meaning, no man could possibly reproduce that feat. Anything similar would be impossible without deep thought and reflection, and long hours of contemplation. But the poetic words of Christ do not tell of the typical beauty one associates with poetry, as the topic is one of great **fury**. It tells of the rage and violence that mankind will succumb to in the future. In those quatrains of *The Prophecies* it must be understood **that** the detail of this fury becomes clear **by** realizing the importance of **order**. Order is paramount in understanding the individual quatrains and the whole story they all tell. It is especially important in respect to the scrambled condition the quatrains have been published in, because that missing order must be recognized, making them all need to be reorganized, like a puzzle.[28] When this organization is done, *The Prophecies* becomes an epic

---

28   This explanation states, in full, "*que par reigle de poesie*," which translates to, "that by order of poetry." The word, "*reigle*" can also mean "rule, canon, method,

tale **of poetry**, on a scale which cannot be found duplicated in literary history.[29]

You must understand that in poetry **there** is **more** meaning behind what the poet writes, than is often immediately apparent. The use of metaphor and symbolism can turn the ordinary into the extraordinaire. Poetic license also allows for many standard practices of language to be waved; and, *The Prophecies* takes full advantage of this license. In the poetic style Christ imparted to me, everything equals an important **part** of the whole, making full understanding of each part most important. Each quatrain is one part; but, so too are each line of one quatrain and each word in one line, including all marks of punctuation. This is a key element in what has brought on the confusion, as the majority of the quatrains are out of order, making each appear to be a free-standing part. The method which was used to present *The Prophecies* in such a confusing manner was as such: the whole was first **composed** in a concise and chronological order, in poetic style; then, after its completion it was then separated into parts, and placed in a random presentation. Any book ever written would be equally confusing, if this same method was applied. The answer to the confusion is then to see it as a puzzle, where it must be reassembled to be read, as it was originally written. While this may seem to some to be an overwhelming task to perform, there is a key to determining this order. This key comes from the positions of the planets which have been **accorded**, or granted, within the text. This allows one **to** affix a specific timeframe to several of the quatrains, which then can be aligned to form the framework for the body of text. It should be understood that **the** physics of **Astronomics**, or the study of the stars and the movements of the heavenly bodies, proves that the cyclic movements of each planet is determinable; and this movement can be fixed, well into the future. This is where my physical **calculations** come into play, as I have reviewed the text I have written, to check the planetary

---

instruction or manner," but the use of "order" is most important. The ordering of the quatrains is just one element of order in *The Prophecies*, as line order in the verses is very important, as is word order too. I call this the System of Order.

29   The classic epic tale of Beowulf is comparable, at 3182 lines, and it was written prior to Nostradamus' lifetime (circa 700 – 1000 AD); but, it was not discovered until the 19th Century and not deemed an important literary document until the 20th Century. Another more contemporary comparison would be to *Faust*, by Johan Wolfgang von Goethe, written in the 19th Century and considered a literary classic. Interestingly, Goethe wrote *Faust* in two parts, each poetic German, and took 23 years to complete his masterpiece.

positions in reference to the **corresponding** timeframe. That work has proven the poetic-astrological references do provide the proper planetary placements, **to** determine **the** range of **years** that a planet would be in one position, given the cyclic nature of all planets. In some of the references, where some quatrains give combinations of planetary positions, in specific order of occurrence, the overall effect of that quatrain is to show a period of time where they will all act together. This shows a timeframe, for one quatrain, which will spread over a few **months**. But, in certain parts of the story, when several quatrains will tell of a relatively short period of time, the astronomical placements listed will only cover one or two **weeks** of time. When these timing quatrains are seen to establish a framework, the other quatrains can be connected to this framework by realizing the repeating of key terms in both timing and non-timing quatrains. The timing quatrains will have other clues in them, which will tell **of** something specific that is also found in the linking quatrain. This can be as general as mentioning the name of **the regions** of the world which will be affected at that time; or, it can be listing the specific **countries** in one region which will be affected.

As these general connections link the timing elements with the settings of the story, **the majority of** the quatrains have no timing elements to connect to them. The bulk of the quatrains will be related to one another by linking elements related to the countries, by stating the names of **the towns** in those countries. These connecting links will show where this future will manifest. More importantly affected will be the **cities**, as many more people will reside in the metropolitan areas in this future; but, the cities listed will include the capitals **of all** the countries of **Europe**. Many cities will be clearly **understood** to be those surrounding the Mediterranean Sea, from the Strait **of** Gibraltar, where Europe meets **Africa**, to the islands of Greece.

The continent of Africa will be greatly involved in the futures these European cities will face; as North Africa will be united under the **one** main religious **party**, which has been the predominant religion **of Asia** Minor for a long time. Africa and Asia Minor will become influenced **by the** major countries of Europe, when the **changing** times bring new importance to the resources **of** those lands. This will lead to European nations taking dominion over **the** people and countries in both these **regions** of the world. It will not be like the actions of the past Crusades, **which** found Europeans forcing themselves upon Arab lands; but, to those people of the Moon this renewed presence will find again **itself approached** by dominating outsiders. With Europeans **there** in Muslim lands, in numbers **more** than ever before, taking **part** in the government **of** Arab people, this interference will cause **all** the people in **these** Muslim lands to unite against the Europeans. This will have them spreading into the **climates** of Europe, just as the Europeans have spread into theirs.

While the African and Asian climates have long been the regions under the religion of Islam, the whole of this area has been **composed of** many different kingdoms. Those kingdoms have long been hostile towards each other, with times when **one** country has dominated the others, bringing them under one empire. The **natural** nation for an Arab empire to be formed, under an Islamic banner, would be the land of Arabia. This is where Mecca, the Muslim's most holy city, is located; but, this nation of Arabia has a long reputation of peaceful neutrality. However, in this future one Muslim nation will rise to unify all of the Muslim nations; and, it will be influenced by a **faction** of Islam that will not be peace loving.

This faction of Muslims **will answer** the call for a renewed Arab power, in response to what will be seen by them as a renewal of the Christian Crusades. They will blame the religion of Christianity as the force which coerced Europeans to dominate its peoples. For this faction to rise up and unite the others, it will require **someone** of great leadership abilities **who** will inspire all Muslims, of all factions, to follow his lead. As many Muslims are very devout believers in the rule of peace, this leader **would have** to be seen as a **good** Muslim and follower of Allah. He will have to show a valid **need** for unity, from which retribution against the enemies of Islam will be administered. Above all, he will have to make an example **of himself**, as able **to snuff** (out) mighty foes, as the Europeans will be. This man will show he has these qualities; and he will show how **there** is a way to defeat the oppressors, by the **meter** of timing one's actions. This will mean one has **to be** able to know what the opponent will do, before they do it. This cannot be a guess, based on how one would possibly act; but, it will have to come from knowledge, from **having fluent** understanding of the opponent's nature and patterns of behavior. This ability to think **like** the enemy will be put to use, testing the enemy in small quantities first, to measure their response; but, this will advance to sending spies into the enemy's camp, to gather **the intelligence** needed. This will be how they will know how the enemy plans its actions. This means sending one **of** one's own people to join with **the** enemy,

189

to make perfect **sense** of the enemy's strengths and strategies. This leader will be able to gain all of this knowledge, such that when he **is** ready to lead the Muslims to war, they will prove to be most **difficult** to defeat.

This difficulty is detailed **inside** the work entitled *The Prophecies*; and, there are many verses which clearly identify this Islamic element. The quatrains also fully explain those troubling times that will come and lead to this strategy of stealth. I briefly mentioned this in **the letter** prefacing **that** work of mine, when I spoke of the people who are guided by the Moon. The past has already seen a rise to empirical power by **these** people of the East. This empire has menaced the people of Eastern Europe and the ships on the seas for **years**. However, the peak of that strength has already passed, and in time, well after the Arab power **passes** into the pages of history, they will **have** another empire which will rise and sweep into Europe. In that letter that prefaces *The Prophecies*, I have **dedicated** most of the text to explaining the purpose of true Prophecy, the end result of mankind's actions and how that end can be avoided by change. In that letter I gave those elements more importance than attempting to details the contents of the quatrains. Some people have experienced difficulty in understanding my addresses **to my son**, who was just an infant then. Presently, he is still just a small child, too young to read. Knowing my addresses to **Caesar** must be seen as allegorical, the instructions given were intended to be understood in the future. Caesar will carry the name of **Nostradamus** into the future, but the contents of that letter will have no significant new meaning during my son's lifetime. The symbolism of addressing my offspring will be felt at a more distant future time, when the one understanding the contents will feel as if a reincarnation of my son. The personal aspect that **I've** included in this letter will be realized when this one has **sufficiently** grasped the systems used in writing, allowing for understanding. Only then will it be **declared** by **someone** that there are main **points** of my work which have gone **without** proper notice. This person will realize the significant differences between **prediction** and Prophecy.

And, with that realization that prediction is not what has been produced in *The Prophecies*, as defined as being by the arts of calculation, it will be clear that accuracy comes **because** of a much higher power. This higher power is **oh** so much greater than any human could duplicate, as it is sourced from Jesus Christ, the Son of God. And, while the story is of mankind's future difficulties, the purpose is **very humanistic**, because it is designed to save mankind. Christ, as the **King**

of all Christians, cares for them deeply; but, He also cares for all souls, of all mankind, and all souls will then be in grave danger. For this reason, He has left His throne, **there** in Heaven, to come here to add **more** to the Prophecy that He has already imparted, in *The Revelation of John*. John's **part** in the telling of this future is just as accurate as those *of The Prophecies*; and, both will prove to be completely infallible, should Christ's warnings not be heeded. However, the version Christ told in **the quatrains** are on a more understandable level than are the **prophetic** visions of John. Both versions **are** clearly making the point the future will be **so dangerous** for mankind that it must change. This danger has found John using obviously harsh language to describe the punishments which will come; but, John wrote in metaphorical terms, as do I. It is **that** extreme danger which makes *The Prophecies* **the one** people will most easily be able to understand; although, **neither** will clearly be **known** as documents able **to give** specific details, **nor** make this future **less** avoidable. This condition will last until the time that understanding *The Prophecies* comes. Before that time, there will be **any** number of attempts **to interpret** both *The Revelation* and *The Prophecies*, with no one being able to correctly tell when this future will be. This inability will **nevertheless** keep many people pondering both documents, for a long time, **hoping** that the meaning **of** either prophecy will be concretely found. Christ has commanded us both **to leave** His message **in writing**, without writing or talking further about the true meaning they each contain. In **the** 1500 **years** which have passed since Christ told His Prophecy to John, so too will many years pass until the message of *The Prophecies* will become clear. This time will pass because the people who will try to find the answers will misinterpret the quatrains, especially in the quatrains where it appears a specific year is stated. They will also misread some of the indications made for **towns**, and look for evidence in history which matches that location. Many of the quatrains will appear to match a historical event, but the **cities** listed will confound that history.[30] Many of the **regions** the quatrains mention will be places **where** the distant past history appears to be the only place in time when any important event ever happened **there**. There will be **more** of these quatrains, which will seem impossible to ever become fulfilled, than will be the **part** which the interpreters will promoted as having been solved. The ones which these people will state **will have happened** as predicted will be a small fraction of the whole; and, this will do nothing to promote the infallibility

---

30   This is a repeating of the Letter of Preface, where Nostradamus also wrote that the times and places will be tricky to understand properly.

of true Prophecy. Interpretations of this nature will continue, with the **same** conclusions drawn, until there will come a change **of** stability in France. This will occur in **the year 1585**.[31] At this point, efforts to interpret my work will be set aside, until France has worked out its leadership woes. This time without focus will be good, as the world will need more time **to** develop, before the first event prophesized will occur. The most important character, who will play an important role in setting this future course, will not even be conceived before **the year 1606**.[32] That date will be the earliest time for **commencing** to make sense of the quatrains. In fact, it will be a long time between prophesized events, **from** the first recorded historical happening, until **the times** of the second historical event. Natural changes do not occur instantly; and, *The Prophecies* tells of a slowly evolved natural change in mankind. It would be best if those interpreters of the **present** period did not waste any time at all, as they stand no chance of making sense of my book. People will think *The Prophecies* are of the times present, because my yearly almanacs have been that way; but, *The Prophecies* will not begin to be recognizable anytime soon. As for my latest almanac, **which is** now available, it was sent to the publisher on **the 14th of March** in **1557**. That manuscript contains this year's predictions. The people should look there for predictions of the present times.[33]

I make mention **of** these dates as **this** is an area in *The Prophecies* where many people will mistake what I have written, in regard to dates. In **that** specific date of 14 March, 1557, I have written the precise date I posted my manuscript to the publisher. I have written this date **by** what is considered to be standard dating

---

31   Henry II died in a jousting accident in the following year, 1559. The changes of leadership led to France entering a period of leadership struggles, particularly in 1585. This lasted until 1589 and is referred to the War of the Three Henrys.

32   Captain John Smith first founded the Jamestown Colony for the British on December 20, 1606. This was the conception of the United States of America, which would be born on July 4, 1776.

33   In the Letter of Preface, Nostradamus wrote the numbers, "*3797*," which I interpreted as meaning a pattern for Nostradamus' publication pattern. This date, showing the month of March, would represent a number 1, as spring begins in March. The number 3 would be May, with 7 being September and 9 being November. It would mean that Nostradamus began preparing the 1558 Almanac in January (month 11). This makes this date here have that meaning, as the date at the end of this letter to Henry is June 27, 1558.

rules; but, in *The Prophecies* it often appears as if I have forgotten **the course** in proper dating, from my days writing theses. In the quatrains which show a listing **of the times** to come, I do not write numerical figures. Especially in the listing of years, it appears that I have shown these **by** spelling out **all** of the numbers, rather than simply writing the figures. In some of the more formal **regions** of written communication, spelling out numbers is the preferred style; but, it is not **the one** style most people prefer. In all of the incidences where I have written dates in this manner, the reader **will know** a timeframe for when the information surrounding the date is **to happen**. While this is certainly so, one needs to realize that **all** of the spelled out words in a date, which make it appear **as it were** meant to be a number, are not so. This is **particularly** the case where one word is used **like** a number, when **it is** used in that normal context and **written** out completely. I warn you now that you will **not have** the result expected, if you do not recognize the full scope of meaning for the words which have been carefully chosen for use. Those words used to denote dates are **mixing** in some numbers with some words, which appear like numbers. This means an obviously clear date will not actually be so clear, as the date could be **anything** which can be signified by the words of numbers.[34] Still, all of the words have valuable meaning towards determining a specific date, as nothing **of** the quatrains is **superfluous**. Every word has meaning and purpose. To get a firm grasp on **how much** these dates are important to understand, since they form the framework of the story line, knowing **that** nothing is superfluous will make one address all of the possibilities which exist, relative to timing. Remember my allusions to the Oracle of Delphi, where **the one** who asked for truth was only given the truth. While this truth was certainly not superfluous, many did not realize the full meaning of what was **said**, until after the predicted even had occurred, infallibly.

Let me paraphrase from the philosopher-theologian Thomas Aquinas, who delved into the mysteries of truth. He found that this time **now** is a time that is **in the course of** revealing the **future**, but this future **is not determined** to occur and not determined not to occur **entirely** as **the truth**. This means that although the future is known by God, it is not entirely fixed. This is why *The Prophecies* was written, so that man can determine what will be the truth.

---

34   One simple example is how the number of years is determined. One number is listed three different ways, with three different meaning, in three separate quatrains. Ponder how different these can be: forty-five years; forty & five years; and, forty five years.

It is amazing how false hopes for a predicted future can still end up being **quite** prophetic, with a twist of words being reconsidered and found completely **true**. The whole of mankind's future has been seen by God, our **Sire**, the Father and Originator of all humanity; and He has sent Christ to give us the truth we need. I have been chosen to carry **that** truth to mankind, **for** mankind will be in need of finding it. For me, it has been **my natural** inclination to honor Christ's spirit and to trust my **instinct**, such that I feel the truth. By instinct, I am talking of inward stirrings, **which** is when I talk honestly to **myself**, to make decisions over issues that I ponder. It is my intuitive self that tells me the truth that I need to know; but, the self is in reality the soul, which is allied **with** the presence of a higher mind. I also have **been given** a talent, passed down to me **by my ancestors**, to whom I was **born**. Their souls have been with me all my life, **weaning** me from an early age to seek the truth by believing in my abilities **to foresee**, through several mystical arts.

Still, it is important to understand that my ability **to foresee** has not been perfect, requiring me to constantly be **adjusting** my mind's eye, along with my calculations, to meet the realities which come. I have developed the ability to make adjustments well, **according** to the judgments which acclaim the accuracy in my predictions. This accuracy comes because I listen and hear **the one** that speaks to me from within. This **natural instinct** has been most easily drawn out **with** my knowledge of the art of astrology, and the meditative state I enter once I begin to view the aspects. Since **my** talents in astrology have been developed over a **long** period of time, the **calculations** I perform have become natural to me, requiring less thought. Reading the planets has become automatic, such that when I see the physical aspects of the planets my intelligent mind has memorized the meaning associated with those aspects. This ease of thought then allows me to become **united** with my inner voice.

This process has allowed me to easily bring forth an **emptying** of **the soul**, and the knowledge it holds. This means that what is known within, which is vastly more than ever possible to be consciously realized, can come out. This inner voice, which speaks through the soul, is **the spirit** that watches over us; and this spirit is connected to God and all that He knows. Allowing oneself to listen to this spirit is what gives man his spiritual essence as well.

The spirit is the source of **the courage** required **of** each and **every** one of us, to face a world of uncertainties; and, when we let this voice lead our outer actions, it works silently inwardly to **cure** the body and keep it well. This spirit is also our source of **concern**, or conscience, which speaks to us when we do wrong; and, it tells us the right way to act. We always hear this voice before we make wrong decisions, just as we do afterwards. These directions come to us as the spirit is concerned for us and the ultimate safety and security of our souls.

When we find that we **quarrel** with ourselves and others, and when we have difficulty **with rest**, this is because we do not have peace of mind. At those times this spirit is reminding us of our failures and directing us to take the necessary actions of atonement. However, we too often resent this frankness in ourselves. Our **quietness** or stillness of mind, when we can find calm in silence, comes when we are at peace with our actions and when we have found trust in our inner self. We have to be confident that this is **of the spirit** of God, and it will not lead us astray.[35]

The whole of *The Prophecies* has been **granted** to all of mankind, which means we are given this assistance as a gift from God. As such, this gift is the truth of God, through His Son Jesus Christ; but, it is not yet close to being recognized at truth, and will not be for a significant period of time. When that time comes, it will require that one connect to the spirit of God, for complete understanding. This is because the truth of God often comes to us as an **omen** for us to recognize. An omen will speak to us as signs and symbols, which are not always easily understood. This is why so many have not been able to make sense of the words contained in *The Prophecies*. Returning to the comparison to the Greek mythological gods, Apollo was the giver of truth; but, Apollo did not speak directly to mankind. To impart his truth, an oracle was needed, or priestess through whom Apollo would speak. The Oracle at Delphi[36] was **the one** temple where a **party**, who sought an answer sure to be the truth, could make an offering to the priestess of Apollo to get the answer. The priestess sat on a **tripod of copper**, suspended over the opening to Delphi, amid the fumes which came from that

---

35   This series of statements is parallel to the Letter of Preface, where Nostradamus wrote of the whispers of the good angels that guide us.

36   Zeus ordered two eagles to fly in opposite direction, east and west, and find the center of the earth. That center was Delphi, as an opening which led to the center of the earth. Originally, it was a shrine to Gaea, the Earth Mother, and her oracles were named sibyls, who also gave forth the truth. Apollo replaced Gaea later.

opening.[37] This would connect the priestess to Apollo; and, she would go into a trance, before stating the truth that was known. However, the truth was often presented in a way that was not fully understood, until after that truth had been realized. This then compares me to the tripod of copper, with Jesus Christ the giver of truth, and *The Prophecies* being the Oracle of Christ.

Although these are the correct comparisons that could be made, the comparison has more often made me the Oracle instead. This ancient situation has seemingly been transferred to me, such that I am seen as an Oracle, readily available to all for a simple offering. Some people hear my name and instantly think that; and there **are many** instances I am reminded of, where I was tested on my psychic abilities.[38] Some of them, **who** know of my reputation, see **me charged with** special predictive abilities; as if I was seated on this tripod of copper and connected to Apollo at all times. As I have explained how I unite the intuitive spirit with my objective skills to find accuracy, many have seen **this** accuracy of mine as a trait **that is** indicative of being an Oracle or a prophet. Either of these monikers **is** a title that means **so much**, they should never be used lightly; but, neither aptly applies **to me**, at this point in time. As far as my yearly predictions are concerned, I am not a prophet. There was no direct contact with God or Christ when I calculated accurately in the past; and, the title should not be bestowed loosely, as to imply that anyone can become truly prophetic alone.[39] Although the accuracy makes it seem **like** it comes easy to me, as seen in **this** ability with my almanacs, **that** is **not** the case. Those have been prepared by considerable work, at some length; and, the accuracy **in** my work **is** not from **anything** that cannot also be done by others, with the same talents with astrology. The source of every prophetic word comes from the grace of **God alone**; because only God is **eternal** and possessing knowledge of all times: past, present and future. It is God **who is** the **examiner of** all humanity; and, it is He who chooses who will become His prophets. In His watching all that we do, He knows precisely **the humans**

---

37 When Nostradamus wrote "tripod of copper," many have translated the metal to brass, taking them away from the true meaning, found in Greek mythology. Further, they have used this single reference to make it appear that Nostradamus had a boiling pot on a brass tripod, as though he was using witchcraft to see the future in the mist.

38 There is the famous lore of Nostradamus and the white pig, black pig test. Check that out online.

39 This series of statements is a reference to the Letter of Preface, where Nostradamus made it clear that he did not deserve the title of prophet.

who are worthy and capable of being encountered. As I stated earlier, when I stated He saw a good heart and frank courage in me, God looks for those with **courage**. The ability to not fear God's presence is important; and, those with this kind of courage are **pious** or religious and believers of God. God is **just**, or fair in His views of mankind, and He also looks for this same quality in humans.

While God is just, above all God is **merciful** and forgiving. The proof of that mercy was the promised Messiah being sent to mankind, to forgive us all of our sins. The purpose of that incarnation was to teach us to be forgiving also. God looks for those who likewise show mercy to his or her fellow man or woman. This is the one trait **in** human beings which **is** most valuable; and, it is **the true judge** one's character, showing how one cares for one's own soul. The true judgment of how successfully one lives a life on earth is shown by the return of that soul to Heaven. This is **to whom** the greatest mercy is received. Often **I pray** for the spiritual guidance I need; and, I ask God to show me the way to give mercy and forgiveness to others. I pray **that it** will bring strength from within **myself**, as I want to always remember to judge others as I would want them to judge me. My **wish** is that I will always be able **to defend** my soul **from** the temptations an earthly existence will bring. Just as Christ faced the temptations to become self-serving, to spare himself from the **false accusations** that were rendered against Him, leading to His crucifixion, we all have our own cross to bear to find salvation. In the normal lives **of** every human being, we are challenged by encountering **the spiteful** ones of humanity, who are filled with hate and maliciousness. These are the people **who** are **wishing** to cause us to lose our souls. They do this by acting unjustly, to see if we will **also** respond unjustly. For those who forgive in the face of anger, they are forever saved; but, evil will know the source of our strength, and will cause people to **slanderously** attack **the one** who represents to Christians the model of passivity. There will be those who will come to you, sire, **to inquire** about how you will treat my book which no one has been able to understand. It is **for** you to decide, as the merciful ruler you are, **who** will be kept clear of disturbing the document which will show the **cause** of **all** the evil that will threaten the world. The time will come when **your** reign over France and your life on earth will cease. You are the sum of the **ancient** blood of Jesus Christ, whose **offspring** have been blessed to become the **Kings of France**; but, your line will also eventually come to an end. This royal blood will be undone by a future sect of slanderous people who will come. What will have **had** acted from a purity of soul will become ill from this slander. The people will be led to believe they can be **cured** of this sickness by removing the royal figures and replacing **them** with people **of** common blood. The last true bloodline King of France will be **overwhelmed** by the people, spurred on by those who slanderously despise all connections to Jesus Christ.

Still, this will not be a phenomenon that will only be found in France. It is important to know that this philosophical thought will also be the cause of the fall **of the** royal houses in **other nations**. The belief they will spread, that they will have somehow **cured** a deadly disease, will actually be the spreading **of** venom, or poison, which comes from **the bite of the** viper or adder. I use **snakes** as an analogy, because it was a snake which tempted Eve in the original sin. Just as that biblical snake represents Satan, those snakes will be his agents, influenced by his evil will. Those snakes will gain control of **the others**, or the common masses, which will be **had**, or under their control. This control will come to them by convincing the masses they **had** a **certain instinct**, or an inherent aptitude, as leaders for and of the people. They will tell **of** their abilities of mind and intelligence and that they are gifted in **the art** of **divination**. This gift will not be from God, the divine; but, they will promote themselves as divine, because of such intellectual prowess.

As important as it is to know **of** how variously the **others** under their control will be treated, each **case** shows a different effect **which would be** too **long** to state **here in** this document. Just know that there will be a prior attempt at establishing this reign of the common man, **to rehearse** the shortcomings of common rule, before France falls to the same plot.[40]

This decision to not relate the details of all of these failures **notwithstanding**, they will come; and, those people promoting mind over religion and royal lineages will bring great suffering to the masses, greater than existed before. They will be led by **those** of the sects, who have served those institutions up till now, **to which** they will have known the benefits of wealth and power. This knowledge will have them ponder a world where such common souls can achieve this position of excellence for themselves; but, this will lead to a lust for material things, creating **the malignancy of** purpose that will spread throughout all of the world's

---

40   The last part of this section repeats the statement in the Letter of Preface that there would come the advent of the common man.

populations. Such material goals will destroy **the spirit**, as it will be virulent to the soul's connection to God. Once this **malignant** state has gone untreated for a significant period of time, it will lead to the death of mankind. Treatment comes from a dedication to Christ, and while wealth can afford many wondrous things to those in need, without a strong Church or the blood of Christ leading the people, it **will not be understood** a malignancy exists until it is too late. It will be understood **by the course of time**, when their world will begin to completely break apart; and, they will realize man is not divine after all, when he is unable to save himself. This course of time will not begin to show the signs of illness until well **after** all of **the earth-born** offspring of **mine** have reached their **extinction**. This means when all my children have died, and their children's children. My bloodline will not last to see the beginning of this malignant growth.[41] However, **more** importantly, my spirit **will** last this course of time, such that when the time of need will **be**, to inject the antivenin into the veins of humanity, **my document**, *The Prophecies*, will be there to let the masses know of their malignant state. It will be **that** document and the revelation **in my** book which will make that book become the offspring of my blood. It will be **living** in my name, by the heartbeats of those who heed its call. While **this** life of mine is still here, the life of *The Prophecies* will be **pending** its time of breath. With that time still being **so** far in the future, it will appear my work is barely alive at times; but, I have placed **in my** verses the first **calculations of** those wanton minds, which will come to control **the ages** which will come. Until those verses have become understood, there will be those who will say **I** have **failed** as a prophet. They will point to **where** my language is so seemingly inappropriate chosen, saying **none** will be able to claim any surety of my meaning, without them having completely **corrupted** my text to suit their wild imaginations. Those corruptions will be promoted as my words, so that **in the opinion** of interpreters **the meaning** will have finally been gained. Still, this will only be possible for a small percentage **of** the whole, as only **some** of what I have written will be seen as worthy of consideration; but, that will be enough to keep the heartbeat alive, until the time it springs to full life.

---

41 Nostradamus is documented as having 6 children, including Caesar, not counting the two that he lost to the plague, along with his first wife. He had 3 sons and 3 daughters by his second wife. Of these, three entered religious orders and did not marry. The three that did marry did not have any children. The last of them to die lost their life around 1636, with Caesar being one of two that died that year.

(It) **Will please** you **to** know that this continuing life will have been spared by you, **your** highness, causing Christ to also be **pleased**. For having refused to censor the work so many think is threatening, you will receive the greatest honor possible, by sitting on your throne in **that imperial** palace in Heaven, as the true **majesty** that you are. You will have stood by **me**, willing **to forgive** me for not making this explanation perfectly clear to you. Despite the **protesting** of others, who wish to sway you to censor everything until I make the explanations clear, you will have placed the matter **before God** and rendered your unchangeable decree from the heart. You are truly one of greatest models of the Christian spirit that mankind has to offer today; and, Christ sees you as one of **his** true **Saints**, even if this honor will not officially be bestowed upon your name by the Catholic Church. I want to assure you **that I** have **not** made any **claims** against the present Church, to warrant their distrust. I have tried to stay away **from** making any of those quatrains telling of the future Church's corruption easy to understand. There is no need to become a catalyst which will act **to put** the wrong ideas in people's heads. I have not made **anything** about the Catholic Church clearly obvious, as I have made most of my words about the Church the most **indifferent**, or unbiased, of the whole. It can be told that I have put nothing derogatory about today's conditions, as seen **by** the verbiage **written in** *The Prophecies*, particularly in the preface. You will find **there** I **offered** strong evidence of Christ as the author, making *The Prophecies* an **epistle**, just as those of the Apostles in the New Testament. However, I did also present that the future would become diametrically opposite from the way things are today, **which** clearly stated the Church **is** one element that will change. Those who will come in the future, and turn **against the** canons of the **true Catholic** Church, are a very long time away. The Church today is still very strongly a center for **faith** in Christ for the people, and I will not concern them with those matters that will take place, naturally, at a distant time. I have been **conferring** with certain members of the Church about **the** mechanics of future **calculations**, by plotting the planetary movements. They believe my work is a product of the physics of **Astronomics** and therefore about the foreseeable future. Since they believe everything in *The Prophecies* is **according to** the limits of my lifetime, and based solely on **my knowledge** of astrology, then when I have passed on the Church will no longer worry about how my words may affect their positions of influence.

But, in regard to that change which will come to the Church, know now that it will be **the** greatest **insult of the** ages. This insult will be to Christ and to all of humanity; and, it will be greater than any other in all of the **times** of man. It will be **oh** so insulting that it makes me moan with sorrow at how the Church, which was founded by those who had personally learned from the **most serene** Christ the **King** himself, could tarnish His image so loosely. Still, Jesus has **required** me to make **that** portion of the story of **such** betrayal **secret**, until the time for exposure has come. The **events** detailed in those connecting quatrains will **not be** made **obvious**, or evident, to those of the Church who will take time to decipher *The Prophecies*. Christ has had me write **that** section **by** using some of the more **enigmatic** verbiage. The interpreters will read those lines as if they were written in a standard **sentence** structure. Those who will read those verses, **not having** the guidance of Christ's Angels, will not know **that** sentence structure is absent from *The Prophecies*. Each word must first be read **alone**, with the full scope of its **meaning** gained, realizing that each word can represent its own sentence. This style of reading is quite **unique**, as it speaks in concepts based on the most primal form of language. While it is written in a truly simplistic style, it yields such an amazing complexity that it goes well beyond the highest levels of human **intelligence**.[42] It will be impossible to decipher **without** understanding this method for reading **it**. For one **to have** misread these instructions, and to try to turn the words into sentence structure, the result could be **anything**. Those who will try to **put** four lines of poetic words into the form **of** one or two sentences will only come up with vague interpretations, leading many to see my work as **ambiguous**. That is certainly not the case, as everything in the book is **neither** ambiguous nor vague, as there is intention and purpose for all of the words that it contains. Not only every word has purpose, but every letter and mark penned as well. I admit many words are **amphibologic**al, such that this degree of ambiguity will leave most scratching their heads; but, this is because they have been coined by Jesus Christ, following the rules of roots, prefixes and endings.[43] No words have been misspelled, as Christ understands prayers in all languages of mankind. Additionally, there are so many words written in *The Prophecies* which have multiple definitions, based on the context, with many noun usages being different from the verb usages. All possibilities have meaning with this style. The

---

42   In the study of problem solving, this can actually fall under the category of "over-thinking" a solution, when the answer is more obvious than we first imagined.

43   This is the System of Manufactured Words. All of these words are rooted only in either French or Latin, with French being a derivative language of Latin.

use of standard sentence structure eliminates or limits this flexibility for double meaning. In many cases, one line of text can be read properly a multiple of ways, with each way adding depth of meaning to the words used. This means one has to realize everything has purpose and is delivered to the reader only after the careful **calculation** of Jesus Christ.[44]

In reference to this careful calculation, I have made several statements to this effect; **but**, until people begin to understand these instructions, people would **rather** scrutinize them **under** the framework of rules that best apply to standard prose. This will **obnubilate**, or confuse even further the **obscurity** that lies in the non-prose format. Failure to recognize this instruction will make them produce wild guesses about the shapes they will see in the fog, **by** turning many statements of great depth into **one** sentence which may or may not be partially intended. The **natural** way people read requires an **infusion** of all of the words of a sentence, so the words are blended and modified in the mind, to grasp the central point the sentence appears to make. That modification is where their errors begin, as **approaching** *The Prophecies* from a perspective that the objective is **to** turn a series of words and punctuation into something understandable, so that they fit **the** structure of a grammatically correct **sentence**, is the wrong approach. The words **of one** line in one quatrain can produce one complete standard sentence **from** each word written, depending on the type of word. One word can even produce multiple sentences, based on its full scope of that word's definition and use. The use of a historical name could require several sentences, to detail the significance of that name's history as why that name was written. When one sees *The Prophecies* has nearly **one thousand** quatrains, thus almost four thousand lines, consisting of well over 15,000 words, this method of turning the quatrains into sentences misses almost 90% of what was stated; and, that is if everything guessed to be a sentence is guessing correctly.[45] It is so important

---

44   This is a reference to the Letter of Preface, where Nostradamus stated that he did not write *The Prophecies* in prose, and that it was written with a minimum of verbiage.

45   Using just a minimum of 4 words per line, or 16 words per quatrains, where a "word" is defined as containing more than 4 letters (I'm sure the number is higher), then this would be 15,168 words, for 948 quatrains. If that turned into that many sentences, verses the 2 sentences per quatrain (that is probably a high estimate), then that would be 1,896 sentences. If all 1,896 were corrected interpreted (impossible), they still would have missed the depth of 13,272 sentences. That is a percentage of 87.5% missed (a low estimate).

to realize that an external clue to understanding how to approach what I have written is the first thing read. This is the title, which clearly states *The Prophecies*. The capitalized article, "*The*," places emphasis on the next word, which is also capitalized, "*Prophecies*." This states that the book contains THE divinely inspired PROPHECIES, which can only mean they are from Jesus Christ. I have never professed to be able to produce prophecy; but, there are many who have produced prophecy in the Bible. Importantly, there are **two**, where many have seen parallels in their separate prophecies; and, these are the books of *Daniel* and *The Revelation of John*. One is in the Old Testament and one is in the New Testament; but, both **Prophecies** tell of similar things to come, using similar terminology. Drawing this connection from the title of my book would be the first correct step towards interpreting it properly; as the basic realization of divinity would cease all reason for blending the words into sentences which have not been written. *The Prophecies* is the third and final telling of the story of mankind's final dangers, **which** means it is not a collection of random visions of the future. Both the other two Prophecies did not have this format; and, neither did mine originally. *The Prophecies* must be reorganized first. When this is done, my book tells a story of the future to come, which has **been** known **since** well before Daniel. In fact, it goes back to **the** time **of** man's **creation**, before Adam and Eve were cast out of Heaven into **the world**. The three Prophecies are all **adjoined** to one another, in style of symbolism and intended confusion; but, when they are viewed together, some parts of one will be seen to be adding more clarity to the whole of the others. All will require the use of **the** mind's abilities for **calculation**, by these instructions I have given, rather than a dependence on literal simplicity for understanding. In the holy **Chronicle** of mankind's time on earth, whenever mankind veered to the ways of evil, through the **Punic** and faithless times when mankind has become lost, God has spoken to mankind. In the Bible's Book **of Joel**, 2:28, he wrote of how God spoke to mankind, particularly when he wrote of God saying, "I **poured out my spirit upon all flesh**." This means God is always with us, as the spirit within the body. He then wrote, literally, "**to speak abundantly to your sons**," which means God, always with us, has abundant ways to speak to us, without appearing before us. But, when God speaks abundantly through "your sons," this is the spirit of prophecy, as divine utterances. We all have this capacity, should we seek God and live as I have previously stated. Then, and equally important, Joel included that God also spoke through, "**your daughters**." This means that not only men have the

203

capability to become prophets, but women do as well. All of mankind has this ability to have God speak through us. The standard translation of this stanza is: "And it shall come to pass afterward, that I will pour out my spirit upon all flesh; and your sons and daughters shall prophesy, your old men shall dream dreams, your young men shall see visions." This is the way of true prophecy; and, it is the way that Christ has spoken abundantly to me.

EXPLAINING THE ROLE THE BIBLE PLAYS IN UNDERSTANDING

From those Biblical records of God and Christ speaking to mankind, a great deal of time will be **passing** before anyone will understand that this line of communication has never ceased. *The Prophecies* will be seen as another event in this history of prophetic exchanges from Heaven. Mankind has not moved **beyond** the need for this form of communication, having had the **benefit** of this guidance for as **far** back as man's history goes. However, mankind will lose confidence that this assistance can still be provided; and, it will increasingly turn a deaf ear to this potential, **until** it has come **to** the point of self-extinction. These communications of prophecy are what give mankind **the chance** it needs for survival; especially when mankind has taken the chance to believe it no longer needs God's advice. The advice of *The Prophecies*, just as is the advice of all of the prophetic language of the Bible, **which** is designed to teach mankind how to remain reverent to God, **will be** seen as nothing more than partially completed prophecy. This will certainly be the case **at the commencement of** the next millennium, which is now another 443 years away. At that time, mankind will have reached **the seventh millennium** since its creation, with 5,000 years of history before the birth of Christ. I know that this time is correct, as it has been **deeply calculated** for me, in my encounters with Jesus. I have not only been allowed to see the times of the future, which is the focus of *The Prophecies*, but **all** of the times of man. By seeing how **that** calculation affected the past, it has enhanced **my** ability to confirm the exactness of the future's **calculation**. All of those calculations have been done by the laws of **astronomic** movements. My calculations, again, are merely to check the mathematics and timing projections; but, the source comes from one **other**, who has **knowledge** of all things and all times. Christ has shown me the history of man; and, this history is the same **one as** has been recorded in all of the holy documents of the three religions which serve the one God: The Christian Bible's Old Testament, the Jewish Torah and the Muslim Koran. While these holy books tell the same histories, **few** agree on the exact times and dates of their occurrences. My being allowed to view this sacred history of mankind was so I would be able **to extend** this knowledge to those seeking to justify these disputes. I will show **where the** errors lie, which become the sources of these **contrary** opinions that exist today. In regard to this error, there is little argument about the time which has passed since the days **of Jesus Christ**; and, especially since the founding **of his church** in Rome. The history of the Catholic Church has been maintained, with it feeling it necessary to take on the **undertaking** of reconciling these differences. They have put **more** effort into tying all of the fragments of times listed in the Bible together than anyone. The official timelines of all of the churches have **strong** connections to the same Patriarchs, starting **from** Adam and then listing all who were **to bud** on the branches of this Tree of Man. On **the whole**, there is no question about the order **in** the list of names which appear on that tree. This is **to be** understood, as this order has been **composed** for them by the books of the Bible. Still, much of the years that have been **calculated** have been modified to fit the way years were counted **in** those **days** of old. This has created many **hours** of debate among the scholars, with some **of** one opinion and some of another. To solve this stalemate, there have been times when a vote has been taken and the majority has been given the right to decide which **choice** of time was used. Obviously, this makes timelines of this nature **quite disposed** to making mistakes, which results in the differences of opinions. Christ has seen that **the more** this difference remains, the more it has an effect on the differing churches being able to see each other as **equally** connected to the same source. Christ sees **that it** is necessary to bind all the faiths equally together. For this reason, Christ showed the correct timeline to me; and, I place **myself at** your service, to show you what has **been** the history of mankind. It is not to be found in *The Prophecies*, but your request for a letter of explanation has made it **possible** for me to let it be known now.

This has been made possible to me **because** in the future **the distance** of man's origin will be argued, relative to the measurement **of time** mankind has been on earth. The future's knowledge will be **of** the opinion that man has existed for a greater number of years than the Bible alludes to. The Bible tells of **our prime** ancestors or those people that make up the principal history of three of the world's great religions. The history of all of life on earth, **which** does nothing to alter what **we had** been led to believe in the Bible's records, **surpasses** all the previous timelines which have been constructed. It is just a matter of time before evidence surfaces which proves these timelines **are** gross miscalculations of man's time on earth. It will be **such** a difference that some will begin to doubt the records of the Bible, and distrust it is indeed a book of truth. I have seen these times for **myself**, through the eye of God; and, what I will recount will be for the purpose of **reviving** any lost faith in the Bible. It must be understood that the Bible, as the Word of God, is completely the truth; and, when its words are put **under** the same scrutiny which the words of *The Prophecies* will have to be viewed, one will find **the correction** that will be made in the future's observation of man's timeline will do nothing to disprove the truth **of** the Bible. This scrutiny will make these words give strength **to the** meanings that come from the words of the Bible, as much **more** detail will be realized. This view of what was written will make faith in the truth of the Bible secure and **sound**; and, that will give reason for how one should be casting **judgment** on why the Bible does not focus on every aspect of life on earth. In **that** judgment, one has to begin with the book of *Genesis*, and its view of the creation of the earth, and when man first began his history on earth. We know that **the first man** to exist was **Adam**, who was created from matter, by God. We also know that Adam **was** dead **before Noah** was born, due to the Biblical chronology of when the Patriarchs begat the lineage that led to Noah. We can calculate this because of the years listed and the Bible stating that Adam lived 930 years. In reality, Adam lived in the **environ** of earth for a total of **one thousand two hundred forty-two years**; but, he was immortal before being cast out of the Garden of Eden, with Eve. The Bible does **not** state how long Adam live as an immortal; nor does it state how long Adam was created, before God created Eve; nor does it state how long Adam and Eve enjoyed the Garden of Eden, before the original sin. The Biblical statements are simply **calculating** the years of mortality, from the time Adam had to face his eventual end, to the time his end did come. Neither Adam nor Eve were born, as God created them both; so, the number stated in the Bible is from Adam's "birth" as a mortal creature, one which needed to procreate to maintain his new species. In the first five verses of Genesis, **the** Bible states (5:1) that man was created by God, in His likeness. Then (5:2) man is made into male and female, when the name Adam originated. Then (5:3) we find that 130 years beyond this ability to bear children Adam bore Seth. Then (5:4) we are told Adam lived 800 years beyond the birth of Seth; and, finally (5:5) we learn Adam died at the age of 930. These **times** also do not reflect the total time other creatures lived on earth, simply **by the calculation of** 930 years of Adam's mortal existence. Prior to God making man in His image, God had previously created (1:20) water and air creatures, followed by (1:24) the living creature after his kind, cattle, and creeping things, and beast of the earth after his kind. These existed for a great number of years, before God created man in his image. Also, the separation of the statement that God created man in his image, before the naming of one man Adam, says that time existed between these steps; but, the Bible is not concerned with this time or the creatures which appeared to be men and women, "after his kind." All of this early timing is written in Hebrew, where much of the meaning is lost in translation. The timeline we are having disputes over are generally the ones produced by **the Gentiles**, who have acted similarly as those who have tried to translate *The Prophecies* into one set statement, without realizing the full scope of meaning. This is one example of how the calculations of people, well beyond the fact of time, have been in error, **like** missing an implied statement of time, like Genesis 5:1 makes. Still, there are other places where people have erred in their calculations, and many of the Bible's stated times are **in-laid**, or overlapping one another, making careful understanding of the text a necessity. Without this care, a stated time, like 930 years of Adam, can be misleading, while still being perfectly true. Understanding comes **by** realizing that there is more to these calculations than is **written**. This inability has kept the keepers of the public records, like Marcus Terentius **Varro**,[46] unable to correctly determine the timeline of mankind.

For example, the Catholic Church **will be able** to determine its own history; but, for it **to object** to the account of prior history by other religions, it will need **someone** of its own religion who can substantiate **this** first. The historical record, from which all **calculation** must come, is the Bible; and, this holy book does not contain all of the books other religions have recognized as historically correct. Some of the books **are** seen by the Church as contradicting one another, such that the two main branches of the Churches of Christ see some books as **not to be** recognized as the **true** Word of God. This means any time references found in those books cannot be officially recognized. The most ancient times have been recorded by the Samaritan Pentateuch, which is the oldest known chronology; but, it is one that only takes into account the first five books of the Bible, all attributed to Moses. This is given credence **because** Moses listed **who all** came into the world, from Adam to the time of Moses' last days.

---

46   Varro was a Roman scholar that is estimated to have written over 620 books on a wide range of topics. Caesar appointed him to be the director of Rome's proposed public library. It is assumed that the reference here, by Nostradamus, is because Varro made the first attempt to reconcile the timeline of the Bible, but no record of this remains today.

The Samaritan Pentateuch, however, has **differed from** two other chronologies: the Masoretic and the Septuagint; and, these also claim calculations of Biblical time. The Church needed to officially recognition one historical timeline, which would become **that** chronology for all Christians to recognize as holy. This was the undertaking **of Eusebius**, who has become known as the Father of Church History.[47]

And, even with this official record of man's history being produced, **so** it takes into consideration all of the other timelines, it still causes debate and uncertainty. Many are still confused **by** how to make sense of **this** timeline which Eusebius constructed; so much so that in the future, when better methods of time **calculation** will have been developed, **that** timeline will be totally disregarded. To help ease the argument which will come, **I have** been given knowledge of those arguments **made** available to me by Christ, which has been for the purpose of having an account of biblical history be **assembled** here for you now. Everything I will present is supported **by these** times which have been used in the past constructions of timelines, sourced from the **sacred** texts of the Bible. The words in those **letters** and documents **are** the sole source that is required to get **around** the arguments for other theories, as the biblical texts capture the true time of man on earth. Since Adam and Eve became mortal, **four thousand one hundred seventy three years** then passed, before the birth of Jesus Christ.

There were some problems with the calculation of the years, because the ancient Roman calendar needed to observe an intercalary period every **eight** years, to adjust it to match the earth's rotation with the Sun's movements. An intercalary period was when an additional 22 or 23 days were added during February. However, before 46 BC this practice of rectifying the time was not kept, meaning many **months** of time were lost, due to time not being recorded correctly. Each year **that** passed, before then, had too **few** days to account for full years, such that researchers have argued there has actually been **less** time pass since the

---

47   Eusebius Pamphili of Caesarea (70 miles north of Jerusalem) was a bishop of the Catholic Church (est. 300-340 AD) and is considered to be the Father of Church History. He documented the *Ecclesiastical History*, which was a 20-volume work on the history of Christianity, from Christ until 324 AD. He also wrote *Chronicon*, which was a chronology of world history, which was the cornerstone reference for world history for a very long time. He was influenced by Origen of Alexdrandia (185-254 AD), who had gone to great lengths, doing meticulous translations of the Hebrew and Greek documents which would become the Bible.

creation of man, because the ancient biblical writers were either using lunar years or not correctly calculating solar years.

I can assure you the estimates of less time will not **hold** true upon close inspection, as **this** was not the way ancient man marked time. God created the firmament of stars and the Sun to mark the seasons, and **that** was how **the sacred** authors calculated the years in the **scriptures**. They **would** mark the time by the equinoxes, when the Sun **would** cross the equator in the spring. They had a firm **hold** on how to understand **that** passing of time, although their months were marked by lunar phases. They **would** know precisely when a new year would **be**, and this year would represent a true **Solar** year.

It is true some attempts by man to accurately record time have been wrong; **but**, with **so many** years to be considered, from so long ago, one is left with the **only** way for determining time, which is by the historical record. The times **according** to the life spans of the Patriarchs have been given **to the** authors, by the **sacred** Spirit, just as I was permitted to know by Christ. This makes the times stated in the Bible **Scriptures** completely accurate and true.

Still, **in the opinion** of those who will come in **the** future, they will see **feebleness** in the validity **of** the Scriptures. They will not be able to prove the holiness of the words, nor be able to prove the sanctity of many of the book's authors, or some of the places and events the Bible's stories account. All of this will have long since passed into the oblivion of a time long gone; but, I can attest that **my** eyes have witnessed all of these times, through the eye of God, accompanied by the **spirit** of Christ. What I have seen I have confirmed **in my calculations**, which are based on the precision of **Astronomics**.

Howbeit my ability to calculate in this manner, it is only to confirm what I have seen; and none of my calculations change the importance of our history, as shown in the Bible. The Bible serves the purpose of **reckoning**, or counting **the** number of **years** that have passed in the line of Adam, **since** he became mortal and had to bless God with his children. This lineage begins in Genesis, with **the creation of** both Adam and Eve, who were then cast into **the world** as mortals with immortal souls. As all beginnings have an end, the Bible ends with the Book of *The Revelations*, at which point that line of Adam will have reached its bitter end. This is **as far as** the Bible needs to go, towards producing a timeline. There have long been other creatures of God's kind that resemble man; but, these creatures do not have the same lineage as man. Man is in the image of God, which means he knows of God's existence, talks to God daily and completely believes in the one God. The branch of God's creation which mankind is today comes from **the** new **birth** that took place after the time **of** the Great Flood. This means that **Noah** is mankind's Patriarch. Still, Noah is of the line of Adam; and, there **are** eight total Patriarchs who have **gone** as the ones before Noah. Those men span a period of **one thousand** years, until Noah was born unto Lamech. Then, when Noah was **five hundred** years of age, he too began to sire children. An important number which follows this is **six**, as Noah begat three sons, over this period of **years**, and it took Noah and his three sons six years to build the ark.

God commanded Noah to build the ark, **since** the earth had been filled with giants and there was wickedness all about; and, God had decided to cleanse the earth by flood. The other lines of Adam had lost touch with God, causing **the birth of** many mutations and creatures which mankind feared more than God. God saw that **Noah** remained good and still listened to God's voice; so, God chose Noah to be the father of this new line of mankind. God waited **until** Noah had mature sons, with wives, before telling Noah to build an ark, on land, where **there** was no water. God gave Noah **perfected** instructions for the **framing** and building **of the ark**, and watched as the work was performed. When they were finished, God had them gather the pairs of animals to load on the ark, as it was **coming close to the** time of the beginning of the **universal flood**. This beginning of the flood was when Noah was **passing** the time that marked **six hundred years** of life for him; **so**, it was in this way that God began **the gifts** of prophecy to mankind. Noah had faith God would protect him, his family and cargo, even though it **would be** after forty day and nights of rain that Noah would again see the **solar** rays at day **or** the **lunar** beams at night. When Noah's ark came to rest, exactly **where** the book of *Genesis* says, the earth had been purged of those creatures which were not **from** the blood of the **ten** Patriarchs, from Adam to Noah. It was the **mixtures** of that bloodline that began the repopulation of the earth.

And, it is this bloodline that will be **in** all of those who will last until **the end** of the world. All of humanity who exists now and those who will exist in the future are **of these** survivors of the Great Flood, on the timeline when Noah was **six hundred years** of age. At the time God commanded **Noah** to enter the ark, Noah acted on faith alone; because, at the time Noah **will enter the ark**, there

211

will be seven days before the rains begin to fall. Noah trusted God's voice **for** his preservation, but he also knew that his family was **to be saved**. Only those who did not heed God's warning perished **from the** devastation of the **flood**.

There were others who God also spoke to, just like He spoke to Noah; and, each one who listened to God **was himself** saved from the **flood**, just like Noah was. The Bible is not about all beings that were saved, but about the lineage of man which would eventually bear witness to Jesus Christ. However, the flood was indeed **universal**, as the water covered all of the land, **over** all of **the earth**; but, there were others who were likewise spared, for the same reasons of goodness.

This universal flood **will last** for **one** complete **year**, especially at the lower elevations. The ark carrying Noah came to rest on Mount Ararat, after seven months; but, the peaks of this mountain range were not above water until another ten months had passed. Noah released a dove three times, to see if the land was dry. The first time it returned because it had no place to land; and, the second time it returned with an olive branch to indicate the treetops were no longer under water. On the third release of the dove it did not return, indicating the earth was dry. This period of drying lasted **two months**, after which point Noah and his crew and cargo left the ark.

And this story in the Bible, of Noah and the ark, is symbolic of what will come again, **since** it has been foretold that **the end of the** world will also find a **flood** ridding the earth of wickedness. But, God will not be the cause of the second Great Flood, as His covenant to mankind is seen in the rainbow. This covenant will last **until** mankind fails to hear God's voice and respond to His wishes; and, this failure has also been repeated in the history of the Bible, following the first flood. Within ten generations, after **the nativity of** ten other men who are branches of the Christ tree, mankind will once again need God to speak to it. On the timeline this takes us to the birth of **Abraham**. All of those men **will pass** the blood of Noah down through **the number** of children they and their children will produce. The number **of** those children will multiply over **the years** of time, until the birth **of** Abraham. That period will cover **two hundred ninety five** years; and, in this time those children will spread around the Near East.

After this seed of **Noah** has been spread, the populations of the world will take root. Those who will have come **from him** will begin to mingle with the other fruit of other survivors. Those children will have come **from** the other survivors who were spared in **the universal** dispersing of mankind that had been, before the time of the **flood**. Of this blood of Noah, some **came** to the land of Ur, to live amongst the people named the Chaldees. This was where **Abraham** was born, with Ur being in the **environ** of the Fertile Crescent. At that time, another **thousand years** on the timeline of man had been passed, beyond the birth of Adam as a mortal man. At the age of seventy-five, Abraham was called by God. He was asked to move from Haran, to the land of Canaan. Before Abraham was called by God to move, **which** is not **to** be found in the Bible, God had already made Abraham His chosen one. By this, I mean that Abraham **was** already of **sovereign** rank in God's eyes, when Abraham lived in the Ur Kasdim. Because Abraham had already proven a worthiness and faithfulness to God, this was why he would be made the father of Israel. Still, by the time of that calling God had already given Abraham a special gift; and, this gift was the gift of understanding the meaning of the planetary placements. This gift made Abraham the first **Astrologer** the earth had ever known. This art was another of God's gifts to mankind, for helping it prophesy the future. With the explanations of the movements being taught to Abraham by God, **according to** the founding principles which He had created, **none** have ever been better at practicing this art, in all the history of mankind. It was **he** who **will invent** the **first** methods of calculation and interpretations for other men to learn. Abraham was the one who taught the people of Mesopotamia, who then inscribed this knowledge into their **documents** of learning, which will be preserved for others to later trace this source. The people who Abraham taught were **Chaldaen**, which is where Abraham lived, before God told him to move to Canaan. The Chaldaens are the people who have since been determined to be the most ancient people ever skilled in this art of astrology. It came to them from Abraham, who learned it from God.

And, with this information, the most difficult periods to retrace have been covered. For the most part, the time **since the nativity of Abraham** has been where chronologists have been in agreement about the times between the children of Abraham, which is the family which would create the nation of Israel. When God told Abraham his seed would inherit Canaan, the Promised Land which would become Israel, Abraham's wife, Sarah, had given no children **unto** Abraham. After he sired a child by a slave girl, Hagar, God told Abraham **of** the coming of a son, by Sarah, who would be named **Isaac**. When Isaac was born,

Abraham was **passing one hundred years** of age, and his wife Sarah was 90. While Noah had produced children at the age of 500, the lifespan of mankind had since become shorter; and, this birth of Isaac was one of the many miracles t God has produced for those who have faith and believe in His powers.

And, as a test of that belief, after Abraham was given Isaac by God, God commanded Abraham to kill Isaac, as a sacrifice to Him. Abraham proved his faith in God; by having Isaac prepared on a sacrificial alter, with the knife raised. God commanded Abraham to stop, as God just wanted this show of true faith. Then, **since Isaac** was not killed, he grew to adulthood and married a woman named Rebekah. Isaac became a wealthy man, as God had blessed him; but, **at the time** Isaac wanted to have children, Rebekah was barren. God again produced a miracle, and Rebekah became pregnant with twins. The first-born **of** Isaac's twin sons was Esau, with **Jacob** a close second, holding Esau's heel. At the time of this birth, Isaac was **sixty years** of age. The first-born male is the owner of the birthright; but, **from the time that** Jacob was born, he was the favored son of Rebekah. Jacob stole his brother's birthright and blessing, due to his mother's prompting, causing Jacob to flee to the land of Haran. There Jacob toke three wives, who bore him many children. God appeared to Jacob and told him that his name was Israel and that he was the father of many nations and kings. God told Jacob that **he will enter in** the land of his father, Canaan, before taking his family into the land of **Egypt**. Jacob did as God commanded, which began their time of captivity and wandering; and, **upon the exit** led by Jacob, **from** Canaan into Egypt, Jacob will have **hence** assumed the name of Israel. He will have **them passing** into Egypt when he is **one hundred thirty years** of age.

And at this age, **since** the land promised to Abraham and Isaac had been left behind, **the entrance** into Egypt meant that the birthright **of Jacob** was lost. Each of the new Israel's sons would labor **in Egypt**; but, **at the time of** Israel's sons selling Joseph into slavery, **the** purchase would send Joseph to the Pharaoh, which would eventually allow them to **exit** Egypt. Form that time **hence** Joseph would introduce **them** (the Israelites) to Moses, who would lead their **passing** out of Egypt. The time between God's renaming of Jacob to Israel, until the Exodus of the Israelites from Egypt, will last **four hundred thirty years**.

Joseph was a prophet of God, who interpreted the Pharaoh's dreams, to bring favor to the Hebrew people; but, **after** a new pharaoh took control, that one chose not to be so benevolent to them. He saw a threat in the Hebrew people building. During this pharaoh's reign, the pharaoh's astrologers **came** and warned of the coming birth of a Hebrew male who would save the Israelites, causing great loss to Egypt. This male was **Moses**, who was raised as an Egyptian, although he was born of Hebrew parents. After Moses grew to adulthood and learned he was Hebrew, he killed an Egyptian for mistreating a Hebrew slave. The news of this murder reached the pharaoh, which meant that Moses had to flee Egypt, to escape the pharaoh's punishment. He went to Sinai, where he spent 40 years as a shepherd. It was there God called Moses, from a burning bush; and, He asked Moses to return to Egypt, to lead the children of Israel to freedom. Moses did as God requested, and with the help of God he performed miracles, to persuade the pharaoh that the Hebrew God's power was absolute, so the pharaoh would release the Israelites from bondage. God led Moses to take the Israelites out of Egypt; and, after 40 years of wandering, the children of Israel were finally returned to the land bordering on Canaan. Moses led the children of Israel back to the edge of the Promised Land, but not into it. God called Moses home to Heaven, leaving Joshua to take the lead. This began a period of time when the Israelites were led by a series of judges. The Hebrew people grew in numbers, and when the children of Israel finally returned to the Promised Land and had King Saul, **about five hundred fifteen or sixteen** years had passed from the time that they first left Canaan. Although Saul was their first king, **between the time of** his anointment and the passing on to **David**, they had to fear their stronger neighbors. David led a stronger Israel, which secured its position; but, David does not compare **to Moses**, as Moses was another prophet of God, whom God spoke with personally. By the time David **had** passed away, the timeline shows there had **been five hundred seventy years** gone by. The difference **there** is the time that David was **about**.

And, the reason David does not compare to Moses is that **since the** Israelite **exit from Egypt**, led by Moses, God had presented the sacred Tablets to Moses, which were housed in the Tabernacle. David did not build a temple to house these gifts from God, as he was instructed to do. It was not until David's son, Solomon, became king of Israel that the land had finally found a great period of peace, which could be used to build. Only **at the time** of Solomon's reign, when the Israelites did not have to worry about the defense **of** their land, did they take **the** time **to** construct a **building of** stone, to replace their Tabernacle

215

which covered the Ark and the Covenant of the Ten Commandments. Before **the Temple** was **made**, peace had to be brought **by Solomon**, with his brothers. This peace allowed for the Temple of Solomon to be built **in the forth year of his reign**. The Temple lasted as a monument to God, before the **passing** of time saw it was destroyed **four hundred** years later. The Temple stayed in rubble for **eighty** more **years**; but, after the end of **that** period of **eighty years**, the Second Temple was built on the same spot.

And, after this eighty year period had passed, **since the building of the** Second **Temple** of Solomon, it existed in an ever more glorious state that it had before. It was this condition which still existed **at the time of Jesus Christ**. It was on the steps of this temple that Christ often taught, and, it was where he also demonstrated anger at the merchants which filled its steps. By the time of Christ's crucifixion, **according to the calculation of the Hierographs**, or official Church historical timelines of Jerusalem, the age of the Second Temple was **passing four hundred ninety years**.

Then, **after** the passing of Jesus Christ to Heaven, the Temple was again destroyed, not to be rebuilt again until after mankind is to enter into the end **times**. The House **of David** will again resurface before that time; and, this will lead to the Temple of Solomon being rebuilt a third time.

However, as this will signal the days of the End Time, when **the times** will signal the return **of our** Savior, the end will be brought about by those who occupy the land the Temple once stood on. This has been the motivation of the Church, causing it to act as mankind's **savior**, by leading attacks against those who now possess the land. Christians have been led by former kings, as knights of the Church, on Crusades to save this Holy Land. Those campaigns were movements motivated by the Church, to act as savior and eliminate the tribes of Abraham; but, this history of persecution will help bring about the end of mankind. The Christian Church has not acted to free the land for the Jews and reinstate the House of David; but instead, it has acted to defeat the followers of the antichrist. They see this person as the false prophet Mohammed; but, those actions have failed, as it is not up to the Church to determine when the **Redeemer, Jesus Christ** will come to save our souls. This land is holy to us, as Christians, because it is the land in which Jesus was **born**; and, it is also the birthplace **of the only virgin** mother, Mary. Mary has been most revered by our Catholic Church.

The purpose of Mohammed and his followers is to ensure, for Satan, that God's Promised Land does not fall back into the hands of the rightful owners. In this past, which **had been** the Church's attempts to remove this evil influence from Israel and Judah, the future will find (**according to any Chronographs** of history in this region) that **this period** which will follow the rise of Islam will last **one thousand three hundred fifty years.** In all of that time, the Muslims will successfully resist all outside challenges to this Holy Land.

And, those calculations are important, as **since the times of** Jesus Christ and **the** time He was born as a **human,** the time from then until now is not disputed. Our records have been maintained since that time, and they will be maintained just as accurately until the future brings the time of **Redemption,** when Christ will return. In this period after the crucifixion and Christ's Resurrection and Ascension, a new timeline for Christians was begun. It has been in this period that mankind has fallen **to the seduction** of Satan. In the future, many of mankind will have degenerated into a love of **detestable** things; but, not all will have been seduced by such obvious means as wealth and riches. Some of mankind will have also been seduced to follow false prophets, such that as time goes on, their beliefs will have been led so far away from God that they will find themselves sided with the Devil. This work **of** Satan has already begun, in the case with **the Saracens,** or the Arabs that make their holy city in Mecca, and who have been seduced by the false prophet Mohammed. As recorded by the chronologists, with all in agreement, there **had** only **been** passed **six hundred twenty** years, since the birth of Jesus, when this false prophet was called to serve Satan. Within **one year,** Mohammed was able to seduce the people of Arabia and have them call him prophet. Over the years since then, the religion of Islam has grown extremely strong **there;** but, in the future it will spread **around** the world. And, **since** we already know the impact this growth has had, **in** the history of the Crusades where Christians tried to defeat **this** evil but eventually lost, **one** can see how impossible it is to defeat evil by using evil. The use of war to defeat evil is not the message Jesus Christ brought to mankind; but, this method is the one most **easily** taken by Christians. This is how Satan seduces mankind, by taking advantage of mankind's emotional attachment to Christ; but, this advantage certainly does nothing to defeat evil. Instead, it is designed **to gather** the souls of believers, to steal them from God. Mohammed is the antithesis of Christ, just as Satan is the antithesis of God. God and Christ are so much stronger and will always overcome such influences; but, it is this power of influence, **which** will steal men's souls, that has been recorded in the records of the **times** that **are past**. There is **so** much evidence of this happening in the world that it cannot be happening by chance. The powers of mind will be at the root of the downfall of mankind; and, this power of mind is nothing more than a **calculation** of influence, to manipulate others. If this letter of **mine** is not to be understood in the future, then that **is** due to the powers of evil influence having effected everyone, so there is **no** longer any **good** left to save. However, if you can understand this now, you know these claims are very **valid**, as you have felt the same way and thought the same thoughts as I write here now. This presence of evil influence existed in the past, which is our biblical history. It dates from the beginning, as told **by** the story of Adam and Eve. It has affected God's blessed children, such as when Jacob fell for the influence to steal from his brother Esau. Remember Satan tempted Jesus too, although He had the powers to resist. My book, which this letter explains, tells what will happen to the world, when a continued inability of mankind to resist the temptations of evil takes hold. The message of the book must have the same effect as when God told Noah to build the ark. There was danger coming, assured by God, and Noah acted on faith alone. He did not question God about why he should build a boat on dry ground, or tell God how much he enjoyed the world as it was then. Noah knew the world was wicked and he acted on faith, to save his life and the lives of his family. This makes *The Prophecies* a continuing Prophecy, **because** the temptation to destroy evil is evil, with **all** seductions of this nature coming **from** Satan, having **been calculated** to trick mankind. There are no commandments **by** God stating it is okay for mankind to take **the course** of war and destruction in the name of the **heavenly**; as **by** an **association** of this nature, with something evil being assigned the properties of good, this is itself evil. When one believes one knows what evil is, but then sees another doing a known evil, for that one to act in evil ways to stop an evil, with the justification being that one is full **of** the **emotion** of good, that is wrong. When one is **infused** deeply with the spirit of Christ, but has come **to some** crossroad of dilemma, the solution is to spend **hours** in prayer and meditation before acting. When one has been faithful to God and Christ, one will then be tempted by Satan, to become emotionally moved against that faith. Satan delights in having driven the faithful to the point of having willfully **abandoned** the teachings of God and Christ. Those kinds of actions are affected **by the emotion** one holds for God and against sin; but, this emotion is what can lead to sin. This is the nature **of** Satan, and **the** number of times that I have seen this failure in mankind, I can tell you it has been so often repeated that it stretches back to **ancient** times. It has always been Satan's subtle way to coerce mankind to sin. The people of this future will be the **offspring** of those who have not have learned this lesson; and, they will have lost the power of guilt, which the motivation necessary to guide them to atonement.

EXPLAINING THE ASTROLOGICAL TIMING

For example, in the timeline I have just concluded it is easy to see **that all** of **these figures** spoke with God, directly or in dreams, and they followed God's requests. This was due to their faith that God existed and that God was all powerful. All of these men were not saints, without sin, so they **are** examples of how we are all expected to act **justly**, when the call to act according to moral standards is heard within. All of those stories can be **adapted** models to each of us, when faced with similar life circumstances. This is why God spoke to those who wrote the books of the Bible, so that mankind would have parallel examples **by** which to have something to reflect on. This is necessary when we all live amid the influences of evil. All of **the** books of the Bible are of **divine** origin, and thus they are perfect **letters**, or documents, free of errors. However, during the times of the Patriarchs, they did not have a Bible for comfort, so God spoke directly to them. God taught Abraham the knowledge of astrology, such that by seeing life's reflection **in the** planets he could imagine the **things** which would come to pass. When one is guided by the inner voice, astrology is just as **celestial**, or Heavenly, as is the Bible. This was God first way of guiding mankind indirectly, before all of the books of the Bible were written; and, it was much later that the books were combined into one volume for mankind to be indirectly led. The Sun and the Moon and the planets are **visible** lights which remove the darkness that surrounds us, and they give us direction when we are lost and in need. I know **it is** a method that has proven itself to me; and, Genesis 1:4 confirms that God is the source, when it states "And God said, Let there be lights in the firmament of the heaven to divide the day from the night; and let them be for signs, and for seasons, and for days, and years." This states the purpose as to light one's way and make there be predictability to life. However, astrology is not for all to understand, **to wit** it is more important to realize the qualities the planets symbolize. This is the majority of the meaning found in *The Prophecies*, although the more experienced astrologers can see the further details the generalizations also state. In this generalization of principles, more importance is found **by** the slower movement of the planets, as the Sun, Moon and the planets inside of the Earth's orbit appear to move through the zodiac much quicker. All have principles of importance, but it is the speed of motion that is relative to the duration of time the symbolized effect applies to the predictability of the future. The planet **Saturn** is the most distant planet from earth, and thus it appears to move the slowest. As Saturn moves through the signs of the zodiac, it is a good indicator of where times of hardship can be foreseen. This planet is known as the Greater Malefic because of its relationship to life's restrictions. However, it also represents the father principle, where it becomes representative of the teacher and master, who tests and grades. Life's tests are difficult to prepare for, so it means discipline and patience are required to successfully pass a test; but, when the time comes for the grade to be passed out, it can either be seen as very rewarding, or seen as the punisher. Saturn also represents Father Time, who is also known as the Grim Reaper, who comes to reap the harvest, to clear the way for a new growth when the season is right. This is the concept of death, which all human beings must prepare for; and as such, Saturn is very symbolic of those qualities found in God, our Father, who will reap our souls when our time is up. The planet **Jupiter** is the next closest planet to Earth, which moves faster than Saturn, but slowly enough to project the happenings of distant times. When it moves through the signs we can see the growths that take place in our lives, as well as the times of good fortune and fair judgment. This planet is known as the Greater Benefic, because it symbolizes the bounties of life and good luck. Jupiter can signify periods of marriage and pregnancy, wealth and the riches of life; but, it also stands for the study of religion and the faith that is required to know there is more than meets the eyes. In Roman mythology, where the name Jupiter is taken, this name was synonymous with the Greek god Zeus, who was the main god of all gods. The same can be said of the planet, as it is the biggest in the solar system, making it represent the King of the planets. As such, Jupiter symbolizes the qualities of God too, where He is the giver of life and all things surrounding that life. This is the expanse of God, where God knows all; and, Jupiter, like God, represents the benevolent King that is unselfish and knows no boundary for His love. Those who do not share, while others suffer and are in need, will know the justice of God and His judgment. The planet **Mars** is the last of the planets that are outside the Earth's revolution, and although it moves much faster through the zodiac, it moves slow enough to predict the coming of important events. Just as the god Mars was the god of war, the red planet Mars is the planet which symbolizes the energy required for war. Mars is very headstrong and is so full of energy that it often acts before thought, giving it the title of the Lesser

Malefic. Its movements show us when the times of action will come and when this energy must be released. Mars is a freewheeling entity, loving sport and tests of courage, which has him outfitted with all of the tools of competition. However, it is when we lose control of this spirit of fire that we get into trouble. Mars energy needs to be harnessed for good, as it knows no right or wrong. It only knows when static energy must be released. As a symbol of God, Mars is that breath of life first breathed into Adam, and the spirit of fire that is within us all; but, Mars is the principle that every action calls for a reaction, such that God will also act, for us or against us, depending on our actions towards God. Knowing these qualities will be most helpful when reading *The Prophecies*; but, I also mention **the other** planets too, when they become **joined** with these three outer planets. I have already written some about the Sun and Moon, but Venus is symbolic of the value of love and beauty, while desiring material things to enhance those qualities; and, Venus is known as the Lesser Benefic, as it soothes the beast in Mars. Mercury is symbolic of the quickness of mind and the thought processes, which are found in both the inner workings of the body and the outer expression of travel and communication. These inferior planets are less used for timing future events; so, I primarily use them when they are in aspect with one of the major planets that I detailed. The most common aspect is the conjunction, where two planets are in the same position, thus adding their essence together. What I have done here, by explaining the qualities of the planets to you, will be helpful, as these uses here are **like** the uses I placed in *The Prophecies*. However, in the book I give **more** specifics of the planetary positions; but, the wording of those positions is designed **to** confuse the novice astrologer. Even the advanced astrologer will misread most, as the usage appears too **plain** to properly understand. The untrained eye will find it impossible to understand the deepest meanings of the aspects; but, with this knowledge I have now conveyed upon you, you can now read the essence of the meaning properly. To those who understand the art and terminology of astrology, understanding the timing elements comes **by** not being locked onto **any** one possibility. One must first understand the text of the other **quatrains** which surround an astrological quatrain. With that known, the timing of this future will not be too difficult to figure out. I know **the** time will come when **one will be able to see** the purpose of all that is written, and then everything will be clearly explainable.

As this future comes **nigh**, mankind has to understand; and, that understanding

only comes **with** Christ in your heart. Christ stated **God** will be waitii mankind to respond favorably; but, Christ was **not pleased** with the dire mankind is headed. I felt so sorry for Christ and **I confessed** my sins and a for the forgiveness of mankind's sins. Jesus responded that I had a **good** he and that all mankind must become aware of the value of **that** act of confessic There is not one act God is not aware of, as he knows **the whole** of each person life. The justice of God is like that of Saturn and Jupiter, where admission o wrong will yield less punishment than a denial of wrong. Each blessing mankind receives **comes from** one recognizing that nothing can be hidden from **God**.

It is so important to know that having **him in** one's heart **renders** that one **grace** and each of us must respect that presence and give back to God His due. Our time on this earthly plane is on the **honor** system, where God has honored us with a life of free will; but, in return for that life, we must always honor God's power and presence. It is also especially so that we must give God **praise**, which churches allow us to officially do. For this dedication to God's power we have the right to join with the **everlasting** in Heaven, upon our deaths. One must consider that **without** this belief, which honors and brings to us God's assistance, one would have chosen a life **of** chance. Living a life of chance is where **it**, the everlasting life, depends on the way one naturally lives while on earth. For one **to have** chosen a life without accepting God, our outcomes become **mixed**. The possibility **of** entering into **the divine state** of Heaven then depends totally on our earthly actions, without God's influence in assistance. If we are naturally disposed to live a good life, free from any knowledge of God at all, then we will still be allowed through Heaven's gate, by living a good natural life. However, should we fall prey to the temptations of the worldly existence, and break God's laws without asking for forgiveness, a life like **that** will have **resulted in** an outcome where **fate**, or destiny, chose for us our end place. We have been given free will, **but** with that gift comes the responsibility for our actions. The blessing is that we all have **in** us the ability to talk with **God**, from the beginning. He is there **in birth**, before our minds allow us free will; and, the **majority** of us sense that presence, whether or not we know it is God. Beyond that, we are all **accompanied** by other spirits who act **with** us, as God's ambassadors. They are our spirit guides and guardian angels, which come and go as needed. What necessitates **the movement of** these spirits to and from us is determined by **the course** our lives take. So, we are always accompanied by a **celestial** presence. I have been

allowed by Christ to see **so much**, by Him and His accompanying assistants, in reference to this distant future that comes. This is because I believe in God, believe in the model of Christ and listen to his good angels. Of **that** great scope I have seen, **seeing** it has made it seem I was involved in it. It was **like** the future was **inside** of me, as I stood in front of this **one** magnificent **mirror**. That reflection was from the eye of God, with the future reflecting before me as though I was a part of it; but, it was without the future detecting my presence. With this future **blazing** before me, I felt the passion and fervor swelling within my heart, as well as the anger from seeing the rage the future holds. I felt **like** reaching out to touch the people or calling out to stop the madness; but, I was limited **by** only my **vision** as I encountered this future. Obsession was present, as I could not turn away; but, those in this future will be likewise **obsessed**, having fallen in love with their own minds, and forgetting the core of their beings. That core is the heart and the soul. This future shows me the elevations of the **great** peoples and nations who will lead this future, and the **events** which will involve them, leading to this end. The ending will be a **sad** one. The future I have seen is **prodigious**, consisting of phenomenal advancements and transpirations, many with marvelous potential; but, mankind will misuse its advancements, bringing prodigious suffering to the planet.

This great suffering will come from **calamitous** events, where a series of destructive powers will be unleashed. This future will cause the people of the world to undertake **adventures** they will not want to make, but **which** they will be responsible for. Their responsibility will come from allowing their leaders to lead them to devastation. Each **one** of those future peoples will have to decide to accept God and change, or accept stagnation. The time they will spend deciding their fate will be while this danger is **approaching**. They will have been misled **by** the leaders of **the principal religions** on earth, such that those believing their souls to be safe will find they must review their previous life decisions.

Now in our times, the vast majority **of** the people in our country revere **Jesus Christ**. In as much, France is solidly a Christian nation, led by you sire, a Christian king. Further, Christianity is predominating all over Europe, making it one of the most principal religions on earth. Still, **in** Europe **this** distinction is now seeing the effects of differing peoples, cities, lands and regions, with many no longer wishing to be subservient to Rome. There are now different branches of Christianity; but, **by the** time this future comes about, there will be greater

diversity in the Christian nations of the world. This diversity will come from the great spread **of the sects** of Christianity. This, in turn, will affect the sects of artisans who serve both the royalty and the churches, of which **I** belong. In my crafts I have tried to be most Christian, while serving both you and the Church. The Church of Christ in Jerusalem is the source, with the Catholic Church being **the lead** branch which has influenced the majority of Western Europe. The Church of Constantinople holds influence is the East. These fractures which exist now, especially following the Great Schism and the splintering of the Church of Rome by the movement of Reformation, is the beginning of the weakening of Christianity. By the time this future arrives, it will have crumbled to pieces. As of now, all of the sects are dedicated to Christ, with the separate divisions being created to serve the needs of the common peoples in each geographic area. The common people willfully will continue to accept Jesus Christ into their hearts, for some time to come, causing it to become the world's most principal religion.

With me **having calculated** the timeline that led from the first man, Adam, to the life of Christ, having presented it to you here, this shows that the Bible is not only promoting belief in the one God, but it is shows how God completed each promise he made to the prophets. Although it took many years before the people were ready to receive God's promises, both positive and negative, God's promises always came true. In the Christian Bible, and through the Gospels of the New Testament, God culminated his greatest promise, with the birth of His promised Son, the Messiah. Since Christ's time on earth, The Jewish people have not added any new book to their Torah, because God no longer speaks to His chosen people like he did in the biblical days. God last spoke through Jesus Christ, making those who follow Christ, the Christians of the world, the ones who must lead the rest of the world to belief in the one God. The Christian churches must understand that the chosen people are those people of faith and belief who will model Christ, through their actions of peace and brotherhood, to bring the world to Christ and God. Religion is not something that is **calculated**, to determine the greatest benefits that are afforded to **those** who worship a particular sect of religion. Jesus Christ has come to me to write a new book that is worthy of being in the Bible, in the form of the **presented** quatrains. Remember that many of the books of the Bible told of the **prophecies** that God gave to the prophets; and, Jesus Christ gave mankind *The Revelation*. Jesus Christ has dictated **the whole** story to me, to pass on to you; and, it is to be understood only **according to** the time Jesus Christ deems. The presentation of the quatrains is not in **the order** the story was told; but, when the time comes for this to be realized, it will be found that each quatrain fits together like the links **of a** necklace or bracelet, before they have become a **chain**. The greatest key to discovering **which** quatrains links to others is found in the common verbiage that is **contained** in the verses. In the example of a pearl necklace, each of **its** separate pearls makes the circular **revolution** possible, by being threaded onto a fine central wire or chain. This is precisely how **the whole** of *The Prophecies* is linked, as the basic timeline is finely weaved by the **doctrine** of timing which is of **astronomic** nature.

The times which the astrological quatrains mark, as the timing framework for the story, is not something that **I've had to** do by myself. All of the astrological wording was told to me by Christ, such that it was already **calculated** by God and Christ; but, as an astrologer it all made perfect sense to me. God and Jesus Christ are much **more** capable of **profoundly** making such calculations, as I am just a simple astrologer. At first they will seem to represent times that are contrary to the times they truly mirror, because one must become **adapted** to the manner in which the wording is read. However, when one understands how to make sense of **those** timing quatrains, the rest will fall into place more easily. The timing quatrains are **ones** that make everything have continuity. From that outline being known, the others more easily combine **with** those, through recognition of **the** key words being used. The rest, which would not be understandable without connecting to the context of those **others**, will then give great depth to the stories within the whole story.

Still, a belief in the philosophy of astrology is necessary to correctly determine the astronomic timing elements. Those with only a shallow understanding of this philosophy will be unable to determine the timing, such that interpreters will base their views **according to** what qualified astrologers will tell them the timing means. This will, for the most part, have them receiving second-hand information, without those astrologers themselves actually being deeply involved with reading **my** astrological clues. Their timing elements will be accurate, according to the information given them by the interpreter; but, the problem will lie in the fact that one cannot read my astrological aspect in a **natural** way, like one would read some normal text. Everything about *The Prophecies*, especially the astronomic verses, requires the use of one's **instincts**, or inner whispers, to begin to see just how amazingly clear my statements are. One can only begin to understand this clarity **after** one has realized the philosophical aspects of each astrological word; and, when they combine that knowledge with an understanding of the systems which are imbedded in the text, the result will bring out amazing clarity. At first, **some** of the statements will appear to represent **times** that will eventually prove to be wrong; but, **in** this kind of practice, **he** or she will be able to gain **understanding** by realizing the errors come from reading the words improperly. They must be read as written, **since** Jesus Christ put them in a perfect order, one which applies to all languages; and, when this is done **the** quatrains will perfectly tell of the **times** past, present and future. When you remember **that** this element of time is representative of the qualities of the planet **Saturn**, you can start to understand how Saturn applies to the movement of all of the planets. Jupiter represents expansion and growth, **which** is symbolized by the forward motion of all planets and luminaries. Saturn is the model for patience and restriction; and as such, it reflects the apparent retrograde movement of the planets. The luminaries represent the life each of us has, so this is never retrograde; but, each of the planets has a regular, predictable pattern of retrograde motion. The following time periods are important to note, as they mark periods of planetary retrogradation, which will mark important specific times in this future to come. Several key events will occur at times when planets go retrograde; and each planet will have significant periods to mark, lasting from the time it goes retrograde until it **will change** its direction and return to direct motion. One first has to look for Saturn **to enter** into retrograde, as this will begin the clock ticking for the final hour of mankind. Saturn is retrograde for a considerable length of time each year; but, **in** the year **seven** of the new millennium, Saturn will be retrograde for all **of the** days in ten **months of April**. In that eleventh year, Saturn will go retrograde on the 6th of April, and this reverse direction will last **until the 25th of August**.[48] Once this critical period has begun, **Jupiter** will slow to a stop **at** the end of the **14th of June**, to go retrograde the next day and remaining this way **until** nearly a week past **the 7th of October**.[49] Before this period of Saturn's retrograde has ended, **Mars** will turn **from** its direct motion on **the 17th of April**; and it will maintain this backwards course **until** a full week

---

48 Saturn will station retrograde on April 6, going direct on August 25, 2017. (*Table of Planetary Phenomena*, Neil F. Michelsen, ACS, San Diego, 1990)

49 Jupiter will station retrograde on June 15, going direct on October 13, 2009. (Same source)

past **the 22nd of June**.[50] To understand the elements that will lead to this ruin of mankind, the future must look to its past, in the decade which began in the year that **Venus** will have reversed **from** direct on **the 9th of April**, lasting **until** it returns direct on **the 22nd of May**.[51] Another year of importance that will lead to this future failure will be when **Mercury** will make the first of its multiple yearly retrogrades beginning **from the 3rd of February**. This one will last **until the 24th** of February; and, in this year it will be **arranged** the last true royal blood King of France will abdicate his throne. This will be **due** to a second revolution of the common people, in just over forty years.[52]

In this century the ruin of royal rule will be completed and the century which will come **after** will perfect the rule of inhuman tyrants, where amazing powers will be maintained by common people, especially behind the scenes. The one year of this century that will mark the culmination of this perfection of corruption will be when Mercury will go retrograde late on the evening of May 31st, being fully reversed **from the 1st of June**. It will continue to move backwards **until** late on the evening of **the 24th** of that same month. In this year many **arranged** deals will be made, with some of the secrecy exposed. Also, a new leader will be elected to the world's most powerful nation; and, its former adversary will be **due** to crumble to this power.[53]

One other important period for Mercury will be during the times when it will go retrograde late in the year, starting **from** the twelve-hour period before or

---

50   Mars will station retrograde on April 17, going direct on June 29, 2016. (Same source)

51   This occurred on those exact dates in the year 1889. (Same source) During that last decade of the 19th Century, in Russia, the Czar's loyalists created *The Protocols for the Elders of Zion*, while Lenin was developing his work on imperialism. These will both play a role in the changes that occurred in the 20th Century, leading to now.

52   This occurred in 1830. (Same source) Charles X abdicated due to another French Revolution. He was the last surviving heir, as the grandson of Louis XVI and son of the would be Louis XVII, who never ruled, due to the French Revolution in 1789.

53   This year was 1988. (Same source) Ronald Reagan began his final year as President and George W. H. Bush was elected to succeed him in 1988. The Iran-Contra deal was exposed and hearings were held. The war between Iraq and Iran came to an end, and the Soviets began withdrawing from Afghanistan. By the time 1989 came, the Soviet block crumbled and the Berlin Wall fell. All of this history is explained in the quatrains, as they will set the stage for what will happen after 2001.

on **the 25th of September**. This will occur six times after the stories of the quatrains have begun, and each of these periods of retrogradation will last **until** twelve hours before or after **the 16th of October**.[54] Those periods will mark such things as an end and a beginning of different European rulers over empires. The last drop of French royal blood will be forever lost. The nature of earth will demonstrate just how powerful it is and how much trouble it can cause to humanity. Things of value will suddenly be valueless, with the world thrown into a deep depression. Prayer will be seen as against the law; war will begin under the guise of advisement; and, the world will prematurely fear doomsday has arrived. All of these events will be repeated in the year when the last of these retrograde periods will set in. In addition to this timing element of Mercury retrograde, the following sign placements will also mark the same times; but, more importantly, the following planets in signs will mark a series of years, which will signal the worst of times for mankind, close to the very end. From the most outer planet, **Saturn** will spend its time **in** the sign of **Capricorn**.[55] It does this for over two years; but, its ingress into Capricorn and its retrograde periods, back in or back out of Capricorn, will signify important changes of hardship. Saturn rules the sign of Capricorn, so it will be strong in either motion direction. Next, the planet **Jupiter** will spend its year **in** the sign of **Aquarius**.[56] The expansive Jupiter moves too fast for the Saturn ruled sign of Aquarius; but, while it can show rapid advances, its retrograde period will expose the weaknesses of such rapid expansion. This will bring the planet of **Mars** to one of the signs **in**

---

54   These have occurred in: 1725, 9/25 - 10/16; 1804, 9/24 (23:52) – 10/16; 1883, 9/24 (12:52) – 10/16; 1929, 9/25 – 10/17 (5:09); 1962, 9/24 (1:47) – 10/15 (14:59). The next to occur will be in 2008, which will also begin 9/24 (7:11) – 10/15 (20:01). (Same source) Checking historical timelines shows many events making up the background history which will later influence this future time.

55   This occurred in the Great Depression years of 1929-1932, as well as during the last years of John Kennedy's full term, from 1962-64. Saturn will next go into Capricorn in the years 2017 – 2020. . (Sources: *The American Ephemeris for the 20th Century (Midnight)*, Neil F. Michelsen, ACS, San Diego, 1995 and *The American Ephemeris for the 21st Century (Midnight)*, Neil F. Michelsen, ACS, San Diego, 2005)

56   This occurred in the first years of the Kennedy administration, with the retrograde causing it to be in Aquarius in both 1961 and 1962. It was in the same sign, retrograding back and forth, between 1937 and 1939, when Hitler was expanding in Europe. It will next go into Aquarius in the 2009-2010 years; but it will not retrograde like Nostradamus is referring to. That period will next come between the years 2020 and 2022. (Same sources)

its domain as ruler, when it transits the sign of **Scorpio**.[57] Mars is the planet of high energy and war; but, in the Water Sign of Scorpio, shrewdness and planning are realized, before acting again. This will bring us to the planet **Venus**, which will be unable to show its full complement of grace and beauty **in** the sign of its Detriment, **Pisces**.[58] In the year that Mars enters Scorpio, Venus will visit Pisces, both before and after the Mars alignment. To set Mars up, Venus will go retrograde from Aries to Pisces and then back to Aries. Then, the planet **Mercury** will spend nearly two months **inside** the same sign, as it will go retrograde in that sign. After it has become direct, in the space of **one month** it will be in three signs. The first of these signs will be the sign it went retrograde **in**, which will be the sign of **Capricorn**. From there is will spend less than three weeks in the sign of **Aquarius**. Importantly, after Mercury will enter into the sign of **Pisces**, the Sun will also be in Pisces, ahead of Mercury. When these two come into close conjunction with one another, **the Moon** will spend its two-plus days **in** the sign of **Aquarius**.[59] This brief aspect will mark the end of a ten-year period of terrible events for mankind; and, this will have begun when **the head of the Dragon**, or the North Node, was last **in** the sign of **Libra**.[60]

To clarify this a little more, **the head of the Dragon**, or the North Node, will not be in the sign of Libra, at this end time. Ten years later it will then be in the sign of Taurus. After Mercury and the Sun **will be** in conjunction **with one** another in Pisces, the Sun will then make another **conjunction**, three weeks later. This conjunction **of the Sun** will be **to** the planet **Jupiter**, and this will last one week. Up to that point of **the year** the earth **will be** relatively **peaceful, without** any signs of the peace being disturbed. However, during the time of an annular total

---

57   Mars will be in Scorpio roughly ever two years. It will enter the sign of Sagittarius in 2016, before turning retrograde and backing into the sign of Scorpio for the second time that year. However, it will also be in Scorpio in 2018, and when sandwiched between Venus in Pisces, this will be the year 2021. (21st Century source from above)

58   Venus goes into Pisces every year; but, it will next be retrograde in Pisces in the year 2021. (Same source)

59   Mercury will go retrograde in Capricorn next in 2009/2010, and this situation (Sun, Moon, and Mercury in same sign) will occur then. However, it will again occur at the end of the year 2022, continuing into the year 2023. (Same source)

60   The North Node will be in Libra next in 2014-2015. In 2023 it will be in the sign of Taurus.

solar **eclipse**, five days later, things will greatly change.[61]

Over three years later the head of the Dragon will be in Aquarius, which means that **the tail** of the Dragon, or the South Node, will be in the sign opposite, which is Leo. The tail of the Dragon will be at a degree that **will be opposite** of the planet Jupiter. Jupiter will remain within the orb of opposition for seven months, due to it going retrograde in Leo.[62] As Jupiter opposes the South Node, **following** the time that it will go retrograde, there will be **one conjunction** that will be made to the tail of the Dragon. This conjunction will be made by Mercury, which will also make an opposition aspect, **of** the planet **Jupiter to** the planet **Mercury** and the South Node.[63] Six months later, **with** the world in its last throes, only **one** more aspect will signify the final days of earth. This will be a **square aspect of** the planet **Mars**, transiting in the Mutable Earth sign of Virgo, **to Mercury**, transiting in the Mutable Air sign of Pisces. On the day that Mercury stations direct, the world will end.[64]

The planets, signs and aspect **in** these listings that I have made here denote the key years Christ showed to me, which will lead to the mankind's end. The events that will come at those times will be by mankind's own cause, as **he** will lead himself to his own ruin. The **times** I have listed here are very specific and very limiting in their possibilities, regardless of the repeatability of the planetary patterns. While I have been fairly specific **in** listing these planetary positions, it must be realized that **these** apply to the whole of mankind, throughout the world. The quatrains related to those times tell when the most significant events will come, as there will be many events in this time span. With this timeframe now known, I am about to tell you the details that will be found in the quatrains of *The Prophecies*, which will name the **countries** that will grow in size and number, unlocking the secrets to **the power** which will eventually destroy mankind. This power will bring out the **infernal** flames of Hell and kill many people in its wake.

---

61   Annular Total Solar eclipse in 2023 will be on April 20th, after the Sun and Jupiter will have been conjunct in Aries, between April 9-15. (Same 21st Century source)

62   Jupiter will come within 175 degrees (180 = opposition) of the South Node on October 24, 2026. It will remain within 5 degrees of exact opposition until May 20, 2027. (Same source)

63   Mercury will conjunct the South Node, while opposing Jupiter, between January 23, 2027 and January 28, 2007. (Same source)

64   This fateful end will occur on July 4, 2027. (Same source)

Once mankind will have learned to harness this power, it **will put** mankind **to** the test, to not become drunk with this power. This drunken lust for power will not be checked by religion, as during this period the Church will fail Christ; and, **the encounter** which will cause that failure will come to **the Church** will also be self-generated, for not promoting the teachings **of Jesus Christ** to these nations with this power. Once one nation will develop this power, other nations will soon follow. There will be other nations which will develop **the** same **power** in this weapon; and, they will become **the opponents** of the nation which will have first had it. That second nation will be one **of** greatest infidel nations in the history of the world, as it will not abide by God's Law. It will have banned religion of all types, forcing the people to submit to **its** manmade **law**. However, it will not be this second nation that will use the great power against its opponent. The first great nation will have another enemy, **who will be** the one to begin the annihilation of mankind. They will have obtained this power from the **second** nation, which will cause both of those nations delight at the possibility of the first great nation being brought down. The nation which will release this power upon the world will be led by the **Antichrist**. As the Antichrist, his religion will be against Christianity, and his people will be those **which will** seek to **persecute** Christians. This evil nation will use its power to bring their persecution to France, to defeat **her** and the rest of Europe, through a planned persecution of the institution of Christianity and Christ's **church**. It is most important to understand that **it's** designed to destroy the one **true** religion on earth, and become the **curate**, or caretaker, of a forced religion upon Europeans. Their plan for conversion and persecution will been seen **by** them as the end justifying the **means**, as the European nations will have themselves been stripped **of the** holy **power** it once held. The combination **of the** true **Kings** of Europe and the Catholic Church will have long faded to memory; but, their deeds of evil will be seen as what their ancestors had done, in the name of religion, many centuries prior. The Christian world's positions of power will be replaced by **temporal** leaders, who will only serve in such a position for a limited time. During their brief reigns they will take full advantage of the earthly gains their power will make possible for them. Those leaders will be of common blood, without any blood allegiance to God or Christ; but, it will be their sect's leaders **who** will come to power, purporting to be the voice of the common class. The commoners of our day, **being** unaccustomed to having any power and wealth, will be easily fooled by such influences, in the not so distant future. This influence will be designed to manipulate by knowing the weakness of the common minds. This power of influence will make them believe they are intellectually born to rule; but, it will be **their ignorance** of the facts, once the truth will be told, that will expose them for what they are and make their demise possible. They will not confess their sins or ask for forgiveness, however, as they will continue to try and influence more people to surrender their souls. The people at that time will be forewarned, so it will have to be their own decisions to make, having been made fully aware of the consequences, to continue to be misled or stand up for God and Christ. The common people will have been **seduced** by the promises of wealth, fame and power, just as was the case in the original sin; and, many will not be able to turn their backs on their false idols. Those seductions **by** the **tongue, which** will be offering the world to the common people, **cutting** the earth up into small pieces of common property, will lead **more** away from the words of Christ and God than ever have been misled before. It will be **that** situation which will have led the first and second nations to fight for world supremacy, with **none** worthy of such a feat. Both of those two nations will realize that this powerful weapon is a very dangerous **two-edged sword**, as it cannot be controlled to only kill one's enemy. This danger will have kept each of them from using the power in anger; but, without either nation being led by a holy influence, the dispute **between** these two nations will be placed in **the hands** of a new empire, led by strong roots in religion. Their zealot leaders will make use **of** this weapon, in the name of their god; but, that empire will be **the insane** one, filled with anger and willing to kill itself to kill its enemies.

EXPLAINING THE QUATRAINS - THE ADVENTURES OF THE SECTS

But, this insanity will not immediately set in, as it will take centuries for the future to develop this suicidal use of power. The stories of the quatrains tell of this development; and, **here** I will explain some of the detail that will be found applying to the verses. You have requested this from me; and, my true **Sire**, the Lord Jesus Christ the Son of God, has allowed me to respond, in the same manner that *The Prophecies* have been presented. Just as the quatrains **are comprised** of many individual pieces that have been split up and reordered to confuse, **several** of the main sections of this letter have been treated in the same style. This letter will be another of the **great** mysteries I have produced; and, this response will make me appear, to some, to have gone insane. However, when the time comes for *The Prophecies* to be understood, this letter will be found a **marvelous** tool for confirming those first inklings of truth. The explanations I will soon give will make it easier for those **coming to** the realization of what I have stated here and in my Letter of Preface, without them having had the benefit of previously understanding either of my letters. This letter, once solved, will confirm certain conclusions that will have been drawn from my quatrains; and, it will clarify the still confusing ones. I say this because those conclusions **that** will be arrived at will make this confusing letter understandable. For all **those** who will have discounted this letter as the ravings of a madman, there will be one **who** will finally realize the puzzle of the quatrains relates to the puzzle that is this letter. Armed with the basic systems of understanding, he **will be** soon after be **coming** to understand this letter, like no other before; and, **after** the pattern is realized in this letter's statements the systems will allow him to rearrange **them** so that everything makes sense. For all those who will have made wild guesses about this letter, **they will be** amazed at how the whole of *The Prophecies* has been completely explained here. This accuracy of interpretation will have not been reached by anyone, since they were first published, until that time when all will become clear. With all of the explanation I have presented in this letter, they will finally be **seeing** the truth of what all of my documents referencing *The Prophecies* represent.

When *The Prophecies* is seen as the true document it is, **lasting** as long as it will in **the same** unrealized condition for centuries, **this** will have to be recognized as a **calculation** beyond the abilities of normal man. It will also be beyond the abilities of any man to see this far and this well into the future by the simple use of **Astrologics**.[65] Everything **conferred** to me by Jesus Christ has to be known by all. With my recount of the timeline which had previously only known to us by the books **in the** Bible, from the histories produced by the **sacred** Patriarchs through their holy **letters** and epistles, my offering of addition information about the past, dating back to creation, works along with the future stories of the quatrains, which lead to the end of time. One can only believe that it is impossible for any one man to have direct knowledge of this great expanse of time; unless one realizes it can only be gained from divine inspiration. Throughout all time mankind will have suffered at **the** hand of those who use **persecution** as a means for controlling **the people**. This was the way Jesus Christ met his fate, as well as all of the Apostles and the **Ecclesiastic** founders of Christianity. In this future, persecution again **will take** the lives of many people; but, as with all things, the source of the future's ills will find **its origin** in the past. During the Crusades, which are part of our past history, the Ecclesiastic people of Rome were themselves the persecutors. While no pope ever carried a sword into battle, they persecuted **by** casting **the power of** influence they held over **the Kings** of Europe. The knights **of the North**, throughout Europe, **united** the common men of their lands, **with** the goal of holy reward if they sacrificed their lives to loyalty and duty, as one with the Church. There was nothing holy in their attempts to persecute **the Easterners** for their barbaric religious beliefs; and, this included the Jews. The Easterners will always remember their persecutors; just as us Christians will always remember the treatment given Jesus Christ, and especially those who persecute us individually. But, the future will bring a new form of Crusade, specifically to the Muslim world.

The future will find two ways for the nations of Christianity to become once again unified in the Eastern lands. **Firstly**, they will sanction the taking **of** Arab land, to rekindle **the temples** of the children **of God**, meaning the descendants of the Israelites. That seed, which will have been scattered by the winds of the

---

65 Astrologics is more than the mathematical calculations of astrology. The root words have to be realized, "*astro-*" and "*logic*." "Astro" means star and "logic" means the art of reasoning. This means the art of reasoning by the stars is impossible for man to achieve, for great distances in time, even though the mathematics can be calculated for any amount of time.

THE LETTERS OF NOSTRADAMUS • *Robert Tippett*

earth, will again take root in the lands of Judah and Israel, through European initiatives. This re-creation of the nation of Israel, with Christian support to stabilize it for growth, will **secondly** keep a Christian influence in the lands where a new form of wealth will emerge. This valuable natural resource will be found **by those** of Europe, **who** will have gained dominion over the Arab lands, through the art of negotiation after war. Once established as protectorate in this region, the Europeans **are** later found to be desiring of this new natural resource there. Since the Arabs will be **terrestrially** simple and this resource being **under**ground **held** riches, they will require the skill of the Europeans to learn how to extract it from the earth and properly stored and upheld. [66] Due to an increasing value placed on this material and the Christian nations' increasing dependency on it, their addiction will cause **them to approach** the Eastern world as expendable pawns. The European nations will bring **such decadence** upon the Arab peoples that all semblance of Christian upbringing will appear to have been lost. Not only will the Christian nations protect the land of Israel, at Arab expense, but **with that** need for the natural resource the Christian nations will commit **one thousand** atrocities against the Muslim peoples. This will cause the Muslim nations to seek the assistance of **other** nations, who will help them cease this persecution. The result of all of this will be **calamitous**, with the story filled with failed **adventures** for all branches of religion, each having lost its spiritual guidance. It is the purpose of *The Prophecies* to tell of **that** series of adventures, which will be caused **by** one pendulum swing after another, with no one able to understand the message of Christ, where retribution should be to let them strike the other cheek. The quatrains will set **the course** which will lead to this calamitous future, by telling **of the times** that will create the foundation for this lack of Christ in Christian peoples. Mankind will have taken a course so differently from the **one** we have taken, to reach where we are now. It will be one which will be an insult to God and Christ, the Kings of nations and the Church of the people. When you **will know** that everything has been known beforehand, including knowledge of the terrible things **to befall** mankind in the future, you will cry, sire, for having no way of stopping it from happening.

---

66   The word written by Nostradamus, "*soustenus*," at first appears to be a misspelling for "*soustenir*," which translates as "to sustain, to uphold." However, when it is broken down into *sous tenu*, with the *s* pluralizing this, it translates better as "under helds." I included the word "upheld" to fill this word's accepted translation, but underground makes perfect sense of the statement.

Oliver Cromwell, 1628 – 1653

The first clarification of this coming change, which will lead to the future, will not be far removed from our deaths, sire; in the next century, in England. **The plebe**, or the common people, will produce **one** of their own, who will be the first to rise to power. He will come from the military sect, rising from cadet to become the general of an army of the people. His military acumen will not be taught to him; but, he will display his own unique abilities, which will be **self** generated. He will lead victories against his King's army, in a civil war, which **will raise** a great following of commoners. His actions will be **supporting** the people's cause. He will then train his soldiers in the skills of warfare that he will have devised; and, his strategies **will chase** the King's army, eventually defeating and capturing the King. The **members of** the English branch of **the law-makers**, or legislatures, with this military man among them, will refuse the King his right of Divine Authority and the King will be killed and the throne abolished. This common man will then take control of all of England, Ireland and Scotland through bloody battles of persecution; but, he will not claim to be king. Once all is conquered, he will make the Parliament of England subservient to him; and, he will eventually reduce this body's power to nothing. There will be uneasiness within, when the common man first begins to steal that which God has provided as the leadership for mankind. Upon this general's death, the throne will be restored; however, with this precedent set, in time there will be others who will follow this model of civil war and revolution.

The Age of Enlightenment, 1700 - 1917

This thirst by mankind will eventually overthrow all royal blood, giving the common man a complete ascension to power and the wealth that this overthrow brings. With this power to rule, the new leaders of the common man will make new laws that will separate the church for the state. The bloodlines of Christ, those chosen by birth as having God's right to rule, will have been maintained **by the** nations of Europe; but, they will all fall. Some nations that are in close **proximity** to France, the nations **of** the North, will have retained their blood; but, it will merely be as figureheads. None will closely resemble any of those royal houses that you know now, in **our century** today. In these future times, the royalty of England, Denmark, Norway and Sweden will be all that will remain of holy blood; but, these lines will have degenerated from marriages with commoners. This future will then be unable to return to true ruling kings, as all will have been dethroned **by** uprisings of the people. In the same **manner** as the first example, the kings and queens and princes will be executed or sent into exile. The royal houses that now would seem to be least in jeopardy **of the** people's anger, France, Spain and the Hapsburgs of Austria; they will become **three** of the first casualties in Europe. Failures to produce male heirs will cause other nations to **unite** in protest, allowing all to become weak from war and peace compromises. The nation of Great Britain, although it will never return to a Republic, it will thrive with more and more Parliamentary power, until one King of England will give all royal power away. Further, the British will spawn a nation, in the New World, which will break from British rule and become founded without ever truly being under royal rule. This nation will grow into the world's greatest power; and, while it will have been founded on the principle of freedom to practice religious beliefs without persecution, by the end times it will have lost touch with those Christian roots. The last monarchy to fall will be what we now see as a vast wilderness nation, which is not closely involved with our region of Europe. This nation is Russia; and, in the future it will begin to covet the Western European culture and higher education. One king will begin the spread of this influence to his country; but, the end result will be the spread of revolution, such that Russia will become a nation completely without religion, thus no morals to guide the common people. This influence of revolution will spread throughout the Christian world, through a strong element of manipulation, by the leaders of sects who will **secretly** plan their strategies to urge the people to revolt. They will find their center of operations in the free city of Geneva, where those leaders will be **searching** for new ideas that will excite the people. Those bankers will finance both wars and revolutions, bringing about **the death** of the monetary systems we know now. They will present their services to the royal figures, while using **deceits** to conceal their practice of usury. Once the king is in debt from war costs, the Genevans will demand payment **by** the threat of interest and premiums due. With the royal houses bankrupt, they will begin to set **ambushes** against the kings, by financing the promotion of philosophical doctrines aimed as inspiring the common masses on the concept of freedom and independence. In France, **the one** king who will fall to this ploy will have also suffered **from** losing touch with the people. Once this king is lost, steps will lead to **the other** form of government that will replace the kings of birthright. This will be an elected form of government, where the common people vote for common leaders. These common leaders will be the ones who will be financed by the Genevans, so none of the royal wealth will ever be known by the commoners.

The Prophecy of Fatima, Portugal and the Three Letters, 1917 - 1943

And, with this other form of government in place, the influence of the Catholic Church will be strongly curtailed. The people **will be given** the opportunity to practice religious beliefs; but, their government will steer away from favoring one form of Christianity over another. This will cause the Virgin Mary to appear before three Portuguese girls, with **the** oldest **girl** told to warn the Church of the dangers that will be coming.[67] The warning will be about the troubles mankind will face, from the changes coming to Russia, making it become an atheist nation. The warning will be written out in a letter, by the girl to the Vatican, **for the** pope to act on its contents. At this crucial time actions will be necessary, for the Church to take steps to secure the **conservation** of religion in Russia, as well as to conserve its influence over the governments of the world. Actions at that time will reinforce the commitment **of the Church** to Jesus Christ, as a vehicle designed for the protection of souls; and, as the one **Christian** sect that most honors the Virgin Mary, it will show they recognize this power of prophecy. At the time of this apparition, the Church will have been **falling** further and further away from being a power of influence. From **its** once great position, as the **governor** of the religious morals of the peoples of whole nations, the Church will have lost touch with the world's leaders, although it will still reach the majority of the world's Christians. Those leaders will have fallen prey **to the** philosophers of **paganism**, in the sense that they will be true gentiles and not acknowledge the one God of all people. This non-belief in God will stem from the secluded practice in the skills of the mind, in secret organizations of selected membership that will promote the power of mind as the one ruler over mankind. Acceptance of this power will mean a denial of religion; and, this will signify the rise of **sects** of this nature to power. This influence of the sects of philosophy will be what

---

67 The word written by Nostradamus, "*fille*," also translates as "daughter." This is a reference back to the Book of Joel quote, where God will fill both our "sons and daughters with prophecy." The event commonly known as Fatima is a prime example of a daughter, or girl, prophesying.

will rob Russia **of** its royal rulers, instilling their plan for **the new** Russia, which will be led by the main sect that will forbid its people from practicing religion. The warning the Virgin Mary will tell the girl is that the Church must stand up against these immoral **infidels**, and demand that the people's souls be protected. The girl will be too young to sway her Bishop to get the letter to the pope; but, when **she** will become older and be serving the Virgin Mother as a nun, she will try again. In her next effort, she **will have** to write **two** letters directly to the pope, warning him of the dangers she has seen. The girl and her sisters were barely more than **infants** at the time of the first warnings; but, two will have died, leaving only **the one** to get this message to the pope. She will succeed in doing this, **from** her position of devout **faithfulness**, in the convent she will live the rest of her life in.

This faithful duty by the nun will be thwarted by **the other** sect that will have risen to power, after the sect in Russia. This sect will bring a tyrant who will rule over the united German lands, and who will be **of** an opposite philosophy than the one governing the Russians. While both tyrants will be from opposite philosophies, both will equally show **unfaithfulness** to the one God. This tyrant will want to limit the influence of religion, while giving Germany the impression of being a Christian nation. He will call upon the Catholic Cardinal for Germany and have him align the Catholic Church to this government; and, he will succeed, **by** coercing an agreement between Germany and the Catholic Church. This agreement will demand **the confirmation of** this Cardinal, making the Catholic Church **the** only legally recognized **church** in Germany. The Vatican will not act to stop this pact; and, by the time the nun is moved to send the next two letters, this Cardinal will have become the new pope. He will serve over the Church during one of the most deadly periods in the world's history; and, the pope's agreement will have sacrificed the lives of many people, gaining the Church nothing but that title.[68] Simply because this tyrant will have been of a philosophical sect that will have had the potential to use warfare against the Russian sect, the new pope will see apathy towards the German leader as a way

---

68   This was primarily done in 1933, when Hitler first became Chancellor of Germany. At that time, Cardinal Eugenio Pacelli signed the Nazi-Vatican Concordant. This made the Catholic Church the official Church of State in Germany, with the agreement that German Catholics would not be persecuted, as the Jews (and others) would be. Cardinal Pacelli would become Pope Pius XII in 1939 and oversee the Church during the heights of genocide and persecution, by both the Nazis and the Soviet Communists.

240

for him to do the Church's business for it. The new pope will not try to back out of his agreement with the German leader. He will not put his faith in Christ, believing that both sects could be stopped by a committed Church. This will be a grievous error on the Church's part and it will begin a rapid decline of the **catholic** membership.

Pope Pius XII, League of Nations, Beginning of World War II

And, with that confirmation given by the Cardinal that will be pope, **the other** religions of Germany will be banished, with a strong persecution of its Jewish population taking place. This persecution, **which** will be known **to** be happening, will be seen as approved by the Catholic Church, keeping the other Christian nations from challenging **its** decision to appease a tyrant. This will especially be true for the **great** nations that will have been powerful enough to stop both the Germans and the Russians, had the Church acted to influence them to do so. The great nation of Great Britain and its New World nation of America will be faced with **confusion** over the political upheaval in Europe. The pope will be given ample opportunity to speak publicly about the threats of the Russians and the atrocities of the Germans; but, his complaints will be too **late in coming**, to help the many suffering people. While he will take private actions to help save a few, those acts of **repentance** will be all that the Pope will do. The sect of Germany will have aligned **there** in Italy as well, when the German Cardinal will have become pope. The people of Italy **will wish** to see the Church brought **to ruin**, with its land and wealth seized; but, the tyrant that will then rule over Italy will save the Vatican for papal rule. This generosity will be due to the increasing power of the German tyrant, with his sect then **being** found adopted in **three** of the **regions** of Europe. Each of these areas will be sharing the same philosophical ideals of military dominance to gain power, leading to quests of imperialism. Those regions will align with the members of this alliance, seeing the need to forcefully expand into smaller foreign territories. Those actions will be seen **by** many people in the world as **the extreme** lusts of inhuman tyrants; but, while some nations will loudly complain, others will voice a **difference** of opinion, openly accepting forced annexation. At this time, several **of the** nations in the world will have formed as a **league** of nations, for the purpose of protecting the sovereignty of the weaker nations against aggression by stronger neighbors. This league will be called upon to discuss those invasions and consider punishment by sanctions, if lands are not returned. One of the nations that will be threatened with such mild reprimands will be Italy; but, **that is to say** that this league did nothing to keep a weaker nation from being dominated by a larger nation. This will be the first test to this league's power, when the leader of Italy will try to revive the **Roman** Empire and invade Abyssinia.[69] The league will not cause Italy to withdraw. Second, **the** leader of **Germany** will invade the lands of Bohemia.[70] The league will not be able to cause Germany to withdraw either. Finally, a civil war will rage in **Spain** for two years, with the league unable to cease arms and men from Italy and Germany going into Spain to help another tyrant seize a nation.[71] All of these tyrannical leaders of nations will have seized power, by taking advantage of a philosophical system that allows political freedoms. The failure of this league of nations will be due to a lack of involvement by the largest nations, **which** will be finding it difficult to act. This difficulty **will be** due to its own people not **making** the necessary commitments to join a league which could require them to make a show of strength. The New World nation of America will have conceived the idea for the league; but, due to the **diverse** opinions that will be found in the many **sects** of political philosophy that will settle in that country, they will not have officially joined the league. Without the strongest nations being joined with the smaller nations, the league will fail to cease the beginning of a world war. Without the unifying element of religion, overseen **by** one strong Church, the Christian nations of the world will not act to stop the blatant expansions that will be made. Even though these expansions will be made by the **hand** of tyrants who will use **military** force to take a foreign land without provocation, no one will be able to prevent a coming war. The nations of the world will end up **abandoning** this process of negotiation. In the case of the Italian invasion of Abyssinia, of **the** 60 member nations of this league, **50** will have voted against such aggression. Without the strength to enforce the majority's rule, this league will stand only as another example of mankind inability to manage itself. This lack of swift action will motivate the leader of Germany to

---

69   Abyssinia is now Ethiopia. This occurred in 1935.

70   Bohemia is now Chechnya, then Czechoslovakia. Germany annexed the Sudetenland, portion of Bohemia. This occurred in 1938. In 1939 Germany then seized the rest of Bohemia and Moravia.

71   The Spanish Civil War lasted between 1936 and 1939, with the Vatican blessing Franco as the leader of Spain in 1937, even though the Republicans were not defeated. Franco finally defeated the majority late in 1938, after Germany had forcibly taken part of Czechoslovakia, without outside intervention. That broke the will of the Republicans.

expand his plans. In his capital city of Berlin, at **52 degrees**, 29 minutes **of** latitude, he will be nearing his **height** of power and confidence. This man will make very important progress in gaining support, as he **will be making** advances to reform the former members of the Holy Roman Empire, all under one German flag. He will spread a charisma that will charm **all** of the nations which will have been of the Austrian Dynasty, requiring them to pay **homage** to their heritage as Germanic people. This heritage will be seen as a pure blood race, such that persecution **of the** people of lesser heritage and those of non-Christian **regions** of the world will be forced to relocate to **far distant** places, a long way from their homes and villages. They will be collected together and sent **to the regions** of the lands **of Europe** that will later be seized by Germany. Many of those persecuted people will be the Jewish people who had settled in those lands long before, and will have been born in the lands in which they lived. With this call for German heritage creating a dream for the people to follow, and **from** the resulting unity of all of the Germanic peoples in Europe, they will hold all of **the** land **North of 48 degrees** of latitude, where Vienna is located. This will stretch from France and Belgium in the west, to Poland in the east. This will reunite much of the land that was representative **of** the **height** of Germany's history, making the German leader call this new height another Reich, or Empire. This new empire will not show signs of being finished expanding its domination, **which** will be a concern for the British and French. The British will be the **first** nation that will attempt to halt the German leader's quests, **by** making a **vain** attempt to reach an agreement for no further expansion.[72] This willingness of the British to concede a foreign land to Germany will show their **timidity**, as they will be fearful of venturing into a new war. The British will have been believed to be the strongest opposition to Germany. France and Russia will have proven their weakness by failing to assist Bohemia, when both had signed treaties of assistance with them. This will lead the leader of Germany to next invade Poland, which will be the first nation to fight back with arms. The British will have had an agreement with Poland, to assist against such an invasion; but, all of Europe **will tremble** as Poland swiftly falls, without any external forces sent to help. From that time

---

72   English Prime Minister Neville Chamberlain met with Adolph Hitler in Munich, Germany for this purpose. Both signed what is called the Munich Agreement, in September 1938, as well as an agreement that England and Germany would settle its differences peacefully. The pact was broken less than a month later, when Hitler took the rest of Czechoslovakia; and in 1939 he began planning to invade Poland.

then, when Germany will have advanced through Poland with military arms, it will only cause the Russians to act. They will also invade Poland, so that two foreign nations will occupy one captured nation. This will force an agreement between the Germans and the Russians, where both will share the land of Poland. With this agreement of nonaggression between Germany and Russia, the German leader will then not have to worry about a threat from **them**, allowing him to focus **more** on the **westerner** half of Europe. This will be Germany's next area of expansion. With Spain a silent ally and under the control of a tyrant of the same sect of philosophy, the tyrant of Germany will then advance on the lowlands of Belgium and Holland. Once this is secured, he will then sweep into France, before later attacking England. Three other **southerner** nations of Europe, other than Italy, will then join with Germany as members of this sect of philosophy, and begin to war in the Balkans, Greece and North Africa.[73] When the whole of Europe will then at war, the **easterner** nation of Russia will be causing the nation of Finland to be **trembling**, as Russia will demand land from them. In the Eastern world, Japan, another member of this sect of philosophy, will begin a war against the Russians and intensify atrocities towards the Chinese.[74] This aggression, involving all of the nations of Europe, as well as nations in Africa and Asia, will create **such** sweeping warfare around the world that there **will be** no short and easy way to end what will have been started. All will have stemmed from the lusts of the German leader and the dreams of the German people. He will have manipulated them by taking **their** pride and making the promises necessary to gain **power**, knowing their willingness to follow. It will be **that** quest for power that will have become the model for manipulating a nation. Germany will have once held great self-esteem and pride; but, that will have been stripped away by the German surrender in the previous war. It will have been **this** loss of pride that will have sent the German people spiraling into a great depression, **which** will have made it possible for the German leader to raise **himself** into the position of leadership. He will have seduced the people by his words of a return to

---

73   In June of 1940 France had surrendered to Germany and Italy had declared war on France and England, while sending Libyan troops into Egypt. Hungary and Rumania joined the Axis in 1940 also, with Bulgaria joining in at the beginning of 1941. Yugoslavia and Greece were the nations that these four nations focused on defeating, until Germany would invade Russia.

74   Russia went to war with Finland and Japan in 1940. Japan had been at war with China since 1937 (Second Sino-Japanese War), but began its "Three Alls" policy: to kill all, loot all, and burn all, in the areas that Japan had seized in China.

glory. The remembrance of this past loss at war, and the suffering that the victors will have placed on the German people, **will make** the German leader seek revenge by war. He will take great delight in his revenge, **by** forcing the French to sign a surrender **agreement** in the same place that Germany will have surrendered to France in the past war. He will have restored the **union** of the Germanic peoples, and inspired them with words, to have them believe that they were **invincible** warriors. This invincibility will be believed by the German people, as the news of each **of the** mounting **conquests** is heard. They will all believe what will have been historically known of the German people, as being skilled in the arts **warlike**.

But, as invincible as Germany's war machine will seem to be, the Cardinal that will have given the Church's consent to this man of war will become pope and read the letter of the Virgin Mary's warning. The girl turned nun will realize that Germany will not be the nation which will prevent Russia from leading the world to ruin. In that original letter, **she** will have made it clear that it was up to the Church to return religion to Russia. Failing to do this will be **endangering** all the peoples of the world. However, with the pope personally committed to **the one** of Germany, **who** will have then aligned with Japan and had the Japanese declare war on Russia, this pope will rely on the plans of this German tyrant. He will let **him** maneuver militarily against the Russians, before responding to the nun's letter. The German tyrant **will be** seeking to restore a German land that will be **adjoined** to Poland, separate from Germany. He will regain this German land **by** quickly moving military strength from Germany into Poland, so that this **hastiness** will overwhelm the Poles. However, Germany will only take half **of** Poland, as the Russians will fear this move by the Germans and also invade Poland. Since this will be the beginning of **the age** when the stronger nations will take from the weaker, at will, both of these acts **of** invasion will mean the **death** of treaties and agreements on paper. Poland will have signed agreements with both Britain and Russia, but Britain will fail to come to Poland's aid and Russia will aggressively invade Poland. The Russians will be **endangering** the lives the Eastern Poles by their actions. When both Germany and Russia will be **inside the** nation of Poland, they will reach another meaningless agreement, splitting Poland between the two of them. The German portion will return to German control its separated land and the rest of Poland will be divided along the **eighteenth** degree of longitude.[75] Naturally, this agreement between Germany and Russia will **not** last. In time, Germany will turn on the Russians and be found **powering** across the Russian occupied Polish land and into the Balkan buffer nations that border Russia. The Germans will then try **to pass** the Russian capital city, at **the thirty-sixth** degree of longitude. As successful as **that** offensive will be initially, it will later be stalled by nature and the refusal of Russia to surrender. This stall will hurt the German troops, as they will become caught ill-equipped, once **in** an early Russian winter. With that stall, the Russians will be given an opportunity to rebuild, while the Russian tyrant will demand that his people fight to the death. At that time, the German military will learn to know defeat and just how vincible they truly are. Afterwards, the German military will know defeat much more than victory. The Germans **will abandon** their quest for Russia and instead fight a war of survival, on **three** fronts. Those three fronts will be led by the three **male** leaders of what will become the three greatest nations on earth: Britain, America and Russia.

It is this male drive that is most important to fully understand. Astrologically, it is symbolized by the planet Mars. This symbolizes the drive to penetrate and be competitive. In Roman mythology, Mars was the god of war. Those three male leaders will set the tone for each of their nations, by instilling that male spirit into the motivation of their peoples, causing them to believe that greatness comes to those that act aggressively. The **one** planet that is opposite to this male drive is Venus. This represents the **female** principle, where love, beauty and aesthetics are much preferred to the mess of war. France will be the nation that will show the signs of this female receptivity and preference not to do physical battle. They will put more importance on the preservation of national treasures. Those three male leaders of powerful nations will all be able to focus on war with Germany, after the German tyrant will sweep into France. Once Germany will sweep into France, defeating its defenses and causing France to surrender, the British will be unprepared to liberate France. Not coincidently, France will have bestowed a monument to the New World nation of America, to symbolize that nation's receptivity to the philosophy of freedom. This monument will be a lady, who will hold a torch high. This will be intended to symbolize the freedom of its

---

75   The 18th degree of longitude refers to East coordinates (18W00 has no land mass to cover – Atlantic Ocean). This covers parts of several countries in Europe and Africa, but it runs through the heart of Poland, Bosnia-Herzegovina and Libya. Basically, it also separates Western Europe from Eastern Europe.

246

people and the light of knowledge. This lady will act as a beacon to the world's oppressed, making America stand for a land offering opportunity and protection to the weak. With France, America's sister nation, under the domination of Germany, and with Britain, America's fatherland, under attack, the leader of America will covertly assist his nations' friends; but, when the Japanese will violently penetrate one of the American territories, this land will respond as a committed warrior.

The British Heritage

When the American nation will enter **in** this world war, it **will have** entered **two** world wars within the space of fifty years. Both of those wars it will have originally chosen initially not to enter. The difference in **this one** war, from the previous war it fought in, is that the previous war was supposed to be the war to end all wars. From that experience, the leader of America at the time of the end of that first great war will be the one **who** will have designed the concept of the league of nations. The design will have been for the prevention of war; but, with America **not in** that league, unable to negotiate international disputes, it **will have had** to fight a second great war. Since its own people **never** officially approved its membership in that league, this concept **of one** league of nations to settle matters of dispute without war will fail. Based on the power and fortitude it will have displayed in the previous war, America could have prevented this second war; but, it will not accept the responsibility of a true world power at that time. The main reason the American influence would have been so strong is that it was of the **same** philosophy as Britain, as its original heritage will have been British. Great Britain will have been the **father** of America, it beginning as one of their extensive colonial quests, as an empire. In fact, the British will have sired three vast colonial nations, which will have been growing in size over the years; and, all will eventually gain their independence. All three of these nations will share a strong resemblance to that common denominator of British heritage. It will have been **the** British wish that those **three brothers** would always remain loyal and follow their lead, by them supporting British actions. However, the nation of America, **being** the first to declare its independence, will have had to fight its fatherland in a war of independence, **such** that there will have remained some **differences** between the father and that son. From that time of independence, to **then** when it will have entered in its first world war, America will have **united** with Britain and its sister nation, France. Then they will have also fought the Germans; and, the presence of America's power will have been the difference between defeat and victory. With the son helping the father at that time, the British will have taken it for **granted** that America would again back Britain; not only in war, but also in its mediation of world affairs, as an empire. With **that** power of mediation being the forte of the British, backed by strength of arms, the second war in Europe could have also been prevented if the Germans knew that all of **the three** brothers would act to back their father's wishes for peace. With the threat of **four** formidable nations willing to force peace on Germany, if necessary, the German leader would not have been so bold. As it will come to be, the lack of American responsibility will have allowed **parts of Europe** to be stolen by force; and, this hesitancy will give rise to the holdings of the British Empire to also be attacked. With two of the brothers helping their father fight in different parts of the world, the people of England will be **trembling**, as the German attacks will reach their soil.

The End of World War II and the Discovery of the Holocaust

And, with this son rising to help defend its father's heritage, a long and very bloody war will be fought, with many lives lost on all sides of battle. What could have been prevented will end with many innocent citizens having been displaced or killed. After five years there **will be** an end to the war, **made** possible due to the presence of America and its vast resources of manpower and machinery. The defeats of the Germans, Italians and Japanese will not have been possible without America's presence; and although their greatness would have been greater, had they ceased this war before it began, they will come out of this war as the one **great** nation in the world. In this distinction, while it will have sacrificed many of the lives of its people, its land will have suffered the least destruction of all. It will be this new great nation of America that will take the lesson of this new period of **peace**, which will cause it to determine that this peace must be more lasting than the last peace, following the first world war for America. America will call for a new **union** of the nations, which will forever prevent war. As the victorious nation, America will rebuild its ally's nations, as well as the defeated nations; and, this effort will be important towards reaching a **concord** between all nations, as equal members in this new union. This agreement will not only be **between** the strongest nations, but also the ones of lesser power, so that all will have to decide by majority vote how disputes will be resolved. This will be seen as the **ointment** that will heal the past wounds of the last league. One of the first issues that this new united league of nations will face will be the discovery of many **of the children of** Israel in German prisoner of war camps and near death. They will have been held as the prisoners of the Germans, in their tyrant's plans for persecution. Those Jewish prisoners will not have warred against Germany, as soldiers on **the fronts** of battle; but, they will have been taken prisoner from the German occupied populations and interred far from their homes. Those prisoners will have been used as slaves, or they will have been awaiting execution, with many having already been killed. The news of this holocaust will have exposed the latest episodes of European genocide, against the people who have been known for their **wanders** across the face of the earth. While many also will have been wandering gypsies, the greatest number of them will have been of Jewish heritage. The Germans will have forced the Jews to leave their homes and property behind, to be moved into those camps. This program will have been said to be for the Jew's benefit, as it **separates** them from the Germanic people. They will promote fear that many of the German people will do the Jews harm, if they were to stay. The real reason will be to separate the Jews from the public eye, so that those people, seen as racially inferior by the German tyrant, can be comfortably abused. The German leader will see the Jewish blood as inferior to the Germanic blood, even though the Jewish people will have lived in the German lands for a great length of time. Simply **by** the element of cross-breeding that will have already taken place, the German people will have already become a very **diverse** racial mix at that time. The Germanic people will be required to prove there was no history of Jewish descent in each of their family trees. This proof will allow one to escape being sent to one of the German camps. This will be in spite of the fact that the German leader himself, and many others of high German rank, will have such a history of Jewish descent. However, there will have been separate **rules** for the Jews, which will have been installed before they will have been sent to those camps. The Germans will have made them wear the Star of David so they could be identified as Jewish. All of this will be exposed when the war is over; but, the number of Jews who will have died in those camps during that war will be a number so great that the world will not be able to overlook it. This will be the first serious issue that the new united league of nations will have to address.

The Oppression of Eastern Europe

The end of the war will also find another international problem existing, **by**

the fact that many European lands will have been occupied by the nations that defeated Germany, Italy, Hungary and Rumania. While the Americans will have occupied Italy and the western half of Germany, the Russians will have swept across the **lesser** nations and peoples of Eastern Europe, to occupy the other half of Germany. Russia will have been ruled by a tyrant, on an equal scale to those who will have just been defeated; and, he will have proven his tyranny by signing the treaty with the Germans, which will have allowed them to attack France. He also will have shown his lust for expansion by his actions against Finland. This Russian leader will not withdraw his nation's military presence from the occupied nations of Eastern Europe, making him no different than the German leader that will have been disposed. All of those eastern lands will have once shined as powers, over the history of Europe, primarily in the times **of** the **age** of the Holy Roman Empire. Most **will be** from strong histories in support of the Roman Catholic Church, allowing the pope to be **the** one who approved an Emperor's ascension, during times when those lands held dear that level of **monarchy** over the people. Each of those nations will have been **Christian**; but, the majority of each nation's people will be of Slavic descent. This term, "Slavic," means that they will be the descendants of slaves. The slaves of Europe will have **supported** the rule of the monarchs and the Church, as dedicated hard-working peasants; but as such, they will have gained little of material value. At the end of this great war, which will have supposedly been for the defeat of tyranny, the element of tyranny will still remain. However, with the victors of that war having become so **augmented** with power during war, at the end they will all have tremendous military arsenals at hand. This will make the Americans and the Russians the two greatest military powers on earth; so great that the stakes for going back to war will be too high, particularly against one another, and for the purpose of freeing slaves. The costs of war will have already been high, in lost lives and lost materials; but, the additional finances required to rebuild the war-damaged nations will make another war economically prohibitive. This will especially be seen as the case when the wealthier nations of Western Europe will look at the impoverished nations of Eastern Europe and their history as slaves. They will see little urgency for action to rescue a neighboring country. The new united league of nations will have to allow those dominated nations to freely voice their concerns; but, while the Jewish situation will be seen as needing immediate attention, those people of Eastern Europe will be seen as economically expendable. This will leave Europe, at the end of the war, in the same situation as it will have been when the war began. Only the tyrants controlling foreign lands will have changed.

The Soviet Union

The greatest example of this augmentation of power will be found in Russia, which was what the young girl prophesized, from the Virgin Mary. The Russian nation will have disposed its Czar before the first world war; and, since that time it will have banished all forms of religion from its land. This will mean it will be the first nation totally influenced solely by the **sects** of philosophy, allowing no royal or religious institutions to retain any power of influence. The Russian tyrants will have claimed to have spread all of the royal wealth to all of the people, by adopting the philosophy that everything within the nation is common to all of the nation's people. With Russia's vast resources and its people's resolve, its inhumane tyrant will have driven all the Russian people, in a mad effort to build military weapons to defeat the Germans and save Russia. When the war will have been won, the people will have become the common owners of one of the two most **elevated** militaries in the entire world. With all of this power in the hands of a tyrant, the world will be fearful of another war, just as it will have feared the German tyrant when he began seeking world domination. This will be because the nation of America will also be influenced by its military sects, to keep its military on high alert. Those military leaders will influence the American government to keep the Russians from surpassing the American elevated level of strength. From this mentality, both nations will be controlled by sects who will have been elevated by war achievements, with no strong association with the religious concepts of peace and harmony.

The Bomb and It's Power

One of the military sects of America will have secretly worked on devising the most powerful weapon ever imagined by mankind. Once this weapon will be developed, its power will have rapidly elevated America over all opponents. Its development **will seem** possible to several other nations; but, the climate in America will have brought the greatest minds of **that** elevated sect of math and science to America, allowing them to successfully create it first. After **the** war in Europe will have come to a close, with the alliance of America, Britain and Russia having crushed the **reigns** of the tyrants in both Italy and German, the

251

European nations will all be exhausted. The British will have also been at war in the Pacific, against the Japanese; and, its wartime losses will have **weakened** its military capacity severely. This will leave the majority of the responsibility up to the Americans to defeat the military sect of Japan. By the time of the German leader's defeat and Germany's surrender, America will have been slowly defeating the Japanese, **by** attacking Pacific islands, one at a time. With many of **the Oriental** islands surrounding Japan occupied by its military, this resistance will need to be broken by force. Japan will refuse to surrender and its military will also be instructed to fight to the death. The soldiers of **that** Oriental land will have had an Emperor, who will be seen as a god to them; and, the Japanese will all be committed to die for that man and the land of Japan. The cost of continuing to fight to the death, one island at a time, would be great, as many lives would be lost on both sides; but, the Americans will have tested their weapon and found that it will have so much power, they predicted that the Japanese would surrender if they were to use it on the island of Japan. When this weapon is tested, the destructive power unleashed will be so great that some will believe it could be a power equal to that held by **God**. The Americans will believe, as **the creator** of this weapon, God will have given them His blessings to use a device. This thought will be with them knowing this weapon will undoubtedly kill great numbers of human beings. Since the alternative **would have** many Americans soldiers die fighting a fierce foe, the Americans will decide to kill large numbers of people on the island of Japan, in the name of God. With that decision, the Christian nation of America will become **unbound** to the principles of Jesus Christ. The Americans will not have realized **its madness** will be generated by Satan; and, it will be that influence which will have allowed for this weapon's development.[76] This weapon's power will have come **from the** depths of the earth, at the very core of the material realm, where this secret has been kept in the **prisons** of hell, purposefully sealed from mankind's reach. The **infernal** blasts of heat and fire those weapons will release, spreading across vast areas of earth, will be tremendous; and, it will bring the inferno of hell to the surface of the earth. The Americans will wait **for** news of a Japanese surrender after one weapon will be used; but, none will come. This will cause a second great weapon

---

76 Nostradamus wrote "*satan*," in the lower case, whereas Satan would have been capitalized. I have bolded this lower case translation, as "*sa tan*," which in Old French can mean "its madness." Surely, Satan is an intended meaning that is applied, but the lower case makes this the human responsibility for sins attributed to Satan's influence.

to be used; and, that weapon will have the same effect as the first, in a different city. With those two efforts **to make** the Japanese end the second world war, the Japanese will unconditionally surrender to the forces of America. The use of those two weapons will forever be known as the time when the greatest evil ever **to be born** to mankind will have arrived in the world. It will be the existence of a weapon that will make **the** whole world fear, and for just cause. The inner voice of everyone will tell them to fear this weapon; and, many will soon feel that they know where this weapon will lead mankind. Even though the world will see America as a **great** nation, for having possession of this most powerful weapon, America's greatness will be seen as its strength and not its compassion. Once in possession of such a great power, America's sect of philosophy will bend to become the world's greatest **Dog**.[77] Once it will have felt the surge of power this use against Japan will bring, it will lust for more and more great weapons. Once the Japanese will have surrendered the world will have finally entered into a period of peace. However, the Russian military sects will have also been working on the creation of an identical weapon, based on the same mathematical principles of power. They will complete their weapon within a few years, which will make them as equally powerful as the Americans; and, it will equally make them a Dog too. At this time, when two nations will have the power of Satan within their grasps, each nation will feel threatened by the other's weapons. This will create the need for a great weapons **Dogma**, as these two Dogs will have to create rules for the use of their creations. Each nation, America and Russia, will keep the world fearing yet another war, until they reach agreement on how to control their unchecked development of weapons, during peace time. Before this agreement is reached, each nation will bait the other, with news of more and more great weapons having been developed, causing a race of armaments. This buildup of arms, **which** the use of only two will have made the world fear its end coming, **will be making** the prospect of another war **so great** that the whole world would surely come to an end, should that war ever begin. Only a very small **fraction** of those very powerful weapons would suffice to threaten the end of the world, as the effect of only one will have been known to be **abominable**. Condemnation of this abominable collection of power will belong **to the** leaders

---

77 Nostradamus actually wrote "Dog" in this statement, but the French word for dog is "dogue." Dog is English, which is the language of America; but, Dog is the English spelling of God in reverse. This makes the distinction as a Dog be like an anti-God, for having used the powers only allowed to deities, to kill and bring fear to the world.

of the world's **Churches**, and especially the churches of Christianity. But, again their complaints will be tempered, as these pious leaders will be unable to make **that** declaration of abomination, while that weapon will be in the hands of **the reds** of Russia. They will **not** be able to condemn the atheist Russians and their build-up of dangerous powers, without equally condemning **the white** knights of Christian world, which will be led by the great nation of America.[78] The Churches will choose to support the evil of America as God's blessing, for their might will keep the Russians in check. The Russians will have given this power to the nations it dominated, and America will have spread it to its allies. They will all act as if they are **without eyes**, becoming blind to the danger of this situation and its growing influence. The leaders of all nations will **not** able to see the consequences of what will have been created, as possession of such power will bring out lusts for greatness. This power will be seen as an equalizer, when the lesser nations will later begin to gain this power. All of the leaders of the nations of the world will be in agreement that this spread of these weapons will eventually lead to the total destruction of mankind; but, those leaders will claim they are **without hands** to stop its spread, as their hands will be bound to respond to the actions of another. This attitude will only add **more** momentum toward this final end, as the pendulum will continuously swing back and forth, with one's possession causing another to desire it. The solution to this threat will **not** be found **in judging** the threats of other nations, as dangerous to oneself; but instead, the solution will be found in judging oneself as a dangerous threat to others.

---

78 Nostradamus uses four primary colors in the verses of the quatrains, and each is repeatedly specific to the types of religious affiliation one has. White represents the Christians, Black represents Islamists, Yellow represents those of polytheistic religions, and Red represents the people without religion. His use of "red" becomes synonymous with Communism, just as they were called "Reds" at the height of the Cold War.

EXPLAINING THE QUATRAINS –
A NEED FOR ARAB DIPLOMACY

The Last Remains of the Ottoman Empire & the Creation of the State of Israel

This inability to properly judge right from wrong will not only apply to the way the leaders of the world accept the presence of dangerous weapons. The domination the Russians will hold over the Eastern European nations will soon be mirrored by the three most Christian powers, the Americans, the British and the French, in the way they will also dominate weaker nations. At the close of the second world war the people of the world will **suddenly** become aware of the gross persecution the Jews of Europe will have suffered, and will still be suffering. This exposure will act to be **lowering** the reputation of the European Catholics and Christians in general, as the Catholic Church will have been the Church of State for Germany, with the pope having failed to publicly condemn the German leader for his atrocities. An association will be made some people, connecting the Church of Rome to that holocaust. This will cause the Church to attempt to regain the approval of the world's people. In this regard, the Church will put its approval behind a movement for a Jewish homeland, which would act to clear its name, as well as become a solution to the problem of European anti-Semitism. That solution will be to move the Jews from Europe back into the Middle East, where they had thrived two thousand years earlier. This concept will have originated many years earlier, following the end of the first great European war. With the Church behind it, this movement will then pick up momentum. At the end of the first war, the British and French will have become named as the protectorates of the lands formerly under the rule of the Turkish Sultan. France and England will be named and approved by the league of nations. These lands, which the Sultan will have had dominion over prior to that war, will include the former lands of the Israelites, Judah and Israel. Those lands will then be called Palestine; and, it will be predominately inhabited by Arab Muslims, who will also be descended sons of Abraham. The British, as the protector of Palestine, will have allowed an increasing level of Jewish immigration into Palestine, due to external pressures for a Zionist state. The British also will have faced internal pressures from the local Arabs, against such immigration. At the end of the second great world war, the British will have become too militarily weak to defend their empire as it will have done before. With them weakened, many more Jewish people will begin illegally immigrating into Palestine, swelling the Jewish population there. The new union of nations will then act to settle the issue of the persecution of European Jews; and, they will reach that solution by voting to give the Jews back their former land. However, for this move to take place, since the land of Palestine being then predominately occupied by **Arabs**, those people will have to be **moved** out of the way and the Jews moved in. At that time, the Arabs will be seen, by the wealthy powers of Europe, as socially lower than either the Jews or the Slavs of Eastern Europe. Beyond that, the Arabs will be powerless to resist a forced move of this nature. This move, **back** to the biblical lands of Israel and Judah, will be made easier due to the fact that no **Kingdoms** will exist in that region. All of the lands east and north of Jerusalem, along the Jordan River, will have been totally subservient to the Turkish Sultan, before the Turks will have surrendered those possessions of land. Since that fall of the Sultan many years before, all decisions of national interest in Palestine, Phoenicia, Judea and Syria will have had to have been approved by the British and French overseers. The regions controlled by the British at that time will have stretched from India to the Mediterranean Sea, including Persia and Mesopotamia, along with Judea and Palestine. The French will have controlled the lands of Phoenicia and Syria. The Kingdom of Arabia, the land of Mohammed, will have been unaffected, as it will have maintained its national autonomy; but, the whole of this Middle East region will be then, as it is now, **united** under the one main faith of Islam. Since Britain will have become weak after two major wars in half a century, it will no longer be able to dominate as it once had. The British will then pass the responsibility of overseeing this transfer of ownership, giving the Jews Palestine, to its eldest son, America. Because the second world war will have not long before ended, America will be a natural successor, having grown into a world dominating power. In addition, with the authority of the new union of nations, America will be supported in its efforts to take measures to ensure the Jews have proper defenses against their Arab neighbors. The British will have moved the Arabs out of Palestine, allowing them to retain Jerusalem; but, this will have caused many Palestinians to become refugees, no longer with a land of their own. Many Palestinians will be found going into Syria and the land across the Jordan River, in Judea. Once the Jews will have been moved into the land previously owned by the Palestinians, they will make **new** laws for their new nation, under the name of Israel. Those laws will be made to circumvent one of the **Laws** of God, where His Law states, "Thou shalt not steal." This land will most certainly be stolen, regardless of what law man will announce; and, it will have been stolen by the children of God, who were given this Law originally. The union of nations will also make new laws, as for the first time a nation will have been created on land where others will have lived, without the necessity of war or payment. Simply by citing man's new law, Israel will again live. This has been predicted in the Bible, as a sign of the End Times nearing. Once this new law will be **promulgated**, making it official by proclamation and declaration, the world's clock will begin ticking in a countdown to the final hour of mankind.

The Arab Response to Israel

To clarify this proclamation of new laws, they will be quite different **from the other** Laws God will have handed down to Moses, for the **children** of Israel. Those Laws of God were to be **the first** and foremost Laws, especially to lead them, as they were a lost tribe seeking the Promised Land. However, the Hebrew people turned away from God's Law and lost their land and their Holy Temple, which was built to house the Law of God. At this future time, the new laws of Israel will be founded on displacing the children of Abraham, to whom God also promised the land. After the Jews will have been scattered to the winds of the earth, the people of Palestine will have made the first claim on that land, having become the rightful owners. To take the land from them in this way is considered stealing by God. This theft, supported by powerful Christian nations, will cause the Arabs to see the Jews and Christians as having no moral, ethical or legal right to take back land which will have no longer been the Jew's land. A war will have been just recently fought to free occupied lands from oppressive tyrants; but, instead of addressing another oppressive tyrant occupying the lands of Eastern Europe, the Christian nation of America will themselves act as an oppressive tyrant, on behalf of the union of nations, to occupy more land. The Jews **will occupy** this seized land and declare their new state; and, after the British **Lions** will have removed themselves from any responsibility of dominion, the Arabs will become **furious** and attack the Jews from all sides. It will be the **crown** of the British Lion, along with its American offspring, who will have assisted the Jews in this creation of a new Israel, particularly by giving them the machinery for war. The British will have also given gifts to the Arabs, to appease

257

them into submission, which will be the gift of the British granting those once overseen lands their independence, as nations. In some of those lands the British will recognize new crowns being bestowed upon new kings, who will then be allowed to sovereignly rule their newly independent nation. This gift will not include any assistance to help secure those Arab nations militarily, as the English Lion will be **holding the paws** of control on the Arabs, playing each against the other, over land ownership. This ploy will have the effect of weakening the Arab resistance to the new Israel, enough to keep the Jews **on top** militarily. By the Jews having two of the world's greatest powers assisting them in **the** obtaining of necessary **arms** to defend their newfound homeland, the new Israelis will easily defeat the other Arab nations at war. Those defeats will allow the Jews to expand the original borders given to them, bringing Jerusalem and other strips of land under the banner of Israel. Once armed, the Jews will become **dauntless**, or fearless, in their actions against the Arabs; but, the Muslims will also be just as intrepid in continuing their war against the Jews. Once the Arabs will be armed adequately and properly unified, there will be a fight to the death over this issue of stolen land.

Shah of Iran, 1945-1979

And, with this constant unrest present between the Arabs and the Jews over this new state of Israel, the growing dependency of the Christian world on the natural resource of the Arabs will become jeopardized. It **will be** up to **the** Americans and British to **head** operations which will secure Israel's position, as well as secure several key nations in that region, particularly the ones with the greatest quantities of this natural material. That security will not only require military and financial aid to Israel, to make it the strongest nation in the Middle East, but it will also require taking steps to alter the focus of the people in other Arab nations. Since the British and French will have ceased to be a military overseer and presence in this region, having freed all of the lands to their own rule, the Americans will begin to act to subvert those reigns which could become a threat to Israel.

The British will have controlled some Middle Eastern lands for several years, as they will have assumed the role of **governor** over most of the lands lost by the Turks. When the Turkish Empire will have collapsed from war, most of the individual countries they held dominion over will not have had rulers of any true power. One land which will have maintained autonomy, although with a high degree of British involvement, will be the land of Persia.[79] Persia will have had a monarch who will have come to the throne through power, not by not having been of true royal blood. During the second world war this king will have preferred to side with the German leader, due to his view on Jews and a dislike for both the Russians and British; but, to avoid an invasion of Persia by so many hostile nations, this king will have declared Persia a neutral nation. Still, under his authority some of the British interests, pertaining to British knowledge of extracting natural resources from the ground, will be sabotaged. This destruction will anger the British, who will then force this king to abdicate his throne, while the war is still going on. The crown will then be passed on to his young son, who will be seen as favorable to the British. Due to his youth, he will be seen as impressionable; and, this young king will follow the British commands, which his father had opposed. By granting favor to the British in his actions as king he will rule for a decade; but, with the British power dwindled by time of the conclusion of the war, they will no longer be able to control the people of Persia. The people will band together to choose a new primary leader, which will **cast** doubt on the king's continued power of authority. The king will flee **from** Persia, fearing for his life, as the new leader will assume **the** majority of the king's duties of state. With Persia being in the **middle** of this Arab region, thus having a strategic location to Israel, the loss of this pro-British Persian king will make it more difficult for the British to assist the nation of America, in their defense of Israel.

For this reason of central location, the British and the Americans will both covertly act to overthrow this people-chosen leader of Persia, and **put** back **in the** king. Once he is back in that **high** position of power, he will make Persia a **place** which will not threaten Israel. With the assistance **of** America, this king will make Persia the strongest Arab nation. The restored king will purchase a military that will be second only to Israel in the Middle East region. To ensure this military power will not be turned against the Israelis, the Americans will insist that the king rule his people with an iron fist. The king will willingly comply, as this style of rule will ensure that he will not be deposed again. The people of his land will see **the air** of lavishness the king will put on; living off

---

79   Persia changed its name to Iran under the first Reza Shah Pahlavi. He assumed power in a coup in 1925, and then changed the name in 1935.

the wealth his nation will reap. The king will profit greatly from selling Persia's natural resources to the British and Americans; but, this resource will also be in great demand all across the world. The king will reward the Persian people with many freedoms and opportunities, which many will have been unaccustomed to. Those freedoms will be like those found afforded to the people of Britain and America; but, several Muslims clerics will claim that the king is **ignoring** the Muslim religious laws, by granting those freedoms. They will state that freedoms can only be granted if they are not contrary to Islamic Law. This will create significant opposition to this king, and especially his alliance with the West; but above all, there will be an elevated concern from Muslims, about this Arab king's lack of hostility towards the Israelis. The king will look for **the** signs of **conspiracy** against his position; and, he will use the military strength he will have purchased to defend his land from hostile neighbors, and to control his own people. With the methods used by his secret police, some **of the conspirators** who will be found will be punished by exile, outside of Persia. This king will act as if he will be one **with the** spirit of a previous Persian ruler, likening him the **second** in the line of **Trasibulus**.[80] Both of these Persian kings will have welcomed a western culture into their land; but, in this American-controlled king's desire to bring the Western culture to Persia, **which** he will see as good, such a move will be strictly forbidden by Islamic Law. Those actions of change will have been deemed unholy by the clerics, making it a source **of** unrest for the **long time** the king will rule. In response to those complaints, the king **will have** exiled one very troublesome cleric, and **handled** the threat of **all this** cleric's followers by the use of strong arm tactics, including torture. Those actions will be kept secret for a while; but, **at that time** that this king will be exposed, and **the filthiness** of his controlling ways will be learned, the people will see the king ruling as a tyrant. The Persian people will see **the abominations** that are **being** created **by** their leader, at by the direction of the **great** Christian nations which he will have become subservient to. To have the king more dedicated to the Americans and British, over his own people, will put a **shame** over his rule. The Americans and British will see that unrest in the Persian people will have threatened the stability of the king's rule. The cleric, who will have been sent into exile for having **objected** to the changes taking place in Persia, will then

---

80   Trasibulus was the first Persian ruler who made his capital the seat of the king, ruling over tributaries, while being culturally connected to the West. The Shah of Iran named his cultural change the "White Revolution," which was a westernization of Iran.

gain significant attention from the land of his exile, France. There he will again publicly object to this king's rule. This cleric will make public a most significant objection, which will command that a revolution be **manifested** by the peoples of Persia, to return the Muslim faith to power. From the cleric's position **in the darkness** of exile, to the people **of** Persia wanting the return of their religion, the cleric's words and proclamations will be seen as **the light** which will lead them to revolt. This will cause a religious uprising and the king's plan to whiten Persia will be **darkened**. The king **will cease** the atrocities against his people and his guards will stop carrying out his commands. The cleric in exile will be called to return to Persia; and, he will begin to move **towards** that goal. Before this cleric makes a triumphant return, **the** king's time will come to its **end**. He will once again clearly see the signs **of** overthrow surrounding him, with **the changing** of the guard necessary. The lavish times **of his reign** will be over.

Saddam Hussein, 1968-1980

And, this changing of the guard will be the cost of doing business, as far as how America will see the situation. The Persian land will have been kept from **standing up** against Israel for decades, due to the rule of a puppet king; but, with him lost, America will have also established other similar diplomatic connections. They will have prepared for that, by other secret maneuvers, in nearby Arab countries. The Americans will have helped install another puppet ruler in the **neighboring** land of Mesopotamia.[81] This action will have placed a dictator in power as the ruler; but, one **of** this dictator's strongmen will be the **one** most in debt to America. This strongman will be prompted by America to attempt one **other** coup, to put a more manageable dictator in power; but, this strongman will have been forced to flee Mesopotamia, for failing to accomplish his mission of overthrowing the dictator. He will seek refuge in Egypt, where he will again receive training and influence from American secret agents. They will prepare him for a second coup attempt, which will then be successful. With this new regime installed, this man trained by Americans will rise in responsibilities, to assume the role of heading the military of Mesopotamia. When he is in this position of power, he will desire to have a military which will surpass the Persian strength, which will have been supplied by the Americans. The land of Mesopotamia will have been one of the lands governed by the British, as it will

---

81 Mesopotamia is the modern nation of Iraq.

have been an important land the Turkish Empire surrendered. In the record of the past, the Persians and Mesopotamians will have had a long history of border disputes. The British will have had to settle several of those, when they had the power of influence over both nations. When the Persian king will have been forced from his position of power, causing him to vacate before the Islamic cleric will return, Persia will have fallen into a position of weakness. This will allow this Mesopotamian military leader to bring great **devastation** against Persia, by the acts and declarations of war. America will have put more trust in the Persian ruler; but, **by** the time the Persian ruler will abdicate a second time, America will not go to his assistance again. The Americans will **then** see the land of Mesopotamian as helpful to their cause, such **that it** will not have to interfere with the military conflict that will turn into war between Persia and Mesopotamia. The military leader of Mesopotamia **will be** the second in command of the nation; but, he will have become **in** closer alliance to the Russians, even though the Americans will have helped place his leader in power. It will have been Russia who will have supplied much of **its** military machinery to Mesopotamia. The old leader of Mesopotamia will then succumb to frailty, after having given **more** and more power to his second in command. With his demise, the military leader will have become the most **high** figure of power in Mesopotamia. The people of Mesopotamia will have given this ruler its adoration, seeing his character as **sublime**. This will have been seen as remarkable, as he will have been elevated into this position of power from one of most common birth. His war against Persia will be promoted as necessary, to restore lost **dignity** to Mesopotamia; but, this long and horrid war will not be dignified, with many people dying needlessly on the fields of battle. While the Americans will have once raised him to the threshold of such power, this common leader will only be loyal to **himself**. He will have been inspired by the leadership model of the past Russian tyrant, who will have murdered many thousands of his own people to maintain his tight control, before his eventual death. The Mesopotamian leader will become another tyrant of his mold, who will terrorize his own people to stay firmly in control of the land. While torturing all who would threaten his power and control, he will be **putting up**, or erecting statues in his own honor, demanding the people pay homage to them. He will promote his name as one **of** the most significant **potentates**, or sovereign rulers, in the history of Mesopotamia; and he will boast of the size of his army. His **hands** will be firmly grasping the wealth of his nation, while opposition against his reign will be quelled by **military** actions.

Saddam Hussein, 1980-1991

It is important to realize that **this** use of military might to control people will have been part of what this tyrant will have learned in his training, before assuming power. He will have seen the failure of the neighboring Persian king as being due to Muslim opposition to that king's connection to the Western culture. To avoid the same fate, he will adhere to the Islamic Law; but, at that time in Mesopotamia, the Muslim faithful will have been from three different sects. The Islamic sect of this tyrant will not hold a majority of the people in Mesopotamia, only amounting to about one-third of the population. Another third of the population will be of the sect who will be the majority sect in Persia; and, those of that sect will protest the war this tyrant will wage against Persians. This will cause him to begin severe **persecution** of the Muslim people in Mesopotamia, of different sects other than his own, to maintain control of his rule. The sect of the other third will also be similarly persecuted, as these will be of the Muslim sect which will be the majority in Turkey. This persecution **will last** from his rise to great power over Mesopotamia, until **eleven years** will have passed.[82] Over this period of time this tyrant will have warred for eight years against the Persians; and, in the war against the Persians and later to control the two sects of Mesopotamia that will not agree with him, the tyrant will use **some** very horrific weapons against both military and citizens. The tyrant will use poisons as a weapon, which will kill all it comes in contact with, including women, children and animals. Finally, once the tyrant will accept the terms of surrender by Persia, the tyrant will turn his full attention to the persecution of his opponents in Mesopotamia. He will kill rape and torture many thousands of Mesopotamians, while teaching his sons his lust for evil. Then, when this tyrant will feel secure in his power over Mesopotamia, his attentions will turn to another land that will have been an area of a border dispute. He will invade a small neighboring land, one with **few** weapons which will match those of the Mesopotamian military. That land will be very rich in the natural resource of the Middle East, causing it to be a valuable asset to Mesopotamia. The tyrant will occupy and pillage this land for several **months**; but, the Western world will depend on that small

---

82 Saddam Hussein took the official title of President in Iraq on July 16, 1979. The First Gulf War began in January, 1991, ending on February 22, 1991. The invasion of Kuwait took place on August 2, 1990, almost exactly 11 years after he became President. This time period before he made that move and was defeated was a "few months."

land remaining free, to ensure a flow of its natural resource to the West. The Americans will lead an opposition, against this tyrant who will have taken land from a weaker nation. At that point in time, America will see those actions as stealing.

The Soviets in Afghanistan, their Withdrawal and Collapse, 1980–1989[83]

In **that** period of months the world will react swiftly. This tiny land will have once been part of Mesopotamia, but it will have been given its independence **by** the British, when they held mandate. Whereas Mesopotamia will attempt to return lost land into its possession, as has been the accepted way throughout history, by war and violence, the world will see the actions of this tyrant as worthy of immediate response. Led by American representatives at the union of nations, it will only take a matter of months before the tyrant of Mesopotamia will be removed from that tiny land, with its sovereignty restored. Between the onset of the Mesopotamian invasion and their subsequent forced exit, **in that time** of just a few months there will be several actions taken against the tyrant. First, the Americans will have established economic sanctions against Mesopotamia, pertaining to its shipments of natural resources. Second, with the sanctions in place, a unified world force will be readied and positioned in the Middle East, to make a show of strength and cause the tyrant to vacate the seized land. Finally, when the tyrant will have refused to leave the tiny land his military will have occupied, a military action of liberation will be taken against his forces. The primary reason the world will react so quickly in this matter of seized land, when it had been so fearful of such actions before, will be because not long before this event will occur the Russian empire **will fail**. This failure of America's greatest challenger will have freed the Americans to use their might to influence the world, without Russian objection. Russia will have failed, partially because of its own invasion into a neighboring nation, which will not work out as well as they originally planned. They will have invaded and occupied a Muslim neighbor of Persia, to their east; and, they will have occupied it for as long as Mesopotamia

83   The previous block and this block should not be separated, according to the system of punctuation. However, they are best separated to avoid two topics in one block. Together, both could fall under one heading of "Middle East Turmoil, 1980 – 1991", but it reads better the way I am presenting it, while still maintaining the integrity of the order written in the block.

will have been at war with Persia. This Muslim land will be the mountainous territory between India and Persia, where both of those bordering nations will have histories of struggle, trying to also possess that rugged land. Additionally, the British will have also spent time attempting to conquest this area, as part of their empirical dominations. At the time of the Russian invasion into this land, the union of nations will have complained about this aggression, with America voicing the loudest complaints; but, no nation will have acted to unify the world and force the Russians back into their own land. The world will have not acted then as they will act against the tyrant of Mesopotamia, when he will invade a tiny land once possessed by Mesopotamia. After eight years of struggle to control this poor land, where none of the coveted natural resource of the other Middle Eastern nations will be found, the Russian control of its own empire will begin to fail. Its sudden downfall will represent the first time in history that one of **the principal** nations of the world will collapse, without the use of arms or revolution. Seventy-two years after the overthrow of its own **King**, to allow the common man to gain philosophical control, the Russian domination will break apart. The Russians will have maintained a pact with the Eastern European nations they occupied following the second world war, while joining the lands from the Baltic Sea to the Black Sea as one with Russia. Russia will rename this unity the Union of the *Aquilonaire*, meaning the people of the North.[84] The areas covered by this unity and pact, **which** will have been maintained for so many **years** that three generations will have been born into it, all will have all been forced to adopt the Russian sect of philosophy. This will have included the removal of all influence of religion from those lands. For everything Russia **accomplishes** during those years of domination, it will be the Muslim influence which **will overcome** their philosophy that denies religion. This will have been most particularly evident in **its** lands it will have been **united** with in the **Southern** regions of Russia, surrounding the Black Sea. Those regions are bordering on the Middle East, where the influence of Islam has thrived for centuries. The people of southern Russia who will have been of the Muslim faith will fight for maintaining their dedication to Islam. Along with those internal fights to retain the influence of religion, the Russian invasion into another Muslim land will cause unrest in many of that invaded land's devout Muslims. This overall unrest will lead to many scattered rebellions, **which** the Russians **will persecute**

---

84 *Aquillonaire* is the people of Aquilon. Aquilon is a Greek mythological figure, who was the god of the North Wind.

by various shows of military strength, at home and abroad. They will seek to destroy all religious sects which oppose their philosophy and their occupation; but, devout Muslims will continue their struggle all along the southern boundary of Russia. For every Russian rejection of protest, Muslims will try **yet** again. Thwarting those rebellions will be economically costly to the Russians, especially while they will be trying to maintain an occupation force in that occupied Muslim nation. Organized groups of rebels in the occupied Muslim nation will become a persistent pain in the side of the Russian military; and, the Americans will put **more** pressure on the Russians, through secret economic and military aid given to the Muslim rebels. For being a nation so **strong** with military might, the Russians will be unable to successfully defeat the bands of Muslim rebels who will not cease fighting to rid a foreign influence from an Islamic land. The Muslim rebels will see the Russian occupation as a step towards installing the Russian philosophy there; and, the Muslims will fight to the death for the right to practice their religion. The Russians will eventually be defeated **by** their inability to provide for their own people, while spending more than it can afford trying to take **the space of** another nation. After **three years** of mounting difficulties, their union will collapse, too poor to fight any longer, too poor to maintain the union of Aquilonaires. With the Russians no longer able to subsidize **the people** of Eastern Europe and the smaller Baltic – Black Sea lands, all of those nations will finally be freed from the Russian domination. This union of the Aquilonaires will have been a great fear for the past popes **of the church**, causing it to disregard the warning told to the girl who saw the Virgin Mary many years before. The church will have feared challenging such a giant evil as this Russian Union; but, the Russian Union will have collapsed by the constant fight of Muslims committed to their religion. The letter to the popes will have shown that the Virgin Mary clearly stated the evil of Russia would come **by the seduction** of the people to its philosophy. That philosophy will have been **apostatic**, causing the people to renounce their faith in religion; but, the Christian nations of Western Europe will have not dared to maintain Christianity in the people of the Slavic nations. Then, without Russia's union to give it strength, the Russian nation will fall in disgrace; but, because the Catholic Church will have failed God, those freed people of Eastern Europe will have no allegiance **to the one** God, not knowing Jesus Christ. The nation of America, which will be the one greatest nation on earth at that time, will call itself a Christian nation; but, it will have also allowed those people to be born without religion in their lives.

266

Only the Muslims, **which** will have kept faith that one day their brothers and sisters would be free to worship as they please, **will hold** the values of God that strongly in their lives. For **all** of the combined **power** that both the Americans and Russians will have held, the Muslim rebels will have been the equivalent of David against Goliath. They will know that the power of God is greater than any nation on earth, because God has **absolute** power. The Muslim victory over the mighty nation of Russia will allow them to see the Christian world as having lost its faith **in the church** of Jesus Christ. They will see this loss of faith in God as the reason the Americans will have aided those who will have taken **militant** actions against Arabs in the past. America will have allowed this apostatic influence in Russia to grow for over fifty years, especially after the two shared victory in the second world war, when America became the world's greatest power. The Muslims will see America's refusal to address the Russian domination of Eastern Europe, along with its support of the theft of Palestinian land, giving that land to the Jews, as America's approval of the domination of the weak by the stronger. To the Muslims, America will have stolen land from the Arabs and be known to have secretly placed tyrants into power in the Middle East, who will have murdered many innocent Arab peoples. With one giant downed in the defeat of Russia, the Muslims will look towards the other giant which represents religious persecution to them.

Osama bin Laden, 1980-1989

The sudden withdrawal of Russia from the occupied Arab land will not be possible without the militant actions taken by the rebels. This defeat **will be** largely made possible because the Americans will have **made** the Islamists capable of being such a thorn in the Russian military's side. The Americans will not overtly make their presence known, **such** that no American troops will assist the rebels. But, a secret American group will hide their presence with the rebels; and, that group will train one Muslim leader in the mechanics of guerrilla warfare and supply his rebels with the necessary weapons for that style of fighting. Once the Russians will have withdrawn and **peace** will have returned to that region, **that** Arab leader will cause his group of Islamist rebels to continue to train, for a plan to later attack the land of America. This Arab leader's hostility against foreign nations **will continue**, as he will persevere against all outside interference into Muslim affairs. While he will be preparing an army for a long war, this army will not be restricted to any one nation of residence, like typical armies are

267

based. The unity will be **attached** to the principles of Mohammed; and, this rebel leader will be closely identified with the lore of a popular Muslim martyr, named Musab.[85] Both Musab and this Arab leader will have given up a private position of considerable wealth, to fight for the public cause of Islam. The commitment to this goal will make this Muslim leader come **to the** point of turning his back on his family, as did Musab. With the defeat of the Russians, this leader will not stop seeking ways to eliminate the opponents of Islam in the Middle East. He will order **more** attacks, in other Middle Eastern lands, by way of the guerrilla tactics he will have learned from the Americans. He will use those tactics on the Americans and plan attacks on Israel too. Sneak attacks will become more and more **profound**, and the symbolism of their targets will represent a greater sign to other Muslims, than will the actual damage done. Many of this Muslim leader's agents will commit suicide in these efforts, which will act **to cheat** the Americans and Israelis of judging those assailants by their laws. From the Arab's Holiest Land, by the deep abysm that is the Red Sea, this Arab **arouser** will awaken the Muslim faithful and unite them behind a cause. The Christian world will see him as **the inciter** of unprovoked violence and the **promoter** of terror in innocent people. But, before he will have risen to this level of religious zealotry, he will have been from simple origin; born **of the** Arab people who will have profited most from the addictions of the Western world to the natural resources of Arabia. He will have not ever served in any military capacity; and, he will have been weak in the knowledge of **martial** tactics. At first, he will lead a small **faction** of Arabs, striving to remove the Russians from one Arab land. As his success and reputation grows, so will the size and numbers of his followers. He will seek to unify the whole of the Muslim peoples, who will have previously remained separated **by the** different nationalities and the **diversity of the** sects of Islam. This instigator will be seen by the Muslims as a high-ranking **religious** leader; and, his beard will identify him as a cleric of Allah.

Most importantly, his efforts **will be** rewarded, as the Arab lands will become

---

85   I have added this, as it directly applied to the famous quatrain that identifies the name of the "third antichrist," which is "*Mabus*." This is an anagram that easily converts to Musab. Nostradamus did not actually name three antichrists, as many people believe; and, neither does the Bible. There is only one antichrist; but, it can come on three levels of the same thing. An antichrist is basically one opposed to Christianity. Iran is the antichrist nation, Islam is the antichrist religion, and Osama bin Laden is the one that has the appeal of Christ, to Muslims.

united for a common goal. That goal will come with a solid plan of approach formulated, knowing they will need to supply themselves with the necessary weapons to fight their foes equally first. They will want to create **the** unity of a new Muslim **Kingdom**, which will once again have empirical powers. Once they will be strong enough to remove the American backing **of the Rabbis** of Israel, they will be able to remove the Jews from their stolen land, at will.[86] To have this plan reach its goal, **which** will not be easy since both the Jews and America will be seeking this rebel leader and his soldiers, the Muslims **will counterfeit** their actions, or disguise them, so that their enemies will not see the growing unity and arms build-up spreading. The Muslim leader will have learned from the masters of deceit, when the secret American group will have trained him in how to defeat a larger foe. In this regard, history will show that **the wise** warriors of history will have consistently disguised their numbers, drawing their prey into a trap, where the element of surprise is a great equalizer.

The Emergence of the United States of America as the World's Greatest Nation

Against the Russians this Arab rebel leader will have learned how wise it is to use deceit against a stronger foe; and, with the collapse of the Russian union, the nation of America will have become the uncontested greatest nation on earth. This Russian collapse will have been so sudden and unexpected that the world will not consider it as a planed act of deception, because much will have been publicized about the Russian citizens being in dire need of economic assistance. America will have **not** foreseen the Russian fall; but, it will gladly take credit for having contributed to their collapse, due to America having greater wealth, enabling them to outspending the Russians in a race of economics. However, with the fallen Russians **wanting** to develop a better relationship with America, America will then show its giving spirit. More than from a friendly spirit of assistance, America will not want to lose this opportunity to promote **itself** as God's chosen one to lead the world. The Russians, without the strength of their Aquilon

---

86 Nostradamus wrote, "*Royaume du Rabieux*," which many people have translated many ways. The word of most confusion is *Rabieux*, which is not a pure word in French. Closest to this has been *rabique*, which means rabies, the disease found in mad dogs. The word actually separates into "*Rabi eux*," which means the plural of Rabbi and they or them. The Old French word, "*rabin*" meant rabbi and becomes a strong reference to the Middle East.

union, will be forced **to yield** to America's new superiority; and, this will primarily be found when the Russians will yield **to them** on matters of international disputes, in the meetings of the union of nations. This immediate change of heart **by the** Russians will cause many in the world to see an **end** has come to the spreading of the Russian philosophy, the one which was **opposite** to religion. The nation **of** America will extend **the hand** of friendship to Russia, ending years of **sharp** opposition. The past will have found the two nations **touching** on many political differences, which will have caused many heated disputes, rarely coming to agreement. But, at this time the **land** of Russia will be in such great need of economic assistance it will hold its opinion on political matters, to allow the Americans to take charge in world affairs. The people of Russia also **will be wanting** to experience the freedoms the Western nations will have enjoyed for many years; and, the Russians will allow many of its people to leave Russia and go to the West, something it would not freely allow before. The new leader of Russia will seek **to stimulate** the Russian economy and stabilize Russia's relations with many foreign nations, which **until** then will have supported America's commands to economically punish Russia. Many nations will then be welcome **to this** new attitude displayed by the Russians; and, they will see **that** a stimulated economy and stabilization will be good business for them. They will view a new Russia that **will be born**, completely different from the one which will have threatened world peace for so many years. The days of Russia that will have been representative **of the** tyrant who ruled through the second world war, when only **one branch** of government existed, will be seen as over. Although none of the Russian citizens will know **of** religion, the prospect of teaching them **the** values of Jesus Christ will seem promising. Still, to the Russian people that branch of philosophy will have been seen as **sterile**, barren and fruitless; and, at this time, they will be looking for material gains, not spiritual rewards. America will be extending a hand of friendship to the new tyrant of a new nation **of** no faith, which will have caused suffering for many, for a **long time**. There will have been suffering to the people of Russia, the people of the lands it will have occupied and dominated, and to the people of the foreign lands it will have manipulated. The nations of Eastern Europe, **which** will have struggled under the Russian domination, finally **will free** themselves and attempt to reunite with their European neighbors. With **the people** of those nations no longer being supported by the vast resources of Russia, those poor nations will see the contrasts of Western lifestyle and feel like they will have come from another **universe**. Before the time **of** the second world war, those Eastern European nations will have been similarly developed, when compared to **those** of Western Europe. However, when the first occupations will have been directed towards them, by the German tyrant, it will have been their history of **servitude** which will have kept the West from acting to save the East. This Slavic descent will not be seen as equal to the other European nations. Once those nations will have become freed again, they will find their welcome back to Europe will be very **minor**, showing this root of persecution still lives. The Christian nations of Europe will have begun to form their own unity by then, much like the unity of states in America; and, each nation in Europe will have to pay to join this union. While membership in this union will be **voluntary**, each nation will be required to meet economic requirements first; and, the wealthiest European nations will then make the judgments on which other nations will be allowed in. This will mean that those poor Eastern European nations will have been freed too late to be valued by the rest of Europe. Meanwhile, at the time this change will be going on in Europe, the tyrant of Mesopotamia will have devised his plan to bring glory and wealth to **himself**, by planning to settle a very old dispute with Arabia. This plan will call for the **restoring** of land that will have once been a part of Mesopotamia; but, this land will have been granted its separate independence by the British. This land will be **in the** coastal region of the Persian Gulf, and will have once been Mesopotamia's southern coastal outlet. Since this land will have been under the **protection of** the British, and later granted its independence, the world will have forgotten that this land will have once been claimed by both Mesopotamia and Arabia. The god **Mars** will be revered by the tyrant of Mesopotamia, and he will enjoy amassing the weapons of war and using them as often as possible. While Mesopotamia will have a great supply of the Middle Eastern natural resource, the neighboring land will have more. The tyrant's plan will call for the **despoiling** of this resource, stealing it for himself and his grandiose plans. The tyrant will believe the god **Jupiter** will bring him good fortune with his plan, such that his expansion into this land will be a success. He will also see the reclaiming of lost land as a measure **of** justice. The tyrant will be known for basking in **all of his honors**, which his conquests will have brought to him and Mesopotamia. He will envision a new honor on the horizon, by retaking this land. With so much natural resource to be gained from his land, the **dignities** of other nations will have to bend to his will, for them to acquire some for themselves. He will plan **for the** one major **city** in this land to remain **free** and open, once the land will

271

have been annexed. With this plan **constituted** and ready to be implemented, the tyrant will move his army and weapons to the border and prepare to invade. He will be **seated** in his room of command, ready to place his nation **in** yet another war. This war will not be expected to be like the **one** he fought with his **other** neighbor, Persia, which lasted eight years. This war will not be expected to last long at all, as the foe will be **cramped** into a very tiny area of land, barely bigger than the capital city of **Mesopotamia**.

The First Gulf War, 1991

With the fall of the Russians having preceded the tyrant of Mesopotamia's invasion into a smaller nation, the world will now depend on the great nation of America to prevent such forced expansions. The world will know of Mesopotamia's brutality caused by this tyrant, like the use of poisons on many people, ordered by **him**. The prospect of this tyrant **being** in control of an occupied nation, which will have been a key exporter of the Middle Eastern natural resource to the West, will not be tolerated by America or Britain. With the Russians unable to oppose the American decisions in international affairs, America will demand support for an immediate militarily response against this tyrant. The nations of the world will unite to oppose the tyrant's actions, at meetings by the union of nations. This shows how easily America could have gained similar support to prevent the second world war, as well as intervene in the eight-years of war between Persia and Mesopotamia, and the Russian occupation of a small Arab nation, had it wished to do so. It will have not acted in those matters, because it saw nothing could be gained from such dangerous actions. Thus, America will be leading a multitude of nations who will mobilize and relocate to the Middle East. America will threaten the tyrant, demanding that he remove his military presence from the occupied land, or face a war of liberation. The tyrant will return his own threats; but, when America begins to invade, the tyrant's forces will rapidly leave the tiny nation and return to Mesopotamia. When the tyrant **withdraws** his military threat from that region, the American-led forces will follow them into Mesopotamia and destroy them savagely. They will steadily advance to the edge of the capital city of Mesopotamia, where the American military will be prepared to destroy the tyrant and remove him from power. However, the American troops will then withdraw from Mesopotamia, leaving the tyrant still in power, although greatly weakened militarily. The Americans and British will determine there will be the need for **the** tyrant to remain in power, as without him the

272

two nations of Persia and Mesopotamia would stand a chance of merging into one nation. This would threaten the Israeli presence in the Arab world; but, more importantly, it would threaten the uninterrupted movement of the West's needed supply of the Middle Eastern natural resource. In the end, the Americans will leave the tyrant in place as a necessary evil. They will know of his murderous mistreatment of his own people and his lust for military greatness; but, they will see the threat of Persia as greater. For those two **two-edged swords**, Persia and Mesopotamia, to equal each other out, as they will not be allies, the tyrant will have to remain intact. The Americans and British will believe this evil situation will keep those two nations from gaining advantage over the Israelis; and, the flow of the natural resource will continue to the Western nations.

The Ceasefire Agreement, 1991-2002

The plan of the Americans and the union of nations will be to **not** leave this tyrant in a position where he will have weapons that will threaten other nations; but, they will allow **him** control over his own people. Therefore, this man's unjust rule of his nation **will remain** for a longer period of time. However, to this tyrant, the fact **that** the most powerful nation on earth will not have killed him, when the Americans will have had the opportunity, he will see this as **the signs** of victory. The union of nations will have put restrictions on his nation, calling for a search for weapons and limiting his nation's ability to sell its natural resources; but, the tyrant will hide his weapons **from those which** the union of nations will send to inspect for weapons. Regardless of the restrictions, the tyrant will secretly sell his natural resources for profit, keeping the profits for himself, while his people starve. When this will be exposed, it will be seen as a violation of the peace agreement made **by** the nation of America. The tyrant will use this **manner** of secrecy, deception and denial, which will have been methods taught to him by the Americans who first trained him for power. This return **of** disrespect will show the nature of **the curvature** of evil, where an evil that one does will come back as an evil that one does in return. It will also represent the curvature of the relationship of this tyrant to America, as that traveled path will lead back to a new war, where the old one was left unfinished. However, the purpose of the union of nations will have been to bring peace and not war, **which** will make it difficult for America to get approval for a new war against this tyrant. Knowing this, **the** tyrant will act to **entice** the Americans to act against him again. He will know that the Americans will strongly covet the natural resources of Mesopotamia; so, he will treat **the people** of Mesopotamia with even more cruelty than before. He will want the American military to return **there** to Mesopotamia; and, he will be **making** plans for those soldiers, once they get close. The union of nations will ask the tyrant **to go** along with the agreement that ended the last war; and, some nations will help make it seem that the tyrant will have been within the **lawful** language of the agreement, just to prevent another war.

EXPLAINING THE QUATRAINS -
THE ADVENTURES OF THE CHURCH

The State of the Catholic Church

In regard to this lawful agreement, where evil is maintained by the written word of man, this will be at the core of the laws of the common man. The laws of man will be why the world will rapidly be falling apart, because those laws will no longer be based on **the holy** influence of the Church and God's Law. Before the second world war will have begun, the majority of the **people of** the world will have still believed in the one **God**; and, many people around the world will have prayed for peace, once that war will begin. That will be the most important time for the Church of Rome to act, to attempt to stop the tyrants who will have spread evil throughout Europe. The Church will have failed to call upon Christian nations to respond to those evils. Instead, the Roman Catholic Church will have taken the safer course, becoming a passive **observer**. For all of the Saints who will have been named by the Church, with so many of them having spilt their blood as martyrs refusing to give in to evil, the Church will have failed to act saintly. The Church will have failed God by refusing to condemn evil. By turning a deaf ear on the cries of pain and suffering it will have done little to ease, the Church will have turned its back on God's Law. The effect of this inaction will be to show the people **of** Christianity that **its** adherence to manmade **law** was justified; and this was further shown when the Cardinal of Germany will sign the agreement with the German tyrant. As pope, he will have made that law come first, above all others. Saving the Church and the pope will have become more important than saving souls.

The Laws of God and the Word of Christ and the Bible are what had set the laws of the Catholic Church previously; and, **all** church law has been designed to establish the **order** of religious life, by establishing rules to follow. Those laws of man become the principles and doctrines which are most applicable as the guidelines for the holy operation of the Church. This is the dogma of religion; but, those laws are not the true founding Laws, brought forth by God; nor are they laws prescribed by Jesus Christ or the Saints of the Holy Scriptures. Those are the true Laws; and, they are fixed and unchangeable. The Church's canons and laws are the dogma **of** its **religion**, which can be changed or left intact; but, when the Church puts more credence in its own dogma, than it does to God's Law, the people are bound to go astray. The Catholic Church will have become more concerned with its own laws, such that it **will be** no longer able to lead the souls of mankind to salvation, as it will have done before. With that loss of trust in the Church, the laws of the Christian nations will begin to evolve into laws which will be completely void of religious context and intent. When the basic Laws of God are no longer the material for the moral fabric of the Judeo-Christian societies, those religions and their members will then become **greatly persecuted**. This persecution will cause many of the faithful Christians to become **tormented** over the directions the many branches of Christianity will be taking; so much so that many will lose their faith. With **so much** evil being clearly seen in the world, but with religion being too weak to challenge it, it will appear **that** torment and persecution, for believing in God, will never end. Many will lose faith and believe evil is the true path to power and comfort. In time, this will cause many Christians to turn their backs on the Church, and question the values of religion. Fewer and fewer Christians will then be taking the Sacraments, so that less and less people will be realizing that **the blood** of Christ Jesus is the new testament which was shed for the remission of sins. The people will not seek forgiveness and there will be no strong Church to show them the path to Christ. The world will doubt the stories **of the** Bible; and, without clear evidence to prove someone or someplace existed many years before, many will doubt the **truths** which are held within the Bible's pages. This will act to make this new future world seem supreme, with all of its focus being on knowledge; and, many people claiming to be Christians will be enjoying the seductions of a material world. Without the truths of the Bible being accepted, there will be fewer truly **Ecclesiastic** peoples found in the churches and in the world. A current will have begun, which will be separating the material realm from the shores of heaven. Only the truly faithful **will swim** this widening distance to save their souls. Those who do not truly believe will fall **by** the wayside, and their souls will drown. The Prophecies of God and Christ will have long been available to **all** to read and know; but, few will have heeded the warnings, when the time of danger will come. This will be especially so after religion will have lost most of its merit in the eyes of man.

276

Pope John Paul I, 1978

The total failure of the Church will not begin until **after** one pope will have come to save the Catholic Church. Following the pope who will have failed the people at the time of the second world war, two other popes will come to reign. It will be those three popes that **will commence** a slow secret process of corruption in the Catholic Church. However, the third new pope in this sequence after the war will be a true Pope of Saint Peter, touched by Jesus Christ and intended to be a true leader of **the** Catholic **people**. This will be the last **Roman** pontiff who will attempt to return the Church to its former glory in Christ's eyes. This pope will soon find that the state **of** the Church will have been corrupted; and, he will take it upon **himself** to correct that situation. He will quickly take measures **to set straight** the bark of Saint Peter, to keep it on the course it was intended to sail.

The pope will have to set straight the direction previously set, where several **of the** Vatican hierarchy will have become involved with known men of evil. Several of those evil men will have come from one of the islands of Italy, seeking to profit from the Church's holy name. This pope will attempt **to drive away** those men of evil and the evil business they have brought, which will have some of those evil men officially placed in the Church's ranks. In addition to this, the pope will find out **some** of the Cardinals will have memberships in a banned secret organization. He will know this by the fancy rings they will wear on their fingers. Those who wear these rings will have been deemed by the Church as the practitioners of **dark** rituals; and, the Church will have created its own dogma against such association with those groups, by Church members. This forbidding will have been administered by papal decree. Those organizations delve into the **darkness** of men's minds, blocking them from **receiving** the whispers which enter through the heart. This pope will inform **some** of those Church officials that they will have to leave the Church; and, a **few** will be stripped **of their** positions and returned to their **former** ranks. The **transparency** of this situation will become crystal clear to this pope, after he looks over the Church's financial records; and, he will **not** allow it to continue. It will be the clearness of this pope's purpose and plan that will bring him immediate opposition from within. The Church will have lost its wealth, from having lost its royal tithing to the rise of the common man; and, **without** the financial support of the **great** powers of Europe, the Church will be near financial ruin. The pope will uncover a **division** within the

Roman Catholic Church, where some will have been influenced to believe it will be impossible to save souls without a solid economic base to support its extensive missions and parishes. From the **continual** erosions of the Church's holdings, since the **exchanges** from shared rule with royal kings, to having to make a pact with a tyrant to save the autonomy of the Vatican, the Church will have divided itself between good and evil. Over the period of twenty years, before this pope will have been elected, this division will have turned more and more evil. This pope's mission will be to cut away the evil and make the Church whole again.

(The Murder of Pope John Paul I, 1978)

This new pope will soon anger **the heads of** the organizations which will be linked with the officials of **the** Catholic **Church**. With the new pope **being in** a position to see **behind** the false fronts that will have been established, he will see the extent **of** this connection. Those participating members of the Church will act aloof over this matter, as they will be far from the holy men their robes will make them appear. The Church will have been moving backwards, away from it intended purpose. However, it will be **the love of God** that will fill the pope; and, he will attempt to set the Church straight, without publicly exposing all of the evil doings he will have found.

Since the pope will uncover involvement by **many** of the highest ranking Vatican officials, **from among** those who will have been closest to the previous pope, he will have to handle their removals carefully. To keep the world from knowing of the Church's wrongdoings beforehand, the pope will not be able to disgrace **them** by immediate discharge and excommunication. He will decide to move them to locations of minor importance, to let them pray on the consequences of their sins against Christ and His Church, before announcing the evil and its removal. However, when those important figures will learn of the pope's plans, they will not have prayer on their minds. Those unholy men will have long before lost all contact with Christ and God, **apostatizing** by abandoning their beliefs in Heaven. All will have sworn a new allegiance to the faith **of** mind and evil, rejecting any belief in **the true faith** of Christianity.

Those rejections of the true faith will have been made by men who will have once been sincere in their religious beliefs; but, some of them will have found entrance into and acceptance by the Roman Catholic Church from invitations coming

from the **three** previous popes. This will have brought purely evil men into the Church and woven them into such positions of prominence that they will have become well-ingrained in the fabric of the Vatican's highest echelons. This will be one of the many different **sects** of philosophy which will have flourished among men, for a very long time. The main focus of **this** one particular sect will be purely dedicated to the philosophy **of** making money; and, the Vatican will become **the center** of their power. They will know no rules in their quests for this material reward, as their hearts will be rooted in the underworld; and, due to this lust for money they will have become completely satanic. They will promote all the vices of mankind for their profit, and they will kill wantonly. The money they make from their enterprises will be handled **by the** Church, which will act as if it were dispersing contributions by the **worshipers** of the Church. For its role in this scheme, the Church and its officials will keep some **of this** dirty money; however, once **one** has taken some of this evil organization's money, one **will be** in debt to the **one** who originally made the pact with the Devil. Since this will not only be against the Laws of God, but also the laws of man, each member will swear an oath of secrecy an allegiance. Once a partner of this sect of evil men, **few** will have been able to escape with their souls intact, much less their lives. When the new pope will threaten to **put** an end to this relationship, the former holy men will fear his exposures. Those who will be firmly **in** this sect of **decadence** will know of only one way to remove this problem which confronts them.

This state of decadence **will be** what will be transferred to the Church and **sustained** for many years. Those coldhearted killers will determine that **the** one who will make a **sacrifice** will be the pope. Those closest to the pope, who will have not yet been moved to other responsibilities, will poison the pope in his bedroom at night. He will lose his life for coming to the defense **of the holy** role the Catholic Church was created to play. This murder will mean the Catholic Church of Rome will have lost its last **immaculate** leader, one who will have had a strong connection to the Spirit of Jesus Christ. His brief stay will be leaving the Church nothing but a **host** for its evil parasites, who will act in unison to tell the world the new pope died of natural causes. The Immaculate Host of Jesus Christ will no longer see the Roman Catholic Church as a Host, representing the body of Christianity, as the next popes to come will be chosen from among the evil member's supporters.[87]

(Karol Wojtyla, 1939-1946 & Pope John Paul II, 1978 - 1981)

With this pope who would have saved the Church gone, **one of the** Cardinals will have to be chosen to become the next pope; but, this man will have to be one who will be trusted to protect the Church against the release of knowledge about the **horrible** sins that will have been committed. While the next one chosen will be given the title of pope, he will not be one of the line of true **Kings** of Rome. While all popes will have only served the Church in that position for a limited time, till their natural deaths, they will have been more than temporal, being holy. However, the next pope will begin a series of **temporal** popes, who will not only hold the position for a brief moment of time; but, while doing so they will be secular, versus sacred, and only concerned with the gains of the material world. This direction will be decided for all subsequent popes; but, the next pope will be selected **by his** direct agreement with the organizations of evil. Together, those **adherents** of evil, as accessories to a murder and cover-up, will become partners in solidifying the new direction of the Church. The next pope will not have won the position by the admiration and worthiness seen in **him** by his fellow Cardinals. With one Cardinal **being** known as very close to the deceased pope and also as a devout Catholic, it will be he who will have received more votes than any of the others in the first ballot. However, that number will not reach the majority needed to make the white smoke rise. The next pope to be will be **given** votes, only by those who will have been closest to the murder; and, without a majority reached, those voters will apply internal pressures to sway the other Cardinals to overlook the most viable candidate. They will promote a little-known Cardinal who will have pastored a church of ghosts. Some of the Cardinals in the Conclave will give this man **such** high **praises** that enough of the other Cardinals will be swayed to vote for him, making him the next pope. It will not be clearly known by the Cardinals **that he** will not be deserving of this praise, as none of the rumors will be verifiable. This little known Cardinal **will have** been serving the Church in a nation which will have had **more** tears **spilt**, from the purges of Germans and Russians, than any other Eastern European nation. That nation will have had strict controls against the influence of religion

---

87   Pope John Paul I served only 33 days, in 1978. There is a great amount of information on the Internet about his murder, which the Church denies.

280

for many years. It will have been such a forbidding nation that few will have believed the Church still existed there. That nation will be that **of** Poland, where the **blood** of the Poles will have been spilled in the second world war, first by the German tyrant, and then by the Russian tyrant. The Russian philosophy of a society free of religion will have banned the Polish Church from official recognition, directing the Polish people towards more **human** goals and influences. In the line of popes that will have served the Christian world before this pope's selection, this pope will be presented as being representative **of the** lasting power of the Church. As a Cardinal in a forbidden church, he will be enhanced to seem as though without offense and fault, fighting against great persecution. This comparison will be made to the line popes known as the **Innocents**. The **ecclesiastic** histories of those popes will symbolically show a comparison, as to how this pope's reign will be viewed in Heaven.[88] Those papal histories actually show a path towards the worst of human nature; and, **that** will be understood as the true affect of this pope; but only after his past will be known. This pope will have come from where **none** will have been **born** who **would know** of the sacraments, as he will rise within the Polish Church after the Russians will have had their philosophy strongly entrenched. His flock will not have been allowed **to have** the symbolic communion, by sipping **of the wine** that is symbolic of the blood of Jesus Christ.

The sacraments from **this one** will later be given, when the Catholic Cardinals will anoint him to become their next pope. But, as the official head of the Church founded by Saint Peter, this pope will not be committed to Christ the **King**. This lack of dedication will mean the Church will have officially died, becoming a body without a soul. That soul will have left when the last true Pope will have been murdered, leaving behind those whose sins will not be confessed. His church will become a heresy to its own orthodox tenets, as under his guidance he **will commit** it to Satan. There will be no guilt expressed **from** the sins it will commit, nor for the ones it had already committed. All future direction

---

88   There have been 13 popes who have used Innocent as their name, with the last being in the year 1721. The first fled Rome, while the Goths sacked it. The second was pope when Saint Malachy had his prophecy of the line of popes. The third was famous for the 4th Crusade. The 7th was pope during the Western Schism, and he appointed his nephew to the cardinalate, against opposition, and his nephew later murdered those against him. The 8th named the man who would lead the Spanish Inquisition into power. That was the last Innocent pope that Nostradamus would have consciously known of.

will be for the purpose of material gain and personal gratification. Under the leadership of this man his church will become publicly known for the **transgressed** priests and other offenses and misdoings that will have been committed by the Priests, Cardinals and Bishops. Many actions will be directed towards innocent parishioners, who will be taken advantage of, for still retaining faith in Catholicism. This corruption will be what will take his church and move it to the **wrong side**, against its original purpose of saving souls. This will be when the Church will have turned around and become diametrically opposite from the position it holds today. During this pope's reign **the church** he will head will become transparently evil to non-Catholics; and, all past failures of popes and priests will become commonplace. The result of this will be less new members coming to Catholicism, especially from the predominately Christian parts of the world. Those people, who will be on the edge of religion, considering a commitment to faith, will see Catholicism as run by **incredible** peoples. Many will see it as unbelievable, the way their discipline of wayward church personnel will be so incredibly lax. And, there will be some who will know of the connection of this pope and his agenda, to others in the Church; such that several pious priests will strongly disagree with his actions as the pope. This will cause some holy men to leave voluntarily, with others being sanctioned or expelled from their positions. Losses of this nature **will slide** this church even further away from Christ and God. Shortly after this trickle will have begun, one will find **the blood** of this man called pope spilled, as a hired assassin will attempt to kill this **human** acting as a holy man.[89] This assassin will be chosen **by** his association to the Islamic faith, although he will not act from religious beliefs. The assassination will be attempted in **the streets** as this pope will parade in plain view of **the public**. The assassin will then be easily apprehended after the pope will be wounded; but, this pope will recover and rule for a long time. It will be important to know that the group which will be behind this assassination will be devoted to the **temples** of Judaism; and, the pope will have been targeted due to his past treatments of the Jews in Poland. There will have been numerous Jews in the city of this man's

---

89 The assassination attempt on Pope John Paul II's life occurred May 13, 1981. Almost one year later, on May 12, 1982, another assassination attempt was made on Pope John Paul II, but he was not harmed. That attempts was by a Portuguese Catholic priest, who claimed that the pope was an agent of Moscow. This attempt occurred at Fatima, Portugal, where the Virgin Mary appeared to the three girls, telling them of the downfall of the Catholic Church. The original date of that apparition was May 13, 1917.

youth; and, he will have won the trust of many. Those secret Jewish avengers will have uncovered this man's past actions, when he will have acted an assistant to his German overseers and their quest to destroy the Jewish race. For this man to act as pope, it will seem to those Jews **like** Satan blessing **the water** and then calling it holy. Survivors of that holocaust will identify him **by** his regular appearance at one of the most notorious camps in Poland. There, the Jews will have been sent to bathe in showers; but, those showers will not have been like those sprinkling like **rain**. Only poisonous gasses will have come out of the bucket, causing all to find a **violent** end.

This man will have supported the violence of the Germans during their occupation of Poland; but, he will later be found **turning red**, once the Russians will put their occupation in place there. This color will be the same as the Russian flag, symbolizing their atheist beliefs. For this man to become red it will mean that he will have changed his color; and, he will have done this to appease his Russian masters, to save his own life. His involvement with the Church will have begun at this time; and, this involvement will have been to escape punishment. This punishment would have come **from** the Russians; and, many of the same **blood** as this man will have been punished, especially those who will be found to have helped **the** Germans. From his position in the Polish Church, he will do **more** to comfort the people of that **neighboring** nation, Russia, than his own people. Meanwhile, the blood of the Poles will often flow like the **rivers** that empty into the Bay of Gdansk.

(Pope John Paul II meets Lech Waleska – 1981)

The city of Gdansk, at the mouth of the Vistula River, will have been called **by** another name by the **other** nation which will have controlled that area for 150 years. That nation will have been Germany, who will have named the city Danzig. On the land by this bay a shipyard will have been built, which will last until the second world **war** will have it become destroyed. German **naval** ships will have used the port around the shipyard. After the Germans, stationed in Poland, will have been overrun by the Russians, Poland **will turn red**. After the war is concluded, that land surrounding **the sea** will be ceded to Poland by Germany and a new shipyard will be built. In **that** port city, where the shipyards will be located, **the** man who will be pope will watch the blood of Polish shipbuilders flow; because this city will become the center of dissidence against

Russian domination. This dissidence will anger the Russians, and they will depend on their **relationship** with the Polish pope for information on the leading dissident. One **of** the shipbuilders will lead a protest which will result in some relief being granted to the workers of Gdansk; and, this **one** leader will be invited to the palace of the **King** of the Vatican. In that meeting between two Poles, the pope will expose **to** the **other** man something about **him** which will have been unknown. The pope will speak metaphorically about his time of war, where the truth **will be told as such**:

"**You see in the times of war** what it is you have to do to survive; and, you find what it is you are capable of and not capable of. If **one does see a bramble bush**, one does not jump into it without expecting to get hurt; but, if it is a time of danger and a bramble bush is offering a place to hide, one will jump into it readily, for cover. When one is looking for **materials for ship-building**, one does not look for planks that have waves. One looks for material that will make **a flat level surface**, for smooth sailing." This conversation will have symbolic meaning, such that the pope will be telling the man, who will have led the shipbuilders in protest, that he will have been making waves for the Russians, who dominate Poland. The man will afterwards be arrested by the Polish authorities, within a year after this cloaked warning.[90]

(The Fall of Religion in the American Way of Life)

And, when the rule of the royal houses will have been completely collapsed and the Church will have been corrupted beyond any influence to good, it will be smooth sailing for the sects of the world. The sects will flourish in all **the countries**, as the philosophies of the leaders of the world will dominate. This will begin the breakdown of mankind, leading it to its ruin; but, the most negative effect the spread by those new philosophers will have will be on the Christian nations. In the countries of the Christian world the **towns** will have once kept the citizens close to each other and close to their religion. The towns will begin to lose their hold over the people; and, the attraction of a simple life will become mostly lost. The **cities** will become such a magnet for wayward souls that people

---

90   Pope John Paul II met with Lech Waleska in Vatican City in January 1981. Some have stated that his 1981 assassination attempt was sponsored by the Soviet Union, through the Bulgarians. However, Pope John Paul II himself claimed that Bulgaria had nothing to do with his assassination, after his visit there.

will fill the cities beyond their capacities, leading to the evils that cities can bring. Freed from all semblance of royal support, as peasants farming the land and learning trades, the people will have to buy land to farm. Without finances for those purchases, the families will splinter, sending the young out alone to find paying work. The **reigns** that will exist then will not be determined by birth, by being born into power. They will be composed of common men who will come from the wealthiest class; and those will be elected by a majority vote of the populace. This will mean that only common men of money will assume the positions of power.

This will especially apply to the reign in the new world nation of America. The leaders of that Christian nation will have to be selected and approved, based on the majority vote of the **provinces**, or states, which comprise it. America, **which** will be primarily of English descent, will have been an independent nation for over 200 years. Its independence will have come after a brief war, between the militia of several unified colonies and the King's army. The impact of this fight for independence will have a very lasting effect on the people of America, as the success of that struggle will become the crown achievement of its one sect of philosophy. After **having** unified the people of the colonies under a banner of rights and freedoms, the people will have **abandoned** the rule of the King and that rule's restrictions and taxations. As a new independent nation, **the first** fathers of America will have established in writing, in the form of a constitution, the principles of their philosophy. The intention will be to mark the **ways** the country will be forever run. As their fight for liberty, from the control of an oppressor, will have been what will have made them determined to win, or die trying, liberty will be at the foundation of their list of rights. Those rights will not be for the collective whole, but personally **for oneself**. Each individual will be equally given specific rights, for life, liberty and the pursuit of happiness. The original swell of people into this new world land will have come from England; with most coming primarily for the purpose **to free** themselves from religious persecution. Their most coveted freedom, for the common masses that will make up those colonies, will be the freedom of religious practice; but, as time will go on, it will eventually be those liberties given to **oneself**, and not to the majority, that will be the downfall of religion in America. By that time, so many citizens of America will have turned their backs on religion, of any kind, that having a government based on religious freedoms will be against the individual rights of the non-religious. This number of non-religious citizens will grow into a sect that will see a nation founded on religious principles as a personal restriction; and, this minority will be seen as forced, against their will, to adhere to the principles of a religion that they will not want to serve. The argument of those non-believers will be presented in the American courts of law, **captivating** the lawmakers with this bewitching point of view. This will lead the courts to declare for the minority, such that this great Christian nation will strike religion from its laws. While there will be **more** people who will feel the need for a strong religion in government, due to law being morality based, the decisions which will be made by the courts will most **profoundly** affect the whole nation's direction, away from religion. The deep-seated intellectual arguments, which will be used to strike away the influence of founding fathers' original religious intent, will allow this fall of religion to happen; with the arguments **being secretly** motivated by those seeking increased power and wealth. The minority will express its **angers** at the religious constraints which will have been put on them; and, they will argue that their lives will have been harmed, because **of** the threat to **their** individual civil **liberty**. This threat will make them fear being restricted by the presence of religion.

This concept of liberty will be so much a part **of** the America **nature** that, when one group claims it is **being** discriminated against, the courts must hear each case. While the majority will have no problem with the laws of their government being morally based on Christian doctrines, their system of law will be designed so that each and every citizen will be considered **equal**. This concept will have come from the first fathers, and their beliefs that all men will have been created equal.

To clarify this equality, it will be designed to protect the weak from being abused by the powerful; **but**, this concept of equality will not have been intended to let the minority rule, which is the way of rule today, under your highness' royal rule. Since the founding fathers will have been trying to establish a government which would have made such select treatment forbidden, they will have only written the most basic of freedoms as the foundations of their law. Unfortunately, as is often found with the laws of man, the intent can only be manageable as far as how clearly the law is written; and, at this time, the minority will realize how to turn the constitutional words against its original purpose. America will have become a nation of great wealth and prosperity; but, those riches will not be distributed equally among all of its citizens. There will also be a minority which will **greatly** differ from the majority of the people, as the wealthiest; and, those few people will have the vast majority of the powers to affect law. This will lead to the promotion of the concept that, while all people are equal, some people will have **different** results towards gaining material rewards. Many will promote stories of rises **from** the bottom to the top, by hard work and a strong **faith** that God would bless them with riches. The true results of this promotion will be that people will begin to work so hard, including on God's day of rest, that fewer and fewer people will be able to go to church, trying to make that false dream come true. God does not reward the faithful with material gains. God rewards the faithful with a return to Him in Heaven. Satan tempts with material gains.

(Striking Down the Ten Commandments and September 11, 2001)

The Christian faiths will suffer as a result of this **perfected** maneuvering and manipulation. After those legal assaults begin, before long the **religion** of a nation will be **lost**. In the **beginning** of this movement the plan will be to take power **from** those who promote a strong Christian religion, by lamenting those elements who are prone **to strike** out in anger against non-Christians. Particularly, those will be of other religions, which do not observe Sunday as a holy day; but, the Jews will be singled out as most affected. This element of anti-Semitism will have been prominent in the atrocities of the Germans in the second world war; and, **in** many of the cities of America many Jewish people will have established important and sizable communities. This will make them an important element inside many of the key provinces. As the elected representatives of the people of America will be chosen by a majority vote of the people, those representatives will be a reflection of the majority of the population. At the time of this change away from religion, the people will be divided into two parties, with one for a strong religious direction to law and one arguing for no religious influence on law. It will be **the party** that will be against religion remaining intertwined with the law that will call for representatives to legislate to the **left**, away from the religious right.[91] There will have been little chance **for** the people to grow strong enough in numbers **to change** the laws of the land and return them **to**

---

91   The word written, "*gauche*," means "left," but also carries the connotations, "wrong, sinister, awry."

the right side. Once religion is removed from the law, there will be no **restoring** the influence of Jesus Christ on the people. Many will point to **the sanctity** of the Catholic Church, which will have been scandalized to the point of ridicule, as reason for this separation. Many of the priests and bishops will have been exposed for their **profligate** and debased lifestyles, **of** great sins and debauchery. Those people will have been shown to have been without any strong moral character, for a **long time**; but, the Church will have done nothing to punish those men. The Church will have supported its priests, **with** minimal punishments administered, such that **their** compassion for the people will appear to be lost. This showing of irresponsibility will be what the left will use to argue against a religious influence on law; and, many of the **former** laws will be stricken down and rewritten. Many of those former laws will have been based on the **written** Laws of God; but, due to that Law interfering with some one's individual liberties, new documents will present the words of man as the new law to lead Americans. The laws **that after** which will be written will be written at a time when America will be determined to be **the** one **great** nation on earth, above all others. Knowledge of this unopposed greatness will cause the people of America to believe they are invincible; but, it will be such greatness that will lead them to lose their religion. After believing that God will have blessed them to greatness, they will turn on religion like a great **dog**.[92] This image of the American dog will be seen by the Muslim nations, who will have suffered from the actions America will have taken against them. To counter the domination of this great dog over the Arab lands, some Muslims will gather to plot revenge; and, they **will bring out** their dog, to bite the American dog when it will be sleeping. This Arab dog will be more dog than the Americans will expect, as it will be a big mastiff.[93] Particularly, this attack of the mastiff will deliver a very harsh blow to

92   This is a reference to the Preface, where Nostradamus quoted the "Give not that which is holy unto dogs, nor cast your pearls before swine, lest they trample them underfoot and turn to rend you." The word, "*chien,*" also carries the connotation of a base, filthy or shameless person. Here Nostradamus wrote the French word for dog, but this also refers back to the advent of the atomic bomb, when America would believe that power made it the Dog, which is God backwards, both words in English, the language of America.

93   Nostradamus wrote, "*le plus gros mastin,*" which translates literally to "the more big (bigger) mastiff." However, when the word *mastin* is read as *matin*, in modern French, this combination of words means, "early in the morning." The symbolism of dog and mastiff certainly applies; but, the timing of early in the morning is clearly in

the Americans, **early in the morning**, as the Americans will be just waking up to get ready for the day's work ahead. The damage which will be done will cause all Americans great alarm, **which will make** the Americans respond with threats to strike those hiding Muslims. Their threats will be on a degree that will demonstrate their position as the greatest power in the world. This series of events will mark the dawning of the beginning of **destruction**, which will lead to the end **of all** of mankind. This dawning of destruction will be the **same** which is referred to in biblical prophecy; and, it is that prophecy which tells **of this** story that I am about to tell. America and the Arabs will be the ones who will take the steps **that have** been written of in the Bible, as the signs leading to the end. Those actions will be **before**, or in advance of the coming doom; and, it **will be** begun when the Muslims will come out early in the morning of one day late in the time of **summer**.[94] That day will mark the first of many acts which will be **perpetrated** afterwards, towards this end. This time of destruction will mark the first second ticking off of the final hour of mankind. This end will not be assured to occur, **being** that God will have bestowed the gift of free will onto mankind. Mankind will have the opportunity to avert this end, if it will make the necessary changes that **makes straight** the Laws of God, allowing mankind to recover from its sins. The most important key to this recovery will be **the** return of the churches, **temples** and mosques to their level of prominence and intended influence. This will be **like** it was **in the** days of the Bible, when God will have **first** talked to the leaders of His people; and, it will highlight the importance of understanding that the **times** of the first coming of Jesus Christ were meant for all people to model, regardless of a dogmatic preference.

---

the quatrains.

94   This simple line is reference to September 11, 2001, which is late in the summer. There are several quatrains that detail this day; and, it marks the beginning of our present, which is leading to the end.

EXPLAINING THE QUATRAINS –
THE PLANNING FOR THE FINAL HOUR

Still, those times since Christ will have greatly changed many Muslims against Christians, especially from a continuing series of Crusades, led by the Catholic Church and armed by Europeans against the Arabs. However, the most significant changes will occur after the second world war will have been completed. The Muslim attacks on America will have originated from the ill-will which will have developed from the American support of Israel on Palestinian land and America's subsequent undermining of the reigns in other Arab nations. The Muslims will attack so Americans will have to admit to this interference. The Arabs **will be** demanding to be given back the land of Palestine, with the American influence removed. They will require the land be **returned** to the control of **the** Islamic **clerk**, or its leading religious cleric. Jews will be allowed **to** remain in this land; but, they will have to succumb to **his** will, as the clerk will be considered to be their voice for Allah, in the peaceful guidance of His people. The Jewish people will have to understand they will hold no claims on the land, as their **former state** of ownership will have been stripped from them, by the will of God. That loss will be seen as punishment for the sins of the Hebrew people, before Christ was born to them. Their failure to recognize Jesus Christ as the Messiah, promised by God to them, and their refusal to follow His guidance will have further stripped them from any possession of that land.

This demand on the children of God, to comply with those terms and return the Middle East to its former state, will be one the Muslims will not expect America or Israel to accept. They will be more intent on retribution; and, their threats of reprisal, should America and Israel not comply, will not be idle threats, but promises to be kept. Thus, when the Americans will refuse to give in to the Muslim demands, this **will begin** the unfolding of a most horrible future. It will be the future which has been foretold by the Prophet John, in the Book of *The Revelation*. There it tells of the time when the world will **in** bed with and bound **to that harlot** riding the back of the beast.[95] The kings of the world will have had

---

95   The word, "*meretricquer*," is from Latin, where *meretrix* means a harlot. This refers to *The Revelations*, Chapter 17.

intercourse with her and the inhabitants of the world will have become drunk on the wine of her harlotry. This will represent how so many will have turned away from God and become enslaved **to lusts**, especially in their quests for material wealth and possessions. America will lead the Christian world in seeking those carnal or worldly lusts, as they will have become more concerned for the personal pleasures and delights, than the constraints of morality. They will see their enjoyment of those delights as the spoils of being the world's greatest power. Christ has foretold that the Lamb will defeat the beast the harlot is seated upon, and as the Lord of lords and the King of kings, all who will be faithful to Him will be saved; but, it will be up to each individual **to make** the decision to be saved. For one **to commit** to the harlot, the beast will rise to leave her naked, to eat her flesh and to consume her with fire. This will mean the destruction of America, by the beast of Islam. From those initial attacks by the Muslims on America, there will come **one thousand** other **infamies** or countless acts of sin to follow; and, those acts will be committed over the whole scope of the world.

Those infamous acts will be sins in the eyes of Christ, **because** the nation of America will still carry the banner of Jesus Christ, as a Christian nation, while it goes to war. For all of its prior sins, **God will behold** the knowledge of all things kept secret; and, He will watch how America will present itself to its own people and to the world. America will have come from the loins of the British, whose empire will have spread the seeds of Christianity to all regions of the world. However, **the long** reign of the British Empire will have begun to crumble, following the end of the second world war. That **sterility of the** British Empire will have God carefully watching the growth of Britain's eldest heir, the **great** nation of America. America will have come into its own greatness, by the blessings of God, for its original commitment to the teachings of Jesus Christ; but, it will have never known of the influence of royal blood or the Catholic Church. Without a belief in the Blessed Virgin, the nation of America will have admired the statue of a **lady** which will represent the sect of philosophy promoting liberty and freedom. This idol will have been given to America by its sister nation, France, after it will have adopted the same philosophy as America, and overthrown its King and the power of the Church. The British will want America to ascend to the throne of an emperor; and, Britain will call for America to use **that** lady as the goddess America stands for. America will then promote its philosophies around the world, under the pretense of acting in the name of

291

Jesus Christ. The world **then** will no longer have any lands of value which will not have been settled under one firm form of religion, whichever that religion will be; but, **after** a new millennium will dawn, America will have been attacked by rebel Muslims. Those rebels will have seen America's secret manipulations and expansions into the Arab lands, with its protection of the Jewish state, as evidence of a new Christian Crusade worthy of retribution. That group of rebel Muslims will have been under the protection of a poor Middle Eastern nation, which will have been where the Russians will have withdrawn in disgrace, before the collapse of their union of nations. With Britain and America desiring the valuable land of the Middle East, with all of its unique natural resources, the perfect conditions will have existed for an American empirical quest to begin. The leader of America and the leader of Britain **will have conceived** a plan to attack this poor nation which will be known to protect the rebels; but, this nation will be poor because of a lack of this valuable natural resource. However, that poor Arab nation will not be far from the land of Mesopotamia, where the tyrant there will have been left in power; and, he will not have followed the terms of his surrender. The plan devised by the Americans and British will be to take both of these **two** nations, one at a time, under the concepts of giving freedom and religion to the people of those Arab lands. Both of those nations will be easy conquests, as they will be like **infants** compared to the might of America. The plan will call for the support of the union of nations, where they will believe that the world will easily be swayed to allow America to remove the governments of those two nations. They will promote that the tyrant of Mesopotamia will have previously upset the world by his past history of aggression. Without the union of nation's full approval, America will take over each of those two nations, and claim the peoples would become the children of the sect of liberty. America will then tout those conquests as the **principal** jewels of America's new imperialism.

After the nation of America will have devised **this** plan with the Britain, it will swiftly act to invade and secure the poor nation. Several of the member nations of the union of nations will assist **the** American troops in those attacks, which will destroy the poor nation's government and capture several rebel Muslims. With that nation defeated within one year, America will introduce the principle of **lady** liberty to that nation's peoples, by a new government which will be established there. They will seek to allow equal representation to the populations, while seeking to kill and capture the remainder of the Muslim rebels. The newly installed government will not have one strong sect of religion in control of the nation, which will have been by design. The Americans will recognize that a **sterile** government, which is unimaginative and uninspired by the absence of the emotion of Islam, will be necessary to have in place before proceeding to the land of Mesopotamia. Without the approval **of** the union of nations, America will then have to act with only the support of the British and a few **more** subservient nations, whose leaders will be pressured by the Americans to give nominal support. America will claim the invasion of Mesopotamia is necessary, to keep America **great** and able to police the world of rebels. It will then make claims that the tyrant of Mesopotamia will have attempted to obtain the feared **power**; but, it will make this claim without presenting any real evidence as proof. There will be a loud clamor made by the union of nations, as **that** power will have been the focus of inspectors for many years; and, they will claim there will have been no such weapons possible in Mesopotamia. So, without the world's support, America will begin to threaten the tyrant of Mesopotamia, while preparing to invade his nation. America will then lead **the second** invasion of Mesopotamia in twelve years; and, after a short time that weak nation will be defeated by the larger, stronger America. While the union of nations will have not given their approval for that invasion, the removal of the tyrant from power **will be accepted by** the other nations of the world. This acceptance of one nation occupying another will be just as it will have been before the second world war, making America appear to be led by another of the many tyrants of philosophy that the 20th Century will sprout. In the space of less than **two** years, America will have successfully conquered two nations of the Middle East, claiming to have freed those **peoples** from the oppression of tyrants and religious zealots. The military of the Mesopotamian tyrant will have been no match for the American machinery; and, the leaders of Mesopotamia will have all run into hiding, shortly after the invasion will have begun. Still, **by the** ease in which America will have defeated the **first** poor nation and installed a model government there, the land of Mesopotamia will be quite **obstinate** towards the American presence. They will continue to resist their occupiers by the actions of rebel assaults, even after the Mesopotamian military will have been defeated. Even **by** the time the American soldiers will find the one most sought after, **the same** tyrant **whom** the American leader will have said was **to have had** the **power** that will have been so feared, the Americans will not find any of the most powerful weapons in Mesopotamia. At that time they will have looked **over**

293

all of Mesopotamia, with no such weapons to display as proof for their claims. When many Americans will question why America will have been sent to war, **by the** lack of evidence which will have proven the need to invade a **second** nation, the American leader will claim those most dangerous weapons will have been moved to another Arab land, next to Mesopotamia. There will then be two lands which will be **by** Mesopotamia; and, one or both of those lands will be assumed to be **the** land which will have taken the power from the tyrant of Mesopotamia. One land will be Syria and the other will be Persia, as both will border Mesopotamia, one to west and the other to the east. However, before the leader of America will be able to suggest that the great nation invade a **third** Arab land, it will have to bring about the cessation of hostilities in Mesopotamia, and install a model government. To do that, the great nation of America **will spread** out over the troublesome areas of Mesopotamia with **its** military **forces**, so they will be able to quell the rebel attacks. But, many of those rebels will not be Mesopotamians; as they will have come to Mesopotamia to resist the Americans, from **around** the other regions of the Middle East. This will make **the tour** of troops from America to Mesopotamia a longer circuit to complete; and, this delay will be planned for, by the Persians. While America will be struggling to maintain control of Mesopotamia, with complaints inside its own nation rising, an envoy of Persians and their supporters will have left **from** the Arab lands of **the** Middle **East** and North Africa, to seek mercenary assistance from other lands, where the defeat of American would be welcomed. They will find willing partners in the masses of Islamic refugees who will have left **from** the Middle East and Africa, to settle in the Christian nations of Western **Europe**. They will also go **to the** people of Eastern Europe and find many willing partners in the non-religious people around the regions of the **Pannons**.[96] The Arabs will entice those poor people, known as the slaves of Europe, with the spoils of war, should they help **them to overthrow** the allies of America in Western Europe. Those people will have mostly been without work and without the comforts of life for a long time; and, that lack will have become especially pronounced after Russia will have dissolved its Aquilon union with those nations. With offers of pay for those mercenaries, as well as offering the material wealth of the West as the spoils of war, those people will be purchased in large numbers, enough to field a powerful army. Their once great connection to the Roman Catholic Church, and the

96 The Pannons is the ancient name for that part of Europe that is roughly between Hungary and the former Yugoslavia.

morals of right it stood for, will have **succumbed** to many years of oppression, under tyrants directed by Russia.

When Russia will have succumbed to the American subversive economic war against them, the Persians will have then had the opportunity to purchase a great number of military weapons from them and their former allied nations. The Persians will have primarily been interested in coming **by** secret ships in Russian naval arsenal, as the Persians will have need for advanced means of **sail**. Those procurements will have included **sea** vessels with the capacity for veiled movement, underwater; and, the Persians will have a great interest in purchasing some of the most feared weapons, which the Russians will have built in their weapons race with America. With those weapons secured, it **will make** the Persians prepared to act militarily against America, as that **one's extensions** into the Middle East will be greatly unwanted by the Muslim world. The Persians will then engage several of the refugees of the Muslim world who will have fled into Italy. Those refugees will not have been allowed onto the Italian mainland, having instead been forced **to the** island of *Trinacria*.[97] That location of the Muslim refugees, in Sicily, will place them near an American naval port, built to be central for the protection of America's Mediterranean fleet of ships. Those refugees will assist the Persians in gathering information which will be helpful to them. The Persians will also have found a very willing volunteer in the lands to the eastern **Adriatic** Sea. The Americans will have used their military strength against those peoples several years before; and, they will be willing to fight against the nations who will have been allied with America then, especially the ones **by** their borders. This will include the European nation of Greece, which will have once been the place of the **Myrmidons**.[98] The Greeks will have long since lost their ability to make war, no longer resembling those ancient undefeatable soldiers. This lack of strength will make the Greeks easy conquests for those Balkan warriors who will still hold a grudge. Finally, in the Persian circuit to find allies, they will have won over support from the **Germanic** peoples too. Since the eastern half of Germany will have been maintained under the Russian domination after the second world war, the people there will have been raised without religion,

---

97 Trinacria is the Latin name for Sicily, due to its triangular shape. Literally: Triangular Land

98 The Myrmidons were the warriors that fought with Achilles in the Trojan War and myth has it that Zeus created them from ants.

strong supporters of the Russian philosophy. The collapse of the Russian union will have freed them to rejoin with the western half of Germany. However, with that reunion not making a smooth transition, the eastern Germans will willingly add their support to the Persians, due to an equal hatred of America. The majority of Germany will have also been a place for immigrant Muslims to find safe havens; and those immigrants will locate in Germany, to plot and plan military actions for the Persian cause. While the Americans will be planning to take the strength of each Arab land away **from** them, one at a time, this plan will be very rudely upset. The Muslims will plan to attack **the whole** of Western Europe and America, at the same time, with hoards of unsuspected assistance. The Muslim commitment to this plan will be so strong that the Muslim warriors will not stop fighting until all Christians will have been completely annihilated. But, the Muslims will also be planning that Western Europe will not have the stomach for war. Once America will have **succumbed** to a surprise attack, the Muslims will plan for the rest to quickly surrender.

(The Christian Treatment of Africa, 1792 - 2000)

The rest which will be planned to succumb will be the major nations of Western Europe; and, those nations will surrender, due to the overwhelming levels of Middle Eastern immigration there, and the promises the Persians will make to all volunteers to the Islamic cause. Europe will be **the prime** target of the Islamic war against Christianity; and, Europe will be prime for accepting many exiles from foreign nations. Although those exiles will make up only a small portion of the population of any European nation, it will be more than enough to establish significant bases in those foreign lands, before the planned Islamic invasions. Also, with the Geneva bankers holding a significant portion of the world's gold, the land of the Alps will be targeted and planned to fall into Muslim hands. That will mean the great nation of America will lose a prime source of its financial holdings, and thus hold less power. All of this will make the capture of Europe the bonus of bounty, all of which will **totally** be yielded **by** the Muslims to their mercenary soldiers. The Muslims will not be seeking the material things that will have been known to be in the possession of the people of Western **Europe**. Their primary objective will be to seek retribution; so, **the more** successful they will be in establishing control of the Europeans, the more they will be willing to **share** the spoils of war. It will be known that the majority of the world's wealth and material objects will be almost exclusively found in the Christian nations of America and Western Europe; although, there will also be significant wealth amassed in the Oriental lands, mostly the ones who shared the philosophy of the sect of freedom and its economy of free enterprise. Those wealthy branches of the world will have not shared fairly with the poor regions, most particularly with those nations on the continent **of Africa**. In that harsh area of the world, many of the African people will have been **exterminated** in great numbers; this will have come either from famine, war or disease, all without significant outside aid and assistance. Many Africans will also have been murdered, in genocidal exterminations by tribal tyrants, without outside prevention. The people of this continent will be so far removed **from** those people of wealth and lifestyle comforts that they will be termed **the third** world. This moniker will be used as **a means for** describing the world of **the poor**, where nations will be viewed as internationally powerless and internally undeveloped. Most of the people of African societies will have not been influenced by any formal religion; and, they will be seen as wild humans, closer to animals in nature, than civilized human beings. The Africans will have been collective peoples who will have worshiped primitive spirits, without the formal guidance **of** the **spirit** of Jesus Christ and the one God. Without this influence, **which** is the source of mankind's moral fabric, many of the African nations will have become ruled **by** the most powerful chiefs of the largest tribes; and, several of the leaders of those tribes will become **raging** tyrants, who will become such **elevated** chiefs they will steal and kill at will. Those mad leaders will be led **by** evil; and, they will not care for **the** lives of the masses, as they will only be led by their own **excess in carnal delights**. They will lust for the power that being the strongest brings, such that a select few of those leaders will find excesses in material rewards of the Western world. Those chiefs will lead their followers into extremely **libidinous** and **adulterating** lifestyles, where they will know of no morals to block them from forcing the weak to satisfy their physical desires.

Those adulterating conditions will have **not** existed in all of Africa, as the very north and very south of Africa will have had strong elements of religion to guide them. Instead, it will be middle part **of** Africa, between **the** Tropics of Cancer and Capricorn, surrounding the equator, where the majority of Africans will be swayed by Islam's promises of material reward. In that zone the tribal customs will have remained the strongest. Still, the **whole** of this region's peoples will have never known of the wealth and advancements of the historical civilized world, although several European nations and several of the churches of Christianity will have established relations in many of the nations of Africa.

This presence of Europeans in Africa will have been said to be for good purposes; but, on the whole, the white humans will look down on the black humans. Some of the African tribal chiefs **will be** the ones who will have sparked **the beginning** of slavery in the future's world, as they will have sold conquered peoples to European traders who will have explored the coasts of Africa. The human beings which will be bought and sold as slaves will have no **understanding** of the worlds they will be transplanted into. Their actions will be seen as animal-like to those buying them for labor; and, **this** will represent the beginning of a long oppression of African natives by whites claiming to be Christians. The Persians will realize the African chiefs will be capable **of that** same level of treachery, which will sell its own kind for profit. From **that** beginning, slavery **will last** in the colonies of America for over two hundred years; but, in the minds of Christians worldwide, that impression of Africa, as an evil continent, will last even longer. The clerics of Islam will have found a need met in the African people; and, they will begin **undertaking** the task of teaching the Africans the ways of Islamic law. While the Africans will find this teaching different from their tribal customs, the Muslims will allow some of the old ways to blend with the ways of Islam, to make the conversions easier. With Islam having been in Africa for some time, taking root with the people of Africa, **this one year** the leader of Persia will be seeking willing volunteers for the Islamic cause against the Christian nations, there **will be made** agreements with many of those lustful African leaders. With Islam having had **more** of an impact on the African leaders than the missionaries of the **great** nation of America, those African leaders will be more easily swayed to follow the Islamic requests. This will begin a period of **persecution** in Africa, where those **of the** African clans, who will be aligned with the Islamic cause, will begin to attack the evangelists and members of the **church** who will be **Christian**. Those Africans will first attack **that** element of Christianity which will have connections to America. Those Christians will have **not had been** preaching the gospel to Africans for very long; and, few will have **done** any good for the chiefs. Those missionaries will be said to be **in Africa**, not for the conversion of souls, but for the manipulation of the African governments and the theft of African assets.

The presence of the Christian Church will begin in Africa in the year 1792,

298

when the first Protestant missionaries will settle there; and, this condition of Christianity **will continue** in Africa from then, until the time of that increased interest in Africa by Islam. It will then be found that African tribal customs will be closer to the belief **that is** in the principles of Islam. This will allow for Islam to begin taking a stronger hold on Africans. The strength of Christianity will be greater **here**, in Europe, because of the strong influence of the Roman Catholic Church; but, the Catholic Church will have greatly neglected attempting to save the African souls. Still, without Islam targeting Africa, the hold of Christianity in Africa will gain momentum and last **until the year** that begins the next **millennium**. In that year, in the month of **September**, the Muslim rebels will have attacked America and caused the Christian nations of the world great panic. Following that date, the Muslim interest in Africa will have influenced **approximately** the whole of the north and central African nations. Many will have already joined the Islamic cause, before those attacks will have taken place; but, the success of those attacks will show that America is vulnerable. The African leaders will be told their assistance will be conditional, and **not before** the great nation of America will have spent **two** years responding to the Muslim warning, made that September, will they be asked to commit.[99] The purpose for **that** period of two years will be to allow **many** leaders of America to decide to cease America's manipulation of the Muslim world; and, this will include the relationships shown by several North African nations. They **will presume** that America will instead decide **to be** acting with anger, as the **one** nation which will have never had any attack of this nature on its soil before. Those first attacks on their soil will come after they will have claimed the title of the mightiest nation on earth. The symbolism of the attacks the Muslims will make in that month of September will be designed to show America that there will have been a **renovation of** Arab power; and, the power on that day will have come from America. When that new **century** will have begun, the Islamists of the world will unite to change the currents of sin which will have begun in the last century.

---

99   Nostradamus wrote, *"l'an mil sept cens nonante deux,"* which is commonly believed to state, "the year one thousand seven hundred ninety two," or 1792. However, in the quatrains, as was stated in the Letter of Preface, about how dates are designed to mislead, we find that this spelling out of a date can be seen as something quite different. I believe that the 1792 is intended, as a secondary meaning. This is an accepted year for the first Christian missionary established in Africa; however, the rest of the verbiage in the statements of this block support the above conclusions, as do the quatrains themselves.

EXPLAINING THE QUATRAINS –
THE EMPIRE OF THE ANTICHRIST

(Arming the Muslims, 1990-2005)

Then, once that century has begun, the Muslims will make their first strike; and, the pendulum will swing again. With each swing the seconds of the final hour will tick away; and, the fate of mankind will be resting in the hands of **the great** nation of America. The people of America will hereby be called upon to decide to return to the teachings of Christ and peace or to proceed to the final end; but, the **Empire of the Antichrist** will have been put into place. This personification of the word "antichrist" means the one person who will have had an equal impact on the people of the world, as has had Jesus Christ; but, unlike Christ, the antichrist's influence will work in opposition to the influence of Christianity. Therefore, the one man who will have had such an equal influence will have been Mohammed, who has created the religion of Islam, taught through his Koran. This religion will have had an equal spread around the world, as will have had Christianity. Over the times of man, since the rise of both Christianity and Islam, the people of these two religions will have worked against each other, in many episodes of persecution. There will have been an Empire of the Muslims, before this one which will be coming, one led by the Turk Sultan; but, that empire will not have been the true empire of the Antichrist. This Empire of the Antichrist **will begin** when the Muslims of Mohammed will have influenced the people of non-Arab lands to fight for their cause, against Christians. This empirical expansion will first take hold **inside** the land of **the Atil River**, also known as the Volga River of Russia.[100] The Russians will provide the Antichrist with the weapons he will need, in order to destroy the world. The land which will purchase those weapons of destruction will be the land of **Xerxes**, who was once a ruler of Persia. Persia has its northern border on the Caspian Sea, across from where the mouth of the Atil empties. Just as Xerxes led a Persian Empire,

---

100   The Volga River is the longest European river and it originates just north of Moscow, flowing eventually into the Caspian Sea. As the primary river of Russia, this river has a strong connection to the Russian people, such that it has been termed "Mother Volga" by the people.

which made ruthless conquests of foreign lands,[101] there will be another example of a Persian leader coming in this future who will act similarly **to descend** upon established nations. Just as Xerxes did against the powerful Greeks, by compiling an army 2,000,000 men **in number**,[102] this Persian leader will lead an astonishing number of soldiers against the **great** nation of America and its Christian allies. The number of men that will be sent against those powerful nations will be so many that it will be **innumerable**, unable to fix a count on them.

There will be **so** many Muslims from all over the world joining in this quest **that** one will be unable to count **the** additional troops which will be **coming** from non-Muslim lands, as mercenaries. It will easily exceed two million men and it will make it the largest expeditionary force ever assembled. The Muslims this Persian leader will send into battle will believe they will have the same protection that many Christians have believed they have had, by wearing medallions **of the** patron **saint** Christopher.[103] Saint Christopher was the carrier of the **Spirit** of Christ; and, he was willing to lose his life for that conviction, becoming a martyr. The Muslim people, under this Persian leader's promise that Mohammed's people will find their souls cared for, will be equally dedicated; and, they will feel protected in battle. This Persian leader will be **proceeding** with his plan to destroy America **from the** safety of his own land of Persia. From that safety, the first attack will be on the American forces which will be stationed at the Mouth of the Tigris River, at the only port in Mesopotamia that will be at the Persian Gulf. It will also include the American forces in the tiny nation next to Mesopotamia, such that all of the Persian leader's first attacks will come at the earth's **48 degrees** of longitude mark. American soldiers will become trapped in

---

101   Xerxes quelled a rebellion by the Egyptians in 486 BC, imposing strict rules there afterwards. He then defeated the Greeks, by preparing for this war three years in advance and then using the strategy of keeping some of Greece's usual allies from joining with Greeks. This was between 483 - 480 BC.

102   This number was stated by Herodotus in his account of the war, but others since deduce that the number was probably closer to 250,000. Still, this would have been a huge force of men.

103   While Nostradamus did not specifically name Saint Christopher, it is interesting to note that some pictures of him (Eastern) show him with a dog head. He was a giant of a man, bigger than all others (18 feet tall) and stronger than all too. The name Christopher means "Christ-carrier," such that he becomes the perfect archetype for the United States of America.

that tiny area of Mesopotamia; and, all there at that time **will make** the **transmigration** of their souls from the body, to the spirit plane. Those deaths will come at the hand of the Persian leader, who will be commanding his army to begin **expelling** horrible weapons against the Americans. This will be the beginning of the promised retribution against America being fulfilled. The weapons which will be used **in** the annihilation of the Americans will be those weapons of **the abomination** that the Americans will have first used against the Japanese, to end the second world war. With the Americans defeated and disabled, the armies and navies **of the Antichrist** will begin to attack all the hated enemies of Islam, in the Christian lands of Western Europe. Muslim troops will then simultaneously begin **making war** along the shores of Spain, France and Italy; but, as all of those nations will be seen as Christian nations, under the influence of the Roman Catholic Church, the Persian leader will have separately sent troops to war **against the** one who will represent the **royal** leader of Christianity, in Rome. It will be the pope who will be targeted, as it will be he **who will be** seen as the one man who should have stood up against **the great** nation of America and demanded they cease their persecution of the Arabs. As the pronounced **curate of** the Catholic Church and the vicar of **Jesus Christ**, who Himself would have never promoted persecution as an answer to problems, the Persian leader will have a special punishment for this leader of the Christian world.

This Persian leader will not only seek to make war against this man, who acts as caretaker of the Catholic Church, but more importantly **against** all of the lands which will have paid homage to **his** rank. This will include all of the people of the churches that will have branched from this **church**. His plan will be abuse the Catholic Church for its past influence on Europeans, leading to the Crusades which will have been mounted in the name of the popes. As those will have caused the unwarranted deaths of Arabs, the deaths of Christians and their leaders will be seen as fair retribution. The Christians of Europe left alive will then be expected to convert to Islam, or face extreme punishments. This will be the ultimate retribution; as Christians will be punished for their failing to cry out against the oppression which will have been put on the world, in the name of Christianity.

This emperor of the Muslim's unified world will not personally lead his troops into battle. Instead, he will manage **his reign** from his satrap in Persia; but, he will communicate with his generals, who will have prepared for this war **through**

303

a series of well-planned strategies and maneuvers, with specific objectives and goals. There will be a **division** of the Muslim forces, with multiple primary spearheads and secondary targets; so, several key generals will be involved, overseeing the Muslim and mercenary forces. Those generals will be coming from the Middle East, North Africa and Eastern Europe. The key element for their plan, for it to achieve maximum effectiveness, will be that it must come at the right time.[104]

(Explaining the Antichrist)

In reference to **the foresaid** division of powers, they will all submit to the general **reign of** the one man who will be the embodiment of **the antichrist**.[105] This man will oversee the persecution of European Christians; but, he will **not** see the end of the world. The world **will last** beyond this coming period of Islamic persecution. It will be **that** time of persecution which will mark the last phase of his life; but, the actions of retribution he will lead will keep the world at war **until** the end of mankind, beyond the demise of the antichrist. Mankind, once started to war will not be able to cease its hostilities. Mankind will continue warring beyond his death, leading **to the** final **wasting away** of the earth. Once the world will learn **of this** level of persecution this tyrant will have committed, leaving horrendous numbers of dead in the wake of his rule, he still will **not** come **close to** killing as many human beings as will be killed by the subsidiary ways of death, up till the final cataclysm. However, the number which will die in this first score of years in the new millennium will make it **the age** of the most ruin of mankind. To further understand the origin **of** the one who will be the primary individual to act as the antichrist; he will not be born in the land of **the other** Antichrist, or the nation of Persia. This man will have been born **in the**

---

104 The last two words in this block were written in Latin, "*per tempus*." This translates both as "through division" and as "through a fit time" or "opportunity."

105 Common interpretations of Nostradamus, popularized on television especially, make the claim that Nostradamus predicted three antichrists, with the first being Napoleon, and the second being Hitler. The third is clearly identified as "Mabus." As far as anagrams go, I have mentioned Musab as Osama bin Laden. He is the embodiment of one person as the "antichrist," with Mohammed and Islam being the "Antichrist" on a greater scale. Nostradamus did not write about Napoleon; and, Hitler, while a bad man, forced the Roman Catholic Church to be the Church of the Nazis, so nothing anti-Christ was about that.

land of the holy **city of Plancus**.[106] This antichrist will have **accompanied** goals set for Islam, which will have been adopted by the Empire of the Antichrist. He will have come **from** common birth, although born to a wealthy family name. He will turn on his family, while using his access to wealth to fund his rebel forces fighting for Islam. His fame will grow so rapidly among Arabs that he will be **elected** by all Muslims as the inspiration that will light the way for an Islamic Empire. It will be the support **of** this **Mondone Fulcy**, or the One to Give the Pillar for an Empire, which will allow him to become the antichrist and be successful. This Mondone Fulcy will give this support by obtaining the power that will come **by Ferrare**.[107] It will be this acquisition which will give the nation of the Antichrist the same power as the Americans and Europeans. The antichrist will be the **handler** of that arsenal of weapons when he will lead the army of Islam into battle. The results will be most realized **by** the waters of the **Ligurian** peoples and the **Adriatic** peoples, where most will be Christian citizens.

The first waves of attackers will be **of** this region, recruited from the lands of the Adriatic Sea and North Africa. The naval ports of those areas will be in **the** closest **proximity** to Italy. The antichrist will know **of the** positions of the **great** nation of America, which will have had a military presence around Italy and on the Mediterranean Sea. He will plan a special attack in **Trinacria**, where the American navy will have a port and base. In this attack, he will be using the hoards of refugees who will have settled there, led by agents that will have been sent by the antichrist to coordinate their attacks.

---

106 The meaning of Plancus comes from Latin, meaning, "lamentation." The city of Mecca is actually derived from the Arabic name, Bakkah, which is listed in the Hebrew Bible as Baca. Baca, in Hebrew, means "weeping." The land of the antichrist's birth is then now called Saudi Arabia.

107 I have derived the meaning of Mondone from the Latin words, "monos dono," meaning "one to give." I have derived the meaning of Fulcy from the Latin word, "fulcio," meaning, "support, pillar." I have derived the meaning of Ferrare from the Latin words, "ferrum rarus," meaning, "iron rare;" and, where "iron" meant weapons, from the French used the word "fer."

EXPLAINING THE QUATRAINS –
THE PRELUDE TO THE POINT OF
DECISION

(The United Nations Prepares to Protect Europe)

When the threat of this danger to the Mediterranean islands will be felt, America will still be in the land of Mesopotamia, struggling to install and maintain the model government it will have forced the Muslims to create. With the Americans' hands full, the Persians will call upon their Arab allies to begin causing local strife near the edges of Europe. This will cause the union of nations to convene and discuss the safety of Europe. The **Cock-like**[108] representative from France will speak as if he will be touched with the gift of an **ogmium**.[109] This man will then have Herculean powers of influence, such that he will offer a resolution that the American military presence in Italy be **accompanied** by the military **of** France. At this time, the unrest in the Arab lands will be escalating **so** rapidly that the **great** nation of America, and its ally Britain, will be too preoccupied by the **number** of territorial disputes which they will need to address. It will be **that** number which will be jeopardizing Europeans, because the American and British forces will be stretched thin. The French will be **of** the opinion that it will be **good** for the security of Europe if French military personnel were to be stationed in Italy. Should the Americans and British be needed in an emergency, their forces would have **a long way** to travel, to reach Europe; and, with the French forces staying in France, they would not be able to quickly shut **off** any trouble

---

108 Nostradamus wrote, "*Galique*," which most have translated as Gallic; however, this word is written a *Gaulois*. The word "*gal*" is Old French for "cock," and the "*-ique*" ending means "like." The capitalization gives it importance, so this is symbolic of an important usage of Cock. According to House of Names, the symbolism of the cock, in Christianity, is the resurrection of Jesus Christ. This understanding makes this a person that is in France, speaking as though another incarnation of Christ, or taken that importantly.

109 A Latin form of the word Ogma, which was a god from Celtic mythology. Ogma is depicted as a mature man, with golden chains connected to his tongue, symbolizing the gift of speech that enslaves. Ogma is considered to be an elderly Hercules, due to the strength of his ability to control the actions of others, with his speech.

that may arise. France will have never had a military presence in the unified Italy; although it will have warred with Austria on Italian soil. That will have been in the days of France's glory, when one common leader will have built **the Empire** for France which will have once dominated Europe. The Italians will not oppose the French ambassador's suggestion, as Italy will be struggling **from** the huge influx of immigrants and refugees that will have come **there** to settle. This French orator will convince the union of nations and its representatives to allow it to militarily occupy a foreign nation, without a declaration of hostility. This maneuver will come well after their disapproval of the **great** nation of America, when it will have sought the world's approval for it to militarily enter into Mesopotamia. America will have gone to war without the **law** of the union of nations allowing it to do so. So, France will make a point of demonstrating this formal process for such actions, by calling for approval to send France's military into Italy. The leader from France **will be** blaming America for the turmoil causing the need for this resolution to be **presented** to the union of nations for security purposes. The orator will sway the union of nations with his speech and gain their approval; but, his words will be meant more as an insult to America, for having caused world unrest, than for planning on French troops actually needing to secure Europe.

The French military will establish a naval base near **Venice**, Italy, which will also be the port of entry for its land personnel. This positioning will be seen as allowing the French to be **in** a strategic position, with rising hostilities in the eastern Adriatic, around the Balkans. The French will not believe those hostilities will become a threat to Italy, especially **after** the French will have become established **in** those northern Italian positions. With the French in Italy, some of the military of the **great** nation of America, which will have already been stationed in Italy, will be summoned to help in the Middle East. This will not be a call to go to Mesopotamia; but instead, American troops will be needed in the Aegean region, where a great **force** of nature will have occurred in the land of Turkey. This severe earthquake will have been felt in Venice and it will have destroyed a large area of land in Asia Minor.

While the world will fear those earth movements, the Turkish leader will announce that a dangerous condition will have been created. Turkey will have built buildings to generate **power**, much like the great dangerous power America will have tried to keep from the Arabs. The earth's movements will have damaged those buildings; and, this dangerous power will have become unstable and threatening the lives of the Turkish people. Turkey will have allowed the American military on its land, to help defend American troops to the south in Mesopotamia. With the danger of this power in Turkey having become unstable, the American military eagles **will raise** up in the air and spread **their wings** to fly and join with their American ships in the Persian Gulf. With this move, and with international tensions **so very high**, the Greeks will begin to enter Turkey, to assist the people of the Eastern Church. This will be seen as an act of provocation by a land **not distant** from Greece, in the Balkans; and, they will then invade Greece. The advances of that neighboring land will be **small** ones, but the Greeks will have their backs turned **to the** Balkan **forces**, while trying to save the Christian victims **of** Constantinople. This branch of the Christian Church will have remained in Turkey since the days of **the ancient** split from **Rome**.

The union of nations will call for major assistance to be immediately sent **in**, to restore the peace and rescue the injured. The British will be **that one** nation called by the union of nations to respond, whereas in **times** past it would have called upon the **great** ones of America. Great Britain will then set the **sails** of its ships for the land of the **Byzantines**, with warships to also quell the uprising by the Greek neighbor. As the **associated** partners of America, the British will have taken lightly the difficulties between the Greeks and their northern neighbors. Just as the earth will have erupted with gas **in the** earthquake, the British will be prepared to treat this dispute between nations with **lovage** herbs.[110] When the British convoy will arrive in the Aegean Sea they will stop **by** Greece and lend **the support** requested. However, once the British are in the Aegean Sea, the earth will open up again; and, this opening will be as great as the previous opening, with **power** so great that the sea will swallow the British ships and then half spit them out. This tragic loss of the British Mediterranean fleet will cause the union of nations to call on one of the former nations of the **Aquilonaire** union for assistance. This nation, north of Greece, will be Bulgaria; and the Bulgarians **will give** the European victims in Turkey and Greece **some** assistance. However, the earth will have created a very new and different terrain with its movements, which will become an **obstacle** for all rescue missions. In addition

---

110   This French word is listed in Randall Cotgraves Old French Dictionary as meaning, the lovage herb. The medicinal value of this plant is primarily for the treatment of flatulence and the reduction of menstrual cramps.

to **that** earth shift creating an obstacle for the northern nations of Europe to reach down into the lower reaches and into Turkey, other parts of the world's geography will have also been greatly changed. In the area **of the** Egyptian land, at the Sinai Peninsula, where the **two** continents of Africa and Asia join, the Red Sea will have been greatly affected by the movement and eruptions. Many of the islands of Greece will have sunk, with only the **Cretans** of Crete **not** having drowned in the waves the earthquake will have created. The devastation those two earthquakes will cause will change the world; so much so that those who will have been unaffected will have great difficulty reaching the missing people of **their** populations. Everyone will be in great distress. No one will know of the true condition in those affected areas, which **will be** out of contact with the rest of the world. The city of Constantinople will have been totally lost; and, **there** will have been the last bastion of the true Christian **Faith**, which will have **held** truest to Christ. The earth movements and waves will have sent many of the ancient documents of Christianity into the lost world of the sea. Some of that will then be found floating on the waves after this earthquake strikes.

The damages which will be caused **by** those earthquakes will be very significant; but, **in that time** they will occur, mankind will still have a chance to save itself. The earthquakes will be a sign that there is a much greater power than any man can ever possess. Still, with mankind having come into the possession of **some** of the most dangerous weapons possible to man, the **times** which will follow will mark how mankind's fate will proceed. The devastation which will be found **after** those earthquakes will have occurred to show how truly powerless mankind is to prevent destruction, by forces beyond its control. Man can only help control the power of nature if peace and brotherhood are shown to those in need of help; but, if man continues to plot its own destruction, then all mankind **will be** found responsible for its own blood, which will be **poured out** uncontrollably. That flow of blood will come **profusely** if mankind's penchant for persecution will not be curbed. It will be **the blood** of all living beings who Jesus Christ sacrificed his life for; and, it has been the Sacrament of the wine that symbolizes the renewal **of the** spirit of Christ within all Christians. Those who will be true to the teachings of Christ will be seen as **the** truly **innocent** peoples of the world; and, it will be those people who will be spared by Christ, should mankind begin to spill the blood of the innocents in acts of persecution, war and retribution. It will be a major challenge for the religions of the world to not be

309

influenced **by the wicked** among them.[111] The ploys those **anointed** wicked will offer, to keep the faithful from seeking peace, will be only **a few** material gains; and, those gains will be useless, when compared to the value of a soul saved for eternal reward. Some of the leading figures of the world at that time will have sold their souls for material gain, and a position of power will give them the illusion of being **elevated** ones; but, there is no earthly elevation that can come close to Heaven. When those earthquakes come, **then** will be the time for mankind to decide its fate, not **by** words, but by actions. The Christian nation of America will be seen as having the **great** things wealth can provide; and, that wealth will make America a powerful nation in the world. But, greatness has been known by many long gone nations in the thousands of years of mankind's history, because nations, like man, are mortal and none will live great forever. The second earthquake will have produced **floods** of water which will uncover the remains of a very ancient nation. That ancient nation is one which will have been just as great and powerful as America. That former power will have survived only through **the memory** of ancient men, who told of the times which had already passed into antiquity. That ancient world will return to the surface to become visible for the first time in many thousands of years. That ancient nation will have also controlled an empire; and, it will have had all **of the** material comforts and **things** that its time will have allowed. But, that nation will have been warned by its gods, of the potential dangers which could bring about the end of mankind. The earthquakes will expose a portion of that ancient civilization; and, among the exposed land will be the ruins of one of its former temples. This temple will be found intact and **containing** elements which will show the greatness **of** its peoples. Included will be documents written to warn the people of a future where **such** grave danger will have faced them. Those documents will tell of **instruments** man will have developed, which **will receive** the power to destroy the world. They will tell of the **innumerable** ways **loss** and damage will happen, should mankind not immediately destroy those instruments and return to living by the ways of peace and brotherhood. Those documents will have been written well before the known history of mankind, before the creation of Adam; but, they will tell of the **same** ways taught by Jesus Christ, as recorded by the apostles in **the** holy **letters** of Christianity.

---

111 Nostradamus wrote the words, "*nocens ung,*" which is a switch to Latin, meaning "wicked anointed." This comes from *nocens ungo.*

310

To clarify this statement of the letters of Christianity, in comparison to the documents that will be found in this exposed temple from an ancient civilization, they will come as replacements for the holy documents which will have been lost in the earthquake's waves. While the earthquakes will have destroyed the holy seat of the Eastern Church of Christ and all of its holy documents, these other documents which will be found in those ancient temples will be more important for mankind to know at that time. They will tell of the history of mankind; but, this history will be so ancient it will tell of **the ancient** part of the Old Testament, as if it were still in the future. It will tell of God and the coming of his Son to lead mankind, such that the discovery of these documents and letters will become a most important **new testament** for the belief in God. It will tell of the troubles that civilization will have faced, with some people of their civilization **being** insanely lusting for power and control. It will tell of the instruments they will have used and will have developed, which will have made the creation of the most dangerous power possible. The documents will tell of their **chases** to eliminate both those wicked people and the instruments, for the purpose of saving the world for a future mankind.

Of those chases, **which will be** efforts to catch those mad people, they will have led **towards** the north. That will have been where a society of people will have lived without religion, like **the** Russians will have, when they formed the union of the **Aquilonaires**. The civilization leaving the documents in those temples will have succeeded in defeating those evil people, not by war, but **by the** peaceful measure of chasing them into designed traps. By their own free **will**, as given to mankind by the **divine** deity, they will have chosen to hide within the depths of the earth. Once that decision will have been made by the evil ones, the earth will have closed up around them, sealing them within the earth's cavity.

This ancient civilization will have not prevented its own demise; but, it will have acted to save the earth, while sacrificing its own life. However, they will have made it clear in their documents that **between** the end of their civilization and the end of the earth, there will come **one** other civilization which will also be in need of warning. This warning will rise from the depths because future man's **time** will then be at hand; and, he must also choose to save the world or die. Just as they will have been **tied** to a self-made dilemma, to save earth and die or let the power of **Satan** ruin the earth forever, this future civilization will face the same choice. The mankind of *The Prophecies* will find that those ancient letters

311

will have been written to them, by a long lost civilization. This civilization will have thrived on the island of Atlantis.

And at the time this ancient civilization will have been lost, Satan will have been cast into the depths of the earth with the wicked ones. The words which **will remain** behind will be entombed in a tightly sealed monument. The engraving above the entrance will be in a language which will have later become the language of Latin; and, it will be this similarity which will make the words understandable. The carvings in stone, on the outside of the building, will identify **the sepulcher** as containing a warning. The documents inside will tell **of so many** comings, of the powerful empires that would come and pass, including the time America would become **great**. The people of Atlantis will have had **veneration** for God, as shown **by** symbolic references to the many aspects of the one God, as many separate deities. It will have been their tales of God's power that will have been passed down to become the mythological gods the Greeks and Romans worshiped. The tales of those gods and goddesses will have taken place within **the space** of earth, as well as the space that expands well beyond earth. The Atlanteans will have been a great civilization **for** a very **long time**; and, they will have lived **under the** guidance of God, in His many forms, in a **clear** state. They will have all been well aware, **in** their earthly existence, of **the** powers of God, and especially His **universal vision**. They knew God was **of the** realm much higher than matter; and, they knew the **eyes** of God could see everything they did. Because of this awareness they will have acted in honor of that power and lived a very long time in peace. While God could see all of mankind's actions, **from the** comfort of **heaven**, He surrounded earth with the visible lights, as extensions of His being, by which mankind could be led to act. The greatest light God provided for mankind was the light **of the Sun**, which was God's way of continuing to give life and light to earth. The Atlanteans worshiped the Sun, as an extension of God; and, they saw the Sun god as the son of God, who only spoke the truth.

The second greatest light God provided for mankind will have been that **of the Moon**. The Moon will have been seen as reflective of the changing natures of man. It is not a true light, as it is reflective; but, it shows the ever changing amount of the Sun's light of truth that is absorbed by mankind. Those changes go from no reflection, in the darkness of inner thought, to stages of waxing and waning, to and from our full emotional expressions. In this way, mankind is both led by inner wisdom and outer signs; and, the full moon represents when little inner thought is shown. The Moon will have been an important luminary to the Atlanteans; but, they will warn that the Moon's light still leaves shadows, keeping man from knowing the full truth.

(The Setup to the Beginning)

In the earth's movements in the Aegean area, the shifts will have exposed a temple with the Sun and the Moon engraved on **the arches** of this long buried building, **erected** years before. All of the buildings surfacing will have been constructed **by the ancient** peoples who will have written the documents of warning. Those buildings will have been built where those peoples lived, near where the islands of Greece will have remained in our times and beyond. Those islands will have been formed when their ancient civilization will have finally been lost, by a huge earth eruption. This lost civilization will have been called Atlantis. The buildings discovered will have been built for their gods; and, their gods will have retained interest, by the surviving people who will resettle the earth. This will be particularly evident in the city of Athens, where the two most favorite gods of that city's peoples were Athena, the goddess of **Martial** strategies, and Poseidon, the god of the seas. The Athenians will have admired those gods because of their ancient ancestry to Atlantis. In both places, those gods were seen as immortal powers which surround and enhance the Withering Ones of humanity. These Marciaux humans were the mortal heroes of Greek mythology.[112] Most of those heroes were also dedicated to the temples erected in honor of Ares, the god of war, as their notoriety came from amazing feats during wars. War will have been the **one accompanying** theme which will have made those heroes stand out in Greek lore, **with the** Greek people being most interested in knowing of their strengths and abilities. Some, like Heracles, were enabled with superhuman strengths, which allowed them to kill many normal mortal beings and strange creatures. However, one enemy those heroes always feared was the **waves** of the seas, which their powers could not defeat. This made them honor the god **of** earthquakes and oceans, who was Poseidon to the Greeks, and who the Romans

---

112 Nostradamus wrote the capitalized word, "*Marciaux*," which is seen as a derivative of Martial. The root is Latin, being *marceo* or *marcidus*, meaning to wither or withering, drooping. The –aux ending means "those of." In this reference block, I believe both Martial and Withering Ones equally apply, following the multiplicity of meaning that Nostradamus wrote into the words.

313

called **Neptune**. The exposure of those temples will be a sign sent by God, as the coming of war will be at hand. Symbolized by those three gods and the state of man believing it to be a superhero, nature will prove to be a much superior foe which must not be angered. Mankind will believe it has conceived the battle plans and strategies, as governed by Athena; but, it will not have foreseen a buried monument foretelling their doom, if they proceed. The use of naval vessels, which will strike with bolts of lightning, will symbolically need the blessings of Poseidon; and, with the Red Sea narrowed in Egypt, the Persians will see this as a sign by their god to act. They will believe that Allah will give them victory over the greater Martial nations. The beginning signs of this war will then be seen **in the Adriatic** Sea, as far north as where the French navy will have felt the shocks of the earthquake, in the port of Venice. With the Persians seeing those earth changes as a sign from Heaven, they will order another Balkan ally to prepare to initiate their plan. With this command, there **will be** then **made** a border **discord** between them and the Christian nation that will cover most of the seacoast on the Adriatic Sea, opposite Italy.[113] This nation will have sought help from the **great** nation of America, when many of their citizens will have been purged by their fellow countrymen. This Christian nation of Dalmatia, which **this** state of Serbia will again threaten, will have **that** association with America used as the motivation for the Serbian discord. Many of the Dalmatians **will be** from the former state which will have once been united with Serbia, in the larger nation of Moldavia. Moldavia will have been under the domination of the Russian sect of philosophy; but, many of its Dalmatians will have retained their Christian values. As a new nation of Christians will have arisen from the ashes of the Russian collapse, Dalmatia will have since become **united** with the union of European nations. It will be seen as a Christian ally with France, Italy, England and America. Dalmatia will look towards Italy for help, as the changes in the earth will have narrowed several sea routes and closed others, making the Adriatic Sea difficult to travel. The American and British navies **will be** outside of the Mediterranean; and, with the destruction of the British fleet in the Aegean Sea, it will be impossible for their navies to reach the Adriatic quickly. The nation of

---

113 Dalmatia is now Croatia (Christian) and Serbia and Montenegro are now what is left of Yugoslavia. Both will have been parts of the former nation of Yugoslavia, which was generally Moldavia. The United States conducted an air-warfare bombing of Serbia, under Bill Clinton-NATO (1998), to control their genocide of Christian Croatians that still lived in Serbia.

Dalmatia will have **separated** from its former nation; and, with the help of its larger allies it will have stood independent. However, now it will stand alone, separated from its Western support, as the French will not leave Italy without the union of nations ordering it to do so. The Serbian aggressors, seeing a failure of the French to respond, **will approach** Dalmatia **from** the east. They will be claiming rights to part of the land along the Adriatic coastline, where a seaport will give them vital access to the Adriatic Sea. Dalmatia will be unable to keep Serbia from establishing its **house** of operations in **this** region, causing many Dalmatians to panic. The Serbians will have acted in **that** manner before, when a greater Slavic nation will have united Dalmatia with Serbia. This will have been **before** that nation will have been broken up. At that time, the non-religious supporters of the Russian philosophy will have persecuted those of all religions, trying to maintain the unity of that nation, as well as keep the dominant philosophy of Russia alive in Moldavia. That persecution **was** after the fall of Russia, so the **great** nation of America will have been free to lead the union of nations to approve the use of militarily force against the Serbians. The union of nations will have granted America the freedom to use military force against them, to cease the hostilities that will have existed in this region before. In that military show of strength, the capital **city** of Belgrade will have been severely damaged by the military of the union of nations; and, the city of Sarajevo will have also been destroyed. This will have allowed Moldavia to become broken apart, with several small pieces gaining independence from the Serbian influence. It is important that you are **understanding** this history of destruction in the Balkans, because those great historic cities will have meant a great deal to the Serbians. The Serbians will have seen the Christian nations as responsible for having destroyed Belgrade; and, they will develop hatred for America, for leading a military against them, on their soil. With America unable to respond to this uprising, the Serbians will demand retribution; and, in settlement for their destroyed cities they will want to take the port city of Dubrovnik, in Dalmatia. This will give them naval capacities on the Adriatic Sea, which will be part of the plan of the **Pempotams**. This word, Pempotam, is defined by understanding the word **mesopotamia**. Mesopotamia is defined, from the Greek, as "the land (meso-) between two rivers (potamia)." The Sanskrit word, "potam," means "the boat for crossing," or that which makes a suitable boat for crossing. The new Persian Empire plans will call for free ports of departure, from which their purchased naval vessels will be able to reach their planned points of entry. Those points of

entry will be several major ports **of** the Mediterranean lands of Western **Europe**.
[114] From this outlet to the sea, the Serbians will then have the capacity to send
military vessels **to** the port of Venice, at **forty five** degrees of latitude.[115] At the
same time of that advancement, the Persians will have coordinated plans for
other advancements, from other ports of departure, to designated points of entry in the invasion. One of those points of entry will be at **forty** degrees of latitude, where the island of Sardinia will have the ancient port city of Oristano.[116]
This will be where the Islamic Empire will begin to apply the **ung**,[117] or the ointment, which will remove the Christian irritation to Islam. However, the most
primary source of this irritation will be located at **forty-two** degrees of latitude,[118]
where the Vatican will be near the coast that leads to Rome.[119] The plan to invade Rome will call for the securing of all of the islands surrounding the Italian
peninsula.

One important point of assault will be at Syracuse, on the island of Sicily, at **thirty-seven** degrees of latitude.[120] This will secure against the presence of American
navy ships, and will allow for the Muslim advances upon Rome. However, while
Rome, as the seat of Christianity, will be the most important target of this Islamic
retribution, the most key element of security will be the control of the entrance
to the Mediterranean Sea. Following the earthquakes, the only way to gain access

---

114　Pempotam is thus the proper name for the purchased military vessels that Iran is
documented to have bought from Russia, following the collapse of the Soviet Union.
Interestingly, in the zoological classification of turtles, the Potamites is the group of
river tortoises, with a soft shell.

115　Venice, Italy coordinates are 45N27, rounds to 45.

116　Oristano, Sardinia coordinates are 39N54, rounds to 40.

117　In the previous statement, Nostradamus wrote "quarante-cinq," meaning "forty-
five." However, in the following statement he did not insert a hyphen, writing "quarante ung." This makes "quarante" mean forty, with "ung" being the abbreviation for the
Latin word, "unguentum," meaning "ointment."

118　If you will notice, Nostradamus wrote in this block, "*quarante cinq*" and "*quar-
antedeux*." These numbers seem clearly to state "forty-five" and "forty-two." Actually, "forty five" means a spread of 5 degrees, from 40 degrees of latitude. This spread
stretches from the toe of the Italian boot to Venice. "Forty-two" specifically means
Rome.

119　Rome, Italy coordinates are 41N54, the same as Vatican City, rounds to 42.

120　Syracuse, Sicily coordinates are 37N04, rounds to 37.

to this body of water will be from the Atlantic Ocean. While the Americans, British and French will have had a weaker presence in the Mediterranean, due to the recent earthquakes, they will still have large navies. Those three naval powers will have many ships able to enter the Mediterranean Sea from the Atlantic Ocean. This will make the capture of the fortress at Gibraltar a very key element in the Persian plan. With the British Mediterranean fleet weakened by the devastation of the earthquake in the Aegean Sea, their possession of that fortress will need to be neutralized by the Arabs. This will come by the North African invasion taking the land that Muslims will have once will have possessed, in Andalusia. This will make an assault possible on the western city of Seville, at thirty-seven degrees of latitude, as well as the port of Malaga, at almost 37 degrees of latitude. Those will be the most important points of initial entry into Spain.[121] This European invasion will find massive waves of Arabs coming from North African nations of Morocco and Algeria.

After **the second** earthquake will have caused such destruction around the waters of the Aegean Sea, Red Sea and Mediterranean Sea, much of the land **itself will sink to the bottom** of these seas. This will have given rise to land which will have been submerged, but at one time in the distant past been above the water line. This will have been **so** long **before** that no history of that land mass will be in recorded history books. Now, with it above water again, that land will appear from the waters **by the Latin** nations. This will not only happen in the Eurasian region. The earth's movements will have been so violent that other earthquakes will have **accompanied** those. There will also be significant geological impact in other regions of the world. It will be **that** accompaniment that **will be made**, where **the** earth tremors that will have **followed next** will carve a **path** of destruction along several of the world's fault lines, causing extensive worldwide **quaking**. This trembling will especially upset the plans of the Arabs, as they will become **furious** trying to make contact with their antichrist leader. He will be out of touch, **in the** safety of hiding and confinement within a **mount**. That mountain will be in one of the lands the Persians will plan to occupy, between France and Spain. With no one aware of what **Uses** the antichrist will make of the earth's major changes, they will be afraid to send someone deep in the

---

121   Gibraltar is at 36N08. Seville coordinate being 37N23 and Malaga at 36N43, making both round to 37.

caves of this mountain to ensure he is aware.[122] The mountain will be where the **descendants** of early mankind will have been found to have lived; and, those ancient creatures will have left evidence of their presence, when they will have descended into the caves and left drawings on the cave walls. The Persians will be desperate to contact the antichrist; so, they will decide to send the antichrist's son to Spain, **for** him **to climb** up to the cave where he can get a message to his father. The antichrist will have been secretly planning and training his elite army **in the Pyrenees** Mountains; and, the presence of his son will anger him. His anger will be for worry of detection; but, in this cave lair, the antichrist will have **not** been able to know of the severity of the earth's movements. The Pyrenees will not have been affected. He **will be** made aware of the documents that will have been found in the new island in the Aegean Sea. The son will tell his father those documents will have been **translated** and understood to be telling warnings against using the most powerful weapons. In those documents, which will be addressed **to** citizens of the future by **the ancient** Atlantean **monarchy**; there will be a specific warning to the users of such weapons. The Atlanteans will have prophesized that if there **will be made** war with those weapons, **there** will result one **third** of the world's peoples being killed. In addition, this use will produce **flooding** which will cause the deaths of many of the ones who will have been the users **of** those weapons. Their own **blood** will drown in the flood waters, from a **human** error of miscalculation. The documents will warn mankind **not** to bring about the demise of **oneself**, as one **will find** this future will have been known **of** for a **long time**. It will have been known well before this future mankind will have ever been born. They will warn of the tricks of **Mars**, who will try to work his way into the hearts and minds of mankind, to make them seek war as an answer. The danger will be clear after Mars has been let **in**, as the first taste of blood will make mankind **wanton**, without rules of any kind to stop the lust. To quench this lust, mankind will become savagely inhuman. The paradox of this discovery will be that the discovery of those documents will have been made in

---

122 Nostradamus wrote, "Iouis," which was the Old French style, where "I" was used for the absence of the letter "J." Also, the letter "u" was written, when it could mean a "v." This has caused many to state that Nostradamus wrote of Mount Jove, or Mount Jovis, which is actually non-existent. The word written is "Joui," with the "s" making it plural. "Jouir" is the word meaning, "to enjoy; possess; hold; occupy; use; to take the profit; receive the fruit; make fruition of."

the month of March, during the time when Christians will be observing Lent.[123]

Then, when the son will have told his father of the earth changes and the warning found, the antichrist will become the one who **will pass** judgment on the fate of the world. The antichrist will have led the poor Arab nation against the Russian domination and won; and, it will have been in that poor nation, filled with rugged mountains, where he will have found the value of mountain caves. Like Mohammed before him, the antichrist will hear the voice of Allah in the caves; and, he will believe those voices will be God. The voices will tell him that the warnings are a fabrication of the Americans and that he should carry out his plan as scheduled. He will hear the voice tell him Allah will close off the Mediterranean Sea to help his forces; but, this voice will not be God. It will be Satan, the same false god that spoke to Mohammed in a cave; but, believing he will be doing good for Allah, from deep inside **the mount** of **Uses** the antichrist will order the onset of attacks which will seal the fate of mankind. When the time for action will come, the antichrist will leave his mountain lair and join with one of his generals in the Mediterranean Sea; and, he will begin to implement his plans of retribution and persecution.

At that time, when the antichrist **of** the Islamic Empire will be **there**, hidden in the mountains of Europe, before he makes that fateful decision based on the words of Satan, the world will have not passed the point of no return. That point will actually not be crossed **until** the first strike will have taken place; and, this means at the time when the use of the most terrible weapon will happen. When that use will occur, huge numbers of American soldiers will have already been destroyed, beginning an irrevocable war of destruction that will bring mankind to its end. However, the world will still be salvageable, should those first strikes never occur. The words I write **here** now are the words of Jesus Christ, for the purpose of preventing that end. The words of the Atlanteans will not save the world; but, my words will be understood, well before that time comes. They will have been made public, in the manner they have been intended to be read, before the use of that weapon will happen. The story that will follow will occur, but only should these warnings be ignored. I have written that all of these words will

---

123 Nostradamus wrote, "*Mars en caresme.*" This translates to, "Mars in wanton," where "*caresme*" means "wanton." However, the word "*caresme*" also means, "Lent," and the word "mars" also means the month of "March." Lent is when Christians control their wanton desires.

be proven infallible; and, when that time of understanding has come, many of the verses will have already been proven as such. But, so many will not have faith and not believe at all; while, many will believe only when some future event will further come true as predicted. That is not the faith that will save mankind, as it will make deaths necessary first, to finally believe it all will have been accurately prophesized. Those American troops who will witness the use of those powerful weapons, should mankind not adopt faith, they will know that the line of no return will have just been crossed. It will be too late to believe in God then, once the use of this weapon will have begun the motion to the end. I have written these words, by the direction of Jesus Christ, to save mankind. The future of mankind can be saved if mankind changes its direction and dedication. The fate of mankind cannot be left up to the antichrist, who will be listening to Satan's enticing promises. Mankind must act immediately, on faith alone, to prevent this first strike from becoming a reality. The future fate of mankind is avoidable; such that all I have written to this point is all that need be known. It will have been the failure to understand the purpose for the passion of Jesus Christ that will haunt the souls of those lost in the very first battle, should mankind fail to act with faith. Failure will haunt all souls that choose to ignore this warning.

If the destruction will be begun **by** the use of man's own devises, **at the time** of the first sign of this power being released man **will be** in the final minutes of life. Those dreadful actions will have **accomplished** the first steps of the End Times, as was written in **the prophecy** of John. In that Book of *The Revelation* this will be when the first of the four horsemen will have appeared from the clouds. And, this prophecy was not only told to John, as all of the prophecies in the Bible will then be found activated and coming true as they will have never been understood before. It was the Prophet Jeremiah who made his warning of these times coming, when he told the king of Judah **of the** coming ruin of Judah and Jerusalem, by the Babylonians. Jeremiah was also summoned directly by the true **Royal** spirit, God, who told Jeremiah what to say. This was just as Jesus Christ has told me; and, it was as He also told John. As a true **Prophet** of God, Jeremiah wrote the *Lamentations*, which told of the coming sufferings of the people of Israel, in captivity. Jeremiah wrote **how**, "they have **heard** that I sigh," which was **a sigh** where "there was none to comfort me." This sigh comes from Jeremiah, because no one listened to his words of God's warning. He **made** his warnings **shortly** before the beginning of the stages of oppression. Jeremiah also wrote about

320

how this wrath of God was due to the **loosened** values of the Jewish societies, where the **sons** and daughters of Israel were literally sacrificed to pagan idols; but, they were also figuratively sacrificed by not teaching their children the laws of God. This failure to save the children would make them **murderers** in the eyes of God, as their own lack of faith and morals will have loosened the sons of murder. The measure of **what** is **great** does not come from one's strength, wealth or the **oppression that** that one can create **by** using force against another. **At the time** Jeremiah made his prophecies to Judah and Israel, the same principles that applied then **will be** just as valid again. In fact, they will be **made** even more relevant in this future. There will be a similar arrogance of domination that will force men to feel the need to show power **over** others; but, this will be the cause of a greater end punishment. Those who will have thought of themselves as **the princes** of royalty, those common leaders far removed from the true reigns, they will all find out just how minor they are. They will see how all of mankind will be treated as common, as the mortals they are. Just as Babylon and Rome appointed **governors** in each **of the kingdoms** their might had conquered, those new rulers will rule as tyrants and oppress their enemies, to keep them enslaved. This **same** lack **of** common courtesy and caring will be found facing **those** on the waters of the Mediterranean Sea, **which** will be awaiting a signal from the Persian Gulf. With warships **being** staged in the **maritime** waters of Western Europe, near the nations that will have oppressed the people of the **eastern** lands, both of Eastern Europe and the Near East, the Easterners will be prepared to attack. They will be awaiting the news of a successful defeat of the American navy, which will be announced only in **their languages**. Those tongues will not be understood by the Christian nations. Their warships will have people on the land awaiting a signal also, as those people will have **intermingled in** these Western European nations which will have supported **the great** nation of America. Those immigrants will have blended into the **society** of the west; and, they will have learned **the language** of their prey. France, Italy and Spain all have different languages; but, each will be **of the** root language of the Romans, with all being **Latin** languages. Those European peoples will not know **of the** language of the **Arabs**; and, when the Arabs will send the confirmation from the Persian Gulf, **by the** use of Arabic in a coded **communication**, the Europeans will be unsuspecting that those words will be **punic**. They will be unaware that those communications of treachery will lead to the horrible actions which will be about to commence against them.

EXPLAINING THE QUATRAINS – THE BEGINNING OF THE JUDEO-CHRISTIAN DEFEATS

(Timing of the Beginning of Armageddon)

This plan will have been in place for some time prior, waiting **until** the time when the best **opportunity** would arise. The element of a favorable moment of **time** will be the key ally of the Muslims, especially against a stronger foe. Given the right space and the right moment, the element of surprise will give the Islamic actions the upper hand.[124] This favorable time **will surpass** even the best planned moments of attack, with all of the global earth changes which will have taken place. In Islam, the Moon is their holy luminary; and, they will have planned an attack to begin when the Moon will be in a favorable aspect for them. It will have been determined that one strike will precede the other attacks, as the first strike; and, this first strike will occur at the time of a total lunar eclipse. Another lunar eclipse will have already occurred, **before** this **one** that will be the chosen, in the same year; and, this previous lunar **eclipse** will have acted as a trial run, before the real plan goes into action. They will wait for the second lunar eclipse, which will follow a partial **solar** eclipse. At the time of this planned lunar eclipse, **the** duration will last longer and the light of the Sun will be made **most obscure**. The Moon will be totally in the earth's umbra for the longest period of time possible. This obscurity will be longer than any of the other lunar eclipses, which will have cast its shadow over the Middle East in that century.

At that time of darkness, the Persian leader will command the beginning of the first onslaught, which will cause **the** soldiers of America to initially panic. Their panic will be caused by a **most** tremendous upheaval. This upheaval's origin will be completely **mysterious**, and it will leave the Americans saturnine, when they will become cold with fear; and, the Americans will be slow to react properly. As mysterious as this upheaval will be, it will be readily recognized by name, **which** will have been the name used to describe the powerful weapon known to

---

124   This sentence fragment was written in Latin, "*in occasione temporis.*" These words can also mean, "at a favorable moment at the right time."

generate the greatest fear in all of mankind. They will know **very well** what it **was** that they will have encountered, having had the same power in their arsenal. That capacity will have been limited to only select nations, as it will have been the most destructive power **since** America will have first brought **the creation** into being. The continued presence of this menace **to the world** will have led other nations to lust for this power. The race for superiority will have brought this power to such heights of presence that this level will have brought fear to the whole world. America will have not destroyed this fearsome weapon; instead, it will have used that fear as its source of power, more than the weapon itself. America will have used this power to gain world superiority; but, that period of domination will have only lasted **until** this use that will occur that dark night **in** the land of Mesopotamia. The fear will have been just, due to **the** known **death** that the weapon will have created in its only use, both immediate and long-term. Originally, the discovery will have been seen as a breakthrough in mankind's **passion** to understand all of the workings of the universe; and, as a nation which will have been dedicated to **Jesus Christ**, it will have been seen that this power could serve as a way to protect His people, against those who would deny Christ. At this moment in time, it will be their failure to understand the passion of Jesus Christ that will have all of Christianity set up for destruction, by its own double-edged sword.

The Islamic plan **will be** ready to initiate when the Moon is eclipsed, because of the breakthrough that will have occurred **in the** prior year, in the **month of October**. Prior to **that** time of eclipse, **some** of the **great** nation of America's communications, which will have been coded for security, will be broken by the enemy. The Persian people, skilled in such communication, will then be able to determine a **translation** of America's military language. When this code is broken, false communications **will be made**, after the advent of this mysterious upheaval will have been unleashed, to further confuse the America's military.

When that false communication will be received by the Americans it will be read **such that the one** reading it **will imagine**, or presume, it is official. This belief that the message is official will place **the burden** on the leaders reading the message to respond accordingly. The message will appear urgent; but, the message will tell **of** more major movements of **the earth**, as a report of another earthquake. There will be no mention of the use of one of the most powerful weapons. For the Muslims **to have** the Americans believing this message,

America's naval fleet will have **lost its** emergency preparedness, and will proceed to sail by **natural movement**, without guard.[125]

This natural course would be planned for by the Persians; and, the communication will be designed **to be** leading the American vessels into a trap. Once inside this trap, the Persian navy will then cause the American ships to be **engulfed** by a surprise attack and sunk. With this occurring during the darkness of an eclipse, the attacks will be on ships that will be **in** the pitch black of night; and, when the attacks begin and the ships slide beneath the waves, their sailors with them, those sailors will be listed in the **perpetual** records of those who met their deaths in the **darkness** of deep waters. In the darkness of the eclipse, the communication will call the ships, with this call **being precedent** to the great evil that will next be unleashed. Those attacks will occur **in the** aftermath of this first strike, and they will destroy the American fleet in the Persian Gulf. It will occur at the **time** of a lunar eclipse, which will occur in the **spring**, after the Vernal Equinox.

The time of this spring lunar eclipse will be close to the great earthquakes, which will occur around Easter; and, the **one in** Greece, which will occur when the Sun is in Taurus, will have recently occurred, before these attacks. All of the discoveries that will be made, **following** the raising of the ancient temples and the realizations of the ancient warnings, will be made public; and, the attacks will occur **after** this. The antichrist will order the execution of these attacks **from the extremes** of his mountain lair. With the news of the recent discoveries received by the antichrist, some will believe he will be **altering** his schedule and changing the plan; however, he will be firm in his decision to transform Europe into an Islamic state, by converting all Christians to Islam. Those plans for change will be great **permutations**, where major fundamental changes will be enforced. The people **of** the Christian nations of Europe, whose **reigns** will be unprepared for attacks, will be forced to choose between submission and fighting to the death. The antichrist will not be led **by** the news of ancient warnings, as his heart will

---

125   In this statement fragment, modern French makes it read, "the gravity of the earth to have lost its natural movement." While this appears clear, gravity was not known in 1558. Newton did his work on gravity 100 years later. The French word written, "pesanteur," means "weightiness, heaviness," more than gravity. However, as that clear statement, it is quite possible that it also means that some kind of jamming system will be employed, making motion detection appear wrong, making it seem that the gravity of the earth did indeed appear lost.

325

lust for the destruction of all that will have made America **great**. The major **tremblings**, which will have raised portions **of** one of the greatest civilizations to inhabit **earth**, will not sway the antichrist. He will know that his plan will be set to spring into action **with** his approval and order. At that time, Europe will become inundated by **proliferations** of Muslims and their mercenary allies. Those invasions will be the beginning steps **of the new Babylon**, or the new Empire of the Antichrist. It will be fed by a newfound spirit of hatred, which will be ignited in the waters next to Persia, below Babylon, against the American dominators. All this hatred will have been born from the artificial placement of the **daughter** of the Jews on Arab land, as the new Israel. The Jews will have lost their land to the King of Babylon ages ago, then to have been freed without a land, to become scattered across the face of the earth. While this lack of a homeland will have made the Jews **miserable**, they will have been too weak and disunited to win their land back by themselves. They will have been **increased** in power **by** other great nations, due to **the abomination of** the German persecution that will have been **the first holocaust**. While they will have thought they had found joy with their receiving of that gift of a nation, with the loss of America's protection their misery will increase so greatly that the abomination of the first holocaust will pale in comparison, to what will be about to come.

And Israel will find it will **not** be able to keep the Promised Land that God had once given them. While **being** strongly covetous of this land, and more greatly possessive of it once they will have taken it **from the** people of Palestine, God will not bless this theft. It will be the Palestinians who will have had taken up rightful residence there. The Jews will have taken the **whole** of Israel as **theirs**, while defending their persecutions, **assaulting** peoples of Arab descent who will have resented losing their land. The Palestinians will have been forced to live in squalor, with few arms of significance to fight with, against a far superior Israeli military. Still, they will not have given up hope or the fight. All of this effort to regain what was lost will make the Israeli attempts to squash resistance become **vain** efforts.

The Zionists will have manipulated others, **to** have had **the place** of Israel regained. Much of **that** land, **in times past**, will have **had** been **the dwelling** of the children **of Abraham**. This was his promised land, which Jacob left from, taking his children to Egypt. The Promised Land that will have been delivered by Moses will have fulfilled God's promise to the children of Israel. It was the

Promised Land that was later divided into Israel and Judah, with Jerusalem being the capital of Judah. All of this land will have been lost by the Jews when they failed to listen to the words of their prophets of God, who warned them to change or be crushed. When they were defeated and exiled to Babylon, that right to their land was no longer valid; and, the biblical symbolism of this is found when Jacob took Esau's birthright and blessing, by the use of deception. Esau was the one to be given the blessing by Isaac; but, when Jacob listened to his mother's commands and was given Isaac's blessings, Esau had no recourse once the blessing was given away. In this way the Arabs, as the children of Abraham, will see the Jewish people given land that was not free to give as unfair. To justify this unfairness, the Jews **will be assailed by** the **people** whose land they will have had stolen and given away. This will not only by the Palestinians, but also by the Arabs who will stand up to defend the Palestinian's right to that land. It will be those people **who will be** continuing to fight back for this stolen land, until they will be **having** the land back in their possession. The success of those attacks on Israel will be seen as being by the will of Allah. Once this land will be taken back, the Muslims will celebrate **in veneration** by erecting holy mosques there. They will see the Jews as **the Jovialists**, who will have not taken the sacred ground seriously; but, the Arabs will be jovial at the time of recovery.[126]

And towards this goal of recovery, after the Muslims will begin their holy war they will immediately target the Jews. As the ground will be sacred, neither side will use the most powerful weapons near Jerusalem; but, without this weapon to use and without external assistance, the Jews will not be as powerful as they will have thought they were. The Jews will be driven back to the shores of the Mediterranean Sea, to their seaport fortress. However, with the damage done by the earthquakes, there will be no escape by sea. This city will be their last refuge of hope; and, it will be **here** that the State of Israel will cease to exist once again. They will fortify **this** fortress area, around the ruins that will have been the **city**

---

126 Nostradamus wrote the capitalized word, "*Ioualistes*," which has been translated as "Jovialists." However, this word is defined as anyone that lives life with joy. The core word is the same as was presented before, where I translated it to be "mount Uses." The possibility exists, in the context of this block of text, that "Jovialistes" is actually "Joui – alites," which means, "used in bed," or "possessed in bed." This would give an Arab perspective of the Jews in a more negative light, with the capitalization being a personification of the Israelis being comfortable with their possession of Palestine.

of Achem.[127] The city **will be surrounded** on all sides, with the Muslims to the north, south and east. The Jews will then be **assailed from all** sides, in **parts** and **in** wholes, by the **very-great power of** the Arab **people**. Each **of** the sides will have tremendous **arms**, making the final battles there most destructive.

(The End of Israel)

The Jews **not will hold** the city of Achem once their arms will have been exhausted. The Arabs will begin a siege; and, they will continue to attack and attack again, looking for the weakest point of entry. Those attacks will become **so much** that the Jews will become too weary to hold any longer. Without the help of another nation coming to their rescue, they will know all will be lost. When the Jews will have finally fallen in defeat the calendar's marks will show they **only** held that land **seventy three years.**[128] They will fight to survive for **seven** more months of war, but the Jews will find themselves pinned down in their last stronghold, gasping for help as their supplies run out. They will finally surrender to the Arabs in the **month** of September.[129] And **then**, when the Israelis will be defeated, **after** so many years of being **in** Palestine and punishing the Palestinians for rejecting their presence, the true Arab anger of hatred **will come out** against those Jews who will surrender. Several **of** the Israeli men who will carry a white flag out of their city walls will be killed by the Arabs. To **them**, the Arabs will use **the rod** of punishment, killing those as sacrificial lambs. They will allow the rest of the survivors to remain alive. The Arabs will do **this** to cease the hostilities between Arabs and Jews. They will say both have come from the **one** Abraham, **which** gave both equal rights to the lands. The surviving Jews **would** be offered to **have** a place of **dwelling** in the land they will have loved **so much**, and **for**

---

127   I see "*Achem*" as Tel Aviv. It was the first Jewish settlement in Palestine in the 20th Century, so fitting to be the last to go. "Achem" appears on Jewish websites in searches, but without a definition. French, however, has the word "*achemes*," which means being dressed up or decorated. This could also be read as "*a' chem.*," where French has the word, "*chemer*," meaning to be on the decrease or in wane.

128   This is a very important timing element, as the modern State of Israel began in 1948. When 70 years is added to that, the year that this war will begin would be 2018. When Israel falls it would then be 2021. The only question is the duration of this war, as the element of a 3-year war in Israel is not certain, but fits the way Nostradamus is read, by his non-use of a hyphen.

129   The French word, "*sept*," means both: seven and September.

such **a long time**; but, to accept those terms of surrender, the Jews will have to allow their religion to become **sterile** and convert to Islam. Those who will agree to **proceeding** with the Arab's offer will remain in Palestine; but, the ones who will refuse this offer will be sent **to** the land of Persia. There, at **the fiftieth degree** of longitude, the New Babylon of captivity will be readied for Jewish prisoners.[130] This defeat of the Jews, **which** will have been the arch enemy of the Arabs for so long, **will renew** the faith of **all** Muslims in Europe that Allah stands with them in battle. This will give them more incentive when they will go to war against **the church** of Jesus Christ, and all people who will be **Christian**.

(The Forces that Will Target Europe)

The greatest Christian target for persecution **will be** the nations of Europe. The Islamic agreements with the Eastern European nations, who will have developed from the **sect** of philosophy not knowing religion, will be purely mercenary. Those volunteers will not see Christianity as a specific cause to defeat. However, they will see all Western Europeans as opulently selfish, while having had exercised economic punishments on the poor nations of that sect for a long time. They will see the war as one of revenge; but, their revenge will be for different reasons. This source of hatred will have made the Eastern Europeans savage warriors, who will use the most **Barbaric** actions against all Western Europeans they will encounter; and, this will be regardless of any religious beliefs one may hold. Still, as the Eastern Europeans will stand united **with the** Islamists and Africans, as allies in a war of retribution, none of them will be controlled by the moral standards of Christianity. This will cause the **whole** of their forces to become equally barbaric, with all allowed to pillage, rape and slaughter wantonly, throughout all European nations. Most specifically horrible will be the persecution **of the Latin** lands, which surround the Adriatic Sea. The Eastern European participants will reap the rewards of their horrible victories, and they will lust **greatly** for the material things of the West. The peoples of Italy, Slovenia, Croatia and Greece will become greatly **distressed** by their Serbian-led invaders. The people of those lands, who will not be killed at the hands of their

---

130 Tehran, Iran coordinates are 51E26 longitude. Rasht, Iran is near the Caspian Sea, to the north, at 49E36, and Arak, Iran is southwest of Tehran, at 49E41. The city of Karaj, Iran is where Iran has a nuclear research center, which is at 51E00, with a reservoir to the west, around 50E25. It would be possible that Israeli prisoners would be located close to this nuclear site, as hostages, in case of attack.

dominators, will be **expelled** from their homes and placed in prisoner camps. From there they will be sent to the islands of the Mediterranean Sea, where they will be left to fend for themselves.

(The Invasions of Rome and Marseilles)

And while the Eastern European allies will be controlling the Balkans and eastern Italy, the primary Muslim forces will be expelling all resistance in the other coastal regions of the Mediterranean Sea. Once they will defeat all military resistance, their primary purpose will be **to** locate **the** men and women of the **Clergy** of the Christian churches, in Italy, France and Spain. When those people will be rounded up there **will be made** great punishment, to **every** one of those people of faith, causing the churches to exemplify the **desolation** of the surrounding area. All will be barren, with sadness felt by all; and, no one will be willing to go near a church for fear of persecution.

Those Arab and mercenary forces will be **usurping** the power of the nations, seizing control without legal support. They will do this by **the** means of **Martial** actions. It will have been **this** same militaristic approach **that** will have previously been used by the West, to forcibly strip the Palestinians of their land. All of this **will be** the planned form of retribution, which will be **returned** to the Christians of Europe; but, as the Catholic Church of Rome will have called for the Crusades against the Muslim people and their lands, this target will get special Muslim attention. The antichrist leader will personally lead the attacks on Rome and the Vatican. He will lead an assault that will take **from the city of** Rome its dignity, causing **the Sun** of Christianity to be darkened. Without protectors any longer at Rome's beckon call, like were the Knights **of Malta**, all Romans will suffer terribly because of their proximity to Vatican City.

Italy and Rome will not be the only places where the Muslims will attack. They will capture all **of the islands** of the Mediterranean Sea, and cause panic in the seafaring boats that will be at sea when the attacks begin. The waters of the islands of Italy will be taken, first from Sicily to Sardinia, followed by Corsica and the **Stechades** islands, near the port city of Marseilles, France.

Here **will be opened** Marseilles to the Arab invaders, where they will attack the French, as one of **the** allies of the **great** nation of America. This will be aided by Muslims living in France, who migrated there prior to the advent of the attacks.

As those attacks begin, the Muslim ships will send rockets far and deep into the West, which will reach America and Britain. Surrounding Marseilles has been said to be a **chain**, which will have protected the city from naval assault for centuries. This has been the lore **of the port** of Marseilles, **which takes its** pride from the **designation** that the chain around its port had never been broken. However, this reputation will be forever lost **to the ox marine** (sea ox), or the Leviathan, the monster of the sea. This underwater creature will have been tamed by the Muslims; and, it will be utilized in all of their coastal invasions.[131]

(The Defeat of the Multinational Forces Stationed in Italy)

Oh it makes me sob at all that will be lost in this future. It is so sad **what calamitous** events will be Christianity's **affliction**, which **will be** brought on **by** the hands of the Muslims. It will come **at the time** least expected; and, the disarray **of** the American and French troops stationed in Italy will send them, along with the Italian military, fleeing from the onslaughts. From a three-pronged invasion plan, the Italian peninsula will be cut off. With the military in flight, there will be many of **the women** who will be in **enclosures** designed for safety, having not been able to escape. Many of those women will have special conditions, as some will be pregnant, or too old and feeble to be able to flee.

The women and the elderly **will be** nervously awaiting the outcomes of the battles across the north of Italy, where the invaders will have been encountered **by** the multinational militaries stationed there. All of those forces will have gone into retreat **during** the invasions, as the Americans, French and Italian forces will have been taken by complete surprise. The results **of the main** points of entry, enacted simultaneously on both the east and west coasts of Italy, will have caused those forces to scatter and run. The **head** of the Italian invasion campaign will be the chief leader of the **Eastern** European alliance. He will place **the majority** of his focus on northern Italy, directing troop movement from the three points of invasion, to pinch across Italy, separating north from south. Those Eastern forces will be **excited by** the successes they will have, forcing the Western allies to attempt to flee to **the northern** regions of Italy, towards the French Alps. This will have been planned; and, with France also surprised and defeated at Marseilles,

---

131 The word "Leviathan" is Hebrew and today translates as "whale." However, it appears five times in the Bible, in reference to a sea monster. This Leviathan is also referred to as the "sea ox," and a submarine perfectly fits this ancient description.

the Italian allied forces will become trapped near Turin, Italy, unable to proceed further. In this retreat, from Venice to Turin, the Western allied troops will be annihilated in savage battles. When those armies will be totally ruined, they will have reached the **western** end of Italy, with no clear pass into France. They will become **vanquished**, as the Muslims will have overcome them.

Those of the militaries who will be defeated, but who will have not died in battle, will be **put to death** upon surrender. All of the forces in Italy to defend Europe will have become totally **ruined** units. All of Italy will have been overcome, with the southern half of France occupied, and all of Spain surrendered.

While those elite attack units of the invasion forces will be chasing the militaries of France, Italy and America, more forces will continue to flow into the invaded nations, to secure **the rest** of the coastlines of the Mediterranean. The citizens of those coastal cities will be left unprotected; and, those citizens who will try to resist the invaders by use of arms will be killed as soldiers. The rest of the civilians will soon be **in flight**, trying to escape. With the news of Europe's losses reaching around the world, the effect of **its** defeat will be to cause fear to set in, especially in America and Britain. Those nations will hear messages of distress from **children** who will be seeking help from the outside world. Those youths will have become responsible for protecting groups **of** people, with each watching over **several women**, younger siblings and orphans. Without any help arriving to save them, those groups will be caught, and they will become the first of the **imprisoned** peoples who will be taken by the Muslims and their allies.

(Securing the Mediterranean)

And, those imprisoned peoples **will be** sent to the various islands of the Mediterranean Sea, which will have been secured by secondary invasions. Sicily will have been **made** secure first, with the high number of immigrants having already been there and prepared to attack on command. The prisoners will be forced to live in the poor slums those immigrants will have vacated. More and more prisoners will be sent to the islands with each **new incursion** of troops to the mainland. This continuous flow of invasion convoys will enter **by the** Mediterranean **coastal** areas, where the **beaches** are wide, flat and open. There will be several good beachheads in Italy, France and Spain; and, those incursions will bring an endless flow of men and supplies from the north of Africa. With the waters of the Mediterranean Sea completely controlled by Muslim warships, they will be blocking any European vessel **wishing** to escape through the Strait of Gibraltar. The Muslims will have made **the leap** from North Africa to Spain, and secured the area of land north of the Pillar of Hercules. The British will have become fortified in **Castulum**, at the center of the rock.[132] The Muslims will attack Castulum **to free** the rock from British control. The British will have held the rock in their possession, **from the** Spanish; but, it will have been Arabs who will have **first** claimed it, many years before. When the Strait of Gibraltar will be taken and under Muslim control, the **resumption** of the plan to invade Europe will find **Mohametans** swarming into Spain, from Morocco.

---

132   The word written by Nostradamus is "Castulum," such that the "-um" ending makes it appear to be a Latin word. However, it is not a clean word in Latin, although one word in Latin, "castellum," is close, meaning "fortress, castle." However, if the word is seen as French, broken down into "*C'astu lum*," it would be a combined form of "*ce astute lumer*," meaning "this crafty light." Supposedly, the airport on Gibraltar has a road that crosses the runway, and when the light turns red it means an airplane is taking off. Still, if Latin, it would be more likely to be a combined form of "castus lumen," meaning "clean light." Gibraltar is the site of the Europa Point Lighthouse.

333

EXPLAINING THE QUATRAINS –
THE PERSECUTION OF EUROPE

(The Aftermath of the European Invasions)

Being that the Iberian Peninsula takes Western Europe to the closest point of the lands of the Mohametans, in North Africa, Spain will have once had a large Muslim population. The Moors ruled Spain for 800 years; but, while they will have been defeated long ago, many Islamic Spaniards will have remained in Spain. The Spanish Inquisition will have driven the rest of the Muslims out, forcing all other Spaniards to convert to Catholicism. While Spain and Catholicism will have thrived together for centuries, the period of time when Spain will have been ruled by its tyrant, the one who will have been assisted by the German and Italian tyrants, this will represent the time when Spain will become largely isolated from Europe. This tyrant will live a long time in power, until his natural death. He will survive that long because he will refuse to declare war on another nation during the second world war. As a result, for many years Spain will have been isolated as the poorest Western European nation, due to his leadership. Spain will not be able to militarily keep up with the rest of Europe as well. The British will have maintained control of Gibraltar, despite this tyrant considering that fortress to be a part of Spain. This will mean that Spain will be **weakened** peoples, unable to force the British out and unable to defend against external attack. The Spanish will have long ceased being an empirical power, as it will have lost all means of protecting itself, should another nation become angered as Spain. They will have been concerned only with that land of **theirs**. As strong as Spain's naval **forces** are today, by the time of this future their **maritime** maneuvers showing superiority will have been long lost; and, Spain will depend on other nations to rescue it, should it be invaded. That invasion will come by the Islamic people, who will bring great forces to Spain, in many small maritime crafts. The Muslims will be assisted internally in Spain **by the western** Basques peoples, who will have long wished to reclaim the lands they lost in Spain. The Basques will help the Muslims to gain their own autonomy again. With western Spain ceded by the Muslims to the Basque, for their assistance, this will make

334

the primary focus of the Islamic waves of soldiers concentrate on the central and eastern portions of the Iberian Peninsula.

The western land of Portugal will not be sought to invade, as to do this will invite a naval invasion from the Atlantic Ocean. The Arabs and Basque will take positions in the mountains of western Spain; and, they will threaten the Portuguese with attack by the most powerful weapon, if they do not declare neutrality. With that agreement made, the Portuguese will be unable to allow the French, British or Americans to land in Portugal. The Muslims will then drive the Spanish into submission; and, with Spain's surrender the Arabs will make claims **to this** land, as the reclaimed Caliphate of Cordoba. The loss of that land will have been deemed due to the **reign** of the Catholic Church, when the kings of Europe thrived; but, with this new reign recognized, Spain **will be made** the first nation to capitulate, becoming the first European nation under the reign of the new Islamic Empire. From this capture of Spain, the Muslims will establish positions for their powerful weapons. Those positions will launch rockets towards the **great** nation of America and Britain, as well as at any ships which would approach from the Atlantic Ocean. The border with Portugal will be converted into a place of extreme **desolation**, to keep the Spanish from escaping and the Portuguese from coming in. This kind of desolation will not only be found in the Iberian Peninsula, as the whole of the Mediterranean coast will be similarly desolated. With the powerful weapons striking the Americans and British from afar, those nations too will know this desolation.

The use of this manmade power will not take place in Europe, as it will be too dangerous for the invaders to operate around its aftermath. Instead, **the** weapon will be directed to **most** of the **great** centers of population in the West, outside of Europe. This will be primarily America's major coastal **cities**, but also London and cities in Great Britain. The Muslims will use their more conventional weapons along the Mediterranean coast; and, once the militaries of those nations will have been defeated, other weapons will be used in the slaughter of those who will continue to resist their presence. With all of those European cities **being** totally unprepared for such great assaults, the cities will quickly be filled with dead. Those who will not be instantly killed will run for safety, outside the cities, leaving all of those cities **depopulated** places, void of human life and military defense.

Of the coastal places of Europe, **these** cities will be attacked by naval bombardment, before the Islamic forces will take land. The cities will then be empty and undefended, **which** will make it easy for the attackers to reach land; and, once they will have left the beaches they will find little resistance **entering inside** the cities to secure them. Anyone **being** resistant to those invasions will be treated as military, which will make them become **included in the** acts of war and battle. Those combatants will be killed, such that they will not be granted the protections the Muslims will grant civilians who surrender. All resistors will be treated with the **vengeance** of the Muslims and their allies. All who will be found bearing arms in Italy will be found worthy **of the ire** of Islam; and, they will be seen as armed protectors **of** Christians and their **God.**

With Spain, Italy and France **being** the nations with the most Catholic peoples, those nations will face **more** of this vengeance than the other Western European nations. The Muslims will install this retribution factor with the most **serious** of planning, and those Western European nations will not have a serious will to do battle. All three will have had difficulties winning past **wars** that they will have fought in. The Muslims and their Eastern European allies will have planned their **battles** wisely; and, quickly all of Italy and Spain will surrender, with the French army barely holding the northern third of France.

Due to the initial waves of battle **being** so swiftly maneuvered and carefully planned, many of the small coastal **towns** will be caught completely off guard and unable to defend themselves. Those towns will not be the primary targets; but, some beachheads will make going through several towns necessary, on the way to the known locations of Western European military units. The towns will become cut off from the greater elements of their nation's military units. Many people who will hear the news of an invasion will immediately run to find greater protection in the **cities**, only to find that such a great mass of people will make it impossible for quick withdrawal. The secondary targets of the Muslims will be the major coastal cities, where large populations could pose rebel threats. This will cause the Muslims to use naval bombardment on those locations. The people in the cities will become easy targets for the great weapons the Muslims and Eastern Europeans will have to use; and, while those weapons will not be the most powerful weapon, they will be other weapons which will still consume whole cities, especially by way of fire. The use of **castles** in this future will not be like it is today; but, the remains of fortifications like those will become strategic locations for the military weapons of the Islamic waves. Once they will have encircled the towns and destroyed the cities, those castles will become their headquarters for launching ground attacks and other assaults.

The invasions of Europe will spur **all** of the **others** united with the Muslims around the world to begin their strategic assaults on key **buildings** in the nations outside Europe. They will represent a hidden enemy, which will try to poison the water supplies and cause the fields and woods to become **burnt** menaces. With the use of the powerful weapons against the major cities of America and Britain, those cities will have been made **desolate** of peoples, with many people dead and many others left without a place to live. The use of those great weapons against the peoples who will have first invented them will cause the will and strength of America to become vanished. The Muslims will have **destroyed** dreams of superiority the Americans once held. Because of this devastation, and **with** the people suffering greatly and in panic, the leaders of the **great** nation of America will go into hiding underground. This will cause a tremendous **effusion** of emotion about their form of government, which will have deserted them in the people's greatest hour of need. After their leaders will have caused this great loss **of** American **blood**, without listening to the pleas of the people to return to their Christian values and remove their troops from Mesopotamia, the defaulting government will give rise to anarchy. People left with nothing will try to take from those who still have something, causing a great spread of bloodshed among the American citizens. Their nation will have been **vestal**, having never been penetrated by a foreign nation upon its soil; and, it will have never surrendered its government in a time of crisis. Their government will have become **married** leaders, wed to the ways of Satan, lusting for power and wealth. They will have separated America's government from all influence of religion. They will have symbolized this marriage by their promotion and acceptance of a degenerated state of marriage among the people. They will have allowed marriages to be based purely based on sexual desires, without the need of any clergy to perform the ceremonies.

For women who will have had been married, only to have lost their husbands to one of the many causes of death then surrounding the world, those **widows** will become **violated** ones. Without the protection of an ingrained moral law to lead the invaders, those unprotected women of the affected lands will lose all rights which they will have once possessed. They will be captured and forced to work for their captors; and, they will have no power to resist advances, with no recourse if raped, beaten, robbed or wounded. Many of the women will have young **children** they will then be unable to care for. This will be largely due to a lack **of milk** and the shortages of good food made available. Those children will be used **against** their mothers, as the pawns of captivity, to get the mothers to serve the soldiers. Those who resist this authority will be lined against **the walls of** the fortresses the invaders will overtake and be killed mercilessly. The invaders will take complete control of **the towns**, within the areas they will dominate. Many of the women and children will make themselves **allied with them**, so they will receive less harm from their oppressors. Those who will resist the oppression will become **broken** peoples, completely despondent and devoid of the spirit of life. All captives will learn that their lives will be of no concern to their captors.

The number of broken peoples will be **so many** that no one will be able to remember the good things **of** life. The **evil** that **oneself** will be caught up in will be overwhelming; and, with this evil all about, the people will be found **committing** more acts of disgrace on their own, **by** believing that **the** consequences of their actions will no longer apply to them. The pains which will be inflicted on others, the harms that will be caused to the innocent, and the troubles the people will find themselves caught up in, all will be by the **means of Satan**. The souls of those people will all find their place in Hell with that **prince** of darkness, in the **infernal** flames. The ones who will choose **that** fiery end will be **nearly** all that will exist in **the world** at that time. The whole of the **universe**, from its stars, moons and planets to the earth's rivers, plants and mountains, will have all been previously connected to **oneself**, all in an intricate system of purpose. All of this cohesion will be lost, just as the molecules of a corpse are no longer connected as one living creature. One **will find** that the death of the soul will bring death to the body, leaving only a matter of time before one's soul will be forever lost. The atrocities of mankind will cause all hope for survival and redemption **failed**. Slowly, as one by one those left in this torment die, the ones still living will find life on earth completely **desolate**. Without God to talk to, they will find themselves all alone, waiting for death.

In that desolation, when the final days will be **before those** still clinging to life, they will know of the end's approach. The weak and tired will hear the sound of death **coming to** them; and, they will be too feeble to resist death any longer.

This sound will be recognizable to **anyone**, but especially to those in this near-death state. They will hear that the end is near by the sounds of the **birds** which will be gathering overhead. There will be **strange** sounds of **crying**, coming from the shrieking birds that will be circling the corpses. Those birds will have been sent **by** the Angel of Death, who will be talking to them in **the air**.

(Aftermath Part 2)

This spread of evil and death will actually come from the airborne particles in a huge cloud that will encircle the Northern Hemisphere. The rain which will fall from this cloud will cause **such** destruction that no country north of the equator will be unaffected; and, this will be including those nations that will not have become involved in this holy war. This effect will be solely due to the use of **that one** weapon so feared, which will **not** have been desired to befall **oneself**. The cloud will stretch for 300 miles; and, the people **will know** when it has recycled back again, by the red rain it will produce. Many poor nations which will **not** have ever seen the effects of this weapon will become **fully acquainted with** the dangers this rain will produce. It will fall like acid from the sky and it will destroy all of **the belongings** which will not be covered. Most importantly, the rain, which will have once been the necessary element for growing crops, will then become the greatest danger to the farmers; and, the yields planned to come from the plants **of the fields** will not materialize. With crops failing from bad water, and the rain also having a deteriorating effect on the **houses**, the people will begin migrating to areas less affected. Those migrants will become unwanted in those areas where the land will barely be able to support the people already there.

It will be from the fear of starvation which **will be born** that people will become overly protective of what they possess. After the onset of attacks will have subsided the people of America and Britain will know where danger zones lie. They will be able to tell by the wild vegetation surrounding former places of inhabitation. In areas where **the weed** will have grown wild, it will show where people have fled. This will especially be found evident **by the** visitors to previously inhabited areas, as along the **streets of the cities**, where the grass and weeds typically will not have taken root due to the number of people on the sidewalks and streets. In many of those places there will be much **more** wild growth than usual, with the weeds growing quite **high**. They will become higher **than the knees**.

(Securing Europe for the Muslim Punishment)

And, while this tall growth will be a sign people will have suddenly fled in America and Britain, it will also be evident in occupied Europe. However, in those areas the tall weeds will indicate where some of the people will have been killed, protecting **their** property. Many people will have been forcibly **removed** from their houses, where they **will be** executed and left in the yards. The occupiers will be more concerned with demonstrating **their power** over those who will have surrendered or will have been captured, than to take time and gather all the dead bodies. They will plan for those minute clean-up details to take place **at that time** when all of the land **will be** secured for their presence. When those invaded lands will have been **made** safe for the invaders, then the citizens who will have been taken prisoner will be forced to work as slaves, performing such menial tasks as disposing of the dead. This form of persecution will find those who will not work as slaves and refuse to do the things thought to be below their social status; but, this will only bring **more persecution**, of the worst possible kind. The Muslims will have the greatest form of persecution designed to be applied **to the** people of Christianity, who will be forced to convert to Islam. They will take over all the **Churches** of Christianity, locating all the clergy trying to console the people, forcing **that** group to convert first. Many of those pastors of the soul will have entered priesthood for the wrong reasons, having **not had ever** truly known Christ in their hearts. Those people will have sold Christianity for profit; and, when they will be forced to face conversion or punishment, they will gladly make the conversions.

Then, once the Muslims and their allies will be firmly **in** control of the majority of Europe, **the same** treatment will be given to Europeans as was administered by the European monarchies to the European Muslim, especially in Spain during the Catholic Church's Inquisition. This retribution will last a full **year**, with a tremendous number of Christians killed. The Muslims will offer Europeans the opportunity to renounce Christianity and convert to Islam, such that **the** ones who will change and begin **following** the laws of Mohammed will be the **ones** who will survive. The rest will be killed, tortured or exiled to prison islands. However, as this process will not have been completed quickly, the proper care **of** the dead will not be possible; so, soon there **will ensue** a rapid spread of disease. Those who will not be kept immune from this spread, being those converts and those in captivity, will cause **the** Europeans to suffer **more** dead. This death will be **horrible**, with huge numbers falling. It will be as bad as it was before in Europe, when the Black Plague swept the continent. There will soon arise a noticeable stench of **plague** about, which will be rampant and everywhere.

With so many dead **at** the hands of the Muslims, being **those** refusing to convert to Islam, the converts will not be prepared to take care of so many bodies, including those killed in the invasions. Bodies will be burned as rapidly as possible; but, **in the mean time** it will become impossible to collect all the dead bodies before they will begin to decay, causing this spread of disease. This lack of response will cause dire consequences, as there **will be born** a very virulent **pestilence**. This destructive spread of disease will be **so** bad that the winds will carry it around the globe; but, it will not have come solely from Europe. This pestilence will have been aided in its growth by the release of the weapons of power, on the **great** nations of America and Britain. The diseases born from the corpses, along with the emanating power of the weapons collected in a cloud, will make all become airborne agents which will cause rain to fall like poisons from the sky. It will be this death cloud **that** will have been generated from **the three** nations which will have had the powerful weapon used on them. From those targets the cloud will be born and it will spread continually to all **parts of** the Northern Hemisphere, greatly impacting all of **the world** and its peoples. The nations of America and Britain will have **more** of those weapons to use in retaliation; but, so will the Islamic allies. Due to the nations of America and Britain having seen the impact **that** those weapons will have irreversibly created, they will not respond by further use of those weapons; and, they will especially refuse to use one of the most powerful weapons against a nation of Europe or Israel. Further, due to any response of retaliation having the potential of causing more of those weapons being used against them, **the two** great nations of the West will not fight back at all. What will have once been two nations closely united, the father will no longer welcome his son. Britain and America will sever their alliance, ending their close relationship. The governments of both those nations will be found **defaulting**, forfeiting their positions as the world's most powerful leaders. With those ends coming, it will allow the Muslims to seal their victory over Europe.

(Plague & Famine)

With the defaults of America and Britain, **the** Muslims will be free to place **more** tortures on their captives. The Muslims will view the disarray that will have been created in such two great powers as **marvelous**, since this result will have been deemed highly improbable before they will have begun their assaults. However, the Muslims will have made plans to defeat the Americans and British indirectly, rather than from direct invasions. Those plans will be implemented **by the** Islamic agents stationed in those lands, when those agents will secretly begin to damage the grain crops of both nations. Before this grain will be found contaminated, it will be fed to livestock, most prominently cattle. This will have the effect of causing the destruction of both meat and grain. This poisoning of the food supply chain will have the effect of turning the world, struggling to find enough good food, to the level of extreme **famine**. The only good food will have been stored; and, this stored food will become so costly that only the rich will be able to afford food. The food chain will collapse, and it will not have time to ever recover. When the weapons of great power will have been used against America and Britain, that effect will have joined with the **previous** damage, making many Americans and Britons face shortages of good food, like they will have never faced before.

(Those Not Dead from Plague & Famine)

The shortages of food will become so harsh in America that **continuing** to exist will be difficult for most of America's poor. The price for good food will rise so high that only the wealthy will be able to afford to eat. The masses will be forced to subsist the remainder of their lives **by** following **the footsteps** of those who will still be able to afford food. They will hunt for scraps fallen from the tables of the wealthy, causing the poor to rummage through the garbage. In many cases, people who will be starving will turn to eating the remains of the dead, both animals and humans, in desperation attempts to survive. Those conditions will be found **in** all the places of the world, but especially in **any** regions where **countries** will have depended on other nations to help them meet their normal food shortages. One nation which will be a neighbor **of** America, to the south, will be extremely distressed; and, more and more starving people in that region will illegally enter America, in search of good food and medicines. Those nations south of America will have been **the** lands discovered by the **Spanish**, and they will speak that language as they beg for food from the Americans.

The deaths by famine will have just begun at that time, and they will not be limited to only those two great nations. The world will have already had **so** many places where food will have long been a problem, such that famine will have long been known in many regions. Most of those lands will have become dependent on the **great** capacities of the nation of America. America will have been known as the world's bread basket. It will be known for having a cornucopia of plenty, which it could share with the world's needy. However, with America now facing its own **tribulations**, from **that** trouble and grief created by the failure of its food chain, it will no longer be willing to share with its own poor. Add to that the cloud of disease and poison which will be destroying more and more arable land, the whole world will soon be thrown into the depths of famine, including America. This famine will be on a level that **never should be** in the first place, as this domino effect could have been avoided. Never in all of the annals of history has mankind caused such purposeful damage to the most basic life support for the people. Everything will have **come to pass** in the world, because **such** lusts for power will make people lose all touch with foresight, simply to create acts of vengeance. Those inabilities to control the emotion of hatred will mean there will be no recovery possible from this famine. Mankind will have caused it all, showing that mankind has never changed its inherent animal instinct, shown **since the first** act of vengeance causing Cain to slay Able. Only with a solid and true **foundation of** religion can one be instilled with the proper moral forethought and responsibility to have foreseen the results of its own actions. This foundation comes from **the Church** which evolved from the presence of Jesus Christ, as a human being teaching peace over war. If the Christian institutions of the world can act to preserve this lesson for all Christians to be led by, this famine will be avoidable. The Church of the most **Christian woman**, the Virgin Mary, who sacrificed her beloved son to cleanse mankind of its sins, will have been founded to save mankind from this end. However, this Church's commission of its own sins will have left the world without moral leadership, dooming all to this fate.

This failure of the Catholic Church of Rome to protect its flock, **by** refusing to live up to its own rules, will affect **all** of **the** people in all **regions** where Christianity will have spread. However, to the ones who will have remained truest to their faith, where Catholicism will have remained the strongest, the Muslims will be most severe to the people of Italy. The **Latin** peoples will pay the highest price for the sins of their Church.

All of the European clergy **will be** forced to become **converted** to Islam, or

343

suffer punishment. A conversion ceremony will occur in **the place** Christians will have deemed **sacred**, as the Muslim clerics will enter **in** cathedrals for these conversions. They will see other churches as an **accommodation** for their needs, as a place of meeting and lodging, but they will not perform any Islamic prayers in Christian churches. Afterwards the church buildings will be modified and consecrated as Islamic mosques. The Christians **of** Europe, who will have been members of a **flock** of those changed churches, will see this as sacrilege; but, the number of worshipers who will still be left alive and free will be so **minor** that they will have much greater concerns. Many who will have been captured alive by the Muslims will be facing exile to Mediterranean islands. The majority of people will blame the **great** nation of America for having caused this grief; but, most of the people will have **adapted** to the Muslim demands of conversion, rather than stand for a religion they will not have believed **in**. They will not have cared for learning the **substances** of any religion, as they will have been **secular Christians**. Most will not have been overly concerned about learning their own religion.

With so many of the people **being** secular Christians, they will have great difficulty being converted to the strictest form of Islam by the Muslims. While they will struggle with those adjustments, several of the Eastern European allies will have their own special targets. Before those nations will have been converted to the sect of philosophy of the Russians, three generations before, they will have had royalty lineage which will have been disposed. Several of those royal families will have sought asylum in Western Europe, such that **all** of the descendants of **these Kings** will be sought out. The **eastern** mercenaries will make a point of **hunting** those heirs down. The purpose will be that they will want any and all semblance of royal blood **stricken down** forever, with no possibility of them ever resurfacing again, to claim royal rights. Once captured, those descendants of royalty will become **exterminated** peoples, such that no traces of royal blood will survive to regain power or claim their lost land and wealth. They will be seen as **not** worthy **of** their heritage, having fled **the whole** of their subjects, leaving them in poverty, while they will have continued to live lives of luxury. Those royal offspring will have been located **by** the **means of** communication which will be popular in this future, gaining locations and information that will lead them to their doors. When **the forces** of those mercenary warriors will take possession **of** one of **the** descendants of those **Kings**, they will be instantly tried and killed, in the name **of Aquilon**, or Mother Russia.

EXPLAINING THE QUATRAINS – THE COUNTER-OFFENSIVE ATTACKS

(The Unity for a Counter-Offensive)

The chases after the descendants of Eastern European royalty **will last** until all royal blood will be exterminated. At that time the rest of the world will have begun to suffer greatly, due to the use of the powerful weapons deployed by the Muslims. By that time the Russians, who will have been largely unaffected and completely noncommittal in this war between religions, will approach the British about joining with them to liberate Western Europe. The nation of America will have also tried to mend its differences with Britain, once a new leader will have become elected by the people. Together, those three nations will bring about **the renewal of** the Roman Empire's concept of shared leadership responsibilities. This renewal will be another **Triumvirat**, or Commission of Three, where each of the nations will share equal roles in a counter offensive to free Europe of Muslim domination. The three nations will each sign a pact that will last for **seven years**. The goal of **that** timeframe will be to force the Muslims out of Europe and back into their own lands. Once accomplished, they will plan to have the Muslims tried in international courts and punished for their actions, putting the world in such a bad condition. The Russians will see involvement in such a plan of this nature as giving them **the** same **fame** the Americans will have had previously enjoyed, following their entrance into the second world war, turning the tide against the German tyrant. In this war, which will have been a holy war between Islam and Christianity, the Russians will have stayed clear **of such** dispute. They will explain their non-intervention as because their **sect** of philosophy saw the influenced of religion as corrupting. The Russians **will make** a commitment to send **its** troops into battle, if it will be **agreed by the** nations of Britain and America that religions must be banned from all future civilizations on earth. With all nations under one similar sect of philosophy this Triumvirat will be able to rule the **universe**, with the three ruling one united world.

With the universe to be shared by three powers and with two of the three **being** greatly weakened by the Muslim attacks, **at the time** of the Russian offer the people of America and Britain will see **the Lords**, who rule over both the religions of Christianity and Islam, as having caused the war. Since America and Britain will have been the **two** nations which will have caused such hatred **in** the Muslims, they will have caused the Arabs scheme to put the world in such jeopardy. Those two Christian nations will then be willing to turn on their religion, to side with the Russians for a chance to get revenge. Since neither America nor Britain will have responded to the Muslim attacks by using their own most powerful weapons, their **number** of those weapons will be as many as those **of** the **Aquilon**, or Russia. The Russians will point out that the Muslims will have been **victorious over the** nations of Europe because of their alliance with the **easterner** nations of Europe; but, those Eastern European nations **will be** more involved in a holy war between Islam and Christianity for separate reasons, with none of those nations caring about either of those religions. They will have aligned themselves with Islam to gain revenge against the West. With news of the Russians being **in** alliance with America and Britain, beginning **here** all who side with the Muslims will be seen as the enemy of **them**. This notice will cause the Eastern European nations to rapidly cease their alliance with the Muslims. Much of the most powerful weapons the Muslims will have **made** use of, the ones causing **so** much damage to the **great** nations of America and Britain, will then be taken away from the Islamic arsenal when the easterners cease their alliance. The three nations will then agree to unify; and, a great **noise** will be made, making the Muslims will become aware. The sound of this news will create a loud **commotion** in the occupied nations of Europe, of a tumultuous nature. The Islamic allies will begin to make **warlike** threats towards one another. Talk such as **that** will again not consider the global effects the war in Europe will have already caused around the world. A renewed use of the powerful weapons will have **all the same** effects again, making the world an even more horrid place. However, the warrior **men** from the **east** of Europe **will** begin to **tremble from the** thought of facing the nation which will have dominated them for so long. Russia will still have the effect of being the **frightener** to those men, such that the thought **of** Russia rising against them will cause them to turn away from the Muslims. From this point **here**, the Eastern Europeans will side with the Russians, as they will see **them** as of the same blood and heritage, like **brothers**. However, the unity of the Russians with the Americans and British will **not** be understood by the Eastern Europeans. Those two western nations will have been related by different blood, as separate **brothers**. Still, as all of those nations will be of the North, they will all rejoin, causing the return of the **Aquilonaires**.

347

When it will be agreed **by** the three great nations, to become unified against the Muslims, **at the time** the relationship between the brothers of America and Britain will be at its lowest ebb. While the Americans will have elected a new leader to arouse the people of America to war, Britain will have neglected this **third** brother, focusing on unifying the two other brother nations as one lone power, under a new young **King** of England. This unity will have been seen by the Russians as a potential threat to their domination of the union of the **Aquilonaire**. However, as all three powers will be **understanding** of the severity of the world's situation, with **the complaint** of ecological and economic hardships **of the people** in all areas of the world, they will plan an attack together. To unify all three under one leader, the Russians will choose the young King of England to head this unity. By naming him as the King **of** Europe it will be **his** decisions, as the one holding the **main title**, which will be judged, should the plan fail. With that decided, the three nations **will draw up** an agreement **so** that the forces of the **great** nation of America will have no voice in the command of the **army**, or land forces, which will be raised to free Europe.

The Russians will have no need to supply land troops, as the Eastern Europeans will have returned to their unity with the Russians. This will mean the Russian involvement will be to supply naval forces in the western assault. With this agreement, the Russian navy **will pass** all of France, going **by** way of the Atlantic Ocean; and, they will prepare to make an assault at **the straits** of Spain, at Gibraltar. The British will lead a build-up of its allied armies in the area of Europe that will not have fallen under Muslim control. This region will be the areas **of** northern France and Belgium, where **its** (England's) **last ancestors**, or kings, had ruled. One of the **great grandfathers** of the English royal line will have ruled both England and the Netherlands,[133] under the name of William. The new young King of England will assume his rule under **that** ancestral name; and, as William of England, he will again assume rule over the Dutch. Once coroneted as King, this William will abolish the Parliamentary method of rule and **he will renew** the total power and authority of a King. As this method of rule will have caused Britain to nearly come to ruin, **the majority** of the British people will support the new young King and England **in its** new monarchal

---

133 William of Orange married Mary the Queen of England and together they were known as William & Mary, with William having the English title of King William III of England. The eldest child of Charles and Diana is William.

state.

William will become a true leader of those lands, and **the** people of the **great** nation of America will also admire his leadership abilities. He will act as the true **Curate**, or protector of the Christian values Europe will have once had. His armies will force the Muslims and their remaining allies out of Europe, flying the flag **of** the cross, which was the flag of **the hooded** knights of the Crusades, in times past. He will drive his troops through France to Italy, freeing that land in hopes a pope **will be restored** in Rome. Once his army will be **in** control of Europe, to **his** great dismay the **former state** of the Vatican will have been destroyed; and, Italy will have been left in total ruin. There will only be a few people left alive there; **but**, their environment will have become so **desolate** that those who will still be alive will be near death and in great need of food. They will need food more than they will need of religion. Just as Hannibal will have salted the earth of Italy after his conquest, the Muslims will have slashed and burned too. After destroying everything of use, they **then** will have departed **from** Italy, across the Mediterranean Sea to North Africa. In their wake they will have left **the whole** of Italy wasted, with most of the survivors found **abandoned** and without any care, on the islands of the surrounding waters.

With Europe freed and the Muslims in flight to their homelands, the Triumvirat soldiers **will turn** their focus towards following the Arabs across North Africa, into the land that will have been Israel. Those liberating forces will be filled with rage after they will witness the atrocities that will have been committed to the European Christians and Jews. They will all vow **to be** the avengers of this cruelty, by responding with savage treatment to all Muslims they will encounter. This brutality will be regardless if the Muslims they encounter will be armed or not. After they will have slaughtered the North African Muslims, they will enter into Jerusalem. At the ruins of the Temple of Solomon, where the Muslims will have built a mosque around the room which once housed the **Holy of Holies**, this mosque will be completely **destroyed**, as along with the clerics still inside. The Ark of the Covenant will not have been in the possession of the Muslims, as this will have been moved long before **by** the rabbis who will have sought to protect it from the Babylonians. After the ancient Jewish temple will have become the home of **Paganism**, a new Holy of Holies will have been built to surround the Ark of the Covenant in Abyssinia.

In every Arab city and town which will be taken by the Crusaders, the Arab people will be tortured and killed. Just as hatred **burns** in the hearts of those invaders, they will administer unmerciful punishment to anyone in their path. The Islamic people who will have supported a war of retribution **in** Europe will tremble when the war comes to their land. The King of Europe will be **after** information leading his troops to where **the antichrist** will be in hiding. The people will tell all they know, under the pain of torture; but, in the end they **will be** killed. They will find the antichrist hiding in a mountain cave, not far from where Noah's ark will have settled, on Mount Ararat in eastern Turkey. After the last great battles of this holy war, the antichrist will be pulled out of the cave by his beard and taken prisoner. With the antichrist captive, the Americans will demand he be tried and executed in America; and, the King of Europe will grant them consent. Once the antichrist has been eliminated, Satan, the **prince infernal**, will take over the role of controlling men's hearts. With so much thirst for blood having **again** been quenched **by the** King of Europe's unified soldiers, few people will have not committed acts of evil which could have kept their souls from Satan. When the **last** stages of this terrible future war will come to an end, the **times** of mankind's rule over earth will be reaching its final stage. The earth will again begin **trembling**, from the weight of mankind's sins upon its crust; and, this trembling will cause the people still alive but starving and sick to tremble once more. In **the Kingdoms of Christendom**, which the King of Europe will have planned to create, the people will be too fearful to pray to God or Christ.

The trembling will **also** be felt by those **of** Eastern Europe, who will have been **the infidels** who will have made it possible for the Muslims to do so much damage. They will not have been destroyed **by** the unified forces of Russia, Britain and America; but, Britain and America will have not forgotten their roles in the war. Their involvement, by the release of the powerful weapons to the Muslims, will have led to a reduction of **the space** that mankind will be able to live in. Due to the release **of** those weapon's deadly emissions, only **twenty** percent of the earth's surface will be able to support life. This will cause those left alive to be suffering greatly from famine, while seeking a safe place to live. In the **five years** that will have passed since the first attack will have been mounted against the American ships in the Persian Gulf, the world will have become unable to support life as it once had. This will make the Americans and Britons begin to make the case for the Eastern Europeans to be removed from their lands.

EXPLAINING THE QUATRAINS – MANKIND'S INABILITY TO ACCEPT PEACE AND LOVE

Because **that** destruction allowed by the Eastern Europeans **will be** the cause for the world's dilemma, this will be the reason America will begin to threaten war against them. So **close** to the worst war ever waged by mankind, the threats of another war will have already begun; but, those threats will not come to pass. As the nations will be arguing over land, from the meeting house in Geneva for the union of nations, a greater threat will be approaching earth. This threat will be coming **from the** Americans playing god, earlier in the **seventh millennium**. In that earlier time they will have tampered with a comet in the heavens. In **that** time, before the beginning of the use of powerful weapons on earth, America will have shown **more** interest in exploring **the sanctuary of** the Sun and the planets, than it will have wanted to explore the lessons of **Jesus Christ**. They will have used another weapon against the glows of two comets, just to see what will have happened; but, the results will **not** have been as expected. The comet will have fractured into pieces and changed course. One could say the comet was angered at the insolence of an unprovoked attack. One comet **will be** separated into several large fragments; and, their paths will be changed, sent on a path to find earth. The news of those new paths headed for earth will have been suppressed, as those who will have wanted the world to know of this danger will have been **oppressed** by America's leaders. The leaders of America will have been controlled **by the Infidels**, or the greatest non-believers of religion, as the heads of the international sects to destroy the Kings and the religions of the world. Those Infidels will have been the masters of the men and women **who will be** the angels of Satan, **coming** to influence mankind to sin, **from** the great abyss below. They will have first made the citizens of Russia overturn their Czar, bringing to life **the Aquilon**, whose cold north wind will have frozen the church from the people. From that beginning they will have evolved to a position of influence over **the** whole **world** and all of its forms of government. Those evil creatures will have instructed the leaders of America not to alert the world of those **approaching** comets, but word will leak out. The warning will be made public, **from some** of the people who will have run the program to study the stars, funded by the

great nation of America. They will tell of the nearness of those comet fragments and the **cataclysm** that will be created, should any one of them strike the earth. They will report **how much** time will be left, before the comets bring an end to all life on earth. There will be those who will support their claims, **by** presenting the understanding which I have recounted here, from **my** astronomical **calculations**. They will point to the clear words which tell of this cataclysm **in** some of the quatrains in **my prophecies**. In those words are told **the course** the fiery comet will take, when it streaks through earth's atmosphere; and, they will tell **of** the place it will hit. To make all that clear, the astronomical clues in this letter will confirm **the times** of danger. By that notification, mankind will have **gone** to the last second of its time on earth. While there will still be some who will suffer **more**, after the impact, the effect of this comet striking earth will last **far** into the future.

And when this comet will strike the earth, at last there **will be made** a lasting **Peace**, throughout all the lands. There will no longer be anyone left to show any anger and hatred to another. This power of peace will vibrate through all souls, in a **universal** sensing of calm. The animosity that will have been felt **between** the peoples of the earth will vanish, as all of **the** remaining **human** beings will have been separated from their souls.

This impact of a comet with the earth will be the final act which will cleanse the world of the inhumanity that will have spread **their plague** through all who will perish with them. The people who will have met their bodily end through the acts of persecution and war the tyrants and soul sellers will have committed, if they will have only retained faith in God and Christ, they will have not lost their souls. The real **victim** of this destruction will have been he who will have taken part in the evil, falling to the **seduction** of Satan. The agony of that decision will be eternal, but the innocent will have all been saved.

While the suffering of the faithful will be terrible, all suffering **will be** only for a brief moment, when compared to those who will receive eternal pain, from have caused the suffering. The sacrifice of body and blood will act **to free** the soul to Heaven, where it can watch the carnage that will be left behind. To those who will have remained true men and women of **the Church**, and comforted the needy and downtrodden, telling them **of** the better reward which will come, if they maintain the faith in **Jesus Christ**, those people will have been saved. All

353

of the faithful who will not have fallen prey to the seductions of Satan, foregoing the temptation of momentary reward in the physical realm, will be saved **from all** of the **tribulation** the earthly plane will bring. The wise people will know **how much** it will take to resist **that** hardship, especially in a land which will covet freedom and liberty so much. That concept of freedom will be thought to only be defended by military might, rather than by the grace of God. This will have been the seduction which will have been used on so many, to get them to support a military buildup in times of peace. This will have been the ploy used **by the Azostains,**[134] who will have been the lovers of war, people far from following the teachings of Jesus Christ. They will convince young minds who **would wish** not to harm others or be harmed without a just and forgivable cause, by telling them tales of war's glory. This will be **to mix** up their minds, shaking them from remembering the lessons taught in Sunday school. The tricked youth will be taught to learn to obey the laws of man; and, they will be convinced that it is within man's right to kill. They will get **inside** the minds of those young men, while they will still be impressionable; and, those Martial tricksters will train the youth like one would train a dog to kill, stripping them of all moral decency. When the youth will be no longer capable of listening to their inner voices, they will have been programmed to act solely on command. Those liars will say that **the honey** of freedom only comes from the sacrifice of defending against the imaginary enemies of freedom. In the sale **of** this fallacy, **the gall** will be the loss of freedom those young people will be talked into choosing; and, the parents will have not taught the young better, to recognize Satan when he slips out his silver tongue. Some parents will even encourage their children to listen.

Today, in our times, Henry, this future is not ours to worry about; but, know that **this day** which will become tomorrow's today will come to our descendants, to France and to the whole of mankind. The now of our **being** will slowly dissolve away, and **after some times**, when revolution will fill the minds of the masses, our way of life will become **faint**, having vanished and slipped away to

---

134 This word, "*Azostain,*" has to be broken down into its French elements, becoming: "*Az ost ain.*" In French, this means, "Ace army hook," and would be the highest ranking military plan to entice volunteers into the army. This is the process of military recruitment, where the hook is used to get young men to resist their natural moral fears of killing and being killed, to join the army and become a real man. This mentality prevails in the American society today. Another possibility would be "*Az o stain,*" or Ace of stain. Same purpose either way. Take your pick.

lost memory.

It will be **after that** when memory of the divine reason and purpose for **such times** as ours **will have** faded. Even though times as these have **lasted** in this condition **for a long time**, the rule of the people **will be** replaced by another rule. For all of the shortcomings our present ways of life present, where the people suffer at times, sometimes **almost** unbearably, this future change will not be for the betterment of mankind. All of the shortcomings will be **renewed**, with **one** becoming even more dependent on this **other reign** for survival. This dependency will be more than your serfs and peasants experience now, where they are dependent on your kindness and generosity for their comforts and needs to be met. This new reign will be one **of** the natures of **Saturn**, cold and unemotional, with masters working their servants long and hard, so their goals of wealth and prosperity can be met.

In our times now it is the royal families and the Church who possess the wealth. That wealth runs the nations and supports the people; but, this future will become the **century** when each person must fight and struggle mightily to establish individual wealth. In that system the quest **of gold** will corrupt, not only those who lead, but those who follow as well. **God** is **the Creator** of all things; and, He has given gold and wealth to the churches and to the kings. This is God's system, where those in power have accepted the responsibility of leading the masses by God's Law. It has then been the responsibility of those royal figures to make atonement for their worldly desires for wealth, and the sins that they commit to gain such material things. In this future, all will have been born into a world where an acceptance of individual responsibility will be required, as the leaders will no longer be serving God. God will have created this system to help Man; but when Man destroys this system, God **will say** He will be **understanding** of His gift of free-will to man. If mankind chooses to seek fulfillment through a quest for individual desires, then each person of mankind will assume all responsibility for any of **the affliction** which may result. This is the price one must pay for the sin of lust. When mankind has lost sight **of** God's purpose and His love for His people, then **his people** will have lost their love of God. Changes, such as those, will come from the temptations of **Satan**, who **will be set** in position to collect the souls of the wayward. He will easily find the **dregs** of society, or those most undesirables willing to take his offers; and, it will be those dregs that will work their tongues for Satan, to get **inside the** minds of others. The purpose will be to lead mankind to the precipice of the **abysm of** Hell. Satan will be asking them to sell their souls for momentary pleasures and comfort. Those who fall prey to those seductions and lose their souls will find that Hell is actually **the deep** empty **gulf** that is **inside** of them, and not the physical center of the earth. Hell is being devoid of any connection to God. This emptiness is **the deep pit** felt in one's stomach when one is sick and upset. It is the stomach that is the emotional center of the body, just as the heart is the spiritual center.

When this deep pit is felt, it will be **then** when one will know the hurt of a soul having been lost. The final judgment day **will begin** at the same time those who will have saved their souls will find redemption and be taken to be **among God**. This glory will be awarded to **the men** and women who displayed their devout faith in the **one** God and Christ. They will find the ultimate reward of **peace** in their hearts, which will be **universal** for all souls which surround them.

This oneness **will live**, with all **bound** together, **approximately** for **the space of one thousand years**. This length of time is in God's time, as linear time will cease to exist as we know it now.

During those years when all good souls **will turn** with God, all will act like the merging of cells in a mother's womb, but **in his** womb. This gestation period will do **more** to cleanse the souls, and allow all of them to know the true **great force** God is and **the power** He commands. This will then develop each soul into a true **ecclesiastic**, which will then be born again as the new man of the future. They will become immortals who will spread the new seeds of religions, which will span a new race of life which will worship the power and the glory of the one true God.

This is the source of true ecclesiastic power **then**, when souls are fully aware of God, without any doubt. The power of Christianity was greatest in those ecclesiastical people who personally witnessed the marvels of Jesus Christ. It was that transferred power which **turned** Christianity into the religion it would become. However, once the source of power has been **unbound** from the earthly realm, the power of a religion diminishes, at some time after those original ecclesiastics meet their natural demise. The power is actually never unbound from the individual, as God is always with us all. This makes the true ecclesiastic the one who not only believes in this power, but teaches others to also get in touch with the source.

PART 3: THE LETTER TO HENRY II

CONCLUDING THE LETTER

And, sire, with that said and understood, know that I have Christ in my heart, and know that God has shown me the future. Christ has come to me and given me *The Prophecies* **because** of His love for mankind. He is our Savior because He wants to save our souls from eternal condemnation. He is the **Sire** of all Christians, or those who will take Christ into their hearts and live a life of peace. I know **that** it is the ultimate purpose of my work to show the necessity for mankind to operate from this center towards love and peace. But, by **this** manner of **speech** I make here now, and also the language that is written in *The Prophecies*, it is obvious that **I** make everything **wear** a veil of obscurity. So many of the quatrains seem **almost** intelligible, being **vaguely** stated; but, they are indeed significantly more than that. This makes **these** seem to be something they are not; with everyone viewing them from the perspective of my previous **predictions**, based on astrological calculations. It will be **when** the time comes that **this** veil will be removed, so that the clouds of mystery can evaporate and the message of *The Prophecies* **will be** clear. At that time, all of the quatrains will be **able to be** understood clearly. It will be seen to tell of **the coming** of Christ for the second time, **from hence** his first incarnation on earth, which led to His crucifixion, resurrection and ascension. Christ will return to save the souls of **them** who have remained faithful, while He oversees the destruction of them who will have ignored the power and glory of His Father, and showed no honor for God or mankind. I have already written here that I was shown the times which are now past. As **for the numbering of the times**, or the day of reckoning, when time will end, I have set forth a timeline here, from mankind's creation to Christ's time on earth. I have also stated the time of the antichrist, whose influence will lead the world to ruin. The timeline of *The Prophecies* is only a tale of the future; but, the times of **which** it tells are a continuation of those past influences, as **it follows** from then and from now. You must know **that** this future is of the end times; but, **it** does **not** imply that all of mankind will have **been** deemed bad or evil. This will **by no means** be the case; but, **where** there will be found **good** in people, that number will be **few** in comparison to the whole. Not many will be living lives **in accordance with the** wellbeing of its fellow man's needs; and, the majority will not be in accordance with God's laws. Mankind will believe it has become **superior** to the commands of God, the true Supreme Being, to **whom**

all owe their existence. Forgotten will be the remembrance that we can only come to be **by** the grace of God. God has also given mankind a tool, through which mankind can glimpse his or her own future, by **way** of the calculations of the stars and planets, or the **Astronomics** that are known. Still, **that** way cannot be perfected by man alone. The art of astrology is as nebulous and confusing as is this letter; such that we can only gain true insights when assisted **by** one of the **other** spirits, assistant to God. With faith and belief we allow those spirits to whisper the guidance we need, telling us what the symbolism of the aspects means, as meant for us personally. For this to happen, one has to be willing to listen to that inner self. The **same** can also be said **of** the messages and lessons that are contained in the **sacred scriptures**. Unless one is a believer and accepting of God's guidance, the written words of the Bible, **which** is God's word, **are not able to** make perfect sense to us. Many of those biblical documents contain parables, where we must be living those tales to **break** through to the true meaning. When that happens, the meaning becomes personal to us, relative to a current condition which surrounds us. Still, **by no means** does God intend for us not to know the message of His words. That is the role of His churches, which train us in the meaning of the Scriptures, and how to understand them. With **that so** understood, my work, *The Prophecies*, is also a book of God's words, and just as holy as the books of the Bible. If allowed, **I would wish** that I could now make the correct adjustments **to each** and every **quatrain**, to make them clear and properly ordered; and, if that was allowed, it would be easy **to put the reckoning**, or numbering, **of the times** and dates, so that **oneself could be able to make** perfect sense of what was written. I would wish to make this at least clear to you sire, as you are my King; **but, to** that end, that would mean **all** would be able to have that knowledge before the time has come; and that is **not** to happen. It is best that I **should be** seen as not **agreeable**, or not well liked, for not being able to state clearly the meaning of the quatrains, in this letter. Christ has stated to me why it should be this way, and I have agreed to those terms. Still, by my **not** making the meaning of *The Prophecies* clear, there will be some who will think it is **less** than it really is; but, on the other end of that spectrum, there will be those who will sense a higher meaning. People will enjoy acting as **the interpreter**, speaking in my place for me; but, they will interpret less than is there. However, there will eventually be one interpreter who will have correctly found the meaning; but, **as far as** to when **this** understanding of what I have written will come, that is for our **Sire** and Almighty Father to decide. Again,

359

I say "Sire" in this letter, as **that** is **your** Majesty's **majesty**, the one to whom you hold homage. For **myself** in this entire matter, I have been **granted ample** and broad **power**, from which to write the words of Christ **for** Him. It is **this** instructed manner that you do not understand; and, this has been expected. I was not empowered **to make** it any other way. Knowing what *The Prophecies* are **for**, and **not** to be able **to give** clearly this future's true **cause** and effect, this will act **to ignite the slanderers**, which will see the title of my book as heresy; and, those who will feel this way will wish to slander God, by wishing ill will to me.

But seeing is believing, sire, and I have seen Christ and I have seen the future through the eye of God. The effect on my conviction is unchangeable; and, my faith is stronger now than could otherwise be humanly possible to obtain. **Oh,** I shout with joy that Christ is the **serenest King** possible, full of peace and love. From the experience of His presence I know **that** I will be cared for, no matter what happens to my earthbound body; and, **whoever** shall try to threaten me will have no effect. I have heard the rumblings **of the** possibility of **censorship**, from those who have been **finding difficulty** making sense of my words. A step in that direction of retribution, **which will be** well within their power, will **cause** me to be further silenced on this subject. An act **of** this nature will force me **to withdraw my pen** from writing more, without a stipend to depend on. Just realize that **in** the event that **my** writing must come to a **rest**, I will sleep easily, at peace in the **nocturnal** hours.

An example of one such punishment would be the reverse of no source of income, making me pay back what I have received. I know that a **mulct**, fine or penalty of this kind is still possible, along with being forbidden to serve your highness and the holy Church as I have before. **Oh,** but sire I have been with Christ the **King**, who has assured me that His Word will not die. It will continue to be **universally** known; and, my work will continue to be known as well. It will remain alive to **powerfully** attract those who will be seeking to solve its mystery. It will be like the tale of Arthur and the sword in the stone, which attracted a new challenger each year, trying to release its power to them. I have seen this **very clearly**. For whatever **noise**, or sound of disfavor I have created to come **towards** me and my reputation now, I know that **shortly**, relatively speaking, the Lord will grant me **favor**. **But all** of that noise and uproar **towards** *The Prophecies* has led to **this**: a response to **you** in a **letter**. If the words that have been published confused you, then you will not understand this letter, which

360

also must be **put together** in the correct order to understand. The point is that all of the yelling and screaming for knowing the meaning **has not** had any **influence** on my decision to remain silent about that meaning. However, this letter will **not** be found useless, as it will be **a** key to unlocking my **book** in the future, because I have fulfilled your wish and explained the meaning of *The Prophecies*, here in this letter to you. In the future, when that key is discovered, this letter will have the qualities of a book, as the explanation you desired.

It may be difficult at first to see a book in the pages of this letter; **but**, as it appears to you, unchanged, this letter will have little effect **towards** yielding the **understanding** that will be **sought** by many over the years. Once that search has been **done**, and the right ideas and formulas have been grasped, this letter will be found to be like an **unpolished** gemstone, just as a diamond in the rough. When this letter will have been refined, it will explain what has to be **done** to refine the order of the quatrains. In that regard, I have given forth **a few samples**, as offerings, to what is found **sewn** into *The Prophecies*; and, my order of presentation here will match the proper order that should be used there. This is important, for **as much as you** had expected a straightforward response in this letter, none was guaranteed. And, although you are displeased with my response, it will eventually **please** your spirit, when your time comes. You will then find that the people I have written about in the future will be **so small** in spirit that you would not wish to be King of France then. Further, they will be so **dry** of soul that they cannot show enough emotion to act **towards** relieving the plights and needs of others. In **every** nation which will exist, in Europe and around the world, when this future time comes, those leaders will pale in comparison to **your** compassion and the **size** of your heart and courage. You are a humane monarch, and the future will not know of leaders like you. It is so important to realize, now, how much our religious convictions have tempered our **human nature**. When there is no conscience to contend with, our souls have been **murdered**. Murderous acts will have become commonplace in this future. Without the fear of an Almighty God who watches over our every move and deed, mankind assumes a self-anointed **godlike** arrogance. When no longer required to show **dutifulness** to an unseen deity, human beings become nothing more than animals. Without a strong emotional bond to others, while ignoring the inner voice's pleas for sacrifice, mankind becomes self-serving. It is amazing just **how** quickly one becomes alone, when one **solitary** human being cannot find comforting reward by talking to Christ or God. This neglect of God will be what **magnifies** the destruction coming in the future. It makes it so important to understand the reason for **Christianity's** existence. It is not to be forgotten that this word bears the **Regal name** of Christ, and stands for those who follow His model; but, this means more than simply someone acting as a middle man for Christ. It stands for a way of life. In this regard, **towards** those who stand in the middle blocking the shining light of the Lord, they are **in** an appointed capacity of **chief authority** for God on earth. But, it is their actions which must not be seen as a reflection of Heaven, as they are only human. It will be **so often** in the future that the **moral scruples** or the integrity of mankind will not be all that people will like to believe it is. Instead of the church lending its **support** to the people, there will be way too much energy put into asking parishioners to **hand over** earning to them. This, in turn, will allow them to live like the elite, as Kings. Those supposed men of morals will find reason to declare such a thing as **worthy war**, to win favor from the leaders of man. In reality, those people who will classify themselves as clergy will only be acting **to deprive** others of a desire to know Christ, by driving people away with their sinful deeds. This is the tragedy that will allow mankind to destroy itself.

But Henry, **all** I have told you here in this letter is **only** an outline of the whole that is found in *The Prophecies*. In this letter **I** have given **you** what you have requested; but, I have given it in the manner that the Lord Jesus Christ **requires**. **Oh**, again I must exclaim what a wonderful **King** Christ is. He is so **very-mild**, graceful, merciful and forgiving. It is completely **by** His blessing that He has come **here**, to speak to me, which has led to **this** letter to you. As the source of **your** blood Henry, He has honored you and your time on earth, by coming during your reign. He has restated to me now this most **singular** version of the Prophecy that I send to you. The explanation in this letter will provide mankind with all of the knowledge it will need to save itself, in due time. While the words are purposefully difficult to understand now, the **prudent** and wise of **humanity** will listen to the whispers **of** God's angels. They will listen **to hear** the true message these words contain. I know that you would **rather** have this explanation more plainly stated and made clear; but, while that is also **the wish of** mine, I cannot break my oath to Christ. Please know that to tell this story in this way, and not in an absolutely clear manner, is a test of **my courage**.

I must pray that the message will be understood in time, to free my conscience of worry. I realize I will have hidden the message well during my time on earth; but, **the** time I have spent in the service of you and your **sovereign** reign has allowed me the luxury of **studying** deeply on this subject. Still, even though I have done **that** studying on your time, and owe you the honor of explanation, **I have** no option but to respond to your request in this manner. It has been my pleasure to be **of** service to you, and my loyalty calls for me **to obey in your** commands. However, I am more loyal and devoted to the one who is your **serenest Majesty**; and, it is His commands I must now obey. Ever **since** the fist moment **that my eyes** fell on Christ's face, knowing that I **have had** an experience so extraordinary, I am still bedazzled by His presence. Knowing that I was selected as the one **to see** this vision so clearly is an honor. I had already held Christ **so close** in my heart; but, to have Him just as close **at hand** is a reward so wonderfully unexpected. Christ is at the core **of your splendor** Henry, but as much as your splendor presents an aura of greatness, Christ's splendor is like looking directly at the **solar** disk, without any pain in the eyes. It is **that** solar disk which symbolizes Jesus Christ; and, it has been Him who has been **the** true **grandeur of my labor**. It is so wonderful to me because I have **not reached** for this Heavenly treatment. Having been touched by Christ there is **no** further reward **required** by me in this world.

From Salon this 27ᵗʰ of June, I write with the Sun in the sign of Leo, the Lion of courage, which is ruled by the Sun, the light of truth. May the courage of truth surround this document as it is born into this world. I send this letter in the year **One thousand five hundred fifty eight**, the time which has passed since our Lord Jesus Christ was born. **Done** was this work **by Michael Nostradamus**, at the bidding of Jesus Christ, from our meetings in the **Solon Part** of the Department of **Province**.

SUMMARY OF THE LETTER TO HENRY II

Now that you have read the Letter to Henry II the amazing depth this letter of explanation has should be evident. I have tried to make it as clear as possible, which for a document that has historically been seen as the lunatic ramblings of a madman is not a small feat. This letter is completely what one would expect it to be, as a response to the King's wishes to have *The Prophecies* explained; but, it is also more than a simple explanation, as would be expected from such a work of relatively short length. While it goes over the general outline of each stage of *The Prophecies*, it also confirms the premises stated in the preface and tells about past Biblical history as well.

I will readily admit to you this is the first time I have attempted to interpret the Letter to Henry. I had begun the translations after I finished *Pearls Before Swine, Volume 1*, because I intended to begin Volume 2 with this letter. I had read enough of the other translations of it to have an idea about how it matched what I have theorized, giving that hypothesis strength and conviction; but, much of what I initially read of it was confusing. I approached the interpretation of it, once I had completed my own translations, with the confidence that I had approached confusing quatrains with before.

This was done by following the systems I had discovered; and, I knew as long as I followed those guidelines I would realize what the intentions were. Still, I did not know what to expect as I began the interpretations; and, the end result, after several changes in editing from new revelations that came to me as I edited, was an amazing piece of work that truly catches the flavor of *The Prophecies*.

I began the interpretations with the entire letter in the order it was presented to Henry in. This was a good way to start, since the first part of the letter made perfect opening statements. It was when I got to the first section that deals with the biblical chronology that it dawned on me that the whole letter was just like *The Prophecies*, in miniature; and, just as the quatrains had to be reordered to make sense, so did the segments of this letter. I will openly admit that this reordering of this letter is just as difficult as the ordering the quatrains were. But, having done that work with the ordering of the quatrains, I could see how to order the segments of this letter.

In the Letter to Henry, excluding the heading and salutation, there are 67 periods, which become the blocks of the text. This separation is the same as I used to separate the blocks of the letter of Preface. However, when I tried to piece those blocks together, I found there was some need to further divide the blocks into shorter segments.

I first found this was easily done at all places where colons appeared in a block, because the segments following a colon act to clarify the previous text. Still, after realizing that a further division was needed, I then realized that where Nostradamus used a comma preceding an ampersand (a form of unnecessary redundancy) this too make an excellent place for block separation. Finally, in the rare use of a semi-colon, I found that qualified as a point of separation as well.

This turned the 67 blocks into 214 segments, which then acted as the pieces of the puzzle that had to be put together. In my organization of the segments, no statement fragments (the words between two marks of punctuation) have been altered; everything has been consistently separated by period, colon, semi-colon and comma-ampersand only; and, all of the words within each segment/fragment have maintained their precise order, as written by Nostradamus.

When you read what someone else has translated this letter to state, you can see why the letter is so confusing. You read fine along to one point, and then it jolts to another topic entirely, before eventually leading back to the original point. In essence, neither of the letters is difficult to translate (for the most part), as Nostradamus wrote in more standard language – almost prose – unlike the style he used in the quatrains. Therefore, the translations of others show each segment still saying about the same thing, only paraphrased differently. Knowing this you can see how one segment matches another, deeper into the text; so, it makes more sense when ordered properly. This is the amazing quality that proper context applies to the interpretation.

In the section about the biblical chronology and the section about the astrological timing elements, those segments are split in the letter, with half appearing in the front half of the letter and the rest in the later half of the letter. They lose all continuity when presented in that way, so placing them together so they can have clear context is an automatic requirement. Perhaps others have thought of this long before me; but, it seems it has been more important to maintain the perfect order of Nostradamus' presentation, than try to solve what he wrote. Regardless of their reasoning, the true difficulty comes in the later half of this letter, when Nostradamus generalizes the story of the quatrains. That is where context plays its most important role, because it orders the quatrains for you.

For me to order these segments, I had to already know the general story. This is what I realized with my first book, which exposed to me the future part of the story and its separate areas of focus. In *Pearls Before Swine, Volume 1*, I added more clarity to that story, by explaining the quatrains which deal specifically with the period of history between 1600 and 2000. I have sorted the remainder of the quatrains to fit the future scenario which my first book offered; and, this letter separates into the same categories of focus, where the subversion of the post-World War II period would lead to the events of September 11, 2001.

This would lead to the ensuing War on Terror and Afghanistan and Iraq. It is clear in the quatrains that Iran is a clear threat to world peace; but, before that threat becomes realized, the quatrains also make it clear that major earth changes will occur. This will be followed by the surprise attacks which will neutralize the United States military, leading to the invasion of Europe and the Muslim occupation. This will be followed by the persecution of the Catholic Church and Christians. This occupation and persecution will finally lead to the eventual attempt at a liberation invasion, followed by the ultimate defeat of the Islamists. Once this stage has been reached, the world will rapidly be spiraling out of control. That is when the comet will strike the earth. I have seen this story for over four years now; and, the Letter to Henry II has completely confirmed that story for me.

Let me reassure you that I am not the first to see many of these future events coming. In my research of other authors, some have seen nearly the same pattern of events happening, in reference to the invasion of Europe and the subsequent invasion of liberation. Another author has focused the title of his book on the comet which is predicted to come. Even though others have seen the same things happening, they have not been able to realize a story, where all of the quatrains connect in one overall order. Without order there is chaos; and, that chaos has been keeping other interpreters from realizing why these events will occur and when. *Pearls Before Swine, Volume 1* explains the why; and, in this letter we now know the time frame of when, from the astrological timing section.

That is a very important part of this letter, as the astrological timing elements are rather rare, when considering the specific placements of the retrograde planets. Still, this letter is equally important for gaining the faith which is necessary to prevent these timing elements from becoming a factor. This letter supports the preface, especially in the way it explains the involvement with Jesus Christ and *The Prophecies*. While the Letter of Preface gives important aspects of the systems that are necessary for understanding the quatrains overall, this letter clearly states some of the most necessary parts of the systems. For me, several of the segments confirmed what I had been led to believe years before.

Perhaps the most surprising sections are those explaining the Bible connection and the Atlantis connection. The two separately can seem to contradict one another; but, they become more powerful together, when we realize that the Atlantis connection proves a different form of man existed before Adam. This shows that science is not wrong, but it cannot discount the story of creation that is in the Bible. The thought processes opened from understanding these two sections can explain several questionable topics that science has chosen to basically ignore.

In my original book, *The Future According to Nostradamus*, I easily saw that there were major earthquakes predicted, which would occur on the eve of war. I saw some ancient ruins would be discovered at that time of the earthquakes. This discovery would have to be around Greece; but, it seemed there would be found Roman inscriptions on the buildings. This letter has allowed me to see those quatrains in a new light, one which makes more logical sense. I previously had no idea about an Atlantis connection, but I received some of those whispers in my head while interpreting this letter. I mention this because this letter has confirmed many of my prior theories about the quatrains; but, it has also enlightened me to new thoughts in several areas.

This has been a typical progression of my thought, since I first began to make sense of Nostradamus. While my basic premise has been unchanged: That the quatrains tell a story of the end of the world and must be linked together properly to know that story, I have consistently stumbled onto one new idea after another. These ideas come to me from my inner voice; and, it comes simply as a flash of thought, which tells me that something I am doing, while not wrong, would be better if I went in a certain new direction. These new directions, at first, became the foundations of the Systems of Nostradamus; and, my subsequent interpretations of the letters have confirmed those new directions, by

Nostradamus' own words.

Many of my edits in *Pearls Before Swine, Volume 1* were to rewrite new systems into the beginning of a document, where I did not realize an aspect of a system until half-way through the book. All of this means my understanding of Nostradamus has come with a willingness to adjust to new ideas, while not believing my own intellect has played any important role in solving this age-old mystery.

I mention this because this is my first attempt at solving the Letter to Henry II. In this book's rendition of the Letter of Preface, one will find there as some new twists in my interpretations that were not included in *Pearls Before Swine*. I still stand behind my first interpretation in that book, while I fully believe that this interpretation of the preface is very sound. The preface still states the same basic principles in both interpretations, although slightly different in places. Since that has been my experience, I fully expect that there will be aspects of this letter to Henry which will need tweaking, from new insights that will come to the reader. I do not expect anyone to take what I have written as a perfect rendition of what Nostradamus intended to convey. Only Nostradamus could have produced that perfection. However, I feel that my version of his intention is well within reasonable expectations.

If pressured to venture a guess to the percent of accuracy that I have achieved in this first attempt on this letter, I do not feel that I would be stretching it greatly to guess 85%. In the area of statistics there is significance in that number, as it shows a high degree of reliability. I cannot apply any scientifically reasonable explanation to why I come up with that number; but, I did not just pull that number out of the blue.

In my edits of this letter I have prayed and meditated on the accuracy of my interpretations; and, more often than I liked, I was given a sign that there was an adjustment here and there, which needed to be made for my interpretation to be correct. Again, I had my method for determining this; but, it was nothing which can be proven, so I will keep it secret at this time. For those of you old enough to remember the Andy Griffith movie *No Time for Sergeants*, my method was about as valid as the method Andy Griffith's character (Pvt. Will Stockdale) used, when taking the NCO exam. I'm not sure I could explain his method; but, it was successful enough for him to pass the exam, when his character was portrayed as highly uneducated. I have faith that my similarly unscientific method will have a similarly successful result; and, my interpretations and piecing of the segments together will be found highly accurate, if not perfect.

The point of this summary is not so much for me to convince you to believe, by how well I believe I have correctly interpreted; but, to explain to you that my belief is unquestioned. In fact, I welcome others to take what I have presented and let me know what areas need to be corrected. In order for someone to do that he or she would have to use the same elements of logic I wrote of, to argue against what I have proposed. However, to simply change some of the segments to another place, because it makes more sense, that is an automatic acceptance of my premise and the majority of what the letter states. It would make me very happy to have someone else become that involved with the importance Nostradamus conveyed to mankind.

The Letter to Henry is indeed the confirmation of the story that is contained in *The Prophecies*, even though many of the important details are still left for the verses to reveal. Those revelations, while new and somewhat shocking, will really add nothing to bring about that inner whisper that faith is needed. This letter, while being only a general explanation of what the quatrains are all about, is really all that is needed to know.

It is my hope that you will feel the misery this letter conveys, because I can assure you the specific quatrains which detail the events that make up this horrid future, will make the misery felt here much more pronounced. If you can feel the need to act now, from reading this letter, then the possibility of avoiding this future makes the realization of those quatrains only so much fiction. If you can hear the whispers from reading this letter, then I feel I have accomplished my goal of making *The Prophecies* understandable to you.

PART 4
THE CONCLUSION

SUGGESTIONS AND RECOMMENDATIONS

This is where the real tricky part comes into play. As tricky as all of the parts of *The Prophecies* have been for me to solve, now that they have been presented as solved it leaves you with the decisions you have to make. These decisions are ones that most people are not prepared to make, because people do not yet know what I have presented to you. They are not in a position to make any life-changing decisions at all. You are; but you have the task now of asking yourself, "Do I believe what I have just read?"

The way you answer that question to yourself will be the key to how you will act in the future. But, don't worry yet. As long as you don't totally reject the premise that Jesus Christ chose Nostradamus to write a cloaked message which was intended for you to know, then nothing has been lost. It is okay to have doubts, because that is normal. You have been conditioned to doubt.

The initial solution comes from following up on your doubts, by doing your own investigations into what has been stated here. From that investigative work you have to come to your own conclusions about believability. I have told you I am thoroughly convinced and my conclusions are completely proven by the rules of logic; but, I have not actually presented any of that proof in this book. That is the longwinded, dry scholastic approach of another book; and, I knew I had to simply tell you the meaning in this book and let you decide for yourself. This is where listening to your heart will come in.

The only way I can help you with this issue of believability is to review with you the clear points which were made in my interpretation of the letters. I feel it is important to look at the greater scope of everything which has been presented and then apply that to what you already know. By that I do not mean what you know about Nostradamus; but, I mean what you know from your own observable universe.

You see and hear the news each day, on television and by talking with friends and family. You watch cable shows that present Nostradamus along with other stories of prophecies, which give reasons to believe danger is nearer than you ever thought before. You also see best-selling books that write of secrecy and war. From this environment that is personal to you, you must amend what your mind thinks with what you feel inside. I believe what you feel inside will make you realize that you know more than you are allowing yourself to admit.

It is that internal knowledge which causes you to question what I am offering you here; and, it is your inner self that knows that you have to provide a clearer reason for belief. In that regard, I will offer some views of the world which will open your mind to possibilities you may or may not have heard before. Significantly, I will challenge you to question several of the most basic foundations that surround your life. Most of these, especially for Americans, in general, and Christians globally, represent principles and institutions that have rarely been challenged before.

The concept of belief in Nostradamus is just one of these challenges, particularly since he has never been seen before in the light of being a prophet of Jesus Christ. This is a challenge to Christians, many of whom have come to think of Nostradamus as somehow representing evil, instead of holiness. You must listen to your heart about this important aspect and ask yourself to identify the source of your fears, which make you want to reject this concept.

As great as this challenge may be, the greater challenges I will present to you will be to ask you to test the true value of several concepts which are seldom questioned in our society. I will raise questions to you about such concepts as freedom, the political philosophies which run the world, the economic standards which control our lives and even ask why we show such blind trust in the need for education, as a means for success. These are all significant pieces in the story that Nostradamus tells, although they do not stand out as clearly as does his writing of the corruption of religion and the persecution that is coming.

There is so much more than just a simple story presented, allowing us to understand what is good versus evil. We all have an affiliation with things and circumstances that are inherently trusted to be good. All which is opposite that perceived good is then seen as evil; but, this blind faith makes us blind to our own shortcomings. You have to be able to look in the mirror, as well as look at the other side. Once you have seen all 360 degrees of what is going to be the cause of the end of mankind, you will be better prepared to make your stance known.

This will bring you to the greatest challenge that I will present to you. This challenge will be to have you convince yourself that you have an important role in changing the outcome of this future, one which has been prophesized as being most bleak. You have to analyze your fears in this respect too. You have to realize just how much you can do to save the world.

With these challenges I want you to know I will not be able to go deeply into any one area. I do want you to think about the aspects that I point out and look for the gaps in my logic. Rather than write a book within a book, I am confident your inner self will lead your logic to fill in the blanks. All blanks will be filled with all of the amazing details your mind knows; all of which will support the general themes I will present. You may even want to keep your paper and pencil nearby, to jot down questions as you read on.

The Question about Nostradamus

The views I have expressed over the last four and one half years have not matched the views of most people claiming to be authorities on *The Prophecies*. That is enough to justifiably raise doubt; but, it is not reason to throw the baby out with the bath water. Everything I have written in this book is backed by the systems I have uncovered and tested. I have published a book which explains those systems, giving examples of how the systems apply to every quatrain and the Letter of Preface. From that point of reference, everything I state here and there is verifiable. I invite you to follow my recommendation and check deeper into what I have stated, to see if you agree whether I am correct or not. While I readily admit I may not be 100% correct on every interpretation I have written, I am certain the basic premises are undefeatable.

As this task may seem difficult to some, I believe there are those who will be more than willing to check my work for accuracy. Call it coincidence; but, I do not think the popularity of Dan Brown's *The Da Vinci Code* was without some divine guidance. Given that Dan Brown is a polished writer with prior works of recognition, the popularity of *The Da Vinci Code* was more than simply a well-written novel.

The theme struck a nerve with the readers, a nerve that is just like the nerve which should be struck in this book. I have presented you with what can be called the Nostradamus Code. Regardless of the anti-Da Vinci Code campaign to alert people to the facts that Brown's book was a work of fiction and that there was no foundation for his portrayal of the Catholic Church as associated with a secret organization which hid the bloodline of Jesus Christ, the public has become phenomenally interested in checking out the places and rumors behind the story. There are now tours in many of the places featured in Brown's book, to accommodate the interest that has arisen.

The parallels between Brown's fiction and this book are several. Both have the name of a 16th Century figure in the title, figures that have remained easily recognizable into the 21st Century, as men of special talents. Brown revealed some of the mystery that has surrounded Leonardo da Vinci, which before was only known by art historians. Da Vinci would write notes in his journal by using backwards handwriting, so only he could understand his notes. Obviously, Nostradamus wrote poetic verses and letters that only he could understand as well. The historians who have poured over Da Vinci's notes have solved the mystery of his backwards letters; but, while several have stated to know what some of Nostradamus' quatrains mean, none have been able to solve them all and no one has put much effort into understanding the letters he wrote. This makes this an area of Nostradamus that should interest scholars of antiquity; but, there is another area where Brown's novel parallels the information revealed in this book.

That area is in the area of secrecy. A main theme in *The Da Vinci Code* was the secret organization, the Priory of Sion, which was a relative of the Knights Templar, which aided the Catholic Church's quest to keep any known descendants of Jesus Christ from ever being discovered. In the letter to Henry II the issue of secrecy is also huge, as Nostradamus wrote that this is how the rulers of the world will operate, without the public having any real knowledge of what is truly going on around them.

The core problem said to be the cause for the end of the world is the covert meddling which has gone on in the Middle East, with the installations of puppet rulers, by the British and the United States governments. It has been this level of secrecy which has been the cause for the ultimate corruption of the Kings, Church and Sects, of which Nostradamus wrote. This includes the part of the story where a pope was murdered, in essence to forbid a true descendant of Jesus Christ (Pope John Paul I and the spirit that filled him) from being discovered. Nostradamus made it clear this was the final act that would make the Church diametrically opposite from how it operated in 1555.

The quatrains also tell of the murders of the Kennedy brothers and Lady Diana. Those stories within the whole story, which are not reviewed in the letters, exemplify the final corruption of the Sects and Kings. The Sects are the common men who would rob power from kings and the Kings are the true royal rulers,

376

as born to rule by birth. The failures to make the public clearly understand the *whys* and *hows* of such shocking murders shows that much goes on behind the scenes that the powerful need to cover up and keep secret. Nostradamus clears up several conspiracy theories that have been circulating since these murders happened; and, you have to realize that it is theory only because no true investigation ever occurred to solve who did it and why.

As far as those royal rulers are concerned, it was that birthright to rule that Brown focused on in his book. The Holy Grail is shown as the bloodline of a child born to Mary Magdalene. While this was not expressly stated by Nostradamus, his words to Henry stated that he was of the blood of Christ, confirming that a bloodline did indeed exist. The uproar that this aspect of Brown's novel created was seen by some Christians as blasphemy.

The publishers of *The Da Vinci Code* and Dan Brown have had to face a trial over the ideas for this having been previously published in the book *Holy Blood, Holy Grail*. In that book the authors concluded there was not enough evidence to confirm the theory of a bloodline, where Mary Magdalene bore Christ's child. However, while the court ruled Brown did copy those ideas, they determined that ideas were not copyrightable. This did nothing to settle the debate over the resurrected Christ being the father of a human offspring, the daughter that was said to have been born and moved to France.

The fallacy of this thought process, arguing against this possibility, is that it does not focus on the spiritual. Instead, it takes a scientific approach, looking hard for hard evidence, making it focus on the mortal aspect of Jesus Christ and the typical way human children are conceived. They make it appear Jesus loved Mary Magdalene in a carnal way; and, through this physical connection Mary Magdalene was pregnant when Jesus was crucified, out of wedlock. The theory of Brown's book begins with Mary giving birth to a daughter and sailing from North Africa to France, where the arrival is celebrated in ritual ceremonies still held in Sainte-Marie-La-Mer. The Church sees this as a threat to Christianity, because it casts Jesus in too human of a form to worship.

This, to me, is ludicrous. Was not Jesus born to the Virgin Mary, who conceived without Joseph having ever had sex with her prior? The answer is yes, as the pregnancy was announced to Mary by an angel. It is hard to understand why the Catholic Church, which reveres the Virgin Mary unlike any other religion, would think that Christ would have to have sex to make babies. The spiritual focus easily sees that Jesus Christ was the Son of God and thereby the bodily extension of God; and, with this recognition admitted, Christ was quite capable of duplicating that feat of a non-intercourse conception (regardless of whether Mary Magdalene was a virgin or not).

With Mary Magdalene a very devout follower of Christ, she was the only woman who held the role of disciple to Christ. It would have been impossible for any of the male disciples to carry this burden of childbirth; so, she would be the ideal candidate for such a mission from Christ. It would have to be a much less publicized immaculate conception, because the child would not be the Messiah, or another Son of God, per se. It would be a daughter (an excellent complement to the Jesus incarnation), which would be born to begin a bloodline that would give rise to the kings of France.

How else could Henry II be identified by Nostradamus as of this line, if this line did not exist? In the book *Holy Blood, Holy Grail*, the authors proposed that this bloodline surfaced in the Frankish rulers of the Merovingian Dynasty. This rule lasted about 300 years, between 447 AD and 751AD; and, it is said to have unified much of northern Europe, in what is now France, Belgium and Germany. This was well before the Valois Dynasty, of which Henry II was born, with the Carolingian (Charles Magne) and Capetians before them. Henry II was actually the one that sired the first rulers of the final dynasty, the Bourbon line, which fell in the French Revolution and later died completely, after Napoleon, in 1850.

When you understand that Nostradamus calls Henry II the blood of Jesus Christ, after having talked directly to Christ, then Henry II was just one of a long line. Knowing this gives a new angle to the story of Arthur and the quest for the Holy Grail. If Uther Pendragon, the blood father of Arthur, is seen as the Merovingian Dynasty, then Arthur is not just one king, but the succeeding four lines of kings that have ruled over France and the Holy Roman Empire. The Holy Grail that later becomes lost is the failure of the Bourbon line of kings to rule from the spirit of Christ and His compassion for the people. The final battle was then fought in the French Revolution, when royal rule left for the Isle of the Dead, or Avalon. In this way the story of Arthur is the story of Nostradamus, as the rise and fall of the bloodline of Christ.

I offer this suggestion simply because Nostradamus clearly identifies Henry II as of the bloodline of Christ; and, *The Da Vinci Code* used ideas from *Holy*

Blood, Holy Grail, both of which bring this bloodline into question. Instead of looking for some physical evidence that would prove a bloodline existed, the symbolism of the Arthurian tales points to the reality that Nostradamus presents. Merlin represents God and the religions that serve God and King. Morgana, the half-sister of Arthur, represents the philosophies of mankind that mimic religion; but, this element is purely evil and motivated by seeking power, by stealing the magic that the bloodline has created. I have strong opinions about the Christian symbols in the tale of Arthur; but, the only answer that can be found on this matter will come through the inner voice. This is how you have to test Nostradamus.

The point of making comparisons to Dan Brown's book is not to prove his theories or premises. It is to show you how there is no difference in the significance that his book exposed and what this book on Nostradamus exposes. The same kind of interest will be found in Nostradamus as has been found in *the Da Vinci Code.* Whether or not anything can be determined to be indisputable is beside the point. While I fully believe that every quatrain will be found to be infallibly predicted, until we change course and avert the horrible future that is foretold, there will always be those who will believe the opposite. It all boils down to the basic argument of belief in God versus no belief in God. This is where being able to listen to your heart comes in handy. God and Christ will be proven to the faithful; and, investigating Nostradamus, like people have investigated Dan Brown's fiction, will lead to that faith.

One other comparison that I find particular interest in, when related to *The Da Vinci Code* comparison, is something that has recently been promoted on television. This phenomenon is called the Torah Code, or (to attract a Christian audience) the Bible Code. This is something that has been studied for many years; but, with the aid of modern computer technology, it has most recently begun to gain recognition. The premise is based on a system of computing an equal-distance sequence in the letters written in the books of the Hebrew Bible. While I do not have a full grasp of the mechanics of this system, when certain key words are input into a specialized computer program some number sequences have yielded some amazing results. These results are said to be more than could ever be expected to be produced purely by chance.

The results come from a narrow field, or matrix, which lists all of the letters of a particular section of the Bible, with a predetermined number of letters per each row. Within one much smaller matrix a very high number of words have very frequently appeared which are related to the key words searched for. For example: When they searched the Book of Genesis for key words related to the John F. Kennedy assassination, the words President, Kennedy, to die, and Dallas all showed in that one matrix group.[1] The people who are very involved in these searches are solidly behind the belief that the results are more than coincidence; and, more importantly, they believe the results could only come from the power of God. It is too amazing for any human being to purposefully construct something like this.

Still, as convinced as some are that the Bible Code has merit; there are those who do not believe. On the show that I saw on the History Channel program about the Bible Code (Decoding the Past I believe) one non-believer said it was like looking at clouds and seeing animals and other objects in them, which certainly are not there. A supposed test that was used to debunk this process proved that when the same system applied to the Herman Melville book, *Moby Dick*, it produced something like the Kennedy results in Genesis.

This only serves to drive home the point that I have gained from Nostradamus, in the Letter of Preface, where he states that man's knowledge is little more than like wading on the sea shore with our feet barely in the water, when God's knowledge represents the ocean of all knowledge. When he stated that man knows nothing that God does not allow man to know, this means that God allowed Herman Melville to write *Moby Dick*, and while he was at it he put in a code, knowing that some disbeliever would check it one day. In the same vein of reason, God has allowed men to discover the Bible Code, just as he has allowed me to understand Nostradamus. This means that Nostradamus, *Moby Dick* and the Bible all have secrets in them that no one ever imagined were there before. When we realize the commonality is prophetic knowledge being released, it shows that there is a need for that knowledge at this time.

You could say what I present is the Nostradamus Code, if you wanted to. You would be right, in the sense his works represent something that has been seen by so many, for so many years, but has not been seen in the proper light. I have just shed light on the proper way to read Nostradamus' two letters of explanation and instruction, which matches what the quatrains tell when they are put in the proper order. However, unlike the need for special computer programs or an ability to read Hebrew and calculate statistics, *The Prophecies* can be

---

1 http://www.exodus2006.com/3code.htm

understood by anyone with a dictionary and the time to read slowly.

One problem the believers of the Bible Code have voiced is that so far it has proven to be more hind sighted than foresighted. This is because it requires guessing the key words that are applicable to future events. The most amazing results have come from key word analysis supporting known past events, making it appear to be predictive of the past. This is precisely like *The Prophecies*, in the sense that interpreters have best determined when a quatrain matches an event, after the event has occurred.

Those who scoff at interpretations of something that has already occurred often enjoy arguing that a prophecy is useless when it only reveals the past. The skeptics say they will be more impressed when a future event can be predicted before it occurs, so it can be measured for accuracy by occurring in the future time, as predicted. Well, the past is how we learn to use the systems, and the future of Nostradamus is easy to see (and even predict if you know the astrology), but this future is one that is so horrid you don't want it to come true. The proof is then found from the accuracy in having predicted the past and that must lead to the faith which will cause the actions which will avoid the future.

This leads to one last book that I will suggest you look into, to help you determine if Nostradamus is worth further investigation. This book is the Holy Bible and it has long been a source of prophecy and of particular interest lately has been the end of times prophecy that the Bible contains. Nostradamus clearly claims that he is not the author of *The Prophecies*. He just wrote it for Jesus Christ, knowing it was holy and prophetic. This claim, without any further comparisons, makes it at least a companion to *The Revelation of John*, which is the final book of the Bible. However, that book was debated as to whether or not it should be included in the Bible, because it cast Christ in a less than loving light.

This debate shows the weakness of human minds, as it misses the point that Christ first appeared to John and told him to write down his warnings for the seven churches. This is exactly like the warning given to Nostradamus, so he could write a prophecy which would be given to the world; and, when this prophecy is understood the warning serves the purpose of giving mankind the opportunity to change. Failure to change will make the final end horrors mankind's own doing; and, it is the role of the churches of the world to lead mankind to awareness of the evil that has become present. If the churches do not fulfill their role, Christ will come to strike down evil, while also saving the souls of the truly faithful. The warning is rooted in love, for salvation, which is a perfect reason to have that book in the Bible.

This debate over whether a document like *The Revelation*, claimed to be from the mouth of Jesus Christ, should be included in a Christian Bible as part of the New Testament also shows how easy it is to fail to capture the full intent of the written word. This is precisely why so many have failed to understand Nostradamus for so long; and, God and Christ know how simple minded mankind can be, without guidance.

The priest, pastor, reverend, minister, rabbi or whatever title a church gives to the one who leads its followers to understand the Bible, Christian or Hebrew, is usually one who has studied the Bible in great detail. Those learned men soon realize the translations from the Hebrew, Greek, Arabic or even Latin become a tricky business, as far as simply stating one meaning to what was written. This dual nature of the Holy Word is what sermons are used to explain; and, it is the root reason why the Catholic Church felt so strongly about protecting the Latin Bible when the Reformation began and people like Martin Luther wanted the Bible translated into the language of the people. More than wanting to keep the people in need of a priest to explain the meaning of the Latin, they did not want the people to over simplify the meaning by themselves. This over simplification is just what past translators of Nostradamus have done, and this is worth investigating yourself.

The Bible is an amazing work and most people honor and respect it, even if they do not fully understand the meanings of the many stories it contains. Those stories, many of which seem to have little association with today's fast-paced lifestyles, are more than they first appear. I have found that many of the passages I now read in the Bible take on new meaning, which I had not seen before; and, this new meaning comes from knowing what I know of how to read Nostradamus for understanding.

These new meanings are too numerous to recount here now; but, I can tell you that all of the last books of the Old Testament, where the prophets of Israel and Judah warned of coming destruction and captivity, has a dual purpose of both predicting that ancient end as well as predicting the end of the world. Those pleas by prophets chosen by God to warn the Jews of their wayward ways becoming ruinous were unheeded and the ruin came. That mirrors *The Revelation*, where Christ told John to warn the seven churches, which was followed by the ruin. The unwritten is as powerful as the written, as in between was the basic lesson that failure to listen and heed a prophecy is dangerous.

One of the problems of biblical prophecy is that it presents some of the most enigmatic verses in the Bible. I know that when I have read those books in the past I came away with visions of wild creatures and bad things happening, but I did not have a clue what it all meant. Many pastors and priests steer clear of bringing *The Revelation* to their flocks because the language is so symbolic that many priests may be too unskilled to preach about the true meaning. There are people who have become specialized in understanding the meaning and they write books and preach to the people about how that meaning applies to modern life.

This is the "fire and brimstone" approach to preaching, but this is only found in a limited number of Christian churches. Without more uniformity in the preaching of the message, fewer people will tend to give credit to that style of preaching because it feels like a blatant casting of guilt over parishioners; using guilt to make them comply with the Bible's word. This threat of burning in hell is forcing people to be good, rather than convincing them they should want to be good. So many of Nostradamus' verses echo this coming destruction that many people have turned a deaf ear to understanding it better, just like the many Christians who now shun *The Revelation*.

Learning how to understand Nostradamus properly will make understanding biblical prophecy something everyone can do, causing it to no longer require a specialist to come in an explain it all. The book by John is not in the proper order and needs to be realigned to make the most sense of it. However, it has been this unwillingness to change the Word of God to make it flow in an understandable manner that keeps much of it unintelligible to most, just like Nostradamus has been. People see the Bible as chiseled in stone, like the Ten Commandments, but the reality is that it is not a stone tablet. It is a living document, and can be rearranged in any way possible. No matter how it is rearranged, it still will have a holy affect, and this will become especially felt when the rearrangements are found to be yielding more clarity of meaning.

It is so very important to see Nostradamus in the same light as any of the authors of the Bible. Through Nostradamus' work, Jesus Christ is telling us that prophecy is to help mankind. When we understand that, we can understand that the Bible shows prophecy as just as helpful, but the bad results always follow a failure to believe a prophet.

Many people will have to come to terms with this fear of Nostradamus as something or someone that he was not. These fears are unfounded, and in comparison, it would be no different if the Mayans feared Jesus Christ because the Conquistadors held a cross over them as then ran them through with swords. That does not make Christ evil. The people of the past who have given Nostradamus a fearful name were wrong. It is time to lose the fear, look at the hard evidence, and above all you must learn to listen to your heart.

The Question of the Concept of Freedom

Once you have realized Nostradamus is truly a prophet of Jesus Christ and his story does nothing to lessen other recognized prophecies, you have to begin to understand that we are living in the times of corruption. If this corruption was not as great as Nostradamus built it up to be, building over 400 years of time, we would not begin to believe our time was the end time. With other prophecies and interpreters pointing to our times as the relevant times, it makes this awareness important. Knowing danger is just around the corner has to make you open your eyes and look how much value you put on such things as freedom, government, money and knowledge. You just might find that things are not as they seem to be.

The concept of freedom certainly sounds good to Americans. In the United States of America we have put a lot of value in freedom, largely because it represents the foundation of our country where we gained freedom from the British. Bumper stickers I have seen claim "Freedom is not free." I take that to mean we have to fight for freedom; but, to further that even more, I see it as meaning America must supply its youth to a military presence, where some of those young soldiers must die to defend our right to be a free nation. If that is indeed what that means, then there is an error of reason.

First of all, the initial fight for independence was won and freedom from Britain rule was gained. Beyond the War of 1812 and the American Civil War, where fighting did occur on American soil, no other nation has since threatened our nation's freedom, as a nation free to rule itself. Maintaining a belief that we still have to be willing to die to defend this freedom is wrong. This is a great error in reasoning that only keeps people willing to join the military, to prove their patriotism.

Second, the American colonies had such a weak military presence that it stood no serious chance of defeating the British, to gain independence. If the English wanted to crush the American Revolution it most certainly could have. If it weren't for the French and their hatred of the British (plus the French liking Benjamin Franklin) causing the French to assist the American colonies by sending officers and troops to help General Washington, along with Prussian mercenaries, there would be an America today more like Canada, with Queen Elizabeth on our coins.

Even with that outside help coming to the American colonies, there is no real explanation for why the British gave up so quickly. It wasn't as if other nations hadn't resented the British Empire's presence on their land. Their domination in other areas of the world constantly caused revolutions, and the British were more than willing to fully commit to quelling all uprisings. They didn't choose do that with the American War of Independence, which makes that hard fought victory seem more like a heavyweight boxer taking a dive than a clear defeat. Still, saying that America won its freedom from Britain, just what does that mean?

The reason for the discontent was generally taxes. Since the British funded the exploration and settlement of the colonies, they needed money in return for their investment. The British then began to tax tea and stamps, which was seen as too much cost for the early settlers. This was when the early Americans preferred to tax themselves, to be able to afford to build the things they wanted and needed; but, money was tight then, when a penny meant something. This was certainly not reason to go to war; but, it did point out that the freedom that early Americans sought was not a freedom from taxation. It was just the freedom not to pay the British. In other words, early Americans wanted the freedom to keep their money in America. America certainly has taxes today, so we gained no freedom from that restriction. We just gained the right to tax ourselves as an independent nation.

In the Civil War, the southern states decided to sever their ties with the entity known as the United States. Slavery was only one part of that whole issue. The main issue was over a strong central government in Washington D. C., which was originally designed to govern 13 states, formerly colonies. By the mid 19th Century this central government was finding it difficult to govern 31 states and 7 territories, while allowing the states to maintain the right to govern themselves.

385

The southern states wanted the freedom to govern themselves; and, to assist each other in this process, they planned to loosely align the southern states with a weak central government, called a confederation. Since the southern states knew "freedom wasn't free," they armed themselves and even asked the French to help out. In that war the British helped the northern states, showing that all was forgiven from just over 80 years prior. Obviously, what worked once doesn't always work. The southern states lost that war and we are what we are now largely because of the union being maintained then. Since then the nation has grown larger and the strong central government has become more grossly inept, while the states have all become powerless as self-sufficient entities. In my mind, fighting for freedom in America took a hit in 1865.

Now freedom does have a meaning which usually has the word "from" following it. Early Americans sought freedom "from" taxation without representation and the southern states sought freedom "from" the union of states that wanted a strong central government. In this way freedom is associated with escaping "from" oppression, responsibility or captivity; and, slavery was a form of forced captivity. This is a concept often longed for by those who fill the prisons of the world; and, the majority of prisoners may want their freedom, but the free people of society put them there and they expect them to pay for their crimes by a loss of freedom. This makes freedom a reward for those who allow themselves to become limited by social rules and mores and act responsibly within that system. In this sense, freedom is the right to be restricted, or suffer being more restricted.

The concept of freedom was used to stir the peasants of France into revolution, so they could become free from the captivity of peasantdom. Supposedly, that would make them be free to own land. After their revolution, the main freedom they enjoyed was called the Reign of Terror. During that period the common class of people was free to watch beheadings, while a select few were free to create new laws, with which to try the royal figures and justly behead them. This freedom lasted until Napoleon ended that madness and gave the peasants a new freedom: the freedom to live under an Emperor rather than a king. When Napoleon was defeated by the British and Austrians, the French slowly began to learn that freedom meant having to pay more to do the same thing they used to do for nothing.

After most of the revolutions had taken place, and everyone in the world had gained what they thought was freedom, Nostradamus pointed out that letting common men become free to rule lands would lead to corruption. The Reign of Terror was one example of this happening, but while public beheadings have slowed down considerable since then, the corruption has not decreased one iota. The inhuman tyrants who rose to power in the 20th Century not only put more restrictions on their own people than had been on them before, but they began putting restrictions on others, of other nations; and, those restrictions were of the harshest kinds.

The Jews of Europe were imprisoned, along with gypsies and homosexuals and other undesirables, and forced into labor in camps, to be gassed in the free showers. The free people of France were captive by the Germans, but were free to operate as Vichy France. The French underground or the French Freedom Fighters would blow up telegraph lines and bridges and kill Germans here and there, not that acts of this nature would free France from German domination, but because it felt good to hurt the oppressor. It was the same way in which Palestinians treat Israelis today; and Iraqis are regularly bombing American soldiers along the roadside in Iraq, even though those soldiers are there to give the Iraqis freedom. As much as these Arab peoples are acting just like the French did against the foreign Germans on their soil, we somehow reserve so much value for the use of the word "freedom" that it's not allowed to call Palestinians or Iraqis Freedom Fighters. That is unless you are Arab.

As ridiculous and oversimplified as all of this sounds, this is how ridiculous you need to see this kind of meaning associated with freedom. God gave mankind free-will and that is all freedom can mean in our physical incarnations. True freedom is the escape of the soul from the body and its return to God. Anything less is simply the individual right that we all have, to choose; do I choose to act as God wants me to act or not?

This is where religion plays a significant role for mankind. It should teach us how God wants us to act, so we can choose to act accordingly, from our own free-will. But if religion does more than teach – say, physically forces people to act a certain way and punishes those who don't act that way – then people tend to act against that force, from the freedom we innately have, to choose how to act. That kind of freedom is flawed and easily manipulated by those not coming from a religious center. Nostradamus wrote of this being at the root of the coming war, which in no way will be holy, but it will be called a Holy War for

387

religious freedom.

The Question of Political Philosophy

This is where the philosophy of man comes into play, because philosophy is like religion, only more slippery. Freedom had a religious meaning before 1776, because the people who settled the original 13 colonies wanted the freedom to practice their separate brands of Christianity as they saw fit, without the restrictions of the Church of England (Anglicans) or (God forbid) the Catholic Church. The founding fathers saw the religious philosophy of Rome as being too much of an influence on kings, and while they believed that allowing freedom to practice religion was an important way to keep the people complacent, they wanted to keep that influence of religion separate from the government of state. That state would be governed by a philosophy that would be new to everyone at that time.

They founded a Republic which was to be governed by the philosophy of a democratic union, where everyone had an equal say in how the government operated.[2] While that form of government maintained a strong affiliation with Christianity (in all denominations) until the 20th Century, it was not foreseen by the founding fathers that America would become such a large melting pot of humanity. That concept of equality was based on 13 states of equal peoples; British descendants and therefore Christian. The fact that religions of all kinds would later grow to have significant influence among the voters in the United States was not considered. Those growth numbers still make religions like Islam, Judaism and Hinduism, et al, and particularly those claiming no religious affiliation (atheists and agnostics, and pagan religions, etc.) still in the minority overall (maybe 15% at best), and the original design of equality was never designed to give the minority rule.

The concept designed a republic of like peoples being ruled by the majority will of those peoples, such that all were ruled equally, even if it made it a better rule for those in the majority. That lack of foresight, to plan for a freedom welcome mat attracting people from all walks of life to America (unless somehow it was planned all along), has led to the corrupted form of government that rules America now. Because of the American lead, every nation on the earth has also been corrupted, and Nostradamus made a specific point of pointing out the

---

2   Everyone in 1776 meant every white male land owner. Women, slaves, indentured servants and white males without land or title were understood, then, to not have any say in anything. Each state also had equal representation in the Senate.

United States, Great Britain and Russia as three of the most corrupt.

All three of those nations have at one time or another been called republics. Nostradamus wrote about the one time that Great Britain was a republic, which was after Oliver Cromwell overthrew Charles I. Charles I had abolished the Parliament for eleven years, which led to the rebellion which brought about his demise. With Cromwell at the head, never taking the title of King, Great Britain was a republic with parliamentary rule, under Cromwell as Lord Protector. That republic lasted almost five years, with no other republics in Great Britain since.

The United States of America was founded to be a republic, which in its most basic definition is simply a rule of the people, without a monarch. The "R" in U.S.S.R. was also used to state that the communists had formed a republic, but as we can see how seldom the word republic is used today, this philosophy of the rule of more than one is just another good idea gone bad.

The United States is more commonly referred to as a democracy, which most basically means rule by the people. However, under the doctrine of communism, where the people own everything in the state, it is hard to explain why the U.S.S.R. was never called a democracy. It is easier to call it a socialist state, especially since one of the "S" in U.S.S.R. stands for socialist. That word is more definitive of the political process the Soviets used to run their democratic state, where the rule was by the people; but, this then gets into the economic controls required to run a state as a pure democracy. All of this shows that the mind of man, where his philosophy originates, is greatly flawed and bound to find where the lack of forethought causes one change after another to evolve something intended into something believed to be what it originally was. This is what lawyers call loopholes.

The democratic process of the United States was modeled after the parliamentary rule of Great Britain, which makes sense since the colonists were all formerly British. This led them to believe that the President would act like a monarch, only on a more temporary basis, and the House and Senate would act like the Houses of Commons and Lords. Since the House of Lords was the parliamentary voice of the relatives of the King, they ruled over the varying districts of the British holdings as lords, dukes and the like. This made there be fewer of them than those chosen for the House of Commons. The parallel was drawn so that the Senate would align with the individual states, which had governors which acted as the American form of royalty. Since those early days of trying to mimic the British form of government, all of this has crumbled into a corrupt form of political favoritism, where the people have very little true representation.

In the West, we got significant training in how poorly the Soviets were running their political form of government. They would be caught red handed doing something contrary to what they said they were doing, but the Soviets would simply deny it and spread propaganda to the Soviet people about how the West was telling lies about them. Our form of reporting was equally propaganda, which caused most Americans to hate the word communist and especially Soviets. The truth is that the American government is just as adept in this form of denial and deception, purposefully misleading its people, because secrecy is the best way to usurp power. When this secrecy becomes obvious to the people, through police stings and newspaper investigative reporting, then the citizenry becomes moved enough to act against the liars and cheats. The tyrants of this world have polished and refined the practice of lying, denying it when caught and killing those who pose a real threat to the powers that be, by exposing dirty secrets.

I suggest you do some thorough work investigating just how much your voice has an impact with your congressmen and senators. Nostradamus wrote that the United States of America would become the greatest power on earth; but, this power will be abused and the true power will not be held by the people. Instead, a select clique of men and women will manipulate the nation's power for their own benefit. As much as elected representatives may appear to be nice honest people, you must realize that election to government connects them to this power and disconnects them from the common people they represent. As much as they will claim otherwise, once connected to this power these elected officials will vote to support this power clique, long before they will vote for something you believe needs to be done to the contrary. In short, power corrupts people.

The need for secrecy is to hide the fact that our government, which is ballyhooed as a democratic process based on a love of freedom, is more in line with a form of government that American and British propaganda publicly states democracies are against. Primarily this form of government is an oligarchy, which is a rule by a minority of people; but, equally disliked is said to be an autocracy, which is the rule of one. When an elected official, like a president, acts in ways that forces the majority to follow his demands, he has become the one who has all power. Traditionally, we call this form of government a dictatorship, where the rule is by a tyrant. America went to war against Saddam Hussein because he was said to be a tyrant with weapons of mass destruction. Remaining in Iraq after no such weapons have been found makes it appear to Iraqis that America is the one run by a tyrant, because opinion polls show the majority of Americas want America out of Iraq. The reason America does not withdraw from Iraq is one person has the power to run the country contrary to majority will. When that one person with power also caused unwarranted deaths, then that technically constitutes a tyrant.

This is what Nostradamus warned of coming and we saw classic examples of totalitarian tyrants ruling Europe during the period that led to World War II. In that period the United States was not immune to this excessive power given to one individual, as Franklin D. Roosevelt became the only president to be elected to four terms in office. Interestingly, one of the closest advisors to FDR was a man named Prescott Bush; and, he was the father of George H. W. Bush, grandfather to George W. Bush; and, he is known to have carried out secrete correspondence with the Nazis, while World War II was going on and America was in a state of war against Hitler. Clearly, all is not as it seems; and, Nostradamus wrote several exposing quatrains about the Bush connections to our government.

As far as an oligarchy is concerned, one has to look at how the political parties vie for control of the House and Senate. When both houses are controlled by a majority of one party and that party is also the party of the president, who appoints Supreme Court justices with the same party affiliations or philosophies, an oligarchy has been begun. This condition arose in 2000, when George W. Bush was elected president with a minority of the popular vote, while both houses became controlled by the Republican Party. The same condition has existed before, where Democrats ran the country; but, the one notable exception is that the elected presidents on those occasions carried a sizable majority of the general population. That rule of the minority was with greater common support; but, now there exists a nation which loudly opposes the direction the Republican Party is leading us, as dictated by the Republican President George W. Bush.

The main direction the majority disagrees with is the war in Iraq. The lies that were used to get the nation into that conflict have been exposed, showing the secrecy that was involved between the American and British oligarchies, to falsely lead the majority to support something that was not true. The occupation of Iraq and the continuing inability to control the violence there has increased the majority's complaints against continuing in this situation; but, the oligarchy of the Bush administration has refused to consider plans to withdraw and admit their wrongdoings. In a nation truly run by majority rule, Bush would immediately act to appease the majority, or he would face impeachment proceedings.

The Bush stance states that America is committed to installing a stable democracy in Iraq; but, this is not a viable form of government in the Middle East. The people there are not accustomed to being democratic; and, they obviously prefer a theocracy. The greatest fear that the Bush spokesmen have pointed out is leaving Iraq and having the new government become theocratic, or a government dominated by religion. The use of freedom as reason for continuing to act is nothing more than doubletalk. How can Iraqis be given freedom by a nation that remains an oppressor in their land?

These statements of fear of a theocracy are the core cause of the future that Nostradamus has predicted. It is the separation of church and state that has become so ingrained in the minds of Americans that American Christians are willing to accept more and more slaps, by entities against recognizing a connection between religious morals and law. The defeat of the defense for the Ten Commandments being publicly displayed in houses of law is not a protection of constitutional rights but another step in an oligarchic process to let the minority make the rules for the majority. As long as the majority sits back and allows these foundations of religious belief be kicked out from under the legal codes, the less the United States will ever have to fear becoming a theocracy. Still, the fears of theocracy are completely unfounded.

The stated fear of the government of Iraq becoming a theocracy, should American soldiers leave too soon, is because without Saddam Hussein's secular Sunni government controlling Iraq, the Shiite dominated government would become closely aligned with Iran and even possibly unify, to form a very formidable foe. The State of Israel is clearly a theocratic nation and the United States has no problem backing the Israelis and their form of government. We just don't want the theocratic nation of Iran to profit from our mistakes.

This becomes another example of the double-edged sword that Nostradamus wrote of, where the American claims of reasons, for a presence of power in the Middle East, are unraveled when the Muslims point out that they only want the same rights that America allows to its ally Israel. The feared theocracy is then better defined as one which puts religious blame on a godless society that uses covert actions to ensure its power standing in the world. In other words, theocracies see America as the great Satan.

The ultimate reason that the United States will seemingly blindly support its ally Israel has nothing to do with a strong love of Jews or their theocratic society. It has to do with the realization that a strong alliance with Israel keeps Middle Eastern oil within the grasp of the Western nations. Israel has become the greatest negotiation pawn for the United States, to ensure that it has open lanes to oil wealth. Clearly, if Israel was located anywhere else on the face of the earth, where nothing of natural resource value was found, the United States would most likely have a different approach to seeking Israel as an ally.

The Jews were given Palestine because by the end of World War II Middle Eastern oil was of much greater importance to a then highly mechanized west. This theft of land is the sole burr under the saddle that will continue to fester until the world has been destroyed. The hostilities between Arab Muslims and Israeli Jews will never go away, unless a true solution is found to remedy this problem. Nostradamus made this clear and the Bible does also.

If it was just a simple matter of giving the Palestinians back their land, a solution could easily be found. There are expansive areas of land in west Texas, New Mexico and Nevada that could be sold to anyone wishing to form a separate sovereign nation; and, nobody would care or be displaced. The United States would have the right to make such a sale, as long as the landowners were properly compensated and the people voted to allow it. The industrious Jews would then be able to make their new holy land become a Mecca of commerce and tourism; and, the problem of illegal immigration into the United States would be forever solved. As ridiculous as this option seems now, it is how both the Israelis and Palestinians can both be placated and cease the continuous wars in the Middle East. Anything that remotely considers the Jews staying put, under the name of Israel, will never work out. A real solution would address the stealing of Palestinian land and giving it away for nothing, admitting that an action like this is clearly illegal, by any law on the face of the earth.

The question that you have to bring yourself to ask is: am I fully aware of what kind of government I live in? To find this answer you have to sift through the hype and get down to the true definition of whatever form of government you think is best for your world. The chances are that you think your government is something it really isn't. You have to listen to your inner voice when it comes time to determine if you have put more faith in that government than you have in God and Christ. Which do you believe is more powerful?

The Question of Economics

In reference to the issue of Israel vs. Palestine, the reason a solution like selling Southwestern badlands to the Jews and giving Palestine back to the Arabs will likely never be sought brings us into the realm of understanding the economic roots of this future's cause. This is not an issue that will easily be defeated, as money is the drug that has the whole world addicted. Just as the Bible states, "The love of money is the root of all evil," the end of the world will be because of the evils that will have been produced in the name of money. We have been conditioned to call the love of money our economic necessities.

The economies of the world are a very tricky study these days. Long ago, when money was first coined from precious metals, most people did not have much money at all; and, this never halted the progress of mankind. The true value of a land was from what that land produced, in the form of crops, livestock and raw materials. The king owned the land, but the people were allowed to live on it and farm and ranch; and, the fruits of their labors were what they lived on. This was enough to afford most people some degree of normalcy, even comfort, after paying a portion of that production to the king. After all, what good is the land if no one works it?

Coined money was created as a simple way for someone who reaped no harvest to pay for what was needed. Soldiers, for example, had no product to trade for wine in the pubs, but they were paid in coins, which was legal tender. This form of simple economy lasted until the governments of the common man took the places of kings.

Metal coins were fairly easy to judge value, because they were basically made of gold or silver and the nations producing coins from precious metals knew how much metal equaled how much money. Of course this made carrying large quantities of money cumbersome and difficult to easily hide. This led to the creation of paper money, which was originally like a promissory note, promising the holder of the note the value stated on the paper in gold. In the United States and other nations around the world, these notes were considered to be valued, based on the gold standard. However, during World War II, Franklin Roosevelt decided that the United States was running short on gold and a recall of all paper money backed by gold was made, replacing those dollars with silver certificates. A dollar was then no longer backed by the gold standard.

During the Kennedy administration, John Kennedy proposed a return to the gold standard. His unfortunate murder forever left that possibility a lost dream; and, shortly after Kennedy was buried, newly minted silver quarters that bore Kennedy's image went into circulation; and, those coins were mostly copper with a silver coating. A fitting tribute to his foresight, by the very people who had him killed. Not long after that, the silver certificates were replaced by Federal Reserve notes. The Federal Reserve Act was something that was signed into law by Woodrow Wilson in 1913; but, there have been questions of its constitutionality, as it transfers power from Congress to an external entity, the Federal Reserve System. With Congress giving away its control over its right to make money, these Federal Reserve notes which are still circulating today are backed by no precious metals of any kind; and, there are complaints that copper pennies are worth more than a penny, making it a possibility that coin money will soon be obsolete, replaced by debit cards or credit cards.

It is very important for you to know that our economy is not based on a metal standard, as the true value behind a Federal Reserve note is you. In essence, you are allowed to spend as much as whatever your value is to the society; and, in most cases this is a greater sum than your income. America no longer can back its currency with bars of precious metals, so it holds its 300 million citizens as precious commodities, with which to stabilize the value of the U.S. dollar. In essence, you are a slave without knowing it; and, you don't know it because they pay you with I.O.U. notes, based on your own worth.

Perhaps you have read reports of some people in poor nations having an average per-capita income of something ridiculously low, like $65 (U.S.) a year. Imagine trying to survive on that little in the United States or Western Europe. It would seem impossible to do; but, the people in many poor nations do it yearly. It is the stuff that class separations are made of, such as "third world" versus "first world" economies.

These third world nations are still on the old style economy, where money is not as valuable as goods. Goods are the true necessities for life. The "first world" has the same necessities; but, our needs are supplemented by enormous wants and desires. These wants are created by our production of things, and we feel is our right to possess the things we make, regardless of the cost. Our government allows us to gain these things by increasing our income; but, these income increases cause the cost of goods to increase equally. This is inflation. The third world does not suffer from inflation like the first world does.

The poverty level in the United States is determined to be around $18,500 for a family of four.[3] The median income for a family of four in the United States (calendar year 2003, fiscal year 2006) was just over $65,000 a year, which was up 16% from the 1998 level (fiscal year 2001). This represents a five year average increase of 3.2%.[4] The average inflation rate since the year 2000 is listed at basically 3%, which matches the increased income. However, the increased income between 2005 and 2006, which was 3.7%, is offset by inflation rates over a 12-month period that averages 4.1%, particularly due to increased costs for energy related products.[5] As you can see, the higher income levels are tied to a higher cost of living, so basically most of us tread water in our economy. Those who don't just drown in a sea of debt or turn to crime and the housing system that is set up for supporting criminals that can't even succeed in that field (i.e.: prisons).

The one thing that keeps everyone from complaining too much is the ease with which we can all buy things that we cannot afford, through the invention called credit cards. Credit has been around a very long time; but, plastic credit with astronomical interest has become a growing disease in America. The average debt per credit card is $8,000; although the Federal Reserve's audit states that only 1 in 20 families actually owe $8,000 or more in credit card debt. When one realizes that many people have credit cards with lower than $8,000 credit limits, due to lower than average incomes, and wealthy people generally pay off their credit cards each month, the result is a much higher figure of average debt in the middle class than the Federal Reserve figure implies. American Credit Counselors reports that the average American household carries $19,000 in non-mortgage debt, with credit cards representing $7,500 of that figure and medical loans and student loans contributing to reach that total figure. They say that this figure is growing rapidly; but, the question now becomes: With inflation matching income and debt increasing significantly, how can it ever be repaid?

---

3   *Federal Register*, Vol. 69, No. 30, February 13, 2004, pp. 7336-7338. The 2004 HHS Poverty Guidelines, which states that figure for the 48 Contiguous States and D.C. Alaska and Hawaii are higher.
4   U.S Census Bureau
5   Inflation Rates for 2000 to present, InflationData.com, Current Inflation.

The answer is found on two levels. First, it is impossible for the debt that is owed (2 trillion dollars in America) to ever be fully repaid. If someone blew a whistle right this very second and said that all debt must be repaid, besides the probability that there is not enough money in the world to match the debt, only the rich would remain free, while everyone else would become a slave, indentured servant or thrown into debtor's prison. This leads to the second level of why debt has been allowed to get so high; and, that answer is the secret leaders of our economy want as many people as possible to be deeply in debt. People that owe money are more inclined to work as instructed. That work is the value of our monetary system; and to live in a first world society we have to do as we are told, once we get in too far. The alternative is impossible, because it is no longer possible to live off the land and $65 a year in the United States of America.

While this might not be deemed a "love of money", per se, it certainly is an addiction to money and the things that money buys. If you think that this is incorrect, then I highly recommend you pay off your debt as soon as possible and refuse to buy anything that you cannot afford to pay cash for. See if you don't get the shakes attempting to do this. The perception is it cannot be done; and, there are a lot of people who have a very dismal outlook for their future because they face years of nothing, to pay off the interest and principal of things already long gone. You have got to be prepared to face this kind of future, one way or another, because you must free yourself from this prison.

This state of debt is precisely what Nostradamus wrote of coming to the greatest nation on earth. The greatness of the United States is its perception of wealth, even though it has no gold to back up its currency. The greatness is its military and the people who keep it strong, along with its machines of war. Once this final war begins, the true value of America will be readily seen by the whole world, but particularly by Americans suddenly thrust into poverty conditions. Nostradamus makes it clear all debts will be impossible to pay off and they will be erased. When this happens all paper money will cease to have value. Our economy is already primed for such a failure. All we need, to cause it to come into being, is to have our leaders lead us into another attack of our land, one much greater and crippling than 9-1-1.

It is this lust for identifying with this greatness that America holds that keeps people in debt and poor; and, the industrious youth of the poor often have no choice but to see the military as a way to escape poverty and earn an honest living. Much is said about welfare mothers who do not work and simply have babies to get more and more government money to live on. But, the subsidized life of someone in the military is not much different than being on welfare. The subsidized things that are afforded to someone making the military a career allows them to live a comfortable middle class existence, when the income is in reality too low to create that condition alone. Our system of economy knows that the people have few options other than supporting the American way of life as it has become, with massive debt. However, it is this lifestyle that is leading the world to ruin.

The level of war that is predicted to be coming will be unlike any other level of war that anyone has ever seen before. The history of the United States in wars has been a profitable one, due to the increases in spending on industries that support the war machine. While wars like the Korean Conflict and the Vietnam War have historically related to more job opportunities and higher wages, the people that reap the most are the wealthy. Ask your parents if they remember World War II and the difficulties that a world war created then. People were asked to make huge sacrifices; and, rationing was the way of the day. Still, that history was related to a war that was fought in other areas of the world. None of the American infrastructure has as yet been seriously affected by bombs and rifle fire (the events of 9-1-1 excluded).

Nostradamus has predicted that the great nation of America will finally face this level of attack. When it does, nothing will continue to operate as it has before. Businesses will close; roads and bridges will be out, disrupting the flow of goods and supplies. The food sources will be contaminated and the cost of the basic necessities will become so high that only the wealthy can afford them. This outbreak of war will lead to a domino effect that will completely collapse of the world's economies, including the economy of the greatest nation on earth. The result of this class separation will be complete anarchy, where no one will be safe; but, all debts will be erased and all paper money will cease to have value.

If you want to know what to expect to come, then look at what happened when Hurricane Katrina hit the gulf coast states of Mississippi and Louisiana. No one wanted to lose everything. Everyone had previous experience with hurricanes and they assumed that the same result would take place on August 29, 2005. They were all wrong and I was one of them. The losses were devastating and many people counted on the government to come to the rescue. That did not happen, because Hurricane Katrina brought a result no one was prepared for. The lesson of Katrina is there will come a time once again, when the best laid plans of men will utterly fail, leaving masses of people distraught and homeless. The Bible tells of the signs which will precede this final war; and, Katrina was just one of the international signs that natural occurrences have brought, to show just how quickly life can change for large numbers of people.

If you think that you can protect what you own and all of your possessions, through the process of insurance or by living in some place thought to be safe, you will be proven wrong. The insurance disaster which resulted from the claims from Hurricane Katrina was an obvious sign that the common people of the United States are meaningless in the grand scheme of the wealthy. More than a year after Katrina struck; millions of people are still fighting for some form of insurance settlement or government loans and grants. All of this happens while people are living in cramped FEMA trailers, with no guarantees that another hurricane will not come and destroy what is left. The potential for earthquakes is just as strong in many places, with tornados, floods, heat waves, fires and volcano eruptions making every place in the United States vulnerable. Nostradamus is saying you can run, but you sure can't hide. Trying to hold onto "things," when you should be opening your eyes to the entrapment that you have been led into is the worst decision that you can make.

The most obvious view of money you have is that yours has been earned honestly; and, this makes it appear to be a good thing to keep around. Most people apply hard work attempting to get into a position of comfort; and, most people fully believe in the concept of capitalism and the laws of supply and demand. However, what is not as obvious to see, although commonly known by all, is the inevitable offshoots that money creates. Those offshoots are the crimes that are driven by a lust for wealth; and, these offshoots are both random (small time) and organized (big time).

There isn't a commandment passed down to Moses by God that isn't broken over the love of money, in one way or another; but, organized crime shows its lack of moral guidance in the ways that it will addict people to drugs (many dying from these drugs in multiple ways), it will imprison women into forced prostitution, it will provide places for legal and illegal gambling and it will murder at will, all to maintain its position as a big business of wealth. Every one of us that falls prey to these vices is more willing to break a commandment to find the money to support those addictions. As long as people will turn their backs on the criminal lusts for wealth, crime will always exist. It would be easier to do away with money altogether than it would be to cease organized crime from existing.

The typical way we have been taught to do away with increasing crime is through increasing laws but less law enforcement. The measure of this success is not found in the swelling of prison populations, as the prison system is like the "minor leagues" of big business crime. When prisoners usually get out of a prison they are hardened and seasoned veterans that go right back to crime, simply because it is nearly impossible to earn a good honest wage with a criminal record. The prison system is not the answer, as it will do nothing to eliminate crime. It is the mindset that teaches us to believe that crime can be attacked in this manner which shows us just how the education system is equally flawed.

The Question of Education

The laws of our societies are so complex that it requires a college degree to fully understand them all; and, this can only be done with specializations in the different divisions of civil and criminal law. The education system that learns the laws and teaches them to students also teaches those students how to use loopholes to turn the law into a defense of a criminal. Success is not measured in how well right and wrong is defended. Instead, it is measured in the amount of money a lawyer makes in a law practice. When a lawyer has become known for his abilities to manipulate the law, through a few sensational cases that make the headlines, this lawyer is often sought out by the organized crime bosses. When someone is obviously guilty and in need of a good loophole finding, if not creating lawyer, those lawyers can name their price. In essence, our educational system acts to help keep crime strongly alive.

In the days of Nostradamus there were universities, some of which still exist today, with prestigious names. Nostradamus attended a couple of universities and acquired degrees and knowledge. Still, Nostradamus had to be able to afford to go to a university, which is just as it is today. Not just anyone was allowed into universities then; and, this practice of restricting education from many people somewhat remains today.

In the creation of the New World settlements in America, schooling was so important that schools were given equal land rights, as were churches. Those were public schools, which were designed to teach the youth the basic skills of reading and writing, with some ability to count correctly. Only the best of those students were able to find acceptance in the higher institutes of education; and, those higher education institutions were not free to attend. While we can say that this structure is still in place today, it really is much different now.

First of all, the public schools are so overworked that the teachers often have minimal qualifications as teachers. Many inner city schools simply pass students through the grades just to graduate them and create an empty desk for a new student. Meanwhile, with the basic scholastic abilities lowered, there have grown a great number of colleges and universities that are not designed to take only the best students. Many seem designed to take just about everyone, to make it appear that everyone can obtain an education; but, the reality is that higher education is now a pure profit business.

Even the most prestigious universities will deny students from enrolling for their courses, due to poor high school scores; but, while they will accept some prospective students, they will then turn around and allow someone with gifted athletic skills to enroll and play a sport, who otherwise would never be admitted. The reason is college athletics brings in big money to the schools, especially when a popular athlete is helping the team win and fill stadium seats, attracting television revenues.

It really doesn't matter if the NCAA punishes a school for having violated the admission standards by playing a student with failing grades, because the punishment is doled out after the season is over. Two NFL star players (James Brooks – Auburn University [6 years] and Dexter Manley – Oklahoma State University [4 years]) went to major universities, playing at least four years each; and, when their NFL careers had ended, both claimed bankruptcy because they were bilked of their fortunes by agents who took advantage of their inability to read. How can anyone attend college for four years and be illiterate? The answer is the money involved in the educational process has entirely changed the focus of why universities exist.

It used to be said that the best opportunity for financial success came with a college education. This was after our parents were able to find 30-40 year careers, with some advancement, from a high school diploma or a 2-year technical school degree. That mindset no longer applies, as many more people are making the investment of going to a college or university for four years and coming out to find

401

long lists of degreed applicants searching for entry level positions. Meanwhile, someone – parents or students – have incurred a very sizable debt for that education (scholarships excluded). This shows that education is not a guarantee for success; and, it never was designed to be that.

The economic structure that exists is a classic pyramid scheme where for each one that reaches the top (the C.E.O.) there are thousands below that level, with increasing numbers occupying each level below. This has led to the recent trend in college graduates to change jobs frequently, in order to more rapidly climb the income ladder. Taking an entry level position is rarely going to guarantee any form of advancement to a higher level (and thus greater paying) job, such that after a year or two these young impatient workers feel the need to pay off their education debt by seeking positions with higher earnings. They seem to have found some success finding these, not because they have a college degree (although one of the pre-requisites may make this mandatory), but because they have actual work experience in that field.

Most companies looking for mid-level managers are looking for people with 2-5 years of experience, not an advanced degree in some field of education. This is because that low level of experience and education will allow them to hire people willing to do the work available for less than a more experienced worker, one who is probably unhappy and still looking for more money. The only true way that a college degree will directly help someone make that career field pay is by becoming basically a self-employed entity, as a consultant or by starting one's own business.

The professions which are the most successful in repaying all costs incurred for becoming educated are those that have the highest restrictions for admission. Doctors must go to medical school and lawyers must go to law school. Architects and engineers also must pass rigorous course loads in the mathematics of physics and calculus, which are usually taught at schools which specialize in those fields. Another successful area that can bring some success is related to the sciences, including biology, archeology, psychology and others; but, these require advanced degree work, with doctorates bringing the most financial success, but bachelor's being worthless as far as career stability is concerned.

If you decide to go to college to major in one of the humanities, then forget about quickly paying off that student loan. Even with the most advanced degrees in such disciplines as literature, history or philosophy, about the most you can ever expect to become is a teacher or professor. For a specific degree in art, film or music, then some can find amazing success; but, these are few, compared to the whole. This is where the education process fails mankind, as it is heavily leaned towards financial rewards, rather than towards developing the human aspect of life.

During the days of Nostradamus the Church was as powerful as the kings of countries. Much of the educational pursuit was designed towards teaching religion, which included studies of the classic philosophers of Christian thought. Schools which taught this were developing young students who would leave school with a purpose which understood that God needed to be respected, no matter how much position and influence the students gained in life. Purposes like that have long since vanished, especially when schools funded by public dollars (i.e.: state universities) have had to become detached from favoring any one form of religion in their classrooms. Separation of church and state has become the separation of Christianity from any university seeking federal dollars.

In these modern times there have been colleges and universities which have been founded by religions, specifically for the purpose of continuing this blending of moral fabric into the mental development of their graduates. However, a recent trend has been for these universities and colleges to sever their relationships with the religions that created them. The reason is politics. The religions want to have a voice in the courses offered (creationism or intelligent design); or, some may even desire some influence in making certain coursework, for learning the dogma of that religion, mandatory for entering freshmen classes. The boards of these institutions of higher learning have found that is too limiting and unattractive to prospective students, and most have broken their relationships with the parent religion.

Once again the reason boils down to power and control, for the purpose of making education a business that is purely focused on net profit figures. For all intent and purposes, Christianity has become void in most colleges or universities in the United States (other than seminaries). Even the schools that offer degrees in religious studies have begun to focus solely on such neutral philosophical religions as Buddhism, rather than offering programs that focus on Christianity. Christianity is only provided in the colleges that still affiliate with a particular religion (Catholics, Baptists, Methodists, etc.).

In my efforts to promote knowledge and awareness of Nostradamus, I have

403

approached schools about how I could gain an advanced degree in philosophy in this area. As far as I can see, logic is the key educational test of my theories; and, logic is a division of philosophy. However, besides Nostradamus being seen as a medieval sorcerer and believer of such disproven medical procedures as using leeches to cleanse wounds (oh wait – they still do use that medically today), they are less concerned with the topic of Nostradamus than they are uneasy with Nostradamus being called a prophet of Jesus Christ. I have scared several deans of graduate studies, in both philosophy and religious studies, at state universities, with my questions of how I can gain the recognition of academia. No one so far has been able to offer a viable recommendation for me to pursue.

The prospect of Christianity being taught in schools is frightening to administrators who could lose many state and federal dollars for not keeping religion separate from education. It is not about having the masses educated; it is about sending students out into the real world with a sizable debt around their necks. The educational process is not concerned with prophecy, or anything that would cause schools to churn out responsible adults that know the true sins of our society. The educational process has to be in synch with the other branches of secret control, for that secret control to continue on as it has. The educational process must create the proper mindset for those who do not enter the military first.

You have to realize that a total population consisting of well-educated people, where everyone is wealthy because of having been educated, is impossible. Someone will always have to run the offices for doctors and lawyers, carry the lumber and mortar for architects, and do all of the menial labors that support the comforts of the wealthy. If everyone were well-educated, then well-educated people would be serving food in restaurants and picking fruit off trees, for next to nothing. This would not be as bad as it first seems, if every one of these highly educated people also had religious values that recognized the true value of each person's work and labor. This is what is missing in our society; and, our attitudes of superiority come from being educated and believing that education elevates us above others. We have come to the false impression that much of the dirty work that needs to be done is well beneath us.

The success of the wealthy depends on a very large middle class and a large-enough-to-still-manage lower class. The middle class is further layered, with upper and lower levels, but basically these people are those most likely to sell their souls for an opportunity to advance. They do this (sell souls) by taking advantage of someone below them, seeing this as the way up the ladder. The lower middle class and the lower class are never satisfied. They are always behind on bills and always wanting more than they can afford. Education only helps one understand that the deck is stacked against everyone who does not forget about caring for the next guy and do what it takes to make it rich. Before there is any chance of improving one's social status, one has to pay in advance for an education that may or may not justify the debt that instantly comes with it.

A Quick Summation of Conceptual Dependency

With all of this said, it becomes important for you to come to terms with everything I have just presented to you. Some people who are very close to me, who are very in-tuned to what I am saying Nostradamus has predicted, can clearly see it moving toward that end each day on the television news. Still, knowing of this end can be just like it is with someone with an addiction, where they know some bad end is coming if they don't act to change their ways. Knowing is not enough for them to bring themselves to quit what they are doing and save themselves. These people I love are not drug addicts or cigarette smokers; they are addicted to the only lifestyle they have ever known. It just so happens that they have based much of their lives, to this point, on honestly pursuing the American dream, by working hard to establish some position of wealth. This, by itself, is not the cause of the problem that will lead to the end of mankind.

I would like to believe that there is some way to keep the foundations of economics, education and the democratic process. After all, in mankind's most basic cultures these elements exist and carry great importance. But, as long as money exists in the world there will be those who will always scheme to get more than others. God has a way of exposing schemers, but Satan has a way of making those schemers try to involve those who have uncovered their schemes. The situation which exists now, believe it or not, is that we all have been tricked into believing in a dream, losing touch with our religious core.

Money brings power, and with power in one's control one can easily sway the masses to choose the most powerful as the leader. This is the problem with party politics. Money is at the root of every campaign, and the people with that money are the true powers behind the candidates. When you begin to trust that system, by lending your money and support behind one person who represents the chosen one for a party, you are placing your soul in that person's hands.

405

Everyone then becomes dependant on the benevolence of the leader. Without a foundation of moral principles instilled in everyone, the leader most probably will not lead for the good of the whole. Without a church completely dedicated to instilling those principles in the leader, there will not be a church to instill them in the people. We are at that point now, and unless there is a major change in the individuals of the populations of the world, things will get worse, not better. Nostradamus saw no recovery from the way we are headed, so please seriously review what I have stated in the conceptual areas of freedom, political philosophy, economics and education. You must begin to evaluate yourself as to how strongly you value each and how much blind faith you put in man, rather than God. If you find yourself sacrificing your moral values in any way, just to advance yourself in this material world, you need to make changes quickly.

The Key to Saving the World is Change

I have now given you reasons to consider that show all is not as it may seem. Nostradamus has made it clear to me the systems we now adhere to so strongly will collapse, and this will be global in nature. The story the Letter to Henry II tells is one which has a direct connection to the history that has led us to this moment in time. The future that his story tells does not veer off into some wild direction that is not plausible to consider. At this point in time, his predictions made 450 years ago are not only possible, but they are highly probable.

The events of September 11, 2001 were very vividly written of by Nostradamus, and those quatrains (at least eight) were to point to the one most specific event that will initiate a rapid series of events (relatively speaking), leading to this end. He then wrote of the retribution that would take the West, led by the United States, into Afghanistan. He also wrote of the secret agreement between President George W. Bush and British Prime Minister Tony Blair, to take this retribution into Iraq.

The condition in Iraq has only worsened over the past two years, causing some authorities to see a sectarian civil war coming. If those predictions are correct, this will make it impossible for Western troops to control the violence against minority Iraqis and American soldiers. Meanwhile, the ongoing hostilities between Israel and the Palestinians, with Hamas and Hezbollah continuing the struggle to return stolen land to its rightful owners, and the other Arab states voicing their support of that effort, has led to a new outburst of warfare that once again gives the Middle East the potential of sparking a greater war effort.

There have been a steady series of wars in this region, for the same purpose, for several decades. All of this is supporting Nostradamus' claims that the Muslims are unifying with other nations which will support their hatred of Jews and Christians, giving them the confidence to reject the objective of talks of peace. There are many people who feel the world is on the verge of global war, and Nostradamus confirms these fears.

Besides the message of *The Prophecies* foretelling of the conditions which exist today, there are many other prophecies which also tell of the same end coming, relating to Israel and her enemies. The Bible prophecies, particularly Daniel, Ezekiel, Isaiah and Jeremiah, as well as the host of "minor prophets", all repeatedly warned of the destruction of Judah and Israel coming. They actually wrote in terms which can be applied to today's circumstances, just as well as they applied to the first destruction and captivity, before Jesus Christ was born.

Still, in another part of the world the Mayan calendar has similarly predicted problems leading to the return of God and complete devastation. This devastation can actually be timed to the year 2012, which makes today's headlines show nothing to counter that prediction. Nostradamus listed quite specific astrological timing clues that go beyond that 2012 date, but not by much. Nostradamus also referred to the prophecy of Saint Malachy, who named all of the popes until the end of the line. We are now only one pope away from that end. He also referenced in the quatrains the vision that occurred in Fatima, Portugal, where the Virgin Mary showed three peasant girls the pain and suffering that would come from losing religion in the world. The writing is on the wall, so to speak; and, it is all from God, warning us to change our direction or face annihilation.

With so much prophecy telling us that now is an important time to realize, the only positive approach can be from also realizing that the purpose of prophecy is to save us, rather than simply to tell us that we have no chance of survival. God is all-knowing and all-powerful, so no reason can show that prophecy is God's way of proving these abilities. Christ is all-loving and as the Son of God, His extension, prophecy can only have the purpose of saving the souls Christ loves. With this purpose understood, then looking seriously at what Nostradamus offered us, as from the mouth of Jesus Christ, has to become a motivator to act as instructed.

As many times as I have told the story of Nostradamus to others, I have consistently found the same response. People feel too small to do anything to correct the problems that have grown to such heights. Believing that they can have no effect on a global scale, they prefer to walk away from the message of warning and pretend it does not exist. This is precisely what Jeremiah found, when he stood on the steps of the temple and preached that Israel and Judah must return to honoring God or be destroyed. They ignored the warning, because it was easier to do nothing than try to do something and be cast down as a rebel. This "head in the sand" mentality is what brought about their destruction, and that same end awaits us, if we take the same approach.

Admittedly, the aspect of change is daunting. For as much as the axiom, "the only thing that is constant is change" is stated, change is the greatest dread of most people. In consulting, particularly in change management consulting, the rule for making something which no longer works better is to identify the problems first. Once the problems are identified, plans can be set in place to eliminate them. This same rule applies as the first step in the 12-step programs established for the defeat of an addiction, like alcoholism. The first step is always to admit an addiction. In both cases, if the admission that a problem exists is not done first, there is little chance of recovery. That recovery can only come through recognizing a real need for change.

I have identified some of the greater problems that exist today, particularly in America and the Christian West, but also for the whole world. They are the easy ones to identify: war, poverty, and crime, and these problems threaten us in some way, both economically and socially. Nostradamus has identified some of the problems which are less obvious. A growing number of people think these problems really do exist, but because they are not obvious, they just cannot prove them. These problems are the conspiracies which are theorized, involving the true power brokers of the world. This true power is held by those who act behind the scenes, controlling the puppets which act as our leaders. These behind the scene puppeteers are masters of the art of secrecy and denial. They cause the problems of corruption which are more concretely known – the elements of crime and war – while promoting the more nebulous conceptual problems, which are their calls for our support for the leaders, especially in difficult times. This is the corruption of such positive beliefs in patriotism, loyalty, national pride, even calling on the name of God for support of evil actions.

These problems, concrete and nebulous, appear to be so great in size that little can be effectively done to formulate a plan to eliminate them. Individually, we are led to believe that we have no real voice that matters. For the most part, people are influenced to be confused intellectually, believing they are not empowered enough to offer solutions to the problems. This confusion is maintained and backed up by piles and piles of meaningless data and statistics, making it appear that someone smarter than we has a real solution. Add to this the aspect of actual effort being put forth, which requires thought in great depth, and few people have the motivation or desire to come up with a solution.

We like the idea of democracy and the opportunity it promises. Of course, most heroine junkies and alcoholics like the idea of getting high and escaping the responsibilities of their addictions, too. We believe the rule of the people is in place, when an oligarchy is leading us into submissive slavery. It does not matter if we think we are immune, because our life feels good; it's just others who have problems. This attitude is the problem. We must all lay down the crutches of excuses and take the first step towards admitting that a problem exists, knowing that it must be eliminated. Following that we all must take some step of action, to confirm we are not just talking a good game.

You cannot be expected to overthrow the government and bring peace to the world by yourself. This is not where you must look for change to take place. The only person on this planet who you control is yourself, and that is where the change must take place. You are quite aware that force has the least effect on making you change, which I'm sure has been mandated upon you at some time in the past, much to your chagrin. You resisted this kind of change in the past, in one way or another. You either flatly refused to be told what to do (accepting the consequences) or you complied, but without your heart into the change. This mechanical type of compliance means, inside you are hoping and waiting for the changes to fail, returning things back to the warm fuzzy way things used to be. All of this means that you cannot force yourself to change; you must want to change.

One of the mainstays in the publishing industry is the latest diet book. You name the methods; people will always flock to the latest lesson in losing weight. Now, common sense says if one book was successful and everyone lost weight then there is no need for another book on the subject to ever be written. The reason diets fail and new books are needed to offer the easiest way to lose weight is because people always try to make diet changes through will-power and not desire. Will-power is a force, making one comply to change, and deep down inside, the people who fail in their diets fail because they still desire food more than weight loss. When one realizes weight control is simply a matter of a combination of metabolism, exercise and eating the foods that best benefit the body, in moderation, it is easy to lose weight. You just first have to desire to follow that regimen.

Similarly, you must desire to change your focus on how you lead your life, and the motivation for desiring that change is knowing, when your life on earth will end, your soul will be held accountable for how you finished your life. The meaning here is that we each have our own Judgment Day, when we are evaluated on how well we honored God by bringing peace and love into the lives of others. The only way to ensure you will be judged fit to go to Heaven, being one with God and Christ, is to evaluate your life before God evaluates it for you. Think of this just as you would if your doctor told you that you must evaluate your eating habits and go on a diet, or you will die of some complication.

You have to determine just how many addictions you have, and a good exercise to determine this is asking yourself what would make your life miserable to go without. Write your thoughts down, and once you have made that list, imagine you were just warned to immediately head to an emergency shelter because a major hurricane was nearing. Other than the necessities - one week's worth of clothes and simple dry and canned food, taken in one car with a full tank of gas – what steps would you take to protect the items on your list?

Then, imagine that you left that shelter one week later, only to find your home and everything in and around it completely gone. Not just damaged and still recognizable as your home, but swept away with nothing but a slab foundation left behind. This condition would not describe just your house, but all in the neighborhood and those 100 miles beyond as well. Imagine all forms of communication were lost, bridges were washed out, banks were unable to open, and gas stations were unable to operate due to the lack of power. Imagine it is during the middle of the summer (hurricane season) and the temperatures hover near 95 degrees, with high humidity. Take your list and see how well those things you thought were important would help your survival.

If you think you may be immune from the effects of a hurricane, then substitute one of the following: widespread wildfires destroying everything along a path to your house, a dam break up-river caused by heavy rains affecting your house, increased seismic activity leading to predictions of volcanic eruption or earthquake near your house, the uncontrollable approach of disease (bird flu or plague) with no known cure, or an outbreak of war or anarchy spreading in your direction including the use of weapons of mass destruction. You pick this imaginary emergency where all that you can take with you is that which can fit snugly in one car. What would you try to save?

Hopefully, this exercise will open your eyes to what is truly most important, which are the other living beings who are close to you, including pets. Once you have identified the fact that your survival would depend on the mutual support that a group of people would bring, you have to ask yourself how well you relate with other people.

If you have family members with you, are you prepared to spend as much time as necessary to protect them? Are any of them very young or elderly, disabled or sick? You have to ask yourself who in the neighborhood will you help and which neighbors will be willing to help you? Have you become a member of a local church where you could seek shelter and help others while being helped in return? Would you be more concerned for your own safety, so much that you would pass by stranded people, leaving them to find their own way to safety? Or, would you try to help strangers along the way?

Once you have asked yourself these questions, write down the names of all of the people you know who would try to help you and your family survive. The sad reality is that too many people these days will not know more than a handful of people nearby who would feel that close to them. This is one area that has just been identified as being in need of change.

When you can create a list of names that is so long that it has hundreds of people named, all truly being friends and family, then you have a real chance for survival. You could begin to meet with these people now, in groups, and plan responsibilities for everyone, should such an emergency arise. With such pre-planning, those closest to you would be prepared to act, so that once the danger had passed there would be a real network of community to begin a true recovery from such a disaster. Everyone would be counted on to work together to help each other. You will then be without a dependence on others to come and rescue you. This is the true essence of what being Christian means. If your list is not this long, then you are not acting truly Christian, regardless of what religion you may claim to support.

This brings you to the point of facing your own faults, towards being truly

Christian. Nostradamus made it clear that accepting his message means the acceptance of Jesus Christ as the Son of God. The books of the New Testament are written to show the actions of Christ, which proved to the apostles and increasingly many others that Christ was the promised Messiah. In those books it is stated that Christ said there is no other way to salvation than through accepting that fact; but, the apostles did not simply believe Jesus was the Son of God. They acted as commanded by Christ, and they acted willingly. All of them practiced the religion of Judaism, making them all Jews, but they were Christians by acting as Christ wished. In your community there can be any number of people of other religions and faiths around, but if you do not count these on your list of family and friends, because they are not considered to be Christians, then you are not acting Christian.

Christ spoke to anyone who would listen and there came an increasing number of Gentiles, especially when the apostles took the message of Christ to the world. Christ was not attempting to get people to convert to a specific religion. He was teaching people how to live together in peace, honoring God by following His Laws. If it makes one more able to treat others with love and understanding, acceptance and forgiveness, if they take the Holy Sacraments of a Christian religion, then that is all well and good. However, it is not a requirement that Jews convert to Christianity and the same goes for anyone of any other religion. Christianity is a way of life, not a club membership.

As long as someone accepts that Jesus Christ was the human form of God, as seen by the miracles that He is known for, and this someone can then act as Christ taught the apostles to act towards others, then this someone can adhere to any religious dogma and still be Christian. Nostradamus wrote in one quatrain that all religions which respect the one God are good. This means none are closer to God than the other; and, in *The Revelation of John*, Christ's spirit sent a message to the seven churches, not just one. This means the true essence of being Christian (i.e.: good) is possible no matter what good religious rituals of dogma you perform, to remind you to be good. If you are truly a Christian, then you will spread this message of goodness to others, keeping in mind that spreading this message is not only done by words, but by deeds.

If you want others to become Christians, then simply act Christian. When someone asks why you are so nice, trying to get down to your ultimate motivation for acting so good all the time, then simply tell them that it is the way of

Jesus Christ. Your actions will speak much louder than your words, becoming much more convincing.

In the world where we now live, the one which is headed toward doom, there are many who would take advantage of someone acting truly Christian. This is because so many of the people of the world are so far from acting Christian that they see a true Christian as someone who is weak. This is what keeps most Christians from fully demonstrating their faith; as they do not want to be taken advantage of. This makes them hide their faith, until surrounded by other Christians on Sunday morning.

When Christ told those who questioned what to do when someone strikes another on the face, since Jesus preached peace and forgiveness, He said the Christian response would be to turn the other cheek. For someone to have people mistreat him or her because of acting Christian, it is wrong to stop acting Christian when one finds out that he or she has just been abused by a non-Christian. To refrain from acting like a non-Christian, especially in times like these (when being struck) is most definitely not a sign of weakness. To continue to act Christian and offer the other cheek is to show a true sign of strength, one that comes from an inner calm and from being connected to the spirit of Jesus Christ. A weak person will stop being Christian and strike back, thus instantly becoming non-Christian. You cannot force yourself to behave in this manner, because you are human and our natural instincts are just like those of animals. When struck we want to strike back or run, but true inner peace is stronger than that natural urge, when we desire to be Christian.

It is this reaction to actions that has the world in the current position it is now. The Muslims, with Osama bin Laden as their spokesman, have claimed that the events of September 11, 2001 were in retribution for American actions against Muslims in the Middle East. In particular, he cited the American support of Israel and their hostilities against Palestinians as reason for this retribution. Those acts were certainly not Christian, but then neither were the acts since committed against the people of Afghanistan and Iraq. The actions of the Muslims, by the use of retribution (not turning the other cheek) are not Christian acts either.

Those acts of retribution are just more swings of the pendulum, where one cheek strike becomes cause for one in return. Instead of peace being achieved, where the strongest striker wins and the weaker one submits to forced humility,

413

this trading of blows will only lead to greater and greater strikes of retribution, until no one is left standing to strike again. The only chance for peace will come when a truly Christian side refuses to strike back, leaving the other side to strike at will.

In the 1960s, America was involved in an escalating exchange of blows with the North Vietnamese, where an increasing number of American boys returned home in body bags or severely wounded from those strikes. One American was drafted to serve his country during that war, at a time when he was reaching his peak in athletic ability. This American was the boxer Cassius Clay who, citing his devotion to the religion of Islam refused to serve his country. In this refusal, Clay claimed to be a conscientious objector, meaning his religious beliefs forbid him from going to war. Under his new Muslim name of Mohammed Ali, he was stripped of his license to box and forced to go through legal proceedings for five years.

This was being struck once (a racially biased draft notice) and refusing to strike back (claiming objector status), allowing the other cheek to be struck (unable to box in his prime, while defending his rights to adhere to his religious principles in court). Even though Mohammed Ali is Muslim, he acted Christian (regardless of any underlying political games that may have been played) and his Christian act was eventually vindicated when the anti-war movement became so strong that America ended its war in Vietnam and Ali regained his title as heavyweight champion of the world. You have to have this same commitment to Christian convictions now, regardless of the consequences that may be used against you. If you do not have this conviction, you will be forced to surrender your religious principles.

Of course this example shows a test of faith, and tests of faith have to be expected. A strong show of faith can often bring about persecution by those who have no faith and fear those who do. It is the resistance to those attacks which will yield the greatest rewards, just as shown by Mohammed Ali. However, the greatest story of faith is told in the Bible, in the Book of Daniel, and his story tells of the test of faith demonstrated by Shadrach, Meshach and Abednego.[6] This is how you have to change, so you can have just as much faith in God as

---

6   I personally think this is the strongest story of faith told by Daniel, although some may feel stronger about the story of Daniel in the lion's den. Either way, the same point is made.

those three men had.

The story tells that King Nebuchadnezzar had ordered everyone in Babel to eat the foods of the festival, but some of those foods were unclean to the Jews. The Jews were in captivity in Babylon, and the Babylonians might not have known about the Jewish eating habits; but, after the order was given several of Daniel's men refused to comply with the king's command. Daniel did his best to influence the king to respect his people's compliance to their religion and not have them follow those commands; but, after some time of delay, the king demanded that everyone comply with his order, including the Jews. Shadrach, Meshach and Abednego still refused to eat the unclean meat which caused the king to sentence them to burn in the furnace.

Now, persecution of this nature seems harsh for such a small crime. It would have been easy for those three men to just eat a small bite of the unclean meat, just to save their lives, and this is how so many people would react today. It is easier to give in to evil, than it is to stand up for one's principles. In the story, those three men refused to bend and were put into the furnace, which was fired to ten times the greatest temperature it had reached before. In the end, all three walked out without a singe on their clothes or hair, and the lesson of this story is how protective a full commitment to one's faith in God will be.

Of course there are those non-Christians who scoff at stories like this, pointing out that the Bible has many stories of unbelievable (beyond the laws of physics) acts taking place, which cannot be proven. Those skeptics point out that no remains of this furnace have been found, to confirm that this story ever actually took place. This is doubt and doubt is what weakens one's faith in God. The story cannot be looked at solely as a story of an actual happening, in order to get its full effect. You have to look at this story by the symbolism of the words, because this directly relates to where you are in your life now.

The story of Shadrach, Meshach and Abednego shows them refusing to consume the food of foreigners. The symbolism of this is that the king's orders asked them to partake of a religious philosophy that celebrated a lesser god than the one God of the Jews. They refused to bite into that knowledge, which would symbolize acceptance of that way of life, had they complied. The three did not comply because it was forbidden by the first commandment - thou shalt have no other gods before me. It was also was forbidden by the second commandment, where worship to idols (for lesser gods) was part of the festival of the Babylonians.

415

They refused to consume a philosophy that was not holy, and this symbolism of eating is also seen in the ritual that many Christians regularly partake in, when they take the Sacraments.

When Christ told the disciples at the last supper to take and eat the unleavened bread, He was asking them to symbolically consume the philosophies He had taught them all. The unleavened bread is in itself a purposeful symbolism, at Passover, being bread made without yeast. It is mandatory for Jews to eat unleavened bread during the Feast of Passover, because the lack of yeast symbolizes the lack of sinful pride or hypocrisy. The lessons which Christ taught His apostles were certainly free and clear of boast and contradiction, thus His teachings were the pure philosophy of God, with nothing added to enhance the basic facts. By taking and eating this bread, Christ was instructing the apostles to partake of the knowledge of His physical manifestation on earth and asking them to reconstruct the times of His life, by each writing accurately, without sinful pride or hypocrisy, of their personal experiences with Christ, in remembrance of that holy life. The unleavened property is to not embellish their memories, making the books of the New Testament unquestionably true.

This command of Jesus Christ to the apostles is then transferred to the Christians who repeat this symbolic event when they eat the communion wafer. This is the symbolic act of having consumed the knowledge of Christ, knowing the New Testament books of the Bible and how to act Christian. This is where the books written by the apostles represent them fulfilling their promise, pledged by their eating the bread and drinking the wine at the last supper. They each put down their knowledge of Jesus Christ for others to know.

Still, the act of knowing is only on an intellectual level, which is why Christ then followed the request to eat with the request to drink the wine. The wine is symbolic of the blood of Christ, as the new covenant, or agreement that Christ is God's Son and holy. The old covenant was between God and Moses with the Ten Commandments being handed down to the Hebrew people to follow. The new covenant of Christ includes the approval of the symbolic act of baptism, when Christ went to John the Baptist to be baptized. The symbolism of wine, being fluid like the water of baptism, shows the symbolic nature of water, with the color purple symbolizing the royalty of Christ the King. This water symbolism is one of emotion, such that what is then consumed is emotion of the spirit of Christ, as the Son of God. This takes the knowledge of Christ the man and effuses that knowledge of mind with the spirit of the heart. This act can only follow the basic acceptance of the knowledge that has previously been consumed, symbolized by the bread. The two symbolic acts together then connect the mind (body) with the heart (blood). With Christ being accepted within each person taking the Sacraments, the symbolic actions strengthen faith in the individual, to believe in the Word which is the body of Christ in the New Testament.

When you look at this symbolism this way, you see that the story of Shadrach, Meshach and Abednego is more than a refusal to eat pork. They refused to perform any act that would honor another god before theirs, as agreed upon in the covenant between the Israelites and God. The furnace then represents the persecution that will inevitably come to those of strong faith, because Satan wants us all to see a sacrifice of faith as just a small thing, like having a small taste of pork to "save our lives." We cannot bend our moral principles to save life on earth. This is the trick which will not only endanger life on the physical plane, but more importantly will endanger the life which exists beyond death, which is that of our souls.

The heat the furnace created was symbolic of the pressures which other people place on the faithful, but when one is filled with the spirit of God, fire has no effect on spirit. The coming out of the furnace unscathed is symbolic of the protection which will be afforded to all of us who faithfully resist the temptations and persecutions of the faithless. While the bodies may burn away, the soul is the spirit form that will be completely unharmed. You have to realize that you must act to change, to strengthen your commitment to protect your soul above all else. Faith will be returned tenfold if you convince yourself Nostradamus wrote the Word of Christ to save you, and to be saved you must act as a Christian, unwavering in your convictions to faith in God.

It is much easier for you to tell yourself to make this change in your life, than it is to for you to actually stand by those convictions. Very few people are able to act truly Christian, which is why we stand on the verge of ruin. Look at that list of things you first thought were important. How many were representative of the material wealth you enjoy? Would you fear stopping to help a stranded motorist trying to flee to safety? Does your list of important people exclude people who you have been taught to dislike, even hate, because they are in one way or another different from you? You must begin to realize all your shortcomings and flaws of reasoning now, so you can begin to make real changes

417

in the way you approach life. This is the most important step you can take, if you want to help the world avoid this predicted end.

The only person you can change is yourself. When you make that commitment and make yourself committed to bringing peace and love into the world which immediately surrounds you, you will find that others will respond in kind. You should not be afraid to tell others about your desires to change and why. This will help others to begin to change just like you, but you must remember you cannot change them. They must come to their own decision to change, just like you did.

If someone rejects your reasons for acting Christian, you cannot fear that rejection. Fear responds with negative actions, such as anger and weakness. Just as Shadrach, Meshach and Abednego were willing to walk in that furnace, you must be willing to smile at rejection. When you master this desire to become truly heart-centered, just as Daniel's story ended, others will see that the power of your God is much stronger than their beliefs. Just as Nebuchadnezzar saw the power of God and changed, your total commitment will make your enemies eventually change. This is the only way to save the planet.

Early in this book I recommended you read it through more than once, taking notes while you read. I want you to be able to make your own decision about saving your soul. I also asked you to give this book to someone you love when you have finished analyzing these pages. I want to repeat that suggestion again here. This book is designed to make everyone aware of this need for change, more than it is designed to tell of the end of the world.

Still, I do not want to give the impression that this book is more important than the Bible. That is the best book to read and read again, as long as you are reading it to help find and maintain your faith. A strong faith will not hold that flame under a barrel, meaning that you hide your fire of enlightenment from others. You must be always willing to tell others of the happiness you have found, with your change of heart, towards a renewed faith in God and Christ.

When you have spread this news to those in your immediate surroundings, so more and more are learning the values of peace and brotherhood you demonstrate, you will see you have less time to worry about things going on in very distant parts of the globe. You will see there is no reason to be associated with a nation which conducts the businesses of intrigue in foreign lands. You must do your part to stay focused on the well-being of those who are most important to you, which are those family and friends in your immediate environment. This may include some locally elected officials, but they must become aware of your unwillingness to support actions which are not Christian.

Beyond giving that notice of a refusal to support non-Christian demands, there is nothing you can do to stop the people who lust for power, from using their power. Those addictions will continue to demand more and more power and wealth for themselves. Still, if and when their demands come down to your level, just as Daniel's people encountered from the Babylonians, and then you must respond as a Christian, refusing to act non-Christian. If this brings about persecution of any kind, you must be willing to trust your soul is protected. In time, if you act to make this change in your life, it will affect many others to respond the same way; and, when many people like you are acting naturally in this method of peaceful resistance, that togetherness will bring the people who lust for power to their knees.

The people who rule the nations on earth now are all alike in their lusts and greed. It is good at this point to look at the Catholic Church's assessment of what is called the Seven Deadly Sins. In that list, lust and greed are joined by wrath, envy, gluttony, sloth and pride. All of these work in support of one another. When our lusts are not fulfilled we become filled with rage and our wrath strikes out. Our lusts are motivated by envying that which we do not already possess. Greed is a failure to share, causing us to excessively delight in that which we have cornered just for ourselves. This is gluttony. When we read here that we must take action to save ourselves and the planet, our hesitations and procrastinations are sloth. This will be just as deadly as everything else. Perhaps the most misunderstood deadly sin is pride. Pride is letting our heads swell with the concepts of freedom and democracy, thinking our nation is the greatest nation in the world. Pride is what makes us strike out with wrath, when that pride gets hurt. We are certainly living in times that are deadly.

Conversely, the Catholic Church also listed the Seven Holy Virtues, which counter those deadly sins. Fewer people know about the virtues, but they are what will continue life. They are: purity, abstinence, generosity, diligence, patience, kindness and humility. Each one of these is the opposite of the deadly sins, and it does not take much thought to see Jesus Christ held all of these virtues. In essence, these seven elements of life together equal the sum of being Christian. I strongly suggest you do some research into the Seven Holy Virtues.

419

When you realize the true motivations for both sin and virtue, you will see that sin seeks immediate gain, while virtue knows the value of a greater goal ahead. In *The Prophecies*, Nostradamus stated the high will become most low and the low will become most high. This is similar to the biblical prophecy that the meek shall inherit the earth, but it cannot be seen as saying only the downtrodden will be raised to Heaven.

In reality the story of Nostradamus is about the changes that will take the highest figures of 16ᵗʰ Century life – the kings and the Church – and making them most low, as corrupted and dissolved. Those rulers have been replaced by the common people and their philosophies, such that from the lowest levels of humanity the tyrants have risen to hold the highest positions. It has been those philosophies of the common man which have sold the world on everyone having an equal chance to move from the lowest ranks to the highest, but those philosophies made their way to the top by their philosophers leading revolutions. The word "revolution" means turning around, but as a word of action the turning never stops. The passages by Nostradamus not only predict this rising to the top of the most low, becoming the most high, but it also shows their fall back to the bottom, too. Just as they rose through revolution, they will fall through revolution. The only question now is will that revolution be one of arms, led by non-Christians or one of nonviolence and peaceful resistance, led by true Christians?

And in the End, the Love You Take is Equal to the Love You Make

I have used this space in the conclusion to bring your awareness to several elements which are at the root of your needing to make the decision to believe and change. You still have the right to accept the status quo, and thus the consequences. I have not tried to go as fully into each area as could be done, in an effort to totally convince you why you should believe and change. The words I have posted here will suffice to start your mind to work on doing this by yourself. With the understanding that Christ and God will always stand by you, with their angels whispering thoughts into your head, you will become enlightened as to how you should act. This enlightenment will let you know personally where you must change. I fully recommend you thoroughly investigate anything I have posed that makes you question its validity. I cannot wave a wand over you and save your soul.

Please know that I am praying you will receive the full benefit of my efforts, and I pray that you will have your eyes opened to the dangers which truly lie ahead. You cannot look at the big picture of world affairs and let the size overwhelm you. All you can control is you, but that control is only possible if you want you to be in control of yourself.

If you want to change and are looking for some moral support, I would love to help you further by helping you answer your questions. You can send me email at RTippett97@yahoo.com. I also have a website, www.pearlsofnostradamus.com, which has some further explanations of what Nostradamus wrote for the world to know. A blog is also available at that address, where others, more than just me, can offer comments to converse with you about your questions. Please feel free to contact me by any of these means.

CONCLUDING GOSPEL

As Jesus started on his way, a man ran up to him and fell on his knees before him. "Good teacher," he asked, "what must I do to inherit eternal life?"

"Why do you call me good?" Jesus answered. "No one is good—except God alone. You know the commandments: 'Do not murder, do not commit adultery, do not steal, do not give false testimony, do not defraud, honor your father and mother.'"

"Teacher," he declared, "all these I have kept since I was a boy."

Jesus looked at him and loved him. "One thing you lack," he said. "Go, sell everything you have and give to the poor, and you will have treasure in heaven. Then come, follow me."

At this the man's face fell. He went away sad, because he had great wealth.

Jesus looked around and said to his disciples, "How hard it is for the rich to enter the kingdom of God!"

The disciples were amazed at his words. But Jesus said again, "Children, how hard it is to enter the kingdom of God! It is easier for a camel to go through the eye of a needle than for a rich man to enter the kingdom of God."

The disciples were even more amazed, and said to each other, "Who then can be saved?"

Jesus looked at them and said, "With man this is impossible, but not with God; all things are possible with God."

Peter said to him, "We have left everything to follow you!"

"I tell you the truth," Jesus replied, "no one who has left home or brothers or sisters or mother or father or children or fields for me and the gospel will fail to receive a hundred times as much in this present age (homes, brothers, sisters, mothers, children and fields—and with them, persecutions) and in the age to come, eternal life. But many who are first will be last, and the last first."

Mark 10:17-31

(New International Version)

Lightning Source UK Ltd.
Milton Keynes UK
IKOW04f1403211215
55142UK00001B/311/P